VICTORIAN MINDS

VICTORIAN MINDS

by Gertrude Himmelfarb

ELEPHANT PAPERBACKS

IVAN R. DEE, PUBLISHER, CHICAGO

VICTORIAN MINDS. Copyright ©1952, 1962, 1964, 1965, 1966, 1968 by
Gertrude Himmelfarb. This edition was first published in 1968 and is here
reprinted by arrangement with the author.

First ELEPHANT PAPERBACK edition published 1995 by Ivan R. Dee,
Inc., 1332 North Halsted Street, Chicago 60622. Manufactured in the
United States of America and printed on acid-free paper.

Library of Congress Cataloging-in-Publication Data:
Himmelfarb, Gertrude.
    Victorian minds / by Gertrude Himmelfarb.
        p.   cm.
    Originally published : New York : A. A. Knopf, 1968
    "Elephant paperbacks."
    ISBN 1-56663-077-0 (alk. paper)
    1. Great Britain—Intellectual life—19th century. 2. Great Britain—
History—Victoria, 1837–1901. I. Title.
DA533.H55   1995
941.081—dc20   94-43053

CONTENTS

INTRODUCTION

Fｒｏｍ ＥＤＭＵＮＤ ＢＵＲＫＥ (1729–97) to John Buchan (1875–1940): the compass of this volume is evidently broader than a literal reading of the title would suggest. One might like to make capital of this, to take credit for flouting the conventional periodization of history and categorization of ideas. Unfortunately nothing is more conventional today than to flout the conventions. Historians feel no more bound by the old fixities of history—dates, periods, political or geographical entities, distinctions of politics, economics, culture, etc.—than the new nations who change at will their names, identities, constitutions, and whatever else may be alterable. The present sense of history, for good and bad, is of history created *de novo*. And this is true of history in both its meanings: as the past and as the record of that past. Historians assert themselves over the latter with the same zeal that politicians do over the former. If the new fashions in historical writing—contemporary history, comparative history, universal history, psychological history, interdisciplinary history—do not always seem as novel or revealing as the claims made for them, it may be because the past itself is more recalcitrant than either politicians or historians like to think. In any event, this volume makes no such claims to novelty. Such few liberties as it takes, with the word "Victorian" for example, have ample precedents in the literature of the subject. G. M. Trevelyan's *British History in the Nineteenth Century* opens in 1782 (although it more austerely closes in 1901); the heart of Elie Halévy's

England in 1815 is the discussion of John Wesley (1703–91); the periodical *Victorian Studies* makes regular incursions into the eighteenth and twentieth centuries; and the currently published *Wellesley Index to Victorian Periodicals* has wisely chosen to antedate by many years Victoria's accession. To extend the courtesy of *Victorian Minds* to the proto-Victorian and neo-Victorian takes no great imagination or daring.

Nor does the designation "proto-Victorian" require much justification. The intellectual and social history of the Victorians is inexplicable without reference to their predecessors. How can one understand Acton without Burke, Mill without Bentham, Darwin without Malthus? And it was not only individual thinkers who lived under and wrestled with the shadows of these giants. The major movements of the time—conservatism, liberalism, and radicalism—also bore the impress of their prototypes, and even in their present form still bear that stamp.

The rubric "High Victorians" may take more explaining. There are so many other persons one would have liked to include. Some of these (Newman, Disraeli, Gladstone) figure prominently in the general essays that make up the concluding section of this volume. Others (Eliot, Carlyle, Macaulay, Matthew Arnold) make more fleeting appearances; and each of these is surely deserving of very much more attention. I hope to repair some of these omissions on future occasions (with the exception, however, of Arnold, of whom I would despair saying anything that Lionel Trilling has not already said so brilliantly).

If some of these worthies have received less than their due, others may seem to have received more. In part this is because of the ambiguous nature of intellectual history. The philosopher need address himself only to the best minds of an age—perhaps only to the best minds of all time. The historian of ideas must also consider the representative minds of an age, which may well be the "second-best" minds. For Victorian England, fortunately, this is no great affliction, the second-best then being better than the best of many other times and places.

But whether the intention is to scale the highest reaches of the age with the best minds or to take the measure of its general contours with the second-best, one must be impressed by the variety of the terrain. The plurality of the title is deliberate. "The Victorian Mind" would have been more euphonious but less accurate. There is, I believe, and as I have argued in the essay of that title, something identifiable as the "Victorian ethos"—if one sees it in contrast to preceding and following ages, if one appreciates its constantly evolving character, and if one makes allowance for the fact that it managed, at different times and in different degrees, to absorb quite distinct and even contrary ideas, ideologies, sentiments, and policies. Perhaps other ages were more single-minded; certainly some historians have suggested so. But the Victorian age exhibited, and not at its periphery but at its very center, all the diversity, and much of the perversity, of which the human mind is capable. If it was an age of unbelief, it was as much an age of belief, and not only because there were believers as well as unbelievers but also because belief and unbelief were so intimately and ingeniously related. It was an age of severe manners and morals, and of considerable latitude in behavior. It has been described by one historian as an age of equipoise, by another as an age of reform, and by still another as an age of revolution; my own sense of it is best expressed in the phrase "conservative revolution." The title of one of these essays is "Varieties of Social Darwinism." The title of the whole might well have been "Varieties of Victorianism."

The essays also testify to the variety of style and method available to the historian of ideas. Had the essays been intended from the start as chapters in a book, they would have been more uniform in structure and tone, comprehensive in scope, and judiciously balanced. Biography, exposition, and analysis would have been meted out in proper proportion and sequence. Much would have been gained; but also (and I hope I am not making a virtue out of necessity), much would have been lost. For the fact is that different subjects are not necessarily best served by similar treatment. Occasional essays may not consort so well together, but they are likely to be better suited to their individual subjects (unless the occasion itself is constricting, which was not the case here). Thus the Mill essay is largely biographical, because it is my contention that Mill cannot be understood except in terms of his intellectual and personal history; I would go so far as to say that a purely textual analysis of any one of his works, without reference to the circumstances of its composition or its relation to his other works, is necessarily faulty. The second of the two Burke essays, on the other hand, is textual and analytical, because it is only thus that the generalities of the first Burke essay could be tested. And the discussion of Bentham is of still another order, a detailed and precise case study of a single reform proposal, because without such detail and precision it might be difficult to credit a reality that accords so little with the conventional view. The other essays are equally varied in approach and style. The long-standing quarrel among historians of ideas between the textual critics and the intellectual biographers seems to me to be as futile as the similar quarrel between narrative and analytical historians. No one method, surely, has an exclusive claim to propriety or superiority, but neither is the choice of method in any particular case a matter of indifference.

Although most of the essays were originally written for other occasions, they have all been revised, some have been rewritten out of all recognition (the only vestige of the original being the opening paragraphs stating the problem), and some have been written expressly for this volume. The only one to escape substantial revision (although even here

I have not been able to resist small stylistic emendations) is the first essay on Burke; this has been retained in its original form to act as a foil to the second, which is in the nature of a self-rebuttal. (Most of the changes in the final essay on the Reform Act have had to be consigned to the footnotes, the recent spate of literature on the subject appearing too late to be incorporated into the text.) Some of my historian-friends professed to be dismayed at the liberties I was taking with my own texts, as if I were tampering with the historical record. But the historical record that is at stake here is not mine—what I may have said or thought at one time or another—but that of the Victorians; and my only responsibility is to preserve that record to the best of my ability, which is to say, the best of my present ability.

Among the friends, historians and others, whom I should like to thank for an intellectual stimulation that may not necessarily be reflected in any particular essay but certainly informs the whole are Daniel Bell, Diana and Lionel Trilling, Melvin Richter, Bernard Semmel, J. H. Hexter, Lewis Feuer, Marvin Meyers, Martin Diamond, my brother Milton Himmelfarb, and my husband, Irving Kristol. I am also indebted to my research assistant, Martin Jackson, for checking the quotations and footnotes. Parts of this volume were written during the years that I was a fellow of the Guggenheim Foundation and of the Rockefeller Foundation, and I am grateful for their generous assistance.

Gertrude Himmelfarb

PROTO-VICTORIANS

I

EDMUND BURKE

*T*he following essays on Burke represent diametrically opposing views. The first was originally published in 1949; the second, written expressly for this volume, is a reprise or re-evaluation. The more normal procedure would have been to emend the first or print only the second. But by no amount of emendation could the first have been made to accommodate the second. And to print the second without the first would have implied a repudiation of the first that I do not now intend. While I am obviously closer to the second view than the first, I find myself even now occasionally responding to Burke as I formerly did. The first still commends itself to me as representing not only a common interpretation of Burke but also a natural and legitimate one.

The two essays, therefore, are presented as alternative interpretations, much as the editor of a disputed text might offer alternative readings of it. Thus the second emerges, not by accident, almost as a mirror image of the first. The heads of the argument are the same; only the thrust is different. Even the quotations are often identical, although used to different effect. In the second, I have, however, confined myself to the analysis of a single work by Burke, *the* Reflections on the Revolution in France. *To have*

3

*permitted myself the freedom of his entire corpus would
have made my argument suspect, since I might have been
tempted to pick and choose those quotations that suited my
purpose. Confinement to a single text has induced, I hope, a
greater rigor of reasoning and more faithful rendition of
Burke's meaning—particularly since the* Reflections *does
not, on the surface at least, readily lend itself to the view of
the second essay, and has, indeed, more often been used to
sustain the view of the first.*

*I should like to make it clear that I do not hold Burke
responsible for the ambivalence represented by these essays.
If I did, I should be implying that there were chronologi-
cally or logically two Burkes (as I shall, in later essays,
argue for the existence of two Malthuses and two Mills).
But however much I myself may be of two minds about
him, there was, I am convinced, only one Burke. It is for
the reader to decide which is the real Burke: the Burke
who, as Paine saw him, "pities the plumage but forgets the
dying bird,"[1] or the Burke who, by his own account,
believed that only the most careful tending of its plumage
would save the dying bird.*

I. THE HERO AS POLITICIAN

CARLYLE's hero appeared in many incarnations—as god,
king, prophet, priest, even as philosopher, poet, and
man of letters; the one form he did not allow to him was
that of politician. The mission of the hero was to reveal
"what of divinity is in man and nature"—a mission quite

1. Thomas Paine, *The Rights of Man* (Anchor edn.; New York,
1965), p. 288.

beyond the capacity, as Carlyle saw it, of the politician.[2] Later generations contemplated with satisfaction their emancipation from Carlyle's heroes and took pleasure in first humiliating and then discarding them. But hardly had men rid themselves of these heroes before another was insinuated into their midst, and he was the one Carlyle had not admitted, the hero as politician. To Carlyle this would be a classic instance of straining at the gnat and swallowing the camel. For the politician has all the moral disabilities of the others with none of their virtues. Pretending to no eternal ideas or divine truths, he revels in the profane. Yet it is his genius to assume at will the mask of king, poet, or philosopher, and he has even been known to appear to some in the likeness of a god.

Only this extraordinary facility for disguise, combined with an obscurity or ambiguity of character, can account for the high esteem Edmund Burke has enjoyed among so many thoughtful men of different persuasions, and the veneration he has inspired among Whigs and Tories (Macaulay judged him the greatest man since Milton, and Disraeli spoke of his "divine effusions"), Socialists (to Harold Laski he was England's greatest political thinker), and devout Catholics.[3] A Jesuit scholar has described him as "the greatest philosopher-statesman thus far known to history," "the last of the great scholastics."[4] And others have found him a repository of all the social principles of Thomism, a "fountain of wisdom" capable of creating in the desert of modern society a moral and political oasis.[5]

2. Thomas Carlyle, *On Heroes, Hero Worship and the Heroic in History* (Everyman edn.; London, 1908), p. 248.

3. John Morley, *Burke* (London, 1904), p. 3; W. F. Monypenny and G. E. Buckle, *Life of Benjamin Disraeli* (London, 1929), I, 241; Harold Laski, *Political Thought in England* (Oxford, 1920), p. 182.

4. M. F. X. Millar, "The Modern State and Catholic Principles," *Thought*, XII (1937), 51.

5. R. J. S. Hoffman and P. Levack (eds.), *Burke's Politics* (New York, 1949), p. xxxiv.

While Catholics revere Burke as a pious defender of the natural and divine order, secularists praise him for his boldly empirical attitude to politics. Liberals derive from him a philosophy of political pluralism intended to prevent statism and tyranny, and conservatives take comfort in his theory of the organic state and his paeans to authority. It is no wonder that his speeches are used as texts in rhetoric for high-school students, for what they lack in logical rigor they make up in persuasiveness. Oliver Goldsmith once said that Burke in conversation was like a serpent winding around his subject—and, it might be added, he cared as little as the serpent about where he attacked or how; the important thing was that the attack succeed. It was left for his commentators to decide what were his purpose and motives, and what were mere devices of strategy and tactics. The fact that he holds the undisputed title of supreme rhetorician in a country distinguished for its rhetoric may account for the variety of virtues imputed to him by so wide a variety of thinkers.

For every citation from Burke demonstrating his submission to "the universal natural law of reason and justice ordained by God as the foundation of a good community,"[6] there are two others conclusively establishing his contempt for theories of natural law and abstract, absolute values. It was not only the metaphysicians of the French Revolution but all metaphysicians who fell victim to his facile pen: "Nothing can be conceived more hard than the heart of a thoroughbred metaphysician. It comes nearer to the cold malignity of a wicked spirit than to the frailty and passion of a man. It is like that of the principle of evil himself, incorporeal, pure, unmixed, dephlegmated, defecated evil."[7] He harangued against philosophers and theorists who confounded questions of practical politics with

6. Ibid., p. xv.

7. "Letter to a Noble Lord" (1796), *Works of Edmund Burke* (Bohn edn.; London, 1909–12), V, 141.

abstract principles of morality, and he professed to hate the very sound of "metaphysical distinctions."[8] The characteristic words in his vocabulary, providing a refrain for every speech he delivered and every pamphlet he composed, were convenience, expedience, prudence, and accommodation. Everything else he jeered at as the "delusive plausibilities of moral politicians."[9]

Philosophy was hateful because, however well-intentioned its practitioners, the very discipline of thinking—to say nothing of philosophical thinking, the examination of first causes and ultimate reasons—was by nature dangerous. To Burke, prejudice and superstition were infinitely preferable to reason, for what reason tends to uproot, prejudices and superstition keep fast: "Prejudice renders a man's virtue his habit, and not a series of unconnected acts. Through just prejudice his duty becomes a part of his nature."[1] Civil society could not subsist long if all men were philosophers. Subordination, not independence, was necessary for the human mind. Burke had more in common with Rousseau than either would have liked to think. Both looked upon science and philosophy in general, and the Enlightenment in particular, as the great peril to society, and Burke would have been the first to agree with Rousseau that "the development of enlightenment and vice always takes place in the same ratio, not in the individuals, but in the people."[2] (Leo Strauss has brilliantly exposed the "praise of ignorance" that governs so much of Rousseau's thinking.[3]) The difference between Rousseau and Burke, contrary to the general impression fostered by Burke himself, was not in method but in ends; where

8. "Speech on American Taxation" (1774), *Works*, I, 432.
9. "Reflections on the Revolution in France" (1790), *Works*, II, 311.
1. Ibid., p. 359.
2. Quoted by Leo Strauss, "On the Intention of Rousseau," *Social Research*, XIV (1947), 464-5.
3. Ibid., pp. 456 ff.

Rousseau was solicitous of a future democractic state, Burke was interested only in making impregnable the existing aristocratic state.

Like another uncongenial predecessor, Hobbes, with whom he would have been quick to deny any affinity, Burke could have said that he and fear were born, as twins, together. But while Hobbes boasted of the relationship publicly and made the most of it, elevating fear, the fear of war and disorder, to the highest position in his philosophical system, Burke permitted it to enjoy only an illegitimate existence in the shady recesses of his mind, from which it emerged now and then, sometimes defiantly, sometimes quietly, almost without his knowledge. Thus he pleaded that England submit to the demands of America, not because America had right or law or liberty on its side, but because the discontent in the Colonies threatened the order and government of the British Empire; for "whether liberty be advantageous or not, . . . none will dispute that peace is a blessing."[4] On the other hand, it was the duty of England to engage in a crusade against France to extirpate the ideas and principles of the revolution which threatened to create a universal ferment and decomposition of society. The fear of disorder pursued Burke so far as to convince him that liberty could be acceptable, as long as it was liberty "with peace and order."[5] Tell me, he requested, what provisions have been made for government, public force, armies, the revenue, property, peace and order, civil and social manners, and I will judge whether the new liberty of France is a good or an evil. (Somewhere in this enumeration appear morality and religion, but these, like manners, are only euphemisms for order.) The English constitution, which he cherished so dearly that he could not bring himself to entertain the most modest proposal for

4. "Letter to the Sheriffs of Bristol" (1777), *Works*, II, 31.
5. "Reflections," *Works*, p. 283.

an extension of the suffrage or reduction of the rotten boroughs, fixed the order of society as well and as permanently as human arrangements could be fixed, and to tamper with them, he was certain, would open the floodgates to chaos. When it was proposed to substitute triennial parliaments for the traditional septennial ones, he warned that the change would have the following ill effects: it would make the members of parliament shamelessly, shockingly corrupt and would bankrupt those with fortunes; it would make the electorate infinitely more venal and the whole body of the people, within and outside of the electorate, lawless, idle, and debauched; in short, it "would utterly destroy the sobriety, the industry, the integrity, the simplicity of all the people, and undermine, I am much afraid, the deepest and best-laid foundations of the commonwealth."[6]

If Burke's rhetoric sometimes obscures the straight line of his thoughts, it often helps trace that line. Single words —liberty, justice, people—shift meaning too rapidly in the eloquent flow of his speech, but his metaphors exhibit a remarkable consistency of tone and subject. The vision is one of impending danger, as when he describes the prudent politician devoted to the security and peace of his government, who scans the political sky to discover the hurricane in a cloud no bigger than a hand at the very edge of the horizon, and who quickly guides his vessel into the nearest harbor.[7] The constitution is pictured as standing "on a nice equipoise, with steep precipices and deep waters upon all sides of it," so that when men seek to correct a leaning to one side, they risk upsetting it on the other.[8] And when the

6. "Speech on a Bill for Shortening the Duration of Parliaments" (n.d.), *Works*, VI, 142.
7. "Thoughts on the Cause of the Present Discontents" (1770), *Works*, I, 336.
8. Ibid., p. 368.

constitution is not precariously poised on high, it is an island surrounded by raging seas.[9]

Where Hobbes feared everyone indiscriminately, on the theory that all men were driven by the same sense of insecurity and insatiable lust for power, Burke, like Machiavelli, feared only those who were deprived of effective governing power and who, presumably, would risk everything to get at the sources of power. Compared with Burke, Hobbes was an exemplary democrat; he assigned to all men the same instincts, distrusted all for the same reasons, and thought of civil society as profiting all equally. However faulty his schemes for promoting the general welfare, however unpersuasive or distasteful his theory of absolute sovereignty, Hobbes did at least have a conception of the general welfare which genuinely comprised all men. Burke, more practical, more conventional, and less visionary than Hobbes, had a more modest sense of his task. If happiness and security were not the lot of all, he thought it only proper that they be enjoyed by at least the privileged few. It would not help the lower classes, it might even work to their disadvantage, to upset the traditional order of society.

In place of the confusing, illogical, and irresponsible doctrine of the rights of man, Burke urged that men reconcile themselves to the realities of social existence, to the fact that government has authority only by virtue of prescription and presumption—the prescription of ancient conventions and sanctions, and the presumption that what exists must and should exist. Philosophy and speculation are at best supererogatory, at worst pernicious. "That which might be wrong in the beginning," he wrote, "is consecrated by time and becomes lawful. This may be superstition in me, and ignorance; but I had rather remain in ignorance and superstition, than be enlightened and puri-

9. "Speech on Reform of Representation" (1782), *Works*, VI, 151.

fied out of the first principles of law and natural justice."[1] It was for this reason, too, that he was partial to religion even when it was tinctured with superstition, for "religion is the basis of civil society" and "superstition is the religion of feeble minds."[2] This also partly explains his benevolent feeling for Catholicism, "the most effectual barrier" against Jacobinism. Any established religion, however, served his purpose, for all the European religions were "prescriptive religions"; "they have all stood long enough to make prescription, and its chain of legitimate prejudices, their main stay."[3]

Prescription and presumption were, of course, admirably suited to the interests of the English aristocracy. It is strange to find one commentator soberly defend the thesis that Burke, the employee of the most aristocratic faction of the Whig party, "stood for government of the people (with their consent), by the people (through the instrumentality of their natural representatives), and for the people (for their common and permanent good, but not for their vagrant and variant whims)."[4] It is not even necessary to quibble about how "their consent" might be construed, considering the fact that they had no opportunity to express or withhold it. Burke himself made no serious pretense to speak for the people. He was proud that his was the most aristocratic party in England, "connected with the solid, permanent, long-possessed property of the country."[5] And he realized, better perhaps than modern readers who delicately refrain from vulgar imputations of economic motives, that the essence of aristocracy was property, and the genius of the system of prescription, as of inheritance, was that it "leaves acquisition free; but it

1. Letter to Mercer, Feb. 26, 1790, *Letters of Edmund Burke*, ed. Harold Laski (Oxford, 1922), pp. 286–7.
2. "Reflections," *Works*, II, 362, 429.
3. "Letter to William Smith" (Jan. 1795), *Works*, VI, 52–3.
4. Hoffman and Levack, p. xxi.
5. *Letters* (Jan. 31, 1792), p. 328.

secures what it acquires."[6] "The means of acquisition are prior in time and in arrangement" to government, he argued, and acquisition is secure only when the people are "tractable and obedient," when the authority of the magistrate and the law are unquestioned, and when those who have failed in the struggle for acquisition are not tempted to rebel against their "natural subordination." "They must respect that property of which they cannot partake. They must labor to obtain what by labor can be obtained; and when they find, as they commonly do, the success disproportioned to the endeavor, they must be taught their consolation in the final proportions of eternal justice.[7]

Burke may, indeed, be taken as a proponent of "government of the people, by the people, and for the people"—if one understands his definition of "the people." At the start of the French Revolution, he calculated the number of landed proprietors in France at 70,000, and remarked: "I am sure, that if half that number of the same description were taken out of this country, it would leave hardly anything that I should call the people of England."[8] Elsewhere, in a more generous temper, he estimated that "those who, in any political view, are to be called the people" amounted to 400,000 in England and Wales (of a population of eight or nine million).[9] Burke's was not even the normal conservatism of the eighteenth-century Whig. The majority of the Whig party, feeling secure in its power, could complacently suggest minor reforms in the franchise, but Burke was consumed by a fear bordering on hysteria, and the most innocent proposal for liberalizing the state evoked images of mass expropriation and murder. If there were to be any constitutional changes, he pleaded, they

6. "Reflections," *Works*, II, 307.
7. Ibid., p. 514.
8. "Remarks on the Policy of the Allies" (Oct. 1793), *Works*, III, 423.
9. "Letters on a Regicide Peace" (1796), *Works*, V, 189-90.

ought to be in the direction of reducing, rather than increasing, the number of voters.

There has been a curious leveling of academic controversy in recent years. Political philosophers have borrowed from each other so liberally that there are only differences of emphasis rather than of categories to distinguish them. They no longer quarrel about the merits of political pluralism; they only compete for the honor of having originated it. The old arguments about the organic *versus* the atomistic state have peacefully given way to the idea of a corporative society. The utilitarian theory of self-interest has been discovered to be not inconsistent with the idea of social purpose and value. The concept of the tyranny of the majority has been incorporated into the philosophy of democracy. Secularists have been impressed with the urgency of faith, and religious thinkers tend to be, if anything, too receptive to the gospel of pragmatism. The virtues of tradition and history, the complexities of human nature and social arrangements, the uses and abuses of power, the extent and limit of intelligence, are the common denominators of all philosophical parties. Machiavelli and Hobbes no longer excite apprehension or Rousseau derision, Augustine and Marx are associated in a single eschatological tradition, and people are no longer born to be either Platonists or Aristotelians. A bland tolerance characterizes most academic inquiries in political philosophy—an atmosphere particularly favorable to the enhancement of Burke's reputation.

It is easy enough for the political pluralist to forget that Burke had the heretical idea of the state as "a partnership in all science; a partnership in every virtue, and in all perfection."[1] The moralist can ignore Burke's idealization of the past and his identification of what is with what ought to be. The hard-headed realist manages to gloss over Burke's fanciful flight of rhetoric in describing the beauty and

1. "Reflections," *Works*, II, 368.

innocence of Marie Antoinette and the charms of an age of chivalry in passages reminiscent of the magnolia-and-Old-South school of writing. When liberals finally came to admit that conservatism might be a storehouse of political wisdom, they settled upon Burke as the arbiter of politics and morality.

But the insights of conservatism might have been more readily found in a Metternich, who did not delude himself into believing that his aristocracy was the natural, eternal ruler of the universe; or a Tocqueville, for whom the march of democracy was a necessary if ominous, event; or a Burckhardt, who boldly announced that salvation lay not in a tenacious grasp upon property, but in the rejection of a vulgarized, mass-minded, materialistic, industrial society; or an Acton, who set absolute morality against history, democracy, and even religion; or a Carlyle, who searched for the soul of the world's history in the souls of great men.

2. THE POLITICIAN AS PHILOSOPHER

IT IS a neat and plausible logic that denies to Burke all claims to philosophical seriousness. By this logic, his solicitude for tradition and history, expedience and prudence, was a confession of pure opportunism, and his contempt for the metaphysicians of the French Revolution was a contempt for all metaphysicians, a contempt, by implication, for philosophers and philosophy per se. The logic is plausible but not compelling. A closer more sympathetic reading of Burke suggests that his contempt was reserved for those metaphysicians who confused natural law with natural rights and absolute values with absolute will. It was precisely in the interests of natural law and moral values that he deplored this confusion. The exercise of power, he insisted, "to be legitimate must be according to that eternal and immutable law in which will and reason are the same."[1] And while he conceded the difficulty of defining the limits of "the mere *abstract* competence" of sovereign powers, he insisted that the "limits of a *moral* competence, subjecting . . . occasional will to permanent reason, and to the steady maxims of faith, justice, and fixed fundamental policy, are perfectly intelligible, and perfectly binding upon those who exercise any authority, under any name, or under any title, in the state." If there were no limits determined by natural law, "competence and power would soon be confounded, and no law be left but the will of a prevailing force."[2]

It is customary to quote, as I have in the preceding essay, the sentence in which Burke declared the state to be "a partnership in all science; a partnership in all art; a partnership in every virtue, and in all perfection"—as if this were an incongruous lapse into metaphysics on his part, attributable only to his overriding authoritarianism. And the sentence extending the partnership to "those who are living, those who are dead, and those who are to be born," is often cited—and derided—to the same effect. But the rest of the passage is rarely quoted, although it is this that clarifies the idea of the partnership and that puts his politics in the context of his philosophy:

> Each contract of each particular state is but a clause in the great primeval contract of eternal society, linking the lower with the higher natures, connecting the visible and invisible world, according to a fixed compact sanctioned by the inviolable oath which holds all physical and all

1. "Reflections on the Revolution in France," *Works of Edmund Burke* (Bohn edn.; London, 1909–12), II, 366. Unless otherwise noted, all the page references below are to this edition.
2. P. 295.

moral natures, each in their appointed place. This law is not subject to the will of those, who by an obligation above them, and infinitely superior, are bound to submit their will to that law.[3]

The famous metaphor of a "partnership," then, was part of a larger image of a "contract"—a contract far more inclusive than the "social contract" of Hobbes or Rousseau (still more than that of Locke, who required two contracts to effect the establishment of government). When Burke spoke of a "contract" or "compact," he was invoking, in effect, the venerable metaphysical idea of a "great chain of being." His "primeval contract" was conceived of as the link not only between society and the state, but also between the lower and higher natures, the visible and the invisible, the physical and the moral, the temporal and the eternal. So far from denying the philosophical enterprise, he was insisting upon it; he was, in fact, in the very best philosophical company, of his time and all time.

His objection to metaphysicians was that they perverted what he took to be the true task of philosophy, which was not to assert absolutes but to establish relations, to show how the various orders, natures, and conditions were related in the great chain of being. The "thoroughbred metaphysician" represented the "Principle of Evil," which was an "incorporeal, pure, unmixed, dephlegmated, defecated evil." And metaphysical abstractions were dangerous because they falsified reality by reducing it to such an incorporeal, pure, unmixed state.

> I cannot stand forward, and give praise or blame to anything which relates to human actions, and human concerns, on a simple view of the object, as it stands stripped of every relation, in all the nakedness and solitude of metaphysical abstraction. Circumstances (which with some gentlemen pass for nothing) give in reality to every

3. Pp. 368-9.

political principle its distinguishing color and discriminating effect.[4]

A later generation, having itself fought and won the battle of "existence" against "essence," should be sensitive to the distinction between the "thoroughbred metaphysician" and the philosopher as such. Indeed, Burke might well be regarded as a "premature existentialist," and one would not be surprised to find him installed in the Pantheon of the new philosophy.

If Burke had a more complicated sense of the relations of philosophy and politics than I once allowed him, he also had a more complicated sense of religion and faith. In my earlier essay I implied that his devotion to religion was inspired by philosophical obscurantism and political utilitarianism: skeptical of either the validity or the utility of reason, he was partial to religions that accommodated themselves to the social establishment and to superstitions that bolstered those religions. It may be, however, that this view of Burke reflects nothing so much as our own religious incapacities. We may credit, although we do not ordinarily respect, the simple utilitarian argument for religion; but the idea that a religion to be useful must also be true, or that an established religion is nonetheless divine for its establishment, we find hard to credit or respect. Yet if we could suspend our own disbelief, we might find Burke's belief both more credible and more creditable. There is no reason to doubt the sincerity of his professions, unexceptionable certainly in his time, that atheism was against "not only our reason but our instincts," or that religion was not a "mere invention to keep the vulgar in obedience," or that religious toleration should reflect a "zeal" for what was common in all religions rather than an "indifference" to all,

4. P. 282.

or that a church establishment was a "consecration of the state."[5]

Nor can it be assumed that superstition was as disreputable in Burke's scheme as it might appear in ours. By superstition, he meant a popular version of religion—not a species of irreligion but an impure variant of religion, impure as most of reality was impure. "Superstition is the religion of feeble minds," I had quoted. But Burke had prefaced this remark with the warning that excess superstition might be a "very great evil"; and had followed it with the observation that an "intermixture" of superstition and religion was desirable, "else you will deprive weak minds of a resource found necessary to the strongest."[6] Superstition and religion, then, were part of a continuum—a social continuum of the weak-minded and the strong, and a metaphysical continuum of belief and truth. They were, indeed, part of the great chain of being itself: "Every sort of moral, every sort of civil, every sort of politic institution, aiding the rational and natural ties that connect the human understanding and affections to the divine, are not more than necessary, in order to build up that wonderful structure, Man."[7]

Burke has similarly been taken to task for belittling reason and exalting prejudice, for joining Rousseau in the "praise of ignorance." The example of Rousseau is very much to the point—but perhaps to the opposite point. Rousseau praised ignorance for the same reason that he praised natural man, man as he was presumed to be primevally and instinctually before reason and civilization had corrupted him. Burke praised not ignorance but prejudice, the prejudice that was inherent in social man. Rousseau identified

5. Pp. 363–4, 372–3.
6. Pp. 429–30. Earlier he had warned the French, prophetically, as it turned out, that the proscription of the Church would create a void favorable to the development of an "uncouth, pernicious and degrading superstition." (P. 363.)
7. P. 364.

reason with civilization and condemned them both on the same ground. Burke condemned reason only when it arrogantly assumed such an identification, when it refused to accredit the other resources of civilization, of which prejudice was one.

As religion and superstition coexisted in a single continuum, so, for Burke, did reason and prejudice. Prejudice was the means of complementing or implementing reason; it was not false reason but popular reason, collective reason. There was nothing paradoxical or ironic in Burke's expression, "wise prejudice";[8] nor did he intend "wise" merely to signify approbation, as the equivalent, say, of "sensible," or "judicious," or "prudent." Prejudice was not only sanctioned by wisdom; it was part of wisdom. Thus he defended the church establishment as "the first of our prejudices, not a prejudice destitute of reason, but involving in it profound and extensive wisdom."[9] And in the passage culminating in the sentences I quoted in my earlier essay, every reference to prejudice placed it firmly within the context of reason and wisdom:

> We are afraid to put men to live and trade each on his own private stock of reason; because we suspect that this stock in each man is small, and that the individuals would do better to avail themselves of the general bank and capital of nations, and of ages. Many of our men of speculation, instead of exploding general prejudices, employ their sagacity to discover the latent wisdom which prevails in them. If they find what they seek, and they seldom fail, they think it more wise to continue the prejudice, with the reason involved, than to cast away the coat of prejudice, and to leave nothing but the naked reason; because prejudice, with its reason, has a motive to give action to that reason, and an affection which will give it permanence. Prejudice is of ready application in the emergency; it previously engages the mind in a steady

8. P. 368.
9. Pp. 363-4.

course of wisdom and virtue, and does not leave the man hesitating in the moment of decision, sceptical, puzzled, and unresolved. Prejudice renders a man's virtue his habit; and not a series of unconnected acts. Through just prejudice, his duty becomes a part of his nature.[1]

"Virtue and wisdom": the words were constantly on Burke's lips. Had I considered them at all in my first reading, I would have dismissed them as part of that rhetoric which permitted him to appear to be all things to all men. The operative words in his vocabulary, I was then convinced, were of a quite different order: convenience, expedience, prudence, accommodation, prescription, presumption, tradition, history. . . . Virtue and wisdom hardly seem consonant with this unredeemed relativism and opportunism. Yet another reading of Burke might suggest that it was precisely his intention to bring the two vocabularies into a meaningful relation. As prejudice was consistently defined in terms of reason, so the practical, empirical values were consistently defined in terms of virtue and wisdom. Thus "experience" was the "wisdom of unlettered men"; "prudence" was the "first of all virtues"; the English revolutionists were praised for their "practical wisdom"; government was a "contrivance of human wisdom to provide for human wants"; the function of ancestors was to provide a "standard of virtue and wisdom." . . .[2]

The most dramatic confrontation of these two orders of values appears in the memorable sentence of the *Reflections:* "There is no qualification for government, but virtue and wisdom, actual or presumptive."[3] Burke's problem was the problem of all classical philosophy: the relation of the ideal to mundane reality—of "actual" (that is, absolute,

1. P. 359.
2. Pp. 331, 335, 306, 333, 309.
3. P. 323.

perfect, authentic) virtue and wisdom to "presumptive" (approximate, probable, inferential, existent) virtue and wisdom. It was the problem of legitimacy, the legitimization of what is in terms of what should be. This was very different from the view attributed to him in the first essay: that "government has authority only by virtue of prescription and presumption—the prescription of ancient conventions and sanctions, and the presumption that what exists must and should exist." For prescription and presumption, it would now appear, had authority and legitimacy for Burke only so far as they were related, by natural law, to ideal virtue and wisdom. Indeed, the purpose of government was precisely to establish and maintain this continuum: "The doctrine of prescription . . . is a part of the law of nature. . . . The positive ascertainment of its [prescription's] limits, and its security from invasion, were among the causes for which civil society itself has been instituted."[4] The mistake of the French Revolutionists was in supposing that they were free to locate authority where they liked, to conjure up by sheer will or imagination the "virtue and wisdom of a whole people collected into a focus":

> But no name, no power, no function, no artificial institution whatsoever, can make the men of whom any system of authority is composed, any other than God, and nature, and education, and their habits of life have made them. Capacities beyond these the people have not to give. Virtue and wisdom may be the objects of their choice; but their choice confers neither the one nor the other on those upon whom they lay their ordaining hands. They have not the engagement of nature, they have not the promise of revelation, for any such powers.[5]

Because the potential power of the people was so great, it was "of infinite importance that they should not be suffered to imagine that their will, any more than that of

4. P. 422.
5. Pp. 313-14.

kings, is the standard of right and wrong." They had to be taught that power could only be legitimately exercised "in an higher link of the order of delegation," and could only be legitimately conferred on those who, in spite of the "great and inevitable mixed mass of human imperfections and infirmities," represented the "predominant proportion of active virtue and wisdom."[6]

The legitimization of prescription in terms of natural law, and of presumptive virtue and wisdom in terms of "actual" (i.e., ideal, absolute, or authentic) virtue and wisdom, would be of little importance, certainly of no political importance, if it could be assumed to have occurred once and for all, in some mythical or remotely historical past. But in fact Burke allowed for a continuing process of legitimization, a chain of being that was, so to speak, in a constant state of re-creation. Just as he insisted that reform was best promoted not by revolution but within the framework of established institutions ("a state without the means of some change is without the means of its conservation"[7]), so he located the mechanism and process of legitimization in the very strongholds of legitimacy. Aristocracy and property, which were the tokens of presumptive virtue and wisdom, were also the means by which "actual" virtue and wisdom were transmitted to their presumptive heirs; they were the material rewards of ability, transforming philosophers—or, more often philosophers' sons—into rulers. Actual virtue and wisdom, "in whatever state, condition, profession or trade," were the "passport of Heaven to human place and honor."[8]

The power of perpetuating our property in our families is one of the most valuable and interesting circumstances belonging to it, and that which tends the most to the perpetuation of society itself. It makes our weakness sub-

6. Pp. 365–6.
7. P. 295.
8. P. 323.

servient to our virtue; it grafts benevolence even upon avarice. The possessors of family wealth, and of the distinction which attends hereditary possession . . . are the natural securities for this transmission.[9]

But this transmission, Burke insisted, must not be made too lightly. Actual virtue and wisdom, being the "rarest of all rare things," could only be determined by subjecting it to "some sort of probation": "The temple of honor ought to be seated on an eminence. If it be open through virtue, let it be remembered, too, that virtue is never tried but by some difficulty, and some struggle."[1] Such an ordeal was necessary not only to eliminate the spurious claimants to

9. P. 324.
1. Pp. 323–4. "Difficulty," in Burke's scheme, was not only a means to an end—in this case, virtue—but very nearly an end or virtue in itself. One of his principal criticisms of the French Revolutionists was that they were simplistic on principle:

> Their purpose everywhere seems to have been to evade and slip aside from *difficulty*. This it has been the glory of the great masters in all the arts to confront, and to overcome; and when they had overcome the first difficulty, to turn it into an instrument for new conquests over new difficulties; and thus to enable them to extend the empire of their science; and even to push forward beyond the reach of their original thoughts, the land marks of the human understanding itself. Difficulty is a severe instructor, set over us by the supreme ordinance of a parental guardian and legislator, who knows us better than we know ourselves, as he loves us better too. . . . This amiable conflict with difficulty obliges us to an intimate acquaintance with our object, and compels us to consider it in all its relations. It will not suffer us to be superficial. It is the want of nerves of understanding for such a task; it is the degenerate fondness for tricking short-cuts, and little fallacious facilities, that has in so many parts of the world created governments with arbitrary powers. . . . With them defects in wisdom are to be supplied by the plenitude of force. . . . Commencing their labours on a principle of sloth, they have the common fortune of slothful men. The difficulties which they rather had eluded than escaped meet them again in their course; they multiply and thicken on them; they are involved, through a labyrinth of confused detail, in an industry without limit, and without direction; and, in conclusion, the whole of their work becomes feeble, vicious, and insecure. [Pp. 437–8.]

23

actual virtue, but also to prevent the legitimate claimants to such virtue from overwhelming the equally legitimate claimants to presumptive virtue. For the actually virtuous and wise—the possessors of "ability," as he now termed them—were more powerful and aggressive than the presumptively virtuous and wise—the possessors of property. The former, therefore, had to be curbed lest the balance of society be impaired:

> Nothing is a due and adequate representation of a state, that does not represent its ability, as well as its property. But as ability is a vigorous and active principle, and as property is sluggish, inert, and timid, it [property] never can be safe from the invasions of ability, unless it be, out of all proportion, predominant in the representation.[2]

"Compared with Burke," I had said in the first essay, "Hobbes was an exemplary democrat; he assigned to all men the same instincts, distrusted all for the same reasons, and thought of civil society as profiting all equally." By the same token, it might now be claimed that, compared with Hobbes, Burke was an exemplary liberal. For where Hobbes thought of all men as equal under the Leviathan, all having equally yielded their natural rights to the omnipotent ruler, Burke denied the omnipotence of the ruler as well as the natural rights of the ruled. Rulers and ruled alike were bound by convention and law: "That convention must limit and modify all the descriptions of constitution which are formed under it. Every sort of legislative, judicial, or executory power are its creatures."[3] Sovereignty was not located in this or that institution but in the whole complex of government. Thus neither house of parliament could infringe upon the other, or, for that matter, abdicate its own power. "The engagement and pact of society, which

2. P. 324.
3. P. 332.

generally goes by the name of the constitution, forbids such invasion and such surrender. The constituent parts of a state are obliged to hold their public faith with each other."[4]

As Hobbes assumed sovereignty to be absolute, so he assumed liberty to be meaningless. Burke, on the other hand, rejecting absolute sovereignty, affirmed both the possibility and the desirability of liberty—not absolute liberty, but "rational liberty," a "rational and manly freedom."[5] In this respect, the *Reflections* was directed as much against Hobbes as against Paine:

> To make a government requires no great prudence. Settle the seat of power; teach obedience; and the work is done. To give freedom is still more easy. It is not necessary to guide; it only requires to let go the rein. But to form a *free government;* that is, to temper together these opposite elements of liberty and restraint in one consistent work, requires much thought, deep reflection, a sagacious, powerful, and combining mind.[6]

Burke, I had written, "realized, better perhaps than modern readers who delicately refrain from vulgar imputations of economic motives, that the essence of aristocracy was property, and the genius of the system of prescription, as of inheritance, was that it 'leaves acquisition free; but it secures what it acquires.'" Such imputations of motive, however, may be untrue as well as vulgar. For the subject of Burke's remark, the thing that left acquisition free while securing what had been acquired, was the "idea of inheritance." And inheritance, in this context, applied not to the inheritance of property or title but to the inheritance of liberty and reform—what he earlier called "the pedigree of our liberties."[7] The discussion of "acquisition" opened

4. P. 294.
5. Pp. 278, 325, 282, 308.
6. P. 515. Italics in original.
7. P. 305.

with the statement: "It has been the uniform policy of our constitution to claim and assert our liberties, as an *entailed inheritance* derived to us from our forefathers, and to be transmitted to our posterity."[8] Property entered the discussion only metaphorically: as property was transmitted and secured by inheritance, so were liberty and reform:

> The idea of inheritance furnishes a sure principle of conservation, and a sure principle of transmission; without at all excluding a principle of improvement. It leaves acquisition free; but it secures what it acquires. . . . We transmit our government and our privileges, in the same manner in which we enjoy and transmit our property and our lives. . . . We have derived several other, and those no small benefits, from considering our liberties in the light of an inheritance. . . . This idea of a liberal descent inspires us with a sense of habitual native dignity. . . . By this means our liberty becomes a noble freedom. It carries an imposing and majestic aspect. It has a pedigree and illustrating [*sic*] ancestors. . . .[9]

It is readily admitted by many commentators that Burke was a liberal—if liberalism is conceived of in opposition to democracy. Against the democratic claims of popular sovereignty, he urged the claims of ancient liberties—the countervailing forces of institutions, traditions, conventions, laws, and interests—whatever imposed limits on democratic as on autocratic power. Yet there is a sense in which Burke went beyond this negative species of liberalism, beyond the limitation of power, to an affirmation of communality that was something more than the usual organic, hierarchical society.

Again this side of Burke reveals itself by contrast to Hobbes. And again my earlier argument may be turned on its head. Burke, I had said, was as much the twin of fear as

8. P. 306. Italics in original.
9. Pp. 307–8.

Hobbes, and more the slave of his obsession because he was the less candid about it. "Where Hobbes," I had argued, "feared everyone indiscriminately, on the theory that all men were driven by the same sense of insecurity and insatiable lust for power, Burke, like Machiavelli, feared only those who were deprived of effective governing power, and who, presumably, would risk everything to get at the sources of power." This is the conventional image of the antidemocratic Burke. But a recent brilliant study by Harvey C. Mansfield, Jr., puts the subject in a quite different perspective.[1] Burke, he says, was in fact engaged in counteracting the Hobbesian obsession by denying the pre-eminence of fear in civil society. This thesis is particularly striking as it is applied to those passages of the *Reflections* most often singled out for ridicule and execration—the paean to Marie Antoinette, which had given rise to Paine's remark about pitying the plumage instead of the bird (and which I had consigned to the "magnolia-and-Old-South school of writing"). What Burke was extolling, this thesis has it, was the variety of sentiments evoked by the spectacle of royalty—honor, chivalry, reverence, manners—sentiments that, unlike fear, were benign and humane. "All the super-added ideas, furnished from the wardrobe of a moral imagination," Burke wrote, as if in direct rebuttal to Hobbes, were "necessary to cover the defects of our naked shivering nature." It was this "mixed system of opinion and sentiment" that gave law and authority a higher sanction than that provided either by private interests or by "their own terrors":[2]

> It was this, which, without confounding ranks, had produced a noble equality, and handed it down through all the gradations of social life. It was this opinion which mitigated kings into companions, and raised private men to be fellows with kings. Without force or opposition, it

1. *Statesmanship and Party Government* (Chicago, 1965).
2. "Reflections," p. 350.

27

subdued the fierceness of pride and power; it obliged sovereigns to submit to the soft collar of social esteem, compelled stern authority to submit to elegance, and gave a dominating vanquisher of laws to be subdued by manners.[3]

Honor, chivalry, reverence, manners—all that which is generally thought to reveal Burke at his most aristocratic, his most snobbish, precious, and pretentious—may be taken as part of his argument for the amelioration of tyranny and inequality. In one passage after another, the tokens and tributes of rank were praised as the means of subduing superiors as much as inferiors. Thus "opinion . . . mitigated kings into companions," and the "chastity of honor . . . mitigated ferocity." The "old feudal and chivalrous spirit of *Fealty* . . ., by freeing Kings from fear, freed both kings and subjects from the precautions of tyranny." It was these "pleasing illusions, which made power gentle and obedience liberal, which harmonized the different shades of life, and which, by a bland assimilation, incorporated into politics the sentiments which beautify and soften private society." If ever these sentiments and illusions were dissipated, if power were stripped of "its own honor, and the honor of those who are to obey it," there would be no redress against tyranny. "Kings will be tyrants from policy when subjects are rebels from principle."[4]

Thus what is generally taken as an effusive and fatuous display of rhetoric may be read as a sober statement of principle: the need for sentiment, and rhetoric itself, to take the place of fear. And what appears to be an excessive veneration for rank and power may be interpreted as a calculated attempt to pacify rank, domesticate power, and temper the inequalities of life. Burke's rhetoric, hysterical and shrill in tone, was suprisingly muted and conciliatory

3. P. 349.
4. Pp. 349-50.

in substance; the key words were "mitigate" and "subdue," "gentle" and "liberal," "harmonize," "assimilate," and "incorporate."

The panegyric over Marie Antoinette was only the most dramatic illustration of a quality of mind, an intellectual strategy, that Burke exhibited again and again. On the surface, he seemed to go deliberately against the grain of liberal, democratic thought; beneath the surface, by means that were not so much oblique as unconventional, he gave effect to values that were significantly liberal and democratic. His conception of party may be understood in these terms. In my earlier essay, I introduced the idea of party only to suggest that Burke's association with the "most aristocratic faction of the Whig party" made nonsense of any democratic pretensions on his part (or on his behalf). Had I pursued the subject further, I would have endorsed Goldsmith's famous judgment of Burke,

> Who, born for the universe, narrowed his mind,
> And to party gave up what was meant for mankind.[5]

Mansfield makes exactly the opposite point. He sees the legitimization of party, the idea of party as a necessary and proper instrument of politics, as Burke's unique contribution to modern political thought—and by implication, to the liberal, democratic state. Moreover, he continues, this legitimization, and liberalization, of party derived from the same idea of presumption that is commonly associated with Burke's conservatism—the idea of presumptive virtue and wisdom. Bolingbroke, Burke's antagonist on the subject of party, could not admit the legitimacy of party because he could not admit the legitimacy of any such presumptive attribution of virtue and wisdom: as he sought for "first

5. Oliver Goldsmith, "Retaliation."

principles" in philosophy, so he sought for first principles in politics; as he repudiated prejudice and superstition in the name of reason, so he repudiated party and faction in the name of statesmanship. Thus Bolingbroke was committed to the ideal of a patriot-king personifying absolute virtue and wisdom. Burke, on the other hand, opposed the patriot-king and justified the existence of party because he allowed for the existence of presumptive virtue and wisdom.

Similarly, Burke's partiality for prejudice and superstition is susceptible to the same double reading. It may be taken, as I once took it, as part of the conservative strategy —an assertion of the intellectual and political incapacity of the populace, a device for keeping the people in their place and "making impregnable the existing autocratic state." In another sense, however, it was a necessary part of the liberal strategy. The legitimization of prejudice and superstition enhanced the moral authority of the populace by minimizing intellectual differences, bridging social barriers, and creating, once again, a continuum of all men. There was a democratic undertone in Burke's constant appeal to the "common feelings," the "natural feelings," the "moral constitution of the heart," the "wisdom of unlettered men."[6] These common feelings and common wisdom were the basis of what he called the "true moral equality of mankind."[7]

One might say that it was the ostensible democrats (Paine, most notably) who, by insisting upon the radical disparity between prejudice and reason, between superstition and religion, were effectively denying this moral equality. Paine, of course, would have repudiated such a suggestion, decrying prejudice and superstition as the excrescences of a corrupt society, and affirming the ability of the common man to conduct his personal life and public affairs

6. "Reflections," pp. 352-3, 331.
7. P. 310.

in accord with pure reason and religion. The question at issue between Paine and Burke was whether the common man, or any man, did in fact have this ability—and ultimately, whether the common man had more in common with, more to hope from, the principle of absolute virtue and wisdom or that of presumptive virtue and wisdom.

THE HAUNTED HOUSE OF

JEREMY BENTHAM

> Never does the current of my thoughts alight
> upon the Panopticon and its fate, but my heart sinks
> within me.—Bentham, *History of the War between
> Jeremy Bentham and George III.*[1]
>
> I do not like to look among Panopticon papers. It
> is like opening a drawer where devils are locked up—
> it is breaking into a haunted house.—Bentham,
> *Memoirs*[2]

THE Panopticon that so obsessed Jeremy Bentham was
the plan of a model prison. He pursued it more en-
ergetically than any other project and mourned its failure
more passionately. He complained of a conspiracy of persecution; today he might more legitimately complain of a
conspiracy of silence. Historians and biographers, plodding
through his vast tomes and mass of manuscripts, have ignored the readily available and far more readable material
on the Panopticon. They have so resolutely closed their
minds to the devils haunting Bentham that they can hardly

1. Jeremy Bentham, *Works*, ed. John Bowring (London, 1843),
XI, 103.
2. Ibid., X, 250.

credit the reality of his obsession, let alone the reality of the devils.

Thus no one has adequately studied the actual plans of the Panopticon, its role in Bentham's private life, or its function in his philosophy and politics. His admirers invariably place it high among the credits earning him the title of the greatest reformer of modern times, without feeling the need to inquire into the exact nature of his proposed reform or the reasons for its rejection. His critics, preoccupied with his philosophical deficiencies, concede without argument the merits of this and other of his practical reforms. Even the smaller group of irreconcilables, who deride his facility for alternating between grand schemes of social reconstruction (constitutions, codes, and judiciaries created *de novo*) and what seem to be the crotchety schemes of a crank (Panopticon, Frigidarium, or Chrestomathia), are naturally more interested in the former than in the latter. As a result, the documents on the Panopticon have gone largely unnoticed. Not only historians and biographers but even legal and penal commentators seem to be unfamiliar with some of the most important features of Bentham's plan.

The structure of the Panopticon is sufficiently well known: a circular building with the cells at the circumference and the keeper in a tower at the center. And the opening words of Bentham's book have been widely quoted: "Morals reformed, health preserved, industry invigorated, instruction diffused, public burthens lightened, Economy seated, as it were upon a rock, the gordian knot of the Poor-Laws not cut but untied—all by a simple idea in Architecture!"[3] But even his admirers have not taken him seriously enough to find out how this "simple idea in

3. Ibid., IV, 39. The punctuation here, as elsewhere, has been slightly altered, mainly to eliminate the many dashes and commas. All italics, however, are in the original.

Architecture" could have so revolutionary an effect.[4] Yet Bentham was nothing if not serious. The title page of his book announced that the Panopticon was intended as a model not only for prisons but for "houses of industry, work-houses, poor-houses, manufactories, mad-houses, lazarettos, hospitals, and schools." And the second page elaborated upon its suitability for any establishment in which a number of people had to be kept under inspection, "no matter how different or even opposite the purpose: whether it be that of punishing the incorrigible, guarding the insane, reforming the vicious, confining the suspected, employing the idle, maintaining the helpless, curing the sick, instructing the willing in any branch of industry, or training the rising race in the path of education."[5] Subsequent chapters of the book showed how the plan was uniquely fitted to serve each of these purposes.

Indeed, the Panopticon had not originally been conceived as a prison at all. Bentham had borrowed the idea from his brother Samuel, who had constructed a workshop on Potemkin's estate in Russia. It was while visiting his brother in Russia in 1786 that Bentham thought of adapting the plan to other uses, particularly to that of a prison. He christened it Panopticon, from the Greek words meaning "all seeing." (Most of his inventions were subjected to this baptismal rite, as if Greek were a token of scientific grace.)

Certainly this was a fitting name for the "Inspection House," as the subtitle of his book described it. A remarkable quotation from the Psalms prefaced one of his sketches of the Panopticon—remarkable as much for its unlikely

4. Nor have his critics taken him seriously in his own terms. Aldous Huxley, for example, by considering only the architectural features of the plan, which suggested to him a "totalitarian housing project" ("today every efficient office, every up-to-date factory is a panopticon prison"), has trivialized both the subject and the criticism. (Huxley, "Variations on 'The Prison,'" *Themes and Variations* [New York, 1950], pp. 203–6.)
5. Bentham, *Works*, IV, 40.

source (Bentham was little given to scriptural citation) as for its perfect aptness:

> Thou art about my path, and about my bed: and spiest out all my ways.
> If I say, peradventure the darkness shall cover me, then shall my night be turned into day.
> Even there also shall thy hand lead me; and thy right hand shall hold me.[6]

Bentham did not believe in God, but he did believe in the qualities apotheosized in God. The Panopticon was a realization of the divine ideal, spying out the ways of the transgressor by means of an ingenious architectural scheme, turning night into day with artificial light and reflectors, holding men captive by an intricate system of inspection. Its purpose was not so much to provide a maximum amount of human supervision, as to transcend the human and give the illusion of a divine omnipresence:

> It is obvious that the more constantly the persons to be inspected are under the eyes of the persons who should inspect them, the more perfectly will the purpose of the establishment have been attained. Ideal perfection, if that were the object, would require that each person should actually be in that predicament, during every instant of time. This being impossible, the next thing to be wished for is that, at every instant, seeing reason to believe as much, and not being able to satisfy himself to the contrary, he should *conceive* himself to be so.[7]

This was the genius of Bentham's scheme. Aspiring to the "ideal perfection" of complete and constant inspection, he preferred to simulate this ideal rather than to compromise it. And this simulation was achieved by adopting another attribute of God—invisibility. Because of the inspector's "invisible eye"[8] each inmate would "conceive"

6. Ibid., XI, 96.
7. Ibid., IV, 40.
8. Ibid., IV, 79.

himself in a state of complete and constant inspection because he would never be able to "satisfy himself to the contrary." All the architectural details so elaborately worked out by Bentham—the exact arrangement of partitions, passages, floor levels, doors, and windows—were designed for this end: to combine "the *apparent omnipresence* of the inspector (if divines will allow me the expression), . . . with the extreme facility of his *real presence*."[9]

For schools, factories, and the like, the inspection principle was a necessary and sufficient condition. As a prison, however, the Panopticon required the addition of another principle, a "law of solitude." The old adage "Never less alone than when alone" was to be rendered "Never more alone than in a crowd." The multitude, that is, was to be transformed into a mass of "solitary and sequestered individuals."[1] This effect would be achieved by confining each prisoner to a private cell set off by walls and partitions in such a way as to block out the view of every other cell. Here the prisoner would sleep, eat, and work. He was even to have private toilet facilities so as to eliminate that occasion for gregariousness. To be sure, no ingenuities of architecture or plumbing could create an inviolable sound barrier, but that difficulty would be overcome by gagging the obstreperous—a humane and painless deterrent, Bentham argued, compared with the irons used elsewhere to enforce solitude.

The Panopticon was also superior to other penitentiaries in not having to suspend the law of solitude even for Sunday-morning religious worship. There was to be "no thronging nor jostling in the way between the scene of work and the scene destined to devotion; no quarrelings, nor confederatings, nor plottings to escape; nor yet any

9. Ibid., IV, 45.
1. Ibid., IV, 47.

whips or fetters to prevent it."[2] Instead, the prisoners would enjoy the benefits of religious worship, "without stirring from their cells," by the simple expedient of observing and hearing the services rather than actually attending them. For this purpose, the chapel was located in the center of the structure just above the inspector's lodge, the chaplain himself (unlike the inspector) being visible to the inmates, and his voice made audible by means of the same system of speaking tubes used by the inspector to transmit his orders.

As Bentham was pleased, for reasons both of humanity and of economy, to dispense with the conventional chapel, so he was also pleased, for the same reasons, to do without the usual costly dungeon. In the Panopticon, he announced, "the man is in his dungeon already (the only sort of dungeon, at least, which I conceive any man need be in), very safe and quiet."[3] The mode of reasoning was typical. If inspection was good, surely a maximum amount of inspection was best. If solitude was good, absolute solitude was best. And if safety and quiet were desirable, what could be safer, quieter, and better than a cell that was virtually a dungeon?

It could only be, Bentham argued, because "consistency is of all human qualities the most rare" that men might resist his plan. Thus most parents would agree that "children cannot be too much under the master's eye"; if parents were consistent, they "should be fonder of the principle the farther they saw it pursued." Instead, they provokingly drew back "when they saw that point screwed up at once to a pitch of perfection so much beyond whatever they could have been accustomed to conceive." They suddenly developed scruples and doubts:

> Whether it would be advisable to apply such constant and unremitting pressure to the tender mind, and to give

2. Ibid.
3. Ibid., IV, 54.

such herculean and ineludible strength to the gripe of power? Whether persons, of the cast of character and extent of ideas that may be expected to be found in the common run of schoolmasters, are likely to be fit receptacles for an authority so much exceeding anything that has been hitherto signified by *despotic?* . . . Whether the irretrievable check given to the free development of the intellectual part of his frame by this unintermitted pressure may not be productive of an imbecility similar to that which would be produced by constant and long-continued *bandages* on the corporeal part? . . . Whether the liberal spirit and energy of a free citizen would not be exchanged for the mechanical discipline of a soldier, or the austerity of a monk? And whether the result of this high-wrought contrivance might not be constructing a set of *machines* under the similitude of *men?*

But these scruples, Bentham protested, were all beside the point. The only pertinent question was: "Would *happiness* be most likely to be increased or diminished by this discipline?" His answer was unequivocal; and if it was intended for schoolboys, it applied *a fortiori* to prisoners: "Call them soldiers, call them monks, call them machines: so they were but happy ones, I should not care. Wars and storms are best to read of, but peace and calms are better to enjoy."[4]

"Safe and quiet," "peace and calms"—the Panopticon, like Hobbes's Leviathan, was born out of fear. Bentham was not the first prison reformer to discover the virtues of safety and quiet. But he was the first to make absolutes of these virtues, to take refuge in the dungeon as Hobbes had taken refuge in the absolute state. The Panopticon is so dramatic a scheme that less dramatic proposals tend to be ignored, or if not ignored then subtly denigrated, as Bentham himself denigrated whatever fell short of the

4. Ibid., IV, 63-4.

absolute "pitch of perfection." In fact, the Panopticon was so far from being the only plan of prison reform current at the time that it was itself a response to an earlier plan that had actually been approved by parliament.

The state of the penal law and of the prisons had occupied reformers in and out of parliament long before Bentham. A translation of Beccaria's *On Crimes and Punishments*, with a preface by Voltaire, appeared in England in 1767, affirming the purpose of all law, and specifically penal law, to be "the greatest happiness of the greatest number."[5] It was followed in 1771 by William Eden's *Principles of Penal Law*, in which "public utility" was taken to be the practical measure of punishment.[6] Six years later, John Howard's exposure of *The State of the Prisons* led to new penal legislation. A bill of 1778, drafted by Eden and the famous jurist William Blackstone, provided for the construction of "Houses of Hard Labour." These were to be administered by men appointed by and responsible to the government, and the prisoners were to be confined in moderate solitude and employed at varying degrees of hard labor.

This bill is interesting as an exhibit not only of the general tenor of penal reform at the time but also of Bentham's attitude toward the subject before he had seized upon the idea of the Panopticon. In spite of his recent attack on Blackstone only two years earlier, Bentham was so well disposed to this bill that he published it together with a commentary by himself under the title *View of the Hard-Labour Bill*. In this pamphlet of 1778, he endorsed the bill's provision for "solitary confinement" (separate cells for sleeping and in special cases for work),[7] and for labor of the "hardest and most servile kind" for those physically

5. Cesare Beccaria, *On Crimes and Punishments* (London, 1767), p. 2.
6. Lord Auckland (William Eden), *Principles of Penal Law* (London, 1771), p. 6.
7. Bentham, *Works*, IV, 3.

capable of it.[8] Where the bill had provided for distinctive clothing to "humiliate the wearer" and prevent escape, Bentham proposed to supplement this with chemical washes applied to the forehead, or cheek, or whole face, possibly spelling out the offender's name and jail.[9] He agreed that visits from family and friends should be prohibited, not only, as the authors of the bill thought, to prevent mischief, but also to shroud the prison in mystery and thus "enhance the terrors" of jail for "persons in such ranks in life" who were themselves potential criminals.[1] For the same reasons of security and terror, he approved of dungeons, although not unhealthy ones. Fresh air, he pointed out hopefully, would not diminish the salutary terrors of isolation, silence, darkness, and strangeness; and if the presence of windows should occasion some small loss of terror, this could be made up for by additional deprivations of diet. For considerations of health, too, he recommended that prisoners be provided with sheets, bedsteads, and steam heating. And finally, "to inculcate the justice, to augment the terror, and to spread the notoriety" of the prison, he proposed the carving of suitable inscriptions and bas-reliefs over the entrance way. "Violence and knavery/ Are the roads to slavery" was one of his suggestions, accompanied by the picture of a wolf and fox yoked together to a cart and being whipped by the driver. "Let me not be accused of trifling," he concluded. "Those who know mankind, know to what a degree the imagination of the multitude is liable to be influenced by circumstances as trivial as these."[2]

The Penitentiary Act of 1779 adopted some of these recommendations (although not the poetic and artistic renditions over the gateway). But mainly because of the

8. Ibid., IV, 16.
9. Ibid., IV, 20.
1. Ibid., IV, 23.
2. Ibid., IV, 32.

obstinacy of John Howard, who was one of the commis-
sioners charged with putting it into effect, no site was
decided upon and the act was left in abeyance. Seven years
later, while visiting his brother in Russia, Bentham saw the
means of implementing the act. Instead, however, of the
penitentiary prescribed by Eden and Blackstone, he now
put forward his plan of the Panopticon. In a sense, the
Panopticon was the penitentiary screwed up to that pitch
of perfection of which only Bentham was capable. It is
tempting to think of it as a fantasy, a mythical utopia, even
a divine vision tainted by divine madness. Unlike Plato or
More, however, Bentham regarded his creation not as an
ideal against which reality might be measured, but as a
practicable, potential reality. His friends in England had
been assuring him that the time was ripe for reform: "Our
ministers, as they have little to do abroad, seem to be full of
schemes for domestic improvement."[3] The Penitentiary
Act was a token of this mood of reform. And the Panopticon, Bentham hoped, would become the new penitentiary.

There was one crucial difference between the Penitentiary Act and the Panopticon, apart from the obvious
differences in supervision and seclusion. The act had meant
to do away with the prevailing practice of confining prisoners to jail without work or farming them out to work
for private contractors. It had been not uncommon for a
contractor to take over an entire prison, hiring out workers
as he chose, exacting fees from the inmates for their keep,
selling them liquor and other amenities, and in general
running it as a private and often exceedingly lucrative
enterprise. The act proposed to change all this by making
the prison what we understand it to be today—a public
institution. A committee appointed by the government was
charged with the general superintendence of the peniten-

3. Trail to Bentham, Feb. 26, 1787, *Works*, X, 172.

tiary and the selection of officers. Two members of this committee were to visit the prison fortnightly to investigate conditions, report abuses, deal with breaches of discipline, and recommend commutation of sentences. In addition, the prison was to be visited by justices of the peace and, once a quarter, by a specially appointed inspector. At the time, Bentham had entirely approved of these arrangements, cautioning only against the delegation of too much power to the governor of the prison: "Jealousy, not confidence," he had written, "is the characteristic of wise laws."[4]

In drawing up the plan of the Panopticon, however, Bentham reversed himself, as well as seeking to reverse the whole trend of penal reform. In contrast to the penitentiary proposed in the act, the Panopticon was to be run entirely by private contract management. The contract system was so essential to his scheme and so paramount in his mind that Bentham later denied having ever favored anything else.[5] Whatever his earlier views, his book on the Panopticon minced no words: "To come to the point at once, I would do the whole by *contract*. I would farm out the profits, the no-profits, or if you please the losses, to him who, being in other respects unexceptionable, offered the best terms." The contractor would continue in possession

4. Ibid., X, 29.
5. In 1830 he claimed that his pamphlet on the Hard-Labour Bill had been a "complete demonstration of its inaptitude" on the grounds of public management. (Ibid., XI, 98.) Yet earlier, in the preface to the second edition of the *Fragment on Government*, he had described the pamphlet more moderately: "The tone, . . . though free, and holding up to view numerous imperfections, was upon the whole laudatory: for my delight at seeing symptoms of ever so little a disposition to improvement, where none at all was to be expected, was sincere, and warmly expressed." (Ibid., I, 255.) Unfortunately, it is the 1830 statement that has been generally credited by most historians. E.g., "the plan of the architecture and management of a convict prison set forth in the bill was subjected to a severe criticism." (Coleman Phillipson, *Three Criminal Reformers* [London, 1923], p. 120.)

of the contract on condition of his good behavior—
"which," Bentham added, "is as much as to say, unless
specific instances of misbehaviour, flagrant enough to render
his removal expedient, be proved on him in a legal way, he
shall have it for his *life*." And as in any other private
enterprise, the contractor would be given "all the *powers*
that his interest could prompt him to wish for, in order to
enable him to make the most of his bargain." There were,
to be sure, "some slight reservations" upon the exercise of
these powers—"very slight ones you will find they will be,
that can be needful or even serviceable in the view of
preventing abuse." These reservations were: the publication of accounts, the obligation not to starve or maltreat
the prisoners, and the promise to keep the establishment
open for inspection at all times. Inspection, however, was
to be not by an official visiting committee as was provided
in the Penitentiary Act, but by "the great *open committee*
of the tribunal of the world*"—that is, private, casual observers without public status or authority.[6]

Even these slight reservations, Bentham reasoned, were
largely supererogatory since the contract system, like the
system of private enterprise from which it derived, was
itself the best guarantee of the public welfare. The contractor, like any employer, had every incentive to keep his
laborers well nourished and in good health, which is to say,
in good working condition. An additional incentive was a
novel insurance arrangement whereby the contractor
would pay the government a fixed sum for the death of
each prisoner—setting his contract, of course, at such a
figure as would recompense him for the normal death rate.
Such devices, Bentham hoped, would redeem prison contractors from the contempt in which they were commonly
held. He himself professed greater trust in a contractor
than in a magistrate, for the contractor in pursuing his own
interest was also promoting the public good, whereas the

6. Bentham, *Works*, IV, 46–8.

magistrate, having no interest but "the exercise of his own power and the display of his own wisdom," was willful and irresponsible.[7]

This plan of the Panopticon, based on the principles of inspection, solitude, and contract, was described in a series of letters written by Bentham while still in Russia in 1786. The letters, in a single packet, were sent to England in December with instructions to his friend, George Wilson, to have them published as a pamphlet.[8] Wilson, who was always urging Bentham on to bigger and better projects but was rarely happy with them when they materialized, refused to assume this responsibility (as he also refused to do anything about Bentham's *Defense of Usury* entrusted to him about the same time).

The letters were finally published in 1791. By that time, Bentham had had many afterthoughts and the pamphlet had grown into a considerable work (three small volumes in its first edition). The letters appeared substantially as they had been initially written, under the dateline "Crecheff in White Russia, 1787"—1787 being the date of their originally projected publication. But they were now accompanied by a preface explaining the circumstances of their composition and by a "postscript" four times the length of the letters. In the preface Bentham explained that

7. Ibid., IV, 51.

8. In the *Panopticon*, published in 1791, Bentham claimed that the letters had been written "without any immediate or very determinate view to general publication." (Ibid., IV, 39.) His correspondence, however, leaves no doubt that they were from the first intended for publication, the letter form being used only as a convention. When he sent them to Wilson, he described them as a "two-penny-halfpenny pamphlet, consisting, I suppose, from 150 to 200 pages," and he made specific suggestions as to publisher, printer, and format. (Ibid., X, 165.) His *Defence of Usury*, also carrying the dateline of Crichoff, 1787, was similarly cast in the form of letters. (Bentham sometimes used the alternative spelling, "Crecheff.")

the postscript altered the original plan in many respects, but that he had permitted the letters to stand because he had not the time to recast the whole, because his "general principle" was equally well illustrated in either form, and because it would be amusing and instructive to exhibit the plan "in an historical and progressive point of view."[9] A more compelling reason, perhaps, which he did not mention, was that the government of Ireland, exploring the possibility of a "Poor Inspection House" to be constructed on the model of the Panopticon, had subsidized the printing of the letters.[1]

Panopticon: or the Inspection House, the title under which the work was published in 1791, included, then, both the original letters of 1786 and the lengthy postscript written five years later. Yet it has always been treated as a unified work, thus ignoring the gap of time separating the two parts and the substantial differences between them. In fact, the two parts are even more distinctive than Bentham intimated. And looking at them from a "historical and progressive point of view," as he suggested, may be more instructive than he thought.

The most obvious of the changes introduced in the postscript may seem at first to have been prompted by an accession of simple humanitarianism. This was the abandonment of absolute solitude. Instead of single cells, Bentham now proposed that each cell be made to accommodate two, three, or four prisoners, the number to depend upon their character, their employment, and the fluctuating population of the prison as a whole. He hastened to say that the Panopticon system itself—the basic mode of architecture, inspection, and management—was unaffected by this change, being equally appropriate to this revised plan

9. Ibid., IV, 39.
1. This also accounts for the fact that the part of the book consisting of the letters was printed in Dublin, whereas the postscript was first printed in London and then reprinted in Ireland.

of "mitigated seclusion" as to the "absolute solitude" of the original plan. Under the original plan, as he now saw it, the Panopticon system "enables you to screw up the punishment to a degree of barbarous perfection never yet given to it in any English prison, and scarcely to be given to it by any other means." Under the revised plan, the Panopticon would have all the advantages of solitude without its "inconveniences." Absolute solitude, he now quoted Howard's earlier work, "is more than human nature can bear, without the hazard of distraction or despair." Its only proper use was "the breaking the spirit, as the phrase is, and subduing the contumacy of the intractable." But as such it could only be a temporary measure. "Why, then," he asked, "at an immense expense set up a perpetual establishment for the sake of so transitory a use?"[2]

"At an immense expense"—this, much more than the "barbarous perfection" of absolute solitude, appears to have been the main "inconvenience" of the original plan. By Bentham's own account, it was neither his belated attention to Howard nor his newly aroused sense of compassion that caused him to reconsider the merits of absolute solitude:

What startled me, and showed me the necessity of probing the subject to the bottom, was the being told by an architect, that the walls alone as expressed in Plate III might come to two or three thousand pounds. It was high time then to inquire what the advantages were that must be so dearly paid for.[3]

2. Ibid., IV, 71-2. Sir Samuel Bentham's wife claimed that it was her husband who persuaded Jeremy to give up the idea of solitary confinement. (Maria Bentham, *Life of Brigadier-General Sir Samuel Bentham, K.S.G.* [London, 1862], p. 100.) But her zeal to enhance her husband's reputation, particularly at the expense of her brother-in-law, makes much of this biography unreliable. If Samuel Bentham had indeed been opposed to solitary confinement, he would have been better able to exercise his influence at the time of the writing of the first plan, when they were in Russia together.
3. Ibid., IV, 138.

Nor was the cost of construction the only expense of solitude, he discovered. Double, triple, or quadruple the occupants of the cells and the costs of heating, lighting, toilet facilities, and such were divided by two, three, or four. At the same time, the working opportunities were multiplied, not only by permitting trades requiring more room than was available in a single cell, but by permitting those requiring the cooperation of two or more workers. And the prisoners would be more productive, it being well known that "the state of the spirits" of the worker was reflected in his work, and that companionship was more conducive to a favorable state of the spirits than isolation.[4]

Bentham had earlier defended the Panopticon against the Penitentiary Act on the grounds that only absolute solitude could prevent the moral contamination of one prisoner by another and thus give the best hope of reformation. Now he was proposing considerably less solitude than that envisaged in the act (which provided for single cells) and claiming for his new plan all the moral superiority of the old. The system of inspection, he now decided, was sufficient in itself to forestall mischief; for while it could not actually prevent the communication of "pernicious instruction," it would make it impossible to act upon such instruction—at least "for many years to come."[5] He also discovered in mitigated seclusion the moral virtues of mitigated association, and was moved to a rare display of eloquence:

> Sequestered society is favourable to friendship, the sister of the virtues. Should the comrades agree, a firm and innocent attachment will be the natural fruit of so intimate a society, and so long an union.
> Each cell is an island: the inhabitants, shipwrecked mariners, cast ashore upon it by the adverse blasts of fortune: partners in affliction, indebted to each other for

4. Ibid., IV, 74.
5. Ibid., IV, 72.

whatever share they are permitted to enjoy of society, the greatest of all comforts. . . .

A fund of society will thus be laid up for them against the happy period which is to restore them to the world. . . . Quitting the school of adversity, they will be to each other as old school-fellows, who had been through the school together, always in the same class.[6]

This paean to the old-school-tie did not survive the occasion that inspired it; certainly there was no reminiscence of it, as will be seen, in his provisions for released prisoners. And in general his newly awakened sensibility failed him when it was not sustained by economic advantage. He did not, for example, go so far in the mitigation of seclusion as to permit prisoners to attend chapel. Now, as before, they were to remain in their cells and worship from afar: "There they are in a state of continued safe custody; and there they are without any additional expense." To be sure, only half the prisoners could remain in the safe custody of their own cells; on his revised plan, only three tiers of cells enjoyed a view of the chapel, so that the occupants of the other three tiers had to be moved to the more fortunately located cells—this double complement of prisoners, he trusted, "awed to silence by an invisible eye."[7] Yet in spite of the obvious inconvenience of this makeshift arrangement—the very "thronging" and "jostling" his plan had been designed to avoid—he refused to consider a more conventional form of worship in a more conventional chapel.

Nor did he relent when he discovered, after the final architectural plans were drawn up, that there was a large unused space in the area of the chapel. For he then found a more profitable use for that space—as a visitors' gallery. He cited the examples of other sightseeing attractions: the Asylum (for the insane), the Magdalen (for retired prosti-

6. Ibid., IV, 74–5.
7. Ibid., IV, 78–9.

tutes), and Lock Hospital (for the venereally diseased). Why should not the Panopticon be as popular as these? "The scene would be more picturesque; the occasion not less interesting and affecting." And the contributions that would be solicited from the visitors would encourage the contractor to "keep the establishment in a state of exemplary neatness and cleanliness, while the profit of them will pay him for the expense and trouble." The presence of visitors would also serve as a form of "gratuitous inspection," thus putting the contractor doubly on his mettle. Bentham did not seem to have considered the possibility that the contractor, so far from being inspired to greater exertions of neatness and cleanliness, might try to compete with the Asylum, Magdalen, or Lock Hospital in picturesque and exotic horrors. He did, however, take into account the criticism of one friend who suggested that this kind of "perpetual pillory" might have a corrupting effect upon the prisoners by hardening them into insensibility. To this objection he had several replies: that as the guilty were less numerous than the innocent, their serving as an example to others took priority over their personal reformation; that their offenses probably merited even more severe punishment than the pillory; that this form of pillorying was nothing to what they had been subjected at trial; and finally, if the objection persisted, that the prisoners might be provided with masks, thus sheathing the guilty while exposing the guilt.[8]

Behind each of these ingenious schemes and explanations was the overriding consideration of economy. The trinity of the earlier plan—inspection, solitude, and contract— gave way to a new trinity—lenity, severity, and economy. The "rule of lenity" prescribed that the conditions of imprisonment not be detrimental to health and life; the "rule of severity" that these conditions be no better than those of "the poorest class of subjects in a state of inno-

8. Ibid.

cence and liberty"; and the "rule of economy" that "no public expense ought to be incurred, or profit or saving rejected, for the sake either of punishment or of indulgence."[9] Economy was the primary rule: "Its absolute importance is great, its relative importance still greater." It was at the same time the measure of lenity (a malnourished or maltreated prisoner being an unprofitable worker) and the measure of severity, "for the ways in which any quantity of suffering may be inflicted, without any expense, are easy and innumerable," and the best punishments were those involving "the imposing some coercion which shall produce profit, or the subtracting some enjoyment which would require expense."[1]

If the rule of economy was paramount in matters of punishment and management it was more obviously so in the question of prison labor. On this subject, the "historical and progressive point of view" that Bentham recommended may be particularly instructive, especially if the history of his opinions is traced back to his *View of the Hard-Labour Bill*. The bill had originally provided for specified forms of servile labor (such as wheel-treading and hemp-beating), a six-day workweek, and a working day equivalent to the hours of daylight. Bentham had then approved of these provisions, adding only that on the Sabbath the men ought to be allowed, if they wished, to work in their customary trades,[2] and that the criterion of daylight might make for too long a working day in the summer and too short a one

9. Ibid., IV, 123.
1. Ibid., IV, 125.
2. In the *Panopticon* he wrote: "In my *View of the Hard-Labour Bill*, I ventured to throw out a hint upon the subject of putting the good hands to their own trades" (ibid., IV, 50)—the implication being that he had then spoken up against the idea of servile labor. But this suggestion had been made only in connection with voluntary work on the Sabbath and had not at all been intended to apply to the ordinary workweek.

in the winter. The Penitentiary Act as finally passed fixed the hours of work at eight, nine, or ten, depending upon the season, but rejected Sabbath work of any nature.

In his first plan of the Panopticon, Bentham departed radically from both his pamphlet and the Penitentiary Act by opposing not only the specified occupations but the idea of any specification of occupation. As the contractor was to run his establishment with a view to profit, he had to be free to choose whatever occupations were most profitable, and as it happened, the servile forms of labor were the least suited to the Panopticon system. The authors of the act, he protested, had thought too much of punishment and too little of economy. He himself did not see "why labour should be the less reforming for being profitable."[3] The question of the hours of work he passed over in silence, and it may be assumed that he intended this matter, like the choice of trades, to be left entirely to the discretion of the contractor.

The revised plan of the Panopticon went much further in this direction. Bentham now explicitly repudiated the idea of a "House of Hard Labour." The term hard labor, he said, gave "a bad name to industry, the parent of wealth and population." "Industry is a blessing; why paint it as a curse?"[4] So much a blessing, indeed, that there could hardly be enough of it. Neither the criterion of daylight of the original bill nor the eight to ten hours of the revised act now seemed adequate. Instead, he proposed that the working hours be "as many of the four and twenty as the demand for meals and sleep leave unengaged."[5] His program for the six working days specified one-and-a-half hours for meals, seven-and-a-half for sleep, one hour for exercise, and fourteen for work. "Are fourteen hours out of twenty-four too many for even a sedentary trade? Not

3. Ibid., IV, 50.
4. Ibid., IV, 144.
5. Ibid., IV, 142.

more than what I have seen gone through in health and cheerfulness in a workhouse by honest poor." Indeed the number could as well be fifteen, "without the smallest hardship," for "let it not be forgotten, meal times are times of rest: feeding is recreation." And the only habit worse than over-sleep was lying in bed awake, which was a "waste of health and time, one may almost say of good morals." It was not often that Bentham was provoked to speak of "good morals" in this fashion; he did so now because he was outraged by the thought of "five, six, seven, precious hours, out of fifteen, thrown away as offal." "As soon would I turn Macbeth and murder sleep, as thus murder health by smothering it under a pillow."[6]

In the new and improved Panopticon, health, morals, and industry all conspired to the same end—that of economy. Air and exercise, for example, were provided for in a minimum amount of space and in maximum seclusion by the device of having the prisoners "walk in a wheel," the speed and number of turns being determined in advance so that "a lazy prisoner cannot cheat you." This salubrious activity had the additional advantage of generating power "cheaper than you can employ even the powers of nature."[7] (Wheel-treading, rejected as a servile occupation, was thus reinstated as a mode of exercise.) Similarly the diet of the prisoners was such that both lenity and severity conduced to economy: lenity in allowing an unlimited quantity of food, thereby satisfying the needs of the laborer; severity in making it of the cheapest, least palatable, and least varied type. (Bentham derided those reformers, like "the good Howard," who tried to specify the quality of food and prescribed "butcher's meat for the lowest vulgar."[8]) And in the matter of beds and bedding, where he had earlier criticized the Hard-Labour Bill for neglecting to provide

6. Ibid., IV, 163.
7. Ibid., IV, 159.
8. Ibid., IV, 154.

sheets and iron bedsteads, he now reverted to sacks in place of sheets, and wooden bedsteads (in spite of the admitted likelihood of their becoming infested with bugs), or better yet hammocks which were cheaper still. It would be amusing as well as instructive to go into these and other details of his revised plan. But this would mean transcribing a good part of the book, which would detract considerably from the amusement, if not from the instruction.

A point that deserves more than passing mention is the payment of the prisoner-worker. Bentham had earlier criticized the Hard-Labour Bill for not giving the prisoners any compensation for their labor, and he had worked out an elaborate formula for dividing one sixth of the gross profit among them. His first plan of the Panopticon, however, spoke not of a distribution of profits but rather of piece-work wages set at a considerably lower level than that prevailing in industry generally: "The confinement, which is his [the prisoner's] punishment, preventing his carrying the work to another market, subjects him to a monopoly; which the contractor, his master, like any other monopolist, makes, of course, as much of as he can."[9] The revised plan, although more detailed in all other respects, was silent on the matter of wages, except for an oblique reference to "earnings" out of which the prisoner would supplement his diet. A footnote explained why this was desirable: "Reward must assume the shape of a present gratification, and that too of the sensual class, or, in the eyes of perhaps the major part of such a company, it can scarcely be expected to have any value; and if it take a sensual shape, it cannot take a more unexceptionable one."[1]

This deprecation of saving, combined with the exhortation to sensual gratification (even if only the gratification

9. Ibid., IV, 54.
1. Ibid., IV, 153.

of the palate), comes oddly from one of Bentham's puritanical bent. It becomes intelligible, however, in the light of
one of the most important innovations of his new plan: the
provision for released prisoners. He had earlier praised the
Hard-Labour Bill for its "foresight and humanity" in
allowing each prisoner a small sum of money upon his
discharge, in addition to a certificate of good behavior if his
prison record merited it.[2] The first plan of the Panopticon
made no mention of the certificate but strongly advised
against the discharge allowance: "It might help to fit them
out for trades; it might serve them to get drunk with; it
might serve them to buy any house-breaking implements
which they could not so well come at to steal." The
interests of the prisoners as well as of the contractor,
Bentham vaguely suggested, would better be promoted by
"continuing the manufacturing connection."[3]

In the revised plan of the Panopticon, the provisions for
discharge were spelled out in great detail. Instead of the
authorities granting the prisoner an allowance and a testi-
monial of good behavior, it was the prisoner who now had
to provide the authorities with proof of his future financial
security and future good behavior. According to this plan,
the prisoner would be discharged only upon satisfying one
of three conditions: enlistment in the army, enlistment in
the navy, or the posting by a responsible householder of a
£50 bond as a guarantee of good conduct. In the latter case,
the bond was to be renewed annually, the failure of
renewal to mean the return of the prisoner to the penitentiary—"though it should be for life." To induce a householder to post such a bond, the prisoner would have to
contract his labor for a specified term (but as soon as the
term was up, the householder would obviously refuse to
renew the bond unless the contract was also renewed),
with the understanding that the householder would have

2. Ibid., IV, 21.
3. Ibid., IV, 55.

the same power as that "of a father over his child, or of a master over his apprentice."[4]

If the prisoner would not or could not meet these conditions, there remained only one recourse for him short of returning to prison. This was elaborated upon in a long footnote, as if in afterthought. "I take for granted," Bentham wrote, that "an establishment of some sort or other" would have to be set up to receive such prisoners. This "subsidiary establishment," he also took for granted, would be set up on the Panopticon principles. And obviously no one would be better fitted to run it than the contractor of the prison who would have "every facility for getting the most work done, and making the most of that work." Such an arrangement would be worth the contractor's while "because the convicts, having by the supposition no other course of life to betake themselves to, or none they liked so well, would serve on so much the cheaper terms." It would also be to the prisoner's advantage since the contractor is "a tried man in every respect, as well as a responsible one." Indeed, Bentham was so impressed by these mutual advantages that he thought the prisoner well advised to make an agreement with the contractor even before the expiration of his sentence: "I had rather the penitentiary governor should get the emancipated prisoners in this way, than any other undertaker, whom the view of profit, and not any particular connexion with, or friendship for the prisoner, might induce to bid for him." It was because he was partial to the contractor, he confessed, that he "viewed with satisfaction, rather than regret" the advantage enjoyed by the contractor in negotiations with the prisoner—although, he added, he would not entirely exclude other bidders since "such a monopoly would be a hardship on the prisoners, and that a needless one."[5]

4. Ibid., IV, 166–7.
5. Ibid., IV, 166.

"Needless" indeed. The contractor hardly had need of a formal monopoly in negotiating with a prisoner who was completely and exclusively under his control, not only for the duration of his sentence but potentially, as it now appeared, for the whole of his natural (or unnatural) life. It would almost seem that the whole matter of the text was really a pretext for the footnote, and that all the provisions for the "liberated prisoners," as Bentham euphemistically described them,[6] were designed to benefit the contractor and promote his subsidiary establishment. It is hard otherwise to account for the many difficulties placed in the way of the prisoners' release: setting the bond, for example, at so high a figure (£50 was a considerable sum at a time when the ordinary laborer received about ten shillings a week; for this sum the bondsman could engage a worker for two years without the expense of his upkeep); or making the contractor the judge of the bondsman's "responsibility"; or providing that those prisoners who chose the option of joining the army or navy be "stigmatized" and separated from other recruits for an unspecified probationary period until a ceremony reinstated them "in solemn form in the possession of lost character."[7] And not only the conditions of discharge but even the conditions of imprisonment seem to have been contrived for the same purpose. One can now understand Bentham's otherwise inexplicable encouragement of prisoners to spend their earnings on "present gratification." One might even suspect that it was more than the rules of economy and severity that dictated the poor and unvaried diet prescribed by him, and that the "liberty" to purchase a "more palatable diet out of his share of earnings" was intended to deplete the prisoner's savings and thus make him a more likely candidate for the subsidiary establishment.[8]

6. Ibid., IV, 165.
7. Ibid., IV, 166–7.
8. Ibid., IV, 153. (See above, p. 53.)

Even in sheer size the subsidiary establishment looms large over the prison itself. There is no figure given in the book for the population of the prison at any one time, but elsewhere Bentham alternated between the figures of one and two thousand. These prisoners would be serving sentences of varying length. (The Panopticon was not intended, as one might think, for long-term prisoners alone; on the contrary, its advantage, as Bentham saw it, was that it could accommodate all degrees of criminals without contamination.) Yet the conditions of discharge were to be the same for all prisoners, so that a man serving even a brief sentence would be, literally, in bondage for life—hence a potential lifelong inhabitant of the subsidiary establishment. How large, then, would this subsidiary establishment have to be to accommodate this turnover of "liberated" prisoners? Bentham did not say, and the mind quails at the thought.

"*Set a beggar a-horseback*, and the proverb tells you where he will *ride*. . . . The Penitentiary Act sets a whole regiment of such beggars on horseback, and it gives them no master to hold the reins." The question, Bentham concluded, was whether beggar or master was better qualified to hold the reins:

> In the convict, you see a man in whose breast the passion of the day is accustomed to outweigh the interest of the morrow: in the contracting governor, you have a man who knows what his lasting interest is, and is in the habit of pursuing it. . . . This man, whom you know, is the man to deal with, and not the convict, of whom you know nothing but what is to his disadvantage.[9]

Bentham distrusted the "beggar on horseback." But he had complete faith in the contractor who would command not a regiment but an army of beggars with not a horse among them.

9. Ibid., IV, 171.

. . .

The contractor was the key to Bentham's scheme, and in more than the sense that is by now all too obvious. As one proceeds in this study of the Panopticon, what emerges is more and more a travesty of the model prison and the model reformer. But the travesty is not yet complete. The final turn of the screw, the final pitch of perfection, is the discovery that Bentham himself actually intended to be the contractor and the governor of the prison.

There is a poetic rightness about this identification of Bentham with the contractor, so that even if it were not the literal fact, one would be tempted to assume it as a psychological fact. How else can one account for the extraordinary powers vested in one man, for the absolute confidence in his integrity, for the shaping of the whole scheme around him? Without some such conscious or unconscious identification, the Panopticon makes little sense.

In fact, the identification was not only conscious; it was also explicit and public. This introduces a subject that is as curious as the Panopticon itself: the strange, almost willful inattentiveness of biographers and historians to the most striking feature of the plan and the decisive cause of its rejection. To them Bentham was a philanthropist who sacrificed years of his life and most of his fortune to the exemplary cause of penal reform and who was inexplicably, as one biographer put it, "not to be allowed to benefit his country."[1] Most books on Bentham and even some of the most respectable histories of penal reform do not so much as mention the contract system in connection with

1. Charles Warren Everett, *The Education of Jeremy Bentham* (New York, 1931), p. 179. It is, perhaps, unfair to single out Mr. Everett's book for citation. The point could equally well have been made by quoting almost any biography of Bentham or history of Philosophical Radicalism. The subject of the gullibility and culpability of these biographers and historians is too vast to be documented here, but I shall deal with it at some length in my forthcoming book on Bentham.

the Panopticon, let alone identify Bentham as the proposed contractor. Yet it was the contract system that distinguished the Panopticon from other contemporary plans for penal reform, and it was Bentham's personal stake in it that distinguished this scheme from most of his other projects of reform. His Chrestomathia (a model school) was quickly conceived and as quickly abandoned, while the Panopticon involved him personally and passionately for the better part of his life. And unlike the constitutions, codes, and legal reforms that he released to the world and that became, so to speak, part of the public domain, the Panopticon was reserved for his private use.

Bentham did not try to conceal his intentions. He could hardly do so while soliciting a contract that would commission him to build, manage, superintend, and literally own the Panopticon. His official proposal to this effect was submitted to William Pitt in 1791. He then undertook to feed, clothe, lodge, employ, and otherwise minister to the physical and spiritual needs of the prisoners, "constantly living in the midst of them and incessantly keeping them in view." In return he was to receive "the produce of their labour" (minus an unspecified share of that produce to give them "an interest in their work"), in addition to a subsistence allowance from the government for each prisoner.[2]

When Edmund Burke was shown the plan of the Panopticon, he remarked: "There's the keeper, the spider in the web!" Recalling this years later, Bentham could only manage the feeble retort: "Always imagery."[3] But the image rankled because it expressed his own suspicion that there was something ignominious in the job. He tried to allay this

2. Report of Parliamentary Committee of 1811, *Parliamentary Debates*. Hansard, 20:cxix–cxxi (1811).

3. Bentham, *Works*, X, 564. According to a recent biographer, Burke made this remark in Bentham's presence at Bentham's own house. (Mary Mack, *Jeremy Bentham* [New York, 1963], p. 204.) But Bentham himself stated that he met Burke only once, at Philip Metcalf's house. (*Works*, X, 564.)

suspicion by insisting, for example, that the inspector's lodge befit a "style of living, equal or approaching to that of a gentleman," since one of that status, "or not much below it," would be occupying it.[4] And in an earlier draft of his proposal to Pitt, he stipulated that the "station of gaoler" be elevated by "a mark of distinction, not pecuniary, such as may testify that I have incurred no ultimate loss of honour by the service, and afford me some compensation for the intervening risk"[5]—presumably a bid for a knighthood or peerage.

It was not only the position of jailer, the "spider in the web," that was felt to be ignominious, but also that of contractor. Thus, in his proposal to Pitt he slurred over the question of profit, alluding to it only in subordinate clauses, while focusing attention on the obligations he was undertaking and the services he promised to perform. In the final paragraph he adopted the voice of the third person and the posture of the altruist:

> The station of gaoler is not in common account a very elevated one; the addition of contractor has not much tendency to raise it. He little dreamt, when he first launched into the subject, that he was to become a suitor, and perhaps in vain, for such an office. But inventions unpractised might be in want of the inventor: and a situation thus clipped of emoluments, while it was loaded with obligations, might be in want of candidates. Penetrated therefore with the importance of the end, he would not suffer himself to see anything unpleasant or discreditable in the means.[6]

4. Ibid., IV, 76.

5. Ibid., XI, 100. I have assumed that the proposal cited in Vol. XI of Bentham's *Works* was an early draft, in spite of his assurance that this was the proposal "in the terms in which it was sent in." (Ibid., p. 99.) It seems reasonable to suppose that the official proposal was that cited in the Parliamentary Committee Report.

6. Hansard, 20:cxxii (1811).

A situation "clipped of emoluments" and "loaded with obligations"—one would hardly recognize the contractor described in his book, who "knows what his lasting interest is, and is in the habit of pursuing it."[7]

Bentham's profession of disinterestedness was less than candid in other respects. While he may not have thought of himself as a "suitor" when he "first launched into the subject," there is no doubt that he not only thought but declared himself as such long before the postscript, at any rate, was completed. As early as January 1791, he was thanking Wilson for "the access you have got for me to the Contracts."[8] And on April 1 he reported to his brother: "I gave in a proposal to our Potemkin [Pitt] two months ago; but the Potemkins never give answers."[9] The proposal, therefore, must have been submitted early in February,[1] at which time only the original letters had been printed. The postscript came from the press in two installments, in May and July,[2] a lag that can only be accounted for by Bentham's delay in completing it. Thus the final plan of the Panopticon must have been written in full consciousness of his personal stake in it.

Nor was there anything of the diffident suitor in his importuning of friends, officials, politicians, even the king himself. To his brother he wrote:

> Cast about with Carew all sorts of measures that appear to hold out a chance of bringing Panopticon to bear here; —the bribery plans, for example, in the event of its not getting a hearing otherwise. This as from yourself: anything of that sort will come better from an intriguing Russian like you, than from a reformer like your betters.[3]

7. Bentham, *Works*, IV, 171. (See above, p. 57.)
8. Ibid., X, 247.
9. Ibid., X, 249.
1. Not, as he later claimed, in March 1792. (Ibid., XI, 99.)
2. Ibid., X, 261–2.
3. Ibid., X, 263.

There is no reason to suppose that he was being facetious: bribery was certainly familiar enough at all levels of public life—as he himself testified in his *Introduction to the Principles of Morals and Legislation* published two years earlier, where he analyzed the different modes of passive and active bribery.

He was equally tireless and ruthless in casting about for measures to improve upon his plan. Some of these he confided to a Scottish friend whom he was trying to persuade to apply for a contract for a Panopticon to be built in Scotland. The Panopticon, he assured his friend, was an even more profitable enterprise than he had ventured to suggest publicly:

> With regard to economy, I will unbosom myself to you without reserve. Part of my expedients you will find in print. I was afraid of giving the whole of them, or placing them in the clearest point of view of which they were susceptible, for fear of being beat down, or seeing others reap the fruit of my labours. A man who begins with saving 50 per cent to the nation, may be allowed to think a little for himself.

Among the "expedients" he had not thought to mention either in his book or in his proposal to Pitt were economies of clothing (the elimination of stockings, shirts, and hats); diet (potatoes could be grown very cheaply on prison land: "I have been afraid to show how immense the saving may be, by the exclusive adoption of this article"—this at a time when potatoes were regarded even by the poorest as animal fodder); bedding (hammocks, straw sacks, and "coat, waistcoat and breeches" used for blanketing); and working hours ("I get sixteen and a half profitable hours, very near twice as many as our Penitentiary systems allow"). In return for these confidences, Bentham exacted a pledge of collusion: "But having thus unbosomed myself to you, I rely on your honour not to make the offer till you have communicated it to me, and till you hear from me that the terms of it will not prejudice my negotiation."[4]

All these ingenuities and machinations seemed to be in vain. The government was too preoccupied with more urgent matters to consider Bentham's proposal. The country was no longer in the happy state described by his friend four years earlier, when ministers, having "little to do abroad," could indulge themselves in domestic reform.[5] Now there was all too much to do abroad. While Bentham was impatiently awaiting a reply from Pitt, Pitt himself was pursuing a foreign policy that threatened to overthrow his government and to precipitate a war with Russia. The crisis came to a head on April 1, the very day Bentham wrote to his brother complaining that "the Potemkins never give answers."[6] That Bentham could have been so oblivious of this crisis is particularly ironic, since only two years earlier he had himself publicly protested against the foreign policy that was now proving so disastrous, and he was later to attribute the failure of the Panopticon to his part in this controversy. At this time, however, he was too absorbed in the Panopticon to attend to anything else, while Pitt was too absorbed in affairs of state to attend to the Panopticon.

Despairing for the moment of Pitt, Bentham decided to offer his plan, and his person, to France. France was in the market for new codes, constitutions, institutions; he himself had already favored her with a manual of parliamentary procedures. Why not a prison as well? The Panopticon, he wrote Brissot, was "a project of improvement for which there is but too much room in every country, and I am afraid, not least in France: it is a mill for grinding rogues

4. Bentham, *Works*, X, 256–7.
5. Ibid., X, 172. (See above, p. 41.)
6. Ibid., X, 249. (See above, p. 61.)

honest, and idle men industrious.["]7 About the same time he suggested to his brother that they invite a French architect "to join us in fighting up Panopticon—his profit being on the building, ours on the management."[8] Later that year he made another appeal to the chairman of the Committee of Legislation of the French National Assembly:

> Allow me to construct a prison on this model—I will be the gaoler. You will see by the memoir that the gaoler will have no salary—will cost nothing to the nation. The more I reflect, the more it appears to me that the execution of the project should be in the hands of the inventor.[9]

He neglected to explain that the jailer, although receiving no salary, would receive the profits of the enterprise. Perhaps this omission accounts for the effusive reply of the National Assembly, which commended his "ardent love of humanity" and thanked him for his offer to serve "gratuitously" as jailer.[1] While his offer was not as altruistic as was supposed, he did give the French government an option he never extended to the English—that of adopting his plan without contracting for his services.

Bentham was more lenient in his offer to France because he had less at stake there. The English Panopticon was important not only for its own sake but for the success of another enterprise in which he and his brother had invested a good deal of capital and hope. This was a woodworking machine that Samuel Bentham had invented in Russia and that was the main reason for his return to England. Patents were taken out for the machine, and a full-scale model was erected in an outhouse in Jeremy Bentham's garden at Queen Square Place. Originally Samuel had planned to work the machine with steam, but its construction proved difficult

7. Ibid., X, 226. Bentham's editor erroneously attributed this letter to 1790.
8. Ibid., X, 264.
9. Ibid., X, 269.
1. Ibid., X, 270.

and costly enough without assuming the additional difficulties and cost of a steam engine. The Panopticon providently took the place of the engine. As Bentham later explained: "Human labour, to be extracted from a class of person, on whose part neither dexterity nor good will were to be reckoned upon, was now substituted to the steam engine, and the system of contrivance underwent a correspondent change."[2] Only the Panopticon could have provided a sufficiently large, cheap, and steady supply of manpower. "Now," Bentham told a friend who inquired about the progress of the woodworks, "is the season for experiment; for till it can be done in Panopticon, it will be hardly worth while to open shop."[3]

There is no mistaking the intimate connection between the Panopticon and this woodworking enterprise. In May 1793, Pitt and his Home Secretary, Henry Dundas (later Lord Melville), came personally to Queen Square Place to view what Bentham called his "raree show,"[4] of which the chief exhibit was not the small table model of the Panopticon but the wood-planing machine in operation. The following year Dundas, recommending Bentham's proposal to the House of Commons, explained that he had been converted from the principle of transporting convicts to that of employing them by the spectacle of "a machine that gave the power of sight without eyes, and touching without hands."[5]

Bentham had assumed that the Panopticon would come under the Penitentiary Act of 1779, and that it would be necessary only to negotiate a contract with the Exchequer. After the visit of Pitt and Dundas, a contract was

2. Ibid., XI, 167.
3. Ibid., X, 296.
4. Ibid., X, 291.
5. *The Senator*, X (1794), 1162.

drawn up. It was not, however, signed, the government having decided that a new act of parliament was required to authorize the plan. In October 1793, Bentham reported that he was busy drafting a bill, "at the recommendation of authority," to be introduced in the next session of parliament.[6] The bill was speedily approved by both houses, in spite of the fact that it completely reversed the earlier act. Instead of the system of public management provided for in 1779, the Penitentiary Act of 1794 lodged entire responsibility for the "care, management, superintendence and control" of the prison in the hands of a single contractor-governor.[7] The act was tailor-made to Bentham's specifications—as it might well be, since it was he himself who tailored it.

The contract naming Bentham as the contractor-governor of the new prison was equally well disposed to him. Some of his more ingenious economies, to be sure, were abandoned. He promised to feed the prisoners "wholesome sustenance, composed of bread and meat, and other articles commonly used for human food" (this presumably ruled out potatoes), to provide them with shirts as well as suits, and to furnish beds, sheets, and blankets. In other respects, however, he was given far more latitude than might have been expected. Neither the woodworks nor the Panopticon itself was so much as mentioned. Thus he was not bound even by his own plans and models. Instead the contract reserved to him the sole right to decide upon the structure of the building, the number of prisoners in each cell, the nature, hours, and conditions of labor, the mode of discipline, exercise, and all the other details of prison life. He was also given complete authority over his staff as well as over the prisoners: "Every officer and servant connected with the establishment is to be placed

6. Bentham, *Works*, X, 295.
7. Hansard, 20:c (1811).

there by his appointment and removable at his pleasure."[8]

Although his original proposal had stated that the government would not be asked to provide any capital, the contract called for an advance of £19,000, which was Bentham's estimate of the total cost of construction. In addition, the government agreed to pay an annual per capita allowance of £12 for a guaranteed minimum of one thousand prisoners, even if the actual number should fall below that. Three quarters of the profits were to be kept by Bentham, the remainder to be distributed among the prisoners as earnings or annuities. The contract was to be Bentham's for life, afterward passing to his brother, and dissolved only after the death of both when their heirs would be recompensed for the value of the buildings, stock, and other assets, minus the funds initially advanced by the government for construction. Provision was also made for the "subsidiary establishment" to house and employ not only released prisoners but also, as one member of parliament put it, "all those persons of blasted character who, though acquitted for want of legal proof, were thought to be guilty."[9]

The contract was to have been ratified upon the acquisition of a suitable plot of land. Here Bentham encountered unexpected difficulties. When he did finally get the necessary deeds, the Treasury refused to ratify the original contract. For ten years he tried first to have the decision reversed and then to be financially compensated.[1] Finally

8. Ibid., p. civ. These quotations are from the summary given in the Report of the Parliamentary Committee of 1811.

9. *Parliamentary Debates*, ed. Cobbett, XXX (1793), 959.

1. A curious episode occurred in 1798, when Bentham proposed that, as an interim arrangement, he be assigned the contract for the Hulks—the moored vessels that were being used as prisons and that were even more infamous than the Bridewells of the time. Having been so long deprived of the "benefits" from the new plan, he argued, why should he not at least reap the benefits from the old? He granted that the Hulks were "too

in 1811, a parliamentary committee reviewed the plan and rejected it, at the same time conceding Bentham's claim for compensation.

For Bentham personally, "a gentleman of great respectability," the members of the committee professed the highest regard. This, indeed, they found to be the main flaw of his plan—that it depended rather upon the personal character of the contractor than upon principles of sound administration. They compared it unfavorably with earlier reform measures which, for example, prohibited the governor from profiting by the sale of articles in the prison, whereas Bentham's contract left it entirely up to him to sell what he chose (except for alcoholic drinks) and at whatever price he pleased. They also compared it unfavorably with the penitentiaries recently established at Gloucester and Southwell, which were publicly managed and which provided for individual cells, moderate seclusion, and hard labor. The physical and moral welfare of the prisoners, they concluded, could be better secured by such a system of public management than by Bentham's, for in the latter there was no "channel of complaint" or "higher authorities to censure or control the keeper," and every measure was "formed and directed by a person whose interest it must be that the prisoners committed to his charge should do as much work as they were competent to execute and that their labour should be exercised in the manner by which most profit would be produced."[2]

Bentham's testimony before the committee did nothing to allay these fears. He declined to be bound by anything but the literal sense of the contract. And since the contract

---

effectually vicious to admit of much improvement"; yet he might be able to do something, and in any case he could surely do no worse than the present incumbent. (*Works*, XI, 117.) This proposal was not the impulse of the moment. Bentham submitted it to the Treasury twice at an interval of several months, and it was twice, if not actually rejected, at least politely ignored.

2. Hansard, 20:ci–cviii (1811).

gave him complete latitude to determine living and working conditions, he "reserved to himself all those advantages,"[3] including the right to assign the prisoners to night
work if that proved economical, to lodge six or eight in one
cell, and to use hammocks in place of beds. He refused to
make provision, as the Act of 1779 had done, for the
commuting of sentences, and it was obvious that any such
commutation would be a violation of contract since it
would deprive him of the labor that was rightfully his. He
also insisted upon the insurance scheme in place of the usual
medical supervision, and upon the visitors' gallery in place
of official inspectors. George Holford, the chairman of
the committee and one of the great prison reformers of the
century, was appalled to hear Bentham speak of the
"promiscuous assemblage of unknown and therefore un-
paid, ungarbled and incorruptible inspectors," who would
be attracted to the prison by such worthy motives as
"curiosity and the love of amusement," and who would
offer the best "security against abuse and imperfection in
every shape." "For such inventions," Holford commented,
"was it gravely proposed to us in the nineteenth-century to
abandon the ordinary principles of prison management."[4]

In a private letter to a member of the committee,
Bentham denied the superiority of public management with
its "channels of complaint" and appeals to "higher authorities." Everyone knew, he said, that in such cases real
power always devolved upon some one individual, the
only effect of an ostensible division of power being to
divide responsibility, "and by dividing and dissipating the
responsibility, to increase that power which in demonstration they are employed to reduce." The committee had
made out the choice to lie between "a company of guardian
angels" representing the public and "one tyrant devil" of a

3. George Holford, *An Account of the General Penitentiary
at Millbank* (London, 1828), p. 14.
4. Ibid., pp. 14–16.

contractor. In fact, he protested, it was between officials appointed by the ministry and "rendering no account but to their assured protectors," and himself:

> An unseated, unofficed, unconnected, insulated individual whose blameless life, known to have been for little less than half-a-century devoted to a course of unpaid, yet unremitted, howsoever fruitless, toil, in the service of mankind, has not been able to preserve his rights from being an object of neglect, and himself an object of silent oppression to every Administration for these last eighteen years.[5]

Thus, his original description of the contractor as a man consciously and entirely devoted to his own interest was replaced by the self-image of a dedicated, disinterested, persecuted toiler in the service of mankind. Disingenuously Bentham even proposed now to assume management of the prison "without a farthing's worth of pecuniary profit."[6] But coming at this late date, after the final rejection of his plan, and even then only in a private letter rather than in his official reply, the proposal was little more than an embellishment of his self-portrait.

For twenty years Bentham fought for the Panopticon; for another twenty he grieved over its defeat. He never faltered in his devotion, at one point urging it upon the government of India (properly adapted for the segregation of castes and religions), at another composing edifying songs for the prisoners, and always fulminating against the "perfidy, waste, peculation and incapacity" of his opponents.[7] He had been thirty-eight at its conception; he was

5. Bentham, *Works*, XI, 160-1.
6. Ibid., XI, 160.
7. Box CXX, *Catalogue of the Manuscripts of Jeremy Bentham in the Library of University College*, London, ed. A. Taylor Milne (London, 1937).

eighty-three when he memorialized it under the title, *History of the War between Jeremy Bentham and George III* (by "One of the Belligerents").[8] Brooding over the affair, he had come to see it as an elaborate plot by the king to exact vengeance for a letter written as long ago as 1789 taking issue with the government's anti-Russian policy. (The letter had appeared in a daily newspaper under a pseudonym, but he was now convinced that George had penetrated his disguise.[9]) While he congratulated himself that his letter had been responsible for the government's abandoning of its warlike policy, he was also certain that it had brought down upon him the merciless wrath of the king:

> I paralysed his hand. I saved the two countries, perhaps others likewise, from this calamity [of war]. He vowed revenge; and to effect it he wounded me through the sides of this his country, not to speak of so many others.[1]

> Imagine how he hated me. Millions wasted were among the results of his vengeance. . . . After keeping me in hot water more years than the siege of Troy lasted, he broke the faith of Parliament to me. But for him all the paupers in the country, as well as all the prisoners in the country, would have been in my hands.[2]

It is tempting to dismiss this idea of a royal plot as paranoia aggravated by senility. Yet Bentham was so far

8. Selections from this work have been published as part of the final volume of Bentham's *Works*.

9. Bentham's letter, signed "Anti-Machiavel," had been followed by a reply by "Partizan," whom Lord Lansdowne identified as the king. At the time and for many years (indeed as late as 1809), Bentham refused to credit this identification, supposing it to be another ruse on Lansdowne's part to provoke him to a more Whiggish and anti-royalist position. (See a note by Bentham quoted by Mack, p. 401.) It was not until 1821, when he first committed to writing the theory of the royal plot, that he assumed as a matter of course that Lansdowne had been telling the truth. (*Works*, IV, 171-2.)

1. Bentham, *Works*, XI, 97.

2. Ibid., X, 212.

from his dotage that these last decades of his life were among his most productive periods. It was then that he developed the doctrine that is his unique contribution to philosophy and politics. The most comprehensive statement of Philosophical Radicalism is his *Constitutional Code*, written at this time and completed in the very years that he was working on his *History of the War between Jeremy Bentham and George III*. Whatever infirmities may be found in the *Code*, they are not those of mental incapacity.

The conjunction of the *History* and the *Code* dispels not only the suspicion of senility but also the notion that the Panopticon was a quirk of mind, a passing eccentricity having no bearing upon the rest of Bentham's life and thought. It is true that the Panopticon was first conceived at a time when he was pluming himself on his good fortune in living "in the age of Catharine, of Joseph, of Frederick, of Gustavus, and of Leopold";[3] when he was confident that in Russia "I could bring more of my ideas to bear . . . in a month than here [in England] in my whole life";[4] and when even his personal experience of the fiasco of Potemkin's model village did not diminish his enthusiasm for Russia: "I have learnt what the human powers are capable of, when unfettered by the arbitrary regulations of an unenlightened age."[5] This was the time, too, when he was most contemptuous of English liberalism, opposing every effort of Fox and of his own patron, Lord Lansdowne, to broaden the suffrage, abolish rotten boroughs, and otherwise, as he put it, "subjugate the well informed to the ill informed classes of mankind."[6] It is of no little

3. Élie Halévy, *La Formation du Radicalisme Philosophique* (3 vols.; Paris, 1901–4), I, 367.

4. Mack, p. 364.

5. Bentham, *Works*, IV, 52.

6. Halévy, II, 316. Mack's claim that Bentham was a "full-fledged radical democrat" by 1790 (*Jeremy Bentham*, p. 17) is refuted by this and similar evidence.

significance that the Panopticon was born out of this amalgam of Toryism and enlightened despotism. But it is equally significant that Bentham did not abandon the Panopticon when he abandoned this ideology, that it survived intact his conversion to radicalism and democracy, and that he could write his *History* and his *Code* simultaneously, without any sense of incongruity.

Indeed, the Panopticon was more than a passive survivor of his conversion to Philosophical Radicalism. It played an active, perhaps a decisive, part in his conversion. William Wilberforce, who witnessed Bentham's travails throughout the affair, was certain that he turned to radicalism out of vexation and resentment over the failure of the Panopticon: "He was quite soured by it; and I have no doubt that many of his harsh opinions afterwards were the fruit of this ill-treatment."[7] The chronology of his conversion would seem to confirm this. In 1808, with the Panopticon obviously a lost cause and feeling thoroughly unappreciated in England, he tried to emigrate to South America, and only after this failed, did he make his first overtures to the radicals. What is striking about this transitional period (which coincided with the final death throes of the Panopticon) was Bentham's disdain for most of the radicals with whom he associated and his personal commitment to radicalism long before he had worked out an appropriate ideology for it. He evidently sought refuge in radicalism as he had once sought it in South America. Later, explaining his early Toryism and belated radicalism, he said: "I was . . . a great reformist; but never suspected that the people in power were against reform. I supposed they only wanted to know what was good in order to embrace it."[8] Disaffected with the "people in power" as a result of the

7. R. I. and S. Wilberforce, *Life of William Wilberforce* (London, 1838), II, 172.
8. Bentham, *Works*, X, 66.

Panopticon affair, he turned to the radicals whom he had so recently and heartily despised.

The Panopticon is interesting not only as it helps explain Bentham's political and philosophical development, but also as it helps elucidate his political and philosophical doctrine. For it was more than a catalytic agent, more than the innocent cause and archaic survivor of his conversion. It endured as much out of conviction and principle as out of nostalgia, loyalty, self-interest, self-vindication, obsession, or any other personal and pathological motives that undoubtedly entered into it. However disenchanted Bentham became with the old people in power, he never became disenchanted with the Panopticon in its various manifestations. The most interesting of these was his Panopticon-poorhouse. *Pauper Management Improved*, originally written in 1797 and reissued in 1812, applied the Panopticon principle to the problem of the poor. A "joint-stock subscription company," on the model of the East India Company, was to serve as a kind of holding company for 250 "Industry Houses," each to accommodate 2,000 paupers under the "absolute" authority of a contractor-governor and under a regimen of life and labor similar to that of the Panopticon-prison.[9]

9. Ibid., VIII, 369–439. This plan is perhaps even more unsettling to the conventional view of Bentham than the Panopticon-prison. The effect would have been to reduce the poor almost to the status of criminals. Not only was the company, for example, to have "coercive powers" to apprehend anyone "having neither visible livelihood or assignable property, nor honest and sufficient means of livelihood" (p. 370), but even the ordinary citizen would be allowed—indeed encouraged—to apprehend and convey any beggar to the nearest Industry-House. And the scale of operations was vast even by the standards of our time, let alone of that time. The Industry-Houses were to take care not only of the 500,000 poor but also of their children, who, after the discharge of their parents, were "to continue bound to the company in quality of apprentices," boys to the age of twenty-one or twenty-three, girls to twenty-one or nineteen, both regardless of marriage (p. 369). These apprentices would

74

The two Panopticons, prison and poorhouse, were closely linked in Bentham's mind, as is evident from his grievance against King George: "But for him all the paupers in the country, as well as all the prisoners in the country, would have been in my hands."[1] Bentham saw nothing unseemly in this complaint, just as he saw no irony, on another occasion, in concluding his diatribe against the king with the warning: "While nations consent to put into any hands an uncontrollable power of mischief, they may expect to be thus served."[2] Neither the self-righteousness nor the apparent incongruity of these remarks should be permitted to obscure their real import. For their juxtaposition, like that of the *History* and the *Constitutional Code*, suggests that the Panopticon was nothing less than the existential realization of Philosophical Radicalism.

There was no real contradiction between Bentham's objection to the uncontrollable power of the king and his objection to being himself deprived of power over all the paupers and prisoners of the country. For in neither case was he objecting to power, even absolute power, as such. He never deviated from the position he had taken in his youthful polemic against Blackstone: that there could be no such thing as a "mixed" constitution or a "balance" of powers because power itself was illimitable. His conversion to radicalism required only a relocation of power. The old "people in power" were to be replaced by the populace empowered—a "democratic ascendancy"[3] represented by an "omnicompetent legislature."[4] The object, he now in-

---

require an additional 250 houses, bringing the total population of the Industry-Houses to one million. (The entire population of England at the time was about nine million.)

1. Ibid., X, 212. See also X, 591; XI, 96–7.

2. Ibid., IV, 172.

3. Bentham, *Plan of Parliamentary Reform* (London, 1817), p. xxxvi.

4. Bentham, *Works*, IX (*Constitutional Code*), 119.

sisted, was not to limit power but rather to reduce confidence in the trustees of power so as to increase the power of the people: "While confidence is minimized, let not power be withheld."[5]

The Tory Bentham and the Radical Bentham agreed upon the principle of the greatest happiness of the greatest number. The innovation of the Radical was to make the greatest happiness of the greatest number dependent upon the greatest power of the greatest number. In his *Constitutional Code*, Bentham explained that the legislature had to be omnicompetent because "any limitation is in contradiction to the greatest happiness principle."[6] But since the greatest happiness of the greatest number meant, in practice, the greater happiness of the greater number, the omnicompetence of the legislature meant the omnicompetence of the majority. One of Bentham's disciples was asked whether the greatest number always had the right to indulge its greatest happiness, whether the twenty-nine out of thirty people who decided to feast upon the thirtieth had the right and the power to do so—to which the disciple, with the impeccable logic of his master, coolly replied, "Yes."[7]

To Bentham, prisoners and paupers were in the unhappy position of this thirtieth citizen. If it was in the interest of society to confine them in a Panopticon, to subject them to an absolute master, to exploit their labor, to attach conditions to their discharge, it was necessary and proper that all this be done. The traditional motive of reformers had been, as it still is, the relief of the unfortunate, those suffering special disabilities or deprivations, the afflicted minorities: Howard wanted to improve the conditions of prisoners, Wilberforce to prevent the enslavement of Negroes, Whitbread to give sustenance to the needy, Bell and Lan-

5. Ibid., IX, 62.
6. Ibid., IX, 119.
7. Halévy, III, 436.

caster to educate the children of the poor. If Bentham concerned himself with the same problems and even, in some cases, advocated similar solutions, it was not out of compassion for these minorities, but rather in the interests of society at large. There was no question of the "rights" of prisoners and paupers, for there was no such thing as rights at all. There were only interests, and the interests of the majority had to prevail. The greatest happiness of the greatest number might thus require the greatest misery of the few.

The principle of the greatest happiness of the greatest number was as inimical to the idea of liberty as to the idea of rights. Just as Bentham attacked those parents whose scruples about liberty made them apprehensive of a Panopticon-school, so he attacked those who expressed the same scruples and apprehensions in matters of government. "Liberty," "liberal," and "liberalism," he wrote toward the end of his life, were among the "most mischievous" words in the language, because they obscured the real issues, which were happiness, security, and good government. The common notion of liberty as "the right to do anything that the laws do not forbid" was nonsense: "For if the laws are *bad*, what becomes of liberty? And if the laws are good, where is its value?"[8]

There is obviously no room here for an adequate discussion of Philosophical Radicalism. These few reflections are introduced only to suggest that the Panopticon was not the anomaly it may first seem, and that for the later Bentham as for the earlier it was neither an aberration of thought nor a weakness of character. It survived his conversion to radicalism as so much else of his philosophy and program survived. Indeed there was little that did not survive, except his faith in enlightened rulers. His conception of law as positive and statutory continued to imply, as it always had, a rejection of common law, of judge-made law, and of

8. Ibid., III, 435.

a fundamental constitutional law to which all other laws had to yield. His conception of sovereignty as total and illimitable prohibited checks and balances in the democratic state as it prohibited channels of complaint or higher authorities in the Panopticon. His conception of self-interest became, if anything, more rigorous; where once he had thought it possible for a ruler to find his satisfaction and therefore his interest in promoting the interests of his subjects, he now denied that there had ever existed or could ever exist "a human being in whose instance any public interest he can have had, will not, insofar as it depends upon himself, have been sacrificed to his own personal interest."[9] (The very idea of disinterestedness appeared to him "as absurd in supposition as it would be disastrous in reality," for it belied the calculations of rewards and punishments upon which all rational behavior and thus all legislation were based.)[1] His economic thought remained what it had always been—a peculiar combination of laissez-faire doctrine that sometimes carried him beyond Adam Smith (as in his *Defense of Usury*), and an older variety of private, monopolistic enterprise (as in the Panopticon prison and poorhouses). And finally, his philosophical method was unchanged: the rationality, universality, simplicity, and consistency that he prided himself on in the Panopticon continued to be virtues he esteemed most highly—and not only as qualities of mind but as the criteria of valid reforms and of a valid political order.

The affinity between the Panopticon and the mode of thought represented by Philosophical Radicalism is further suggested by the attitude of the Radicals themselves. Bentham's admirers today, one might say, are acquiescent

9. Bentham, *The Handbook of Political Fallacies*, ed. Harold Larrabee (New York, 1962), p. 230.
1. Halévy, III, 472.

out of ignorance, having not read the details of the plan or appreciated what they have read. His associates, however, could not plead ignorance. Yet not one of them criticized it or even belittled it as a private idiosyncrasy. The only one to express any hint of misgivings was Samuel Romilly, who had the unenviable task of defending it in parliament; but even he, while conceding the need for changes and personally absenting himself from most of the committee meetings to avoid embarrassment, professed to approve and support it. (His equivocations were not lost on Bentham; perhaps they were the first signs of a deviation that finally led Bentham to read him out of the party.) The other Radicals felt no need for even this degree of equivocation. John Stuart Mill did not criticize the Panopticon even when he was most critical of Bentham. But above all it was James Mill who publicly endorsed it and gave it the imprimatur of the party—and this long after its rejection by Parliament, when the Radicals, if they had been so minded, could have allowed it to lapse quietly into oblivion.

The occasion of its resurrection was an article on "Prisons and Prison Discipline," written by James Mill in 1822 or 1823 and published in the supplement to the *Encyclopædia Britannica*. Bentham's plan, Mill wrote, was "so perfectly expounded and proved that they who proceed in this road, with the principle of utility before them, can do little else than travel in his steps."[2] And Mill did just this, reviewing and recommending every feature of the Panopticon: the architecture, the principles of inspection, labor, and economy, the contract system, the chapel and visitors' gallery, the insurance scheme, and the subsidiary establishment for released prisoners. He even defended Bentham on all the lesser points: the contractor's right to trade freely with the prisoners, to provide hammocks in place of beds, and to put two or four prisoners—"seldom

2. *Encyclopædia Britannica*, supplement 4th edn. (Edinburgh, 1824), VI, 385.

more"—in one cell. (This was the figure in Bentham's book; later it had been increased to six or more.) And he concluded as he had started, abjuring any originality on his own part and praising the Panopticon for being superior to anything that "the imperfection of the human powers" generally allows.[3]

Mill's eulogy was so excessive as to be almost suspicious, particularly at this period of his life, when he was jealous of his reputation and wary of playing the part of the slavish disciple. One might be tempted to interpret his disclaimer of originality as a disclaimer of responsibility, a polite act of dissociation, were it not for a private letter by Mill to the editor of the *Encyclopædia* explaining that he could do no more than recapitulate the details of the Panopticon "which appear to me to approach perfection."[4]

It is instructive to compare Mill's article with another published at almost the same time in the *Quarterly Review*. While Mill was praising the Panopticon as the perfect expression of utilitarianism, the Tory reviewer was congratulating the country on having rejected a plan containing "no proper checks or lasting securities" and based on nothing more philosophical than Bentham's personal character. "If it had been tried," the *Review* pronounced, "it would not have succeeded, and, in its ill-success, might have ruined, or at least indefinitely retarded the progress of the great cause of Prison Improvement."[5] It is also curious to observe that the Panopticon was effusively praised by the then Radical Henry Brougham (in the *Edinburgh Review* of 1813); and that the Whig Brougham later denounced it as "a scheme absolutely and perfectly vicious in principle."[6]

3. Ibid., VI, 395.
4. Alexander Bain, *James Mill* (London, 1882), p. 201.
5. "Prisons and Penitentiaries," *Quarterly Review*, XXX (1823), 428.
6. Henry Brougham, *Historical and Political Dissertations* (London, 1957), p. 254.

If upon re-examination the Panopticon seems to bear out the judgment of non-Radicals more than that of Radicals, it may be necessary to re-examine the conventional image of Bentham as the father of reform and of Philosophical Radicalism as the fount of reform. It may then emerge that the actual history of reform, and the particular reforms we value most highly, were brought about by other men under the impulse of other ideas—by Peel, for one, who was hardly a Benthamite. Similarly, the conventional view of Philosophical Radicalism as the genesis and prototype of our democracy may have to be reconsidered. Benthamism, we may find, has as little in common with either our functioning democracies or our democratic ideals as the Panopticon has with our actual, let alone ideal, prisons.

The devils that obsessed Bentham, it is now apparent, were all too real and far more mischievous than he suspected. The Panopticon was evidently not the only haunted chamber in his house. Those who have solemnly carried out his final instructions for the creation of an "auto-icon"—his skeleton attired in his own clothes, with a waxen likeness of his head and his favorite walking stick in his hand—might make it a mark of respect to a man so solicitous of his afterlife and so credulous, as he admitted, of ghosts, to exorcise those devils. And for our sake, if not for his, to exorcise them not only from the Panopticon but from the entire edifice of his thought, which is our heritage.

THE SPECTER OF MALTHUS

THE "population bomb" is beginning to usurp the place of the H-bomb in the public imagination and conscience. The vision of a world desolated by radiation and reduced to a few isolated survivors is being supplanted by the specter of an earth overpopulated to the point of suffocation and starvation. Indeed there have been suggestions, not entirely facetious, that our most probable salvation from the population explosion will be a nuclear explosion. Demographers conjure up an appalling array of statistics, such as that 65 million people are currently born each year—the equivalent of the total populations of England, the Netherlands, and Switzerland. At this rate of increase, the population of the earth, presently in the neighborhood of 3 billion, will be 7.5 billion by the year 2000, and 14 billion by 2050—an almost fivefold increase during the lifetime of an infant born today. The historical retrospect is almost as startling as the forecast: it took all of human history until A.D. 1850 to reach a world population of one billion; it took seventy-five years for the second billion; thirty-five for the third; it is now taking fifteen for the fourth; and it will take ten for the fifth. Had the human race started at the time of Christ with a single couple and grown at the present rate of 2 per cent a year, there would be 20 million people for every one person alive today.

These figures seem to suggest that the population problem, like the problem of atomic warfare, is distinctively contemporary in its significance and urgency. Yet it was more than 150 years ago, with the publication of Malthus's *Essay on the Principle of Population*, that the alarm was first raised and the public first exercised. And Malthus too had his predecessors duly acknowledged in the *Essay:* Benjamin Franklin, whose *Observations concerning the Increase of Mankind and the Peopling of Countries* was written in 1751, and the Englishman Robert Wallace, who inquired into the *Various Prospects of Mankind, Nature, and Providence* only a decade later. But Franklin, so far from being distressed at the thought of the population of the American Colonies doubling every twenty-five years (as he predicted), rejoiced in that prospect; while even Wallace saw the population growth rather as an impediment to a socialist utopia of the future than as a problem for his own time and place. It remained for Malthus to convert an optimistic proposition into a pessimistic one, and a future hypothetical difficulty into a present and pressing one.

Wallace inspired not only the theme of Malthus's essay but also the occasion for its appearance. For Wallace, having (reluctantly, it must be said) punctured the dream of utopia, provoked William Godwin to rebuttal, and Malthus, in turn, to counterrebuttal. In the utopian tract *Enquiry concerning Political Justice*, published first in 1793, Godwin tried to dispel the "gloomy impression" about population left by Wallace. "There is a principle," he reassured his readers, "in the nature of human society, by means of which every thing seems to tend to its level, and to proceed in the most auspicious way, when least interfered with by the mode of regulation." This principle dictated that "the number of inhabitants in a country will perhaps never be found, in the ordinary course of affairs, greatly to increase beyond the facility of subsistence." If by chance this happy principle of accommodation should fail to operate, he was confident that the problem would in any case arise only in the remote future: with three fourths of the habitable globe still uncultivated, "myriads of centuries of still increasing population may pass away, and the earth be yet found sufficient for the support of its inhabitants."[1] And even in the remote eventuality of a world fully cultivated and inhabited, Godwin did not despair. In a remarkable appendix to his book, he suggested that the ultimate solution to the problem of population lay in that supremacy of mind over matter which would distinguish the utopian society of the future from the materialist society of the present. Without quite committing himself to the idea of immortality, he ventured the "presumption that the term of human life may be prolonged, and that by the immediate operation of intellect, beyond any limits which we are able to assign." And since the characteristic of the more mature person was a "cultivated and virtuous mind," and thus a diminished sensuality, the earth would finally be peopled by a race that would "probably cease to propagate." His was the utopia to end all utopias:

> The whole will be a people of men, and not of children. Generation will not succeed generation, nor truth have, in a certain degree, to recommence her career every thirty years. . . . There will be no war, no crimes, no administration of justice, as it is called, and no government. Beside this, there will be neither disease, anguish, melancholy, nor resentment. Every man will seek, with ineffable ardour, the good of all.[2]

Only a few months after Godwin had released to the English public his idyll of humanity immortalized and unmanned, a French philosopher-revolutionary, respond-

1. Godwin, *Enquiry concerning Political Justice, and Its Influence on Morals and Happiness* (3rd edn.; London, 1798), II, 516–18.
2. Ibid., II, 527–8.

ing to quite different and less congenial circumstances, gave expression to a similar fantasy. The Marquis de Condorcet, whose revolutionary enthusiasm stopped short of regicide, spent his enforced leisure while hiding from the Terror in composing his final testament, a *Sketch for a Historical Picture of the Progress of the Human Mind*. Like Godwin, he contemplated a future in which not only the sciences, arts, and social relations but even the constitution of man would enjoy infinite progress, so that man's intellectual and moral perfectibility would be complemented by a physical perfectibility approaching, although not quite achieving, immortality. Like Godwin, too, he confronted the vexing problem of population that threatened to make a nightmare out of his daydream. "Might there not come a moment," he inquired, "when, the number of people in the world finally exceeding the means of subsistence, there will in consequence ensue a continual diminution of happiness and population, a true retrogression, or at best an oscillation between good and bad?" Such a time, he answered, was so far in the future that it was almost unavailing to speculate about it. (The fantasy of perfection and near-immortality was presumably of a more immediate and plausible order of events). But even conceding that such a time might come, he supposed it probable that the progress of reason would have been sufficiently advanced, the "absurd prejudices of superstition" sufficiently overcome, that men would know it to be their duty to "promote the general welfare of the human race or of the society in which they live or of the family to which they belong, rather than foolishly to encumber the world with useless and wretched beings."[3]

Condorcet's *Sketch* was published posthumously in France in 1795 and appeared soon after in England in an anonymous and faulty translation. A second edition of God-

3. Condorcet, *Sketch for a Historical Picture of the Progress of the Human Mind*, trans. J. Barraclough (New York, 1955), pp. 188–9.

win's *Political Justice* was issued the following year, and a volume of his essays, under the title of *The Enquirer*, in 1797. Among the many English liberals who responded sympathetically both to the French Revolution and to the utopian visions it inspired was Daniel Malthus, an English country gentleman who was a friend and great admirer of Rousseau. One essay in *The Enquirer*, "Avarice and Pro-fusion," propounding the familiar thesis that "a state of cultivated equality is . . . most consonant to the nature of man, and most conducive to the extensive diffusion of felicity,"[4] precipitated a controversy between Daniel Malthus and his son Robert. Against his father, against Godwin, and against all utopians, Robert argued that there was one fatal obstacle to such a state of equality and felicity: this was the inevitable tendency of population to exceed the food supply. Goaded, or encouraged, by his father, he developed these ideas in an essay published anonymously (although generally attributed to him) in 1798.

Thomas Robert Malthus (familiarly known as Robert) was then thirty-two. Having been educated according to the Rousseauistic precepts of his father by a succession of tutors and by his father himself, he had been admitted to Jesus College, Cambridge, in 1784, where he studied mathematics and was graduated with honors in 1788. He took holy orders the same year, after some hesitation—his misgivings prompted not by religious scruples but rather by a serious speech defect resulting from a cleft palate and harelip, a defect that he thought might impair his function-ing as a clergyman. Elected a fellow at Jesus in 1793, he divided his time between Cambridge and a curacy in Surrey, resigning the fellowship after eleven years in order to marry. (The Church of England allowed clergymen to

4. Godwin, *The Enquirer* (London, 1823), p. 157.

marry, but Cambridge was not so lenient toward its fellows.) In 1805 he was appointed to the first chair of political economy in England, at the East India College (later known as Haileybury), remaining there until his death in 1834.

"There is nothing in Mr. Malthus's life which is worth mentioning, or which illustrated his doctrines," Walter Bagehot wrote[5]—meaning, apparently, that there was nothing in his life to suggest or account for the "dismal science" with which he is associated. Malthus's critics, however, eager to exploit every polemical opportunity, spoke caustically of the parson with eleven daughters, who presumed to preach to others the virtue of celibacy—to which his biographer, James Bonar, rejoined that in fact he had only three children of whom one was a son. (And, it may be added, no grandchildren.) Yet the myth about eleven daughters persists to this day in the introduction to a recent edition of the *Essay*.[6] Karl Marx, surprisingly, gave currency to the opposite but equally mythical belief that Malthus observed "the monastic vow of celibacy"—"a circumstance," Marx continued, that "favorably distinguishes Malthus from the other Protestant parsons, who have shuffled off the command enjoining celibacy of the priesthood and have taken 'Be fruitful and multiply,' as their special Biblical mission in such a degree that they generally contribute to the increase of population to a really unbecoming extent."[7]

Nor was there anything in Malthus's life to suggest the ruthless, mean-spirited, hard-hearted man he is often made out to be. His associates all remarked upon his exceptional amiability, good nature, and gentleness, in contrast, it may be said, to the utopian Godwin who was notably incon-

5. Bagehot, "Malthus," *Works* (Hartford, 1884), V, 400.

6. Malthus, *Essay on Population*, ed. Michael P. Fogarty (Everyman's edn.; London, 1958), I, vi.

7. Marx, *Capital* (Modern Library edn.; New York, n.d.), p. 676.

stant in his affections and querulous in personal as in intellectual affairs. Bagehot took a just measure of Malthus: "He was a sensible man educated in the midst of illusions; he felt a reaction against them, and devoted the vigor of youth to dispense and dispel them."[8] Or as Malthus himself remarked in the preface to the *Essay*, anticipating the inevitable recriminations: "The view which he [the author] has given of human life has a melancholy hue, but he feels conscious, that he has drawn these dark tints, from a conviction that they are really in the picture, and not from a jaundiced eye or an inherent spleen of disposition."[9]

The first edition of Malthus's work, published in 1798, carried the title: *An Essay on the Principle of Population, as it affects the future improvement of Society, with remarks on the speculation of Mr. Godwin, Mr. Condorcet, and other writers.* That he intended it very much as a tract for the times is apparent at the start in his description of the prevailing climate of opinion:

> The great and unlooked for discoveries that have taken place of late years in natural philosophy, the increasing diffusion of general knowledge from the extension of the art of printing, the ardent and unshackled spirit of inquiry that prevails throughout the lettered and even unlettered world, the new and extraordinary lights that have been thrown on political subjects which dazzle and astonish the understanding, and particularly that tremendous phenomenon in the political horizon, the French revolution, which, like a blazing comet, seems destined either to inspire with fresh life and vigour, or to scorch up and destroy the shrinking inhabitants of the earth, have all concurred to lead many able men into the opinion that

8. Bagehot, V, 400.

9. Malthus, *On Population*, ed. Gertrude Himmelfarb (Modern Library edn.; New York, 1960), p. 4. Unless otherwise specified, all page references are to this edition, which reprints the first edition of the *Essay* and those chapters of the final (seventh) edition that do not duplicate the first.

we were touching on a period big with the most important changes, changes that would in some measure be decisive of the future fate of mankind.[1]

The combined impetus of an intellectual and a social revolution had made men feel liberated from the bonds that had always constrained them. Everything was in movement, everything seemed possible. Progress and perfectibility appeared to be the destiny of men—unlimited progress and infinite perfectibility, even perfection itself. The "facts of life," or what had always passed as such, the essential conditions of human and social existence, no longer seemed to be beyond the reach of men willing and able to alter them. Indeed the very idea of facts or conditions inviolable and unalterable had become suspect. Those who still argued that perfection was unattainable, that some evils were inescapable, were accused of pandering to their selfish interests and of prostituting mind to base matter.

Malthus hoped to redress the balance, to restore a sense of the practicable as opposed to the ideal, and to rehabilitate those who, from the most worthy of motives, thought it better to cultivate the practicable than to covet an illusory and possibly dangerous ideal. Behind the utopian rhetoric of Condorcet and Godwin, behind their vision of perfect justice, absolute equality, and infinite perfectibility, he saw the fallacy of attributing all social evils to particular human institutions, and the corollary fallacy of assuming that the reform of these particular institutions would remove the objectionable evils. The truth, he protested, was that "though human institutions appear to be the obvious and obtrusive causes of such mischief to mankind, yet, in reality they are light and superficial, they are mere feathers that float on the surface, in comparison with those deeper seated causes of impurity that corrupt the springs and render turbid the whole stream of human life."[2]

1. Ibid., p. 5.
2. Ibid., p. 65.

One of those "deeper seated causes of impurity," perhaps the deepest seated of all, Malthus found in the "principle of population." This was the principle that "the power of population is indefinitely greater than the power in the earth to produce subsistence for men."[3] He claimed to have deduced this principle from two sets of postulates: first, that food and sexual passion were both essential to human existence (Godwin to the contrary notwithstanding); and second, that while food increased only in arithmetical ratio, population when unchecked increased in geometrical ratio. It was this discrepancy, arising out of the two most primitive and powerful human impulses, that had always prevented and would continue to prevent mankind from enjoying that state of felicity which sentimental philosophers thought it ought to possess. Thus nature itself, and not any particular set of social or human institutions, vitiated the utopian schemes of these philosophers.

So far from "ease, happiness, and comparative leisure" being the natural state of mankind, Malthus saw the natural state of at least a considerable portion of mankind to consist of misery and vice: misery when sickness, starvation, and death carried off the excess population; and vice when the immoral practices of men—war, infanticide, and the resources of promiscuity—either prevented procreation or disposed of the unfortunates who could not be fed. Moreover, this misery and vice were as much of the essence of the human condition as the need for food and the instinct for cohabitation, which reacted together in such catastrophic fashion. The evils of overpopulation were not, as Godwin, Condorcet, and even Wallace thought, in the remote future, when every inch of the earth would have been cultivated and inhabited. Population was always and everywhere, in some measure, pressing against the available food supply. If the means of subsistence should suddenly become abundant, either because of the opening up of new

3. Ibid., p. 9.

food resources or because of a plague carrying off large numbers of people, the remaining population, enjoying relative affluence, would be apt to marry earlier than otherwise, have more children, and die later. In a short period of time, population would thus have adjusted to the means of subsistence—and more than adjusted, population reproducing at so much more rapid a rate than the food supply that numbers would soon once again be in excess of available food. The oscillation created by the permanent imbalance between food and people was a feature of every country, county, and hamlet, in every period of its history.

Malthus's conclusion seemed to follow so directly from his premises, and his premises themselves to be so unimpeachable, that most readers saw no ground for dissent. Indeed premises and conclusion were so much of a piece that for many they assumed the aspect of a tautology. This was one of Coleridge's objections to the *Essay:* that it was a pretentious laboring of the obvious. "Are we now," he scrawled in the margin of his copy, "to have a Quarto to teach us that great misery and great vice arise from Poverty, and that there must be Poverty in its worst shape wherever there are more Mouths than Loaves and more Heads than Brains!"[4]

What most attracted attention and compelled assent, even unwilling assent, and redeemed the *Essay* from the charge of being a truism, was the formula in which Malthus expressed that truism. The surplus of mouths over loaves was represented by the relation between a geometrical ratio and an arithmetical one, with mouths increasing geometrically and loaves arithmetically. "A slight acquaintance with numbers," Malthus assured his readers, "will show the immensity of the first power in comparison with the second."[5] And lest his readers lacked even that slight

4. Quoted by James Bonar, *Malthus and His Work* (London, 1924), p. 372.
5. Malthus, *On Population*, p. 9.

acquaintance with numbers, Malthus performed the appropriate calculations: while the population was increasing every twenty-five years at the rate of 1, 2, 4, 8, 16, 32, 64, 128, 256 . . ., the food supply was at the same time increasing at the rate of 1, 2, 3, 4, 5, 6, 7, 8, 9 . . ., so that in two centuries the ratio of population to food, if not checked, would be 256 to 9, in three centuries 4,096 to 13, and so on. These numerical sequences had a mesmerizing effect, not only because the geometrical series soon mounted up to astronomical heights, but also because of their concreteness and precision. The reader reached for pencil and paper, checked Malthus's calculations, found them to be unexceptionable, and felt obliged then to accept his conclusions. It was thus that the historian Henry Hallam declared the basis of Malthus's thesis to be as certain as the multiplication table,[6] while Charles Darwin rebuked one of Malthus's critics because, "mathematician though he may be," he could not follow common reasoning.[7]

Yet there were some who protested that Malthus's thesis was both more and less than the multiplication table—more ambitious and less certain. Since no one could possibly know what the rate of population growth or the increase of the food supply would be in the hypothetical state where neither was checked, the ratio of 4,096 to 13 at the end of three centuries was completely arbitrary. If fifteen years rather than twenty-five were taken as the period in which an unchecked population doubled—and Malthus himself suggested that there was as much evidence for the one as for the other figure—the ratio would work out at something like 1,048,576 to 13—a "margin of error" that is even more impressive than the astronomical figures themselves. Nor, it was pointed out, was the rate of increase of food, although represented by so small and seemingly man-

6. Bonar, p. 85.
7. Darwin, *Life and Letters* (London, 1887), II, 317.

ageable a figure, less arbitary. Too many imponderables
were involved: the amount of land totally or partially uncultivated and the amount that was uncultivable, the time
and labor required to bring this land to cultivation, the point
of diminishing returns, etc., to say nothing of the problem of extrapolating such present unknowns into the
future, under radically different scientific, technological,
economic, and social conditions. The difficulties, as Malthus
might have said, increased geometrically. And these empirical difficulties were only the beginning. The thesis itself
was, by its very nature, inherently unprovable. There was
no way of determining, however hypothetically or im-
precisely, what the rate of increase of the population would
be if unchecked—since it always was being held in check.

What held the population in check, according to
Malthus, was the "misery and vice" that lay in wait for
those who were imprudent enough to exist, as we would
say today, on the margin of society, where there were
more mouths than loaves. The margin of society might be
smaller or larger, the misery and vice more or less acute;
this would depend on the swing of the historical pendulum.
But the oscillation never stopped, and in their happiest
state, when food seemed most abundant and their conditions most favorable, men had to keep in mind that their
present happiness would be the occasion for their future
despair, that the families they were producing so innocently and incontinently today would tomorrow be a
burden and the day after an affliction. Whether by preventive checks discouraging births or by positive checks en-
couraging death, the population was always being forced
down to the level of the food supply.

"Preventive" checks and "positive" ones, moreover,
were almost equally noxious, since both, Malthus maintained, resulted in misery and vice. It was misery for the
mature man to have to deprive himself of the natural
gratification of marriage and children, and vice to indulge

his sexual instincts without benefit of marriage and children; it was misery to watch starvation and sickness deci-
mate his beloved, and vice to hasten their end by neglect or
act. Malthus's conclusion was as inexorable and arresting as
his formula: "It is difficult to conceive any check to population which does not come under the description of some
species of misery or vice."[8] If this conclusion was not
appreciated earlier, if the oscillations of population were
not more often remarked upon, he suggested, it was perhaps because "the histories of mankind that we possess are
histories only of the higher classes," so that we know little
of the conditions of that class which was most subject to
the pressures of population, most susceptible to misery and
vice.[9]

This observation, almost in an aside, that it was the lower
classes who bore the brunt of the "principle of population," was the first intimation of the more immediate and
urgent occasion behind the writing of the *Essay*. Not the
fantasies of Godwin and Condorcet, which were hardly a
matter of pressing concern, but rather the proposals currently being bruited for the reform of the Poor Laws were
what provoked Malthus. The existing Poor Law administration was a patchwork affair inherited from Elizabethan
times and haphazardly adapted to the modern England of
enclosures, industrialism, and laissez-faire. By the end of
the eighteenth century, the workhouse had been restricted
to the aged and unemployable, and poor relief was being
increasingly provided in the form of "outdoor relief":
doles, family allowances, varieties of relief in kind, and "aid-
in-wages." The latter became common as the so-called
Speenhamland system spread. The "system" was not en-

8. Malthus, *On Population*, p. 41.
9. Ibid., p. 15.

tirely novel; nor was it ever systematically applied. But it was formalized and popularized in the decision of the justices of the peace of Speenhamland, Berkshire, in 1795, to provide allowances out of the poor rates for agricultural workers whose wages were inadequate to support their families—the allowances to be geared to the size of the family and to the current price of bread. The Speenhamland measure, or one like it, was soon adopted by other counties in southern and eastern England (not in the north or in Scotland), and bills of similar effect were introduced in parliament. William Pitt himself proposed a bill that would have extended the system of aid-in-wages and family allowances, and would have made relief, as he said, "a matter of right and honor."[1]

From Malthus's point of view, the situation was sheer folly. Measures that were intended to alleviate the distress of the poor he saw as having the inevitable effect of aggravating that distress, since population would increase without any increase in the supply of food. Nor was it only the recipients of public relief who would suffer. With a stable food supply and a growing population, the scarcity of provisions and the accompanying rise in prices would depress the condition of the entire working class, forcing still more families to apply for the dole and undermining still further their independence and initiative:

> If men are induced to marry from a prospect of parish provision, with little or no chance of maintaining their families in independence, they are not only unjustly tempted to bring unhappiness and dependence upon themselves and children, but they are tempted, without knowing it, to injure all in the same class with themselves. A labourer who marries without being able to support a family may in some respects be considered as an enemy to all his fellow labourers.[2]

1. Hansard, 32: 709–10 (Feb. 12, 1796).
2. Malthus, *On Population*, pp. 33–4.

In its own terms and within its own framework, the *Essay* was irrefutable, and William Pitt was persuaded by it to withdraw his bill. Indeed it persuaded not only contemporaries but also generations of historians, who assumed that the Speenhamland system and the old Poor Law had all the disastrous effects Malthus attributed to it, and more: an increase of the rural population, a steep rise in the poor rates, the depression of agricultural wages, the subsidization of the large farmers at the expense of the rest of society, the disappearance of the yeomanry, the pauperization of the agricultural working class, the immobilization of labor and thwarting of industrialization, and in general the perpetuation of economic and social irrationality. More recent studies have shown that these conditions have been much exaggerated, that they were attributable to other factors than poor relief, and that the later adoption of the new Poor Law abolishing most forms of outdoor relief did not notably alter the situation.[3]

Yet Malthus himself is often misunderstood, for if he predicted that poor relief would have these dire consequences, he did so not to promote the interests of the manufacturing class, as is often said, but out of a genuine sense of the national interest. He was, in fact, so little the representative of the manufacturing interests that he shared many of the physiocratic views regarding the inherent superiority of agriculture over manufacturing, the economic "unproductiveness" of industry, and the social evils attending industrial life.[4] (He even went so far as to favor the retention of the Corn Laws.) Nor was he inspired simply by a concern for the soundness of the economy and society in general. It was out of compassion for the poor themselves that he deplored the petty despotism involved in

3. Mark Blaug, "The Myth of the Old Poor Law and the Making of the New," *Journal of Economic History*, XXIII (1963); and Blaug, "The Poor Law Report Reexamined," *Journal of Economic History*, XXIV (1964).
4. Malthus, *On Population*, pp. 116–20, 397, 455.

the administration of poor relief: "The parish persecution of men whose families are likely to become chargeable, and of poor women who are near lying-in, is a most disgraceful and disgusting tyranny."[5] And it was in the interests of the poor that he urged them to heed the inexorable laws of population and economics of which they, more than any other class, were at the mercy. Indeed the very act of his publicizing those laws was in their interests and against the interests of the upper classes:

> It may appear to be the interest of the rulers, and the rich of a State, to force population, and thereby lower the price of labour, and consequently the expense of fleets and armies, and the cost of manufactures for foreign sale, but every attempt of the kind should be carefully watched and strenuously resisted by the friends of the poor, particularly when it comes under the deceitful garb of benevolence, and is likely, on that account, to be cheerfully and cordially received by the common people.[6]

In the final analysis, however, he placed the responsibility for their condition upon the poor themselves. This was not so much, it would seem, because they were poor per se, but rather because, being poor, they were closest to the condition of natural man. An image of natural man— man as he existed, or would have existed, in a state of nature—haunted most of the philosophers of the seventeenth and eighteenth centuries, and if their philosophies differed, it was largely because these images differed. Malthus's quarrel with Godwin and Condorcet was inspired by such a difference in the conception of natural man: Godwin and Condorcet, disciples of Rousseau, believing natural man to be innately good, his corruption a product of society and civilization; and Malthus, in the tradition of Hobbes, believing him to be innately bad, or if not bad, at least recalcitrant and refractory. Virtue was

5. Ibid., p. 36.
6. Ibid., p. 50.

attainable only through great effort, and natural man was disinclined to such effort: "Man as he really is, is inert, sluggish, and averse from labour, unless compelled by necessity."[7] From this proposition Malthus derived both his opposition to the Poor Laws and his vindication of divine providence. To the question of why a presumably benevolent God should have created the fatal discrepancy between the productive power of the earth and the reproductive power of man, his answer was that only by means of this discrepancy, by the pain and anguish it induced and by the effort required to overcome it, was man raised to the level of spirituality and intellectuality. "The original sin of man is the torpor and corruption of the chaotic matter in which he may be said to be born"; and it was the desire to survive that roused him out of his primeval torpor and stimulated the development of his mind and spirit.[8] Hobbes was, perhaps, Malthus's more obvious mentor, but he himself cited Locke in defense of his view of natural man:

> Locke, if I recollect, says that the endeavor to avoid pain rather than the pursuit of pleasure is the great stimulus to action in life. . . . To avoid evil and to pursue good seem to be the great duty and business of man, and this world appears to be peculiarly calculated to afford opportunity of the most unremitted exertion of this kind, and it is by this exertion, by these stimulants, that mind is formed. If Locke's idea be just, and there is great reason to think it is, evil seems to be necessary to create exertion, and exertion seems evidently necessary to create mind.[9]

As the Marxists were later to be criticized for sanctifying in the name of History all that the Party did, so Malthus was criticized for sanctifying in the name of Nature all that Political Economy did—or would have liked to do. Marx himself took Malthus to task for representing a particular

7. Ibid., p. 131.
8. Ibid., p. 128.
9. Ibid., pp. 129–30.

law of population, "peculiar to the capitalist mode of production," as "eternal," "sacred," and "natural." The Malthusian "accumulation of misery," Marx insisted, was nothing else than a means for the "accumulation of capital."[1] And others similarly accused him of sanctimony and hypocrisy, of parading self-interest under the banner of the general good, and of representing an ignoble doctrine of very recent vintage as an eternal and beneficent law of nature. "Parson," William Cobbett addressed him contemptuously, "I have, during my life, detested many men; but never any one so much as you."[2] William Hazlitt accused him of having a "warm constitution and amorous complexion," and vilified the *Essay* as a work "in which the little, low, rankling malice of a parishbeadle, or the overseer of a workhouse is disguised in the garb of philosophy."[3] Disraeli in his novels leveled some of his most biting satire against the self-seeking, self-satisfied employer who smugly justified starvation wages as "all an affair of population."[4] And Dickens, having named the two sons of Mr. Gradgrind ("Facts, sir, facts!") Adam Smith and Malthus, had all his Scrooge-like characters invoke the doctrine of Malthus in defense of their inhumanity; in one of his Christmas stories, the announcement that two young people were about to be married prompted a sour old man to complain:

> Married! Married! The ignorance of the first principles of political economy on the part of these people. . . . A man may live to be as old as Methuselah, and may labour all his life for the benefit of such people as those; and may heap up facts on figures, facts on figures, facts on figures, mountains high and dry; and he can no more hope to per-

1. Marx, pp. 675, 692–3, 709.
2. Cobbett, "To Parson Malthus," *Political Register*, XXXIV (1819), 1019.
3. Hazlitt, *A Reply to the Essay on Population* (London, 1807), pp. 3–5.
4. Disraeli, *Sybil* (London, 1904), p. 155.

suade them that they have no right or business to be married, than he can hope to persuade 'em that they have no earthly right or business to be born. And *that* we know they haven't. We reduced it to a mathematical certainty long ago![5]

These laws of society that pretended to be laws of nature were not, many protested, so inexorable as Malthus made them out. Were misery and vice in fact the only checks on population? Were, indeed, sex and food equally potent and equally irresistible passions? "Shame upon our race," Coleridge fumed, "that there lives the individual who dares even ask the question."[6] This was also Godwin's reaction to the *Essay*. The resources of mind and will, he objected, were not so impoverished as Malthus supposed. In England the population was kept in check not only, perhaps not even primarily, by misery and vice, but also by "virtue, prudence, or pride." From these mixed motives, many people postponed marriage, thus bearing fewer children than they might otherwise have had and avoiding some of the misery and vice that might otherwise have been their fate.[7]

Malthus himself had not entirely neglected the role of prudence in the control of population. Prudence did appear in the *Essay*, although not very prominently, as one of the causes for delay or renunciation of marriage. It figured in the case of the gentleman who enjoyed a high status and a small income, both of which he was reluctant to risk; in the case of the tradesman ambitious to better himself; and even in the case of the servant sharing the home and some of the comforts of his master. The average laborer, however, was presumed to be incapable of such prudence. Moreover, since Malthus believed sexual passion to be as peremptory

5. Dickens, "A Goblin Story," *Works* (Philadelphia, 1843), IV, 41.
6. Bonar, p. 48.
7. Ibid., p. 360.

as the need for food, prudence itself was only another occasion for misery and vice: "The effects, indeed of these restraints upon marriage are but too conspicuous in the consequent vices that are produced in almost every part of the world, vices that are continually involving both sexes in inextricable unhappiness."[8]

This was the Malthus of the first edition. Only of the first, however. For the second edition so drastically qualified and amended the first as to make of it a new book and a new thesis.

Malthus was moved to compose a second version of the *Essay* by the mixed reception accorded to the first. On the one hand, it was far more influential than the casual circumstances of its composition had led him to expect; on the other, it was more effectively attacked than he had anticipated. Inspired by both the praise and the criticism, Malthus addressed himself to the problem of population more seriously than he had done before. He spent the next five years reading, reflecting, and traveling. One European tour, in 1799, took him to Germany, Sweden, Norway, Finland, and Russia. Three years later, taking advantage of the short-lived peace, he visited France and Switzerland.[9] Everywhere he collected statistics, anecdotes, theories. The census of 1801 also provided him with ammunition in revealing the population of Great Britain to be far greater than had been expected. (Since it was the first such census, however, it did not bear upon the important question of the growth of population; this had still to be deduced from figures assembled haphazardly and uncritically.)

8. Malthus, *On Population*, p. 28.
9. The recent publication of Malthus's journals confirm the impression that the later development of his thought had little to do with his discoveries or observations on these trips. See *Travel Diaries of Thomas Robert Malthus*, ed. Patricia James (London, 1966).

The second edition of the *Essay* appeared in 1803 and was the basis of all later editions, of which six appeared in Malthus's lifetime and a seventh posthumously. (The changes in the other editions brought the work up-to-date without materially affecting the thesis.) About three times the length of the first, the revised work was no longer a tract but a proper guinea-and-a-half tome. Most of its bulk was provided by studies of particular societies: primitive peoples, American Indians, South Sea Islanders, the Greeks and Romans, and various modern countries. Even the title was significantly different: *An Essay on the Principle of Population, or A View of its past and present effect on Human Happiness with an inquiry into our prospects respecting the future removal or mitigation of the evils which it occasions.*

"The future removal or mitigation of the evils"—this was surely a startling notion. For had it not been precisely Malthus's thesis that there was no possible mitigation, let alone removal, of the evils implied by the principle of population? Had this not been his main objection to Godwin and Condorcet? The elimination of their names in the revised titles suggested that they were no longer the principal antagonists. It might even be said that they were no longer antagonists at all. This, indeed, is what Godwin claimed, with some bitterness. Malthus, he protested, had appropriated his main point of criticism without giving him credit for it and without acknowledging that in the process he had abandoned his case.

In the preface to the new edition, Malthus prepared his readers for the change: "Throughout the whole of the present work I have so far differed in principle from the former, as to suppose the action of another check of population which does not come under the head either of vice or misery; and in the latter part I have endeavoured to soften some of the harshest conclusions of the first Essay."[1] What

1. Malthus, *On Population*, p. 149.

he did not say was that the additional check to population was essentially that earlier described by Godwin as "virtue, prudence or pride"—now rebaptized as "moral restraint." Nor did he elaborate upon the full import of the change, perhaps because he did not himself appreciate its full import. Only upon careful reading and close analysis does its real significance emerge.

"Moral restraint" Malthus defined as "the restraint from marriage which is not followed by irregular gratifications."[2] That its motives were strictly prudential did not make it any the less moral; what made it moral was that it did not involve "irregular gratification" or "improper arts."[3] Malthus was unalterably opposed to "birth-control" in the sense of mechanical devices to prevent procreation. Moral restraint meant to him solely and simply chastity. It is one of the ironies of history that "Malthusianism" should have come to mean the kind of birth control that Malthus himself found so reprehensible.

Moral restraint took precedence, in this second edition, over both the preventive and the positive checks of the first edition. It now appeared as "the most powerful of the checks which in modern Europe keep down the population to the level of the means of subsistence."[4] And this most powerful check was derived, Malthus insisted, from a perfectly natural as well as perfectly virtuous instinct in man. If it meant the occasional curbing of other natural instincts and therefore some unhappiness, this degree of unhappiness was slight enough compared with the evil and misery of the other checks. Moreover such a curbing of instincts was typical of the "sacrifices of temporary to permanent gratification" that were the constant "business of a moral agent."[5] Moral restraint, therefore, was not the "forced

2. Ibid., p. 160.
3. Ibid.
4. Ibid., p. 338.
5. Ibid., p. 159.

produce of artificial society," but rather a virtue having "the most real and solid foundation in nature and reason."[6]

Thus the "principle of population" ceased to be a fatal obstacle to men's dreams and ideals. Indeed the principle itself was not the inexorable law it had earlier been. It now appeared that population did not necessarily outrun food supply, or necessarily keep up with every increase of food, and that the oscillations of the pendulum were not so invariable as he had made them to be. Men were no longer at the mercy of forces outside their control: "Each individual has, to a great degree, the power of avoiding the evil consequences to himself and society resulting from it [the principle of population], by the practice of a virtue dictated to him by the light of nature, and sanctioned by revealed religion."[7] Liberated from the eternal menace of overpopulation and the eternal evils of misery and vice, society could now look forward to the union of "the two grand *desiderata*, a great actual population and a state of society in which abject poverty and dependence are comparatively but little known; two objects which are far from being incompatible."[8]

As population and prosperity were now found to be compatible, so were population and progress. Progress— "the future removal or mitigation of the evils" alluded to in the title—once more became a practical objective. And not only social progress but also political progress—the progress of liberty. Since misery and vice were the principal causes of despotism, their removal or mitigation also gave hope for liberty:

The pressure of distress on the lower classes of people, together with the habit of attributing this distress to their

6. Ibid., p. 489.
7. Malthus, "A Summary View of the Principle of Population," in *Introduction to Malthus,* ed. D. V. Glass (London, 1959), p. 181.
8. Malthus, *On Population,* p. 500.

rulers, appears to me to be the rock of defence, the castle, the guardian spirit of despotism. It affords to the tyrant the fatal and unanswerable plea of necessity.[9]

Remove all apprehension from the tyranny or folly of the people, and the tyranny of government could not stand a moment. It would then appear in its proper deformity, without palliation, without pretext, without protector.[1]

Here the argument led Malthus far beyond his original intentions and convictions. For if liberty, as he now conceded, was a consequence of the moral reformation of the lower classes, it was clearly also, to some extent, the precondition for such a reformation. He therefore enjoined the government to establish institutions appropriate to the new temper and aspirations of the people. These institutions were to include not only the usual securities for liberty and property, but also the provison of education for the poor (Adam Smith had earlier included this among the proper functions of government) and, more novel (among the political economists, at any rate), the granting to the lower classes of "equal laws, and the possession of some influence in the framing of them."[2]

At this point, Malthus explicitly addressed himself to the problem of the "representation of the people." Representative government, he argued, was traditionally justified by the claim that it was the best means for securing "good and equal laws"—which exposed it to the counterclaim that if the same end could better be attained by other means, by a despotic government, for example, then that other government would be preferable. But the real argument for representative government, he insisted, was that the participation of the people was an end in itself, since it gave to each individual greater personal respectability and dignity,

9. Ibid., p. 513.
1. Ibid., p. 520.
2. Ibid., p. 522.

thereby generating "that prudence and elevation of sentiment by which alone in the present state of our being
poverty can be avoided."[3] With this accession of dignity,
prudence, and industry, the lower classes would have
acquired those qualities that would "approximate them, to
some degree, to the middle classes of society." And with
these qualities would come also a "taste for the con-
veniences and comforts of life," thus further inspiring them
to the exertions, virtues, and, ultimately, the conditions of
the middle class.[4]

Malthus had come a long way from the first edition,
when natural man had been represented as a slothful creature and the natural social order as one which roused him
from his sloth only by applying the most severe and relentless pressures. Then misery and vice had been man's saving,
and luxury and leisure his undoing. And this had been true
not only of the poor but of society as a whole. Had the
lower classes been able to aspire to the condition of the
middle classes, he had then argued, the effect on the health
of the social organism would have been disastrous:

> As in the oak, the roots and branches could not be dimin-
> ished very greatly without weakening the vigorous cir-
> culation of the sap in the stem, so in society the extreme
> parts could not be diminished beyond a certain degree
> without lessening that animated exertion throughout the
> middle parts, which is the very cause that they are the
> most favourable to the growth of intellect. . . .
>
> Leisure is, without doubt, highly valuable to man, but
> taking man as he is, the probability seems to be that in the
> greater number of instances it will produce evil rather
> than good. . . .
>
> The general tendency of an uniform course of pros-
> perity is rather to degrade than exalt the character.[5]

3. Ibid.
4. Ibid., p. 543.
5. Ibid., pp. 133, 135.

In the revised version of the *Essay*, the metaphor of the oak disappeared, and while the distinctions of parts still seemed to Malthus to be "in the nature of things absolutely necessary," he now discovered that there could be a substantial and beneficial shift in the proportion of those parts: "Our best-grounded expectations of an increase in the happiness of the mass of human society are founded in the prospect of an increase in the relative proportions of the middle parts." The natural condition was no longer the necessary condition of mankind—not even of the lower classes of mankind. Luxury itself was now permitted them. And more than permitted; it was prescribed for their own and everyone else's good: "It is the diffusion of luxury therefore among the mass of the people, and not an excess of it in a few, that seems to be most advantageous, both with regard to national wealth and national happiness."[6]

The denaturalization, or socialization, of the lower classes was the first step in their *embourgeoisement*. It was also the final step in Malthus's abandonment of the principle of population. Yet by giving up his principle, he demonstrated his true gift of prophecy. For the *embourgeoisement* of the lower classes, more than the inexorable pressure of population, has been the saving both of the lower classes and of society. Toward the end of his book, Malthus ventured the speculation:

> If the lower classes of people had acquired the habit of proportioning the supplies of labour to a stationary or even decreasing demand, without an increase of misery and mortality as at present, we might even venture to indulge a hope that at some future period the processes for abridging human labour, the progress of which has of late years been so rapid, might ultimately supply all the wants of the most wealthy society with less personal effort than at present; and if they did not diminish the severity of individual exertion, might, at least, diminish

6. Ibid., pp. 584-5.

the number of those employed in severe toil. If the lowest classes of society were thus diminished, and the middle classes increased, each labourer might indulge a more rational hope of rising by diligence and exertion into a better station; the rewards of industry and virtue would be increased in number; the lottery of human society would appear to consist of fewer blanks and more prizes; and the sum of social happiness would be evidently augmented.[7]

Was it deliberate on Malthus's part, or unconscious poetic irony, that the final sentence of the last edition should have echoed, but in reverse, the opening sentence of the first? The fallacy of the age, the first edition had proclaimed, was to suppose that "the great and unlooked for discoveries" in scientific affairs were a portent of progress in social affairs.[8] The hope of the age, he now concluded, was that these discoveries would, in some measure, be such a portent of progress: "Although we cannot expect that the virtue and happiness of mankind will keep pace with the brilliant career of physical discovery; yet, if we are not wanting to ourselves, we may confidently indulge the hope that, to no unimportant extent, they will be influenced by its progress and will partake in its success."[9]

It is curious that so drastic a change as that between the two versions of the *Essay* should have been largely ignored, both by Malthus's contemporaries and by later commentators. There were some, to be sure, who remarked upon it. Godwin did not fail to take credit for Malthus's conversion, even while continuing to attack him. And Walter Bagehot, perceptive as ever, went to the heart of the matter: "In its first form the *Essay on Population* was conclusive as an argument, only it was based on untrue

7. Ibid., p. 585.
8. Ibid., p. 3.
9. Ibid., p. 594.

facts; in its second form it was based on true facts, but it was inconclusive as an argument."[1]

Most readers of Malthus, however, did not take seriously the revisions of the later editions. Or at least, they did not take them seriously as affecting the central thesis of the book. There were those who merely recorded the shift from the theoretical to the empirical, as if the second edition were little more than a documentation and amplification of the first. Others, remarking upon the introduction of moral restraint as "another check to population," as Malthus had modestly put it in his preface,[2] were gratified that an obvious flaw had been put to right, so that the theory, corrected and refined, could more successfully withstand criticism. Still others were so intransigent in their hostility that they were blind to the change; no tinkering with so odious an idea, they protested, could make it any more acceptable. Partly the fault lies with readers, or non-readers, who find in a book what they expect to find in it. The principle of population was so widely advertised by critics and admirers alike that only a particularly vigilant reader would be aware that something drastic had happened to that principle. Although it was the revised edition that was read by most of his contemporaries and by subsequent generations, the shock effect of the first edition persisted and indelibly imposed itself on later editions.

Nor did Malthus clarify matters. It may be assumed that he was unaware of the magnitude of the change brought about by the introduction of moral restraint as a check upon population. In any event, he gave no indication of it. What has here been described as an abandonment of the principle of population emerges only from close analysis of his argument. Certainly he himself never drew this conclusion. Explicitly he only reaffirmed his thesis—in, as he supposed, an improved form. The essential propositions of

1. Bagehot, p. 387.
2. Malthus, *On Population*, p. 149.

the first edition, including the principle of population itself, the formula and ratios, survived intact into the later editions. The changes were introduced almost *en passant*, blurring into and swallowed up by the original.

Thus it came about that the familiar Malthus remained the Malthus of the first edition. The year of his death—1834—was also the year of his greatest triumph. It was then that the new Poor Law was passed. Public poor relief was not abolished, as he would have liked, but it was considerably reduced. Outdoor relief was replaced by workhouse relief, with the workhouses designed to discourage even the most determined of malingerers, and the sexes segregated to prevent the population increase he had warned against. Within only a few decades, however, Malthusianism ceased to be a vital issue. The growth of the economy permitted an unprecedented growth of population; the prosperity of the lower classes was not undermined but strengthened by social reforms; the Poor Laws were relaxed without any encouragement to pauperdom; and the principle of population was largely forgotten or ignored.

We have now, after a hundred years, come full circle. The apocalpytic exhortations of a few eccentrics have become the daily admonitions of journalists and scientists, and the catastrophes of a morbid imagination seem today uncomfortably imminent. Yet if our current anxieties seem to vindicate Malthus, we may take comfort in the fact that his "mathematical certainties" were not, after all, so certain, that his argument was not altogether logical, that the inexorable developments he predicted have not, for this century and a half at least, come to pass. It may be still more comforting, however, to appeal from the Malthus of the first edition to the Malthus of the second. For in the second may be found not only a corrective of the first but also a possible solution for our present dilemma. We may yet have reason to be grateful to Malthus—less for diagnosing our disease than for prescribing its cure.

HIGH VICTORIANS

THE OTHER JOHN STUART MILL

JOHN STUART MILL is thought of today as the archetype of the liberal, the author of that classic of liberalism, *On Liberty*. But there was another John Stuart Mill, who was anything but the perfect liberal and whose writings were of a quite different character. The drama of his life was the alternation of these two Mills. The "periods" of his work were as well defined as those of a Picasso. Yet the drama has been insufficiently appreciated and the periods have been imperfectly distinguished, so that a single stereotyped image has come to prevail. In part, the fault has been with critics and commentators who have been so overwhelmed by *On Liberty* that they could not seriously attend to his other writings. Partly the fault was with Mill himself who, in his *Autobiography*, rewrote his own past at the same time and in the same spirit that he wrote *On Liberty*.

Mill's responsibility for the creation of his own stereotype is only now becoming apparent. The publication of his correspondence with Harriet Taylor, for twenty years his intimate companion and later his wife, and the more recent publication of the original draft of his *Autobiography*, are enormously revealing. It remains for scholars to collate these materials, as well as to re-examine his early writings in their original versions. These early essays have been known, if at all, from their later appearance in his collected essays, the four volumes entitled *Dissertations and Discussions*. This work is now rare and unavailable to most readers. But even were it available, it would give a faulty sense of the development of his thought. For before the publication of the first two volumes in 1859 (the same year that saw the publication of *On Liberty*), the essays had been carefully selected and edited by Mill and his wife. In his preface he represented them as the only ones worth preserving from an earlier period of his "mental progress": "I leave them in all their imperfection, as memorials of the states of mind in which they were written." And this is how they have been taken—in spite of his own contradictory admission that he had "endeavored to clear the present pages" of statements he "altogether ceased to think true."[1] In fact, both the selection and the editing of the essays present a more biased record of his intellectual development than is generally suspected. While he included some essays that were no longer entirely congenial but were too memorable to omit (perhaps also because he still had a private fondness for those essays), he told his readers that he hoped they would find the "balance restored" by others of a different cast.[2] To restore that balance—in effect to weight the volumes in favor of his later views—he included some essays of little intrinsic merit and excluded other more meritorious ones. The same balancing, or overbalancing, effect was achieved by an inconspicuous yet effective process of editing, in which the omission or addition of crucial sentences, even of single words, altered the sense of the original.[3]

1. Mill, *Dissertations and Discussions* (London, 1859), I, iv.
2. Ibid.
3. The more important of these essays, plus some not included by Mill in the *Dissertations*, are reprinted in their original versions in *Essays on Politics and Culture*, ed. Gertrude Himmelfarb (New York, 1962). References below are to this edition of the *Essays* rather than to the Anchor edition (1963), which is differently paginated.

Mill's *Autobiography* is similarly deceptive. He seemed to be so forthright in the description of his father's personality and ideas, the account of the "crisis" that alienated him from his old world and initiated him into a new one, the portrayal of his "most valuable friendship" with Harriet Taylor, and the discussion of his "mental progress," that biographers have tended to take him at face value. But his candor was disingenuous. What he has often given us are half-truths that are no less misleading than half-lies. His relations with his father and with his wife were far more tortuous than he made out; his long and fascinating account of his crisis deflects attention from a later, more serious crisis which was never so much as mentioned; and the shifts and turns, the vacillations and equivocations of his intellectual history were blurred. It is not generally realized, or enough is not made of the fact, that the greater part of the *Autobiography*, and by far the most interesting part, was written almost concurrently with *On Liberty* and, like *On Liberty*, was minutely supervised by his wife. Thus it, too, perpetuates the stereotype of the later Mill even while professing to describe the earlier one.

The "earlier" Mill and the "later" Mill are convenient but not literally accurate designations. The "conservative" and the "liberal" Mill would be better, if these were not party labels and had no pejorative overtones. But even these are misleading, for while Mill's liberalism is familiar enough, his peculiar brand of conservatism is not. "Liberal-conservatism," "conservative-liberalism," "radical Toryism": none of these is quite to the point. "Coleridgean conservatism" would be preferable, if Coleridge's philosophy were better known; but even this is too derivative. The "heterodox" Mill and the "conventional" Mill would be better yet, if people could bring themselves to think of conservatism as heterodox and liberalism as orthodox. For in fact it was his liberalism that was orthodox and his conservatism that was distinctly unorthodox—unorthodox not only by the standards of liberals but by those of conservatives as well; neither in his day nor in ours could the conventional conservative derive much satisfaction from either Mill. "Earlier" and "later," then, the distinction remains, on the understanding that it refers on the one hand to the remarkable and lesser known essayist of the 1830's and early 1840's, and on the other to the more familiar author of *On Liberty*.

It must not be supposed, however, that the later Mill was the final and therefore the more "real" Mill. After the death of Harriet Taylor late in 1858, and the publication of *On Liberty* shortly afterwards, Mill reverted, in many ways, to his earlier philosophical temper. The last fourteen years of his life were among the most active and productive he had ever enjoyed, and can no more be ignored than the earlier years of efflorescence. The mode of thought that both periods largely shared has as much right to the claim of representing the "real" Mill as that characterizing his interim period, the period of *On Liberty*—when, it may fairly be said, he was not entirely a free agent.

The earliest Mill of all, the aboriginal Mill, was the product of the strenuous system of education devised by his father and Jeremy Bentham for the creation of the perfect utilitarian. If Mill was never really the "Saint of Rationalism"[4] that some of his admirers made of him, nor the "logic-chopping machine"[5] of his denigrators, it was because his education ultimately failed in its purpose. That purpose was not primarily to read Greek at the age of three, or to have mastered a formidable body of classical,

4. John Morley, *The Life of William Ewart Gladstone* (New York, 1903), II, 544.

5. J. A. Froude, *Thomas Carlyle: A History of His Life in London* (London, 1884), II, 420.

historical, and ecclesiastical literature by the age of eight. It was rather to cultivate the faculties of reason and critical analysis to the exclusion of all else, on the premise that the thoroughly rational and analytic man would be the consummate utilitarian. The function of the utilitarian was to reduce the whole complex of human behavior to a simple calculus of pleasure and pain, the "greatest happiness of the greatest number," which would solve all the vexing problems of morals, politics, law, and society. And in this enterprise, in the pursuit of and identification with the greatest happiness of the greatest number, the utilitarian was expected also to find his personal happiness. Until the age of twenty, Mill managed to fill this prescription, to his own satisfaction as much as to his father's.

In the autumn of 1826, Mill suddenly experienced the crisis of faith that is so movingly described in his *Autobiography*. As the evangelist is smitten by the conviction of sin, so he was smitten by the sense of futility. Utilitarianism became meaningless, and with it his whole life collapsed. For months he lived in a state of severe depression, his misery compounded with shame, so that he could not even take comfort in confessing to his misery. "Mine," he later, pitifully recalled, "was not an interesting or in any way respectable distress."[6] Just as life was beginning to seem unendurable, relief came as dramatically as had the crisis itself. He was reading Marmontel's *Mémoires*, when he came upon a passage relating the death of the father, the distress of the family, and the inspiration of the young boy that he "would be everything to them, would supply the place of all that they had lost." Vividly recreating the scene and participating in the emotion, Mill was moved to tears. "From this moment," he wrote, "my burden grew lighter."[7]

Mill himself attributed his deliverance to the discovery

6. Mill, *Autobiography* (New York, 1924), p. 95.
7. Ibid., p. 99.

that all feeling was not dead in him, that he was "not a stock or a stone."[8] A later, Freudian-minded generation may be tempted to see more in it than this. Not just this one episode but the whole pattern of Mill's life shows the same obsession with his father: this early fantasy of his death, the awe and fear that persisted through childhood and well into maturity, the conspicuous lack of love or even compassion for his mother that was a legacy from his father, the abortive attempts at rebellion, and the coincidence of his second breakdown ten years later with his father's impending death. The pattern is commonplace enough; what makes it so fascinating is its bearing upon Mill's intellectual history.

The fantasy of his father's death was more effective in liberating Mill from his father's philosophy and politics—Utilitarianism and Philosophic Radicalism—than from his person. The son was made acutely conscious of the poverty of a philosophy that was tirelessly analytic, that thought all virtues and sentiments to be willed rationally into existence, and that assumed all of society to be subject to the simple and rational principles of the reformers. This philosophy he now believed to be as ill conceived for society as it was deadly to his own spirit. For a time, however, he continued in the unsatisfactory state of rejecting the old without having anything new to replace it. Wordsworth finally released him from this limbo. In Wordsworth's poems he found a fusion of nature and poetry that suggested to him the possibility of a fusion of thought and feeling, a "culture" that would embrace both. The poems acted as an antidote to the old melancholic doctrines, a "medicine" for his soul.[9]

Wordsworth opened the door to others: to Comte, Carlyle, and Coleridge. Comte impressed upon Mill the idea of the necessary development of social systems and the

8. Ibid.
9. Ibid., p. 104.

historical relativity of social institutions, thus condemning to futility the efforts of the Philosophic Radicals to reform society according to a preconceived plan. Carlyle undermined the utilitarian faith in mechanical progress and laissez-faire liberalism. And Coleridge taught him a respect for history and tradition, for an organic society in which religion and authority were no less important than reason and liberty.

In 1829, when Macaulay launched his famous attack on James Mill's *Essay on Government*, John Mill found that while he might deplore the tone of the attack, he could not help but agree with its main theses: that self-interest was not necessarily conducive to, let alone identical with, the social interest, that good government did not necessarily depend upon an identity of interest between the governed and the governors, and that in any case such an identity was not a matter of electoral arrangements alone. The idea of representative democracy, which was the basic dogma of Philosophic Radicalism, Mill no longer regarded as inviolable; it had become "a question of time, place and circumstance."[1] Indeed politics in general, he now believed, was subordinate to culture, more an affair of morals and education than of material interests. By 1831 he had deviated so far from his old position that he confessed to feeling closer to the Tories than to the Radicals: "All my differences with him [Wordsworth] or with any other philosophic Tory, would be differences of matter-of-fact or detail, while my differences with the Radicals and Utilitarians are differences of principle."[2]

It was at this time and in this frame of mind that Mill wrote a series of articles on "The Spirit of the Age" for the Radical weekly, the *Examiner*. The theme of the articles was adopted from Saint-Simon and Comte: the distinction

1. Ibid., p. 120.
2. *The Earlier Letters of John Stuart Mill*, ed. Francis E. Mineka (Vols. XII–XIII of *Collected Works*, Toronto, 1963), I, 81 (Oct. 20–22, 1831).

between a "natural" society (what Saint-Simon called an "organic" society), in which "worldly power and moral influence are habitually and undisputably exercised by the fittest persons whom the existing state of society affords," and a "transitional" society (Saint-Simon's "critical" society), which Mill took to be the character of his own time, in which there was no recognized authority and every man believed himself to be the intellectual and political equal of every other.[3] What passed as the virtues of liberalism, he wrote, might turn out to be only the delusions of such a transitional period. An increase of discussion did not mean an increase of wisdom; error might be weakened without truth being strengthened; the right of private judgment too often became the right of ignorance; truth was not democratic since it was generally available to precious few; and even power was not democratic if that assumed that it was a virtue to deny all natural authority, for in fact such a denial was, for most people at most times, an absurdity and a vice. A hundred voices, in short, did not add up to one genuine authority, any more than a hundred voices necessarily added up to one truth.

A second series of articles by him the following year lost the *Examiner* some two hundred Radical readers because of such provocative statements as: "The test of what is right in politics is not the *will* of the people, but the *good* of the people, and our object is not to compel but to persuade the people to impose, for the sake of their own good, some restraint on the immediate and unlimited exercise of their own will."[4] To Carlyle Mill wrote, after the first few months of the Reformed Parliament, that he hoped this experience would disabuse the Radicals of the "infallibility of Constitution-mongering."[5] And as if in anticipated refu-

3. *Essays on Politics and Culture*, pp. 20–1.
4. Quoted by J. H. Burns, "J. S. Mill and Democracy," *Political Studies*, V (1957), 161.
5. *Earlier Letters*, I, 145 (March 9, 1833).

tation of *On Liberty*, he confided: "I have not any great
notion of the advantage of . . . the 'free discussion' men
call the 'collision of opinions,' it being my creed that Truth
is *sown* and germinates in the mind itself, and is not to be
struck *out* suddenly like fire from a flint by knocking
another hard body against it."[6]

One must be careful, at this point, to identify Mill as
precisely as he identified himself. If he felt closer to the
"philosophic" (or "speculative," or "ideal") Tory than to
the radical utilitarian, he did not feel in the least drawn to
what he called the "practical" Tory. "Practical Toryism
simply means, being *in* and availing yourself of your comfortable position *inside* the vehicle without minding the
poor devils who are freezing outside." Such a Tory was
either a vulgar place-hunter or a complacent enjoyer of
privilege. The "philosophic" Tory, on the other hand,
venerated "old England as opposed to the new, but it is old
England as she might be, not as she is." Philosophic Toryism, the Toryism of Wordsworth, Coleridge, and Southey,
was based on a reverence for "government in the abstract":

> It means, that they are duly sensible that it is good for man
> to be ruled; and to submit both his body and mind to the
> guidance of a higher intelligence and virtue. It is therefore
> the direct antithesis of liberalism, which is for making
> every man his own guide and sovereign-master, and let-
> ting him think for himself and do exactly as he judges
> best for himself, giving other men leave to persuade him
> if they can by evidence, but forbidding him to give way
> to authority; and still less allowing them to constrain him
> more than the existence and tolerable necessity of every
> man's person and property renders indispensably neces-
> sary. It is difficult to conceive a more thorough ignorance
> of man's nature, and of what is necessary for his happiness,
> or what degree of happiness and virtue he is capable of
> attaining, than this system [of liberalism] implies. But I

6. Ibid., p. 153 (May 18, 1833).

cannot help regretting that the men who are best capable of struggling against these narrow views and mischievous heresies should chain themselves, full of life and vigour as they are, to the inanimate corpses of dead political and religious systems, never more to be revived. The same ends require altered means; we have no new principles, but we want new machines constructed on the old principles; those we had before are worn out.[7]

It is curious to find Mill not only identifying himself as he was at this time, but also identifying himself as he was to become. For in criticizing the liberal, he was describing, with uncanny prescience, the author of *On Liberty*. He was also, to be sure, describing his father and the Philosophic Radicals. James Mill was then still very much alive, but Bentham died in 1832, and shortly afterwards Mill wrote a critique of Bentham and Benthamism that was even harsher and more devastating than the longer, better-known essay published five years later. He was frankly contemptuous of an "ethical philosopher" who failed to recognize conscience, or the sense of duty, as a human motive: "One would never imagine from reading him that any human being ever did an act merely because it is right, or abstained from it merely because it is wrong."[8] And he was frankly fearful of the effects of such moral insensibility:

> By the promulgation of such views of human nature, and by a general tone of thought and expression perfectly in harmony with them, I conceive Mr. Bentham's writings to have done and to be doing very serious evil. It is by such things that the more enthusiastic and generous minds are prejudiced against all his other speculations, and against the very attempt to make ethics and politics a subject of precise and philosophical thinking; which attempt, indeed, if it were necessarily connected with

7. Ibid., p. 84 (Oct. 20–22, 1831).
8. *Early Essays of John Stuart Mill* (London, 1897), p. 401.

such views, would be still more pernicious than the vague and flashy declamation for which it is proposed as a substitute. The effect is still worse on the minds of those who are not shocked and repelled by this tone of thinking, for on them it must be perverting to their whole moral nature. It is difficult to form the conception of a tendency more inconsistent with all rational hope of good for the human species, than that which must be impressed by such doctrines, upon any mind in which they find acceptance.[9]

Yet, when this essay was published, as an appendix to Bulwer Lytton's *England and the English*, Mill was most anxious that its authorship not be divulged: "It is not, and must not be, known to be mine."[1] Nor did he write anything else for publication during the next few years that would suggest the extent of his heresy. On the contrary, his public role was that of a devoted son and disciple. He continued to live at home, to work under his father at India House, and to be associated with the Philosophic Radicals. In 1835 he even undertook to edit their new journal, the *London Review*. (The title was changed the next year to the *London and Westminster Review*.) And the first few numbers of that *Review*, including Mill's own contributions to it, were such as to satisfy all but the most fanatical utilitarian and Radical. He wrote a defense of the utilitarian theory of ethics that is difficult to reconcile with anything else he wrote in the years immediately preceding or following it; one would be tempted to doubt his authorship were it not for its inclusion in the *Dissertations and Discussions*, where Mill felt obliged to comment on the discrepancy—although not to explain it. Another essay, on the "Rationale of Representation," advocated the principles of universal suffrage, self-interest, and the identity of interests. And a

9. Ibid., pp. 403–4.
1. Michael St. John Packe, *The Life of John Stuart Mill* (London, 1954), p. 221.

laudatory review of Tennyson concluded with the advice that Tennyson "strengthen his intellect" and "cultivate . . . philosophy," lest he be carried away by mere imagination or poetic imagery.[2]

Even Mill's public response to Tocqueville's *Democracy in America*, the first volume of which appeared early in 1835, was equivocal. His review of it was appreciative enough. But mingled with praise was a counterpoint of dissent: whenever Tocqueville's analysis of democracy became overly critical, Mill tried either to refute the criticism or to reinterpret democracy so as to evade the criticism. And when he met Tocqueville personally, in company with a leading Radical, he took the conventional Radical position. In private, however, he was far more sympathetic to Tocqueville. He besieged him with requests for articles and urged him to become associated with the *Review*, in order to counterbalance, he said, the influence of the Radicals who were sadly lacking in general ideas and who might "excite the democratic spirit without giving it any principles to guide it."[3]

Later Mill wrote in his *Autobiography* that he was not really, at this time, as far apart from his father as might seem, that his new views "were reconciled with and seemed to confirm while they modified" his old ones, "in no essential part of which I at any time wavered."[4] This, however, is patently the judgment of hindsight. It is clear that at the time he was living what might bluntly be called a double life, conforming to his father's views in public while placating his conscience with private asides of disagreement.

. . .

2. *Early Essays*, p. 266.
3. Tocqueville, *Oeuvres Complètes* (Paris, 1954), VI, 292–3 (June 11, 1835).
4. *Autobiography*, p. 118.

In the summer of 1835 matters came to a climax when his father was seized with a severe attack of tuberculosis. Almost immediately the younger Mill succumbed to a variety of ailments that stubbornly persisted, in varying degrees of severity, for almost a year—until after, that is, his father's death. He developed an infection in the lungs, intense pains in the head and stomach, and disturbing and unsightly muscular twitches in the face. "An obstinate derangement of the brain," his friend and biographer, Alexander Bain, described it.[5] Carlyle put it more graphically: "His eyes go twinkling and jerking with wild lights and twitches; his head is bald, his face brown and dry."[6] Although there were intervals when he could carry on with his work in London, he spent most of the long period of his father's illness abroad or in the country, in the hope, as he said, that a "complete change of scene" would help his recovery.[7] Of this breakdown there is not a word in his autobiography, although in many respects it was worse than the first crisis of which he made so much. Its physical symptoms were far more severe, and it left him with a permanently disordered stomach and with facial twitches and eye tics that disfigured him for the rest of his life.

The imminent death of his father not only brought to a head all the anxieties of a tortured and guilt-ridden relationship, but also coincided with—and aggravated—another equally tortured and guilt-ridden relationship. This was Mill's affair with Harriet Taylor. Any affair with any woman, given the exacerbated state of his emotional life, would have been difficult. Harriet Taylor was the most difficult of women under the best of conditions. And an illicit affair with Harriet Taylor compounded the difficulties almost beyond endurance.

5. Bain, *John Stuart Mill* (New York, 1882), p. 42.
6. Froude, *Carlyle*, I, 74.
7. Tocqueville, *Oeuvres*, VI, 313 (June 15, 1836).

It was as if Mill had willed her into existence. In 1829 he complained to a friend of the terrible loneliness of his life and his unsatisfied longing for "perfect friendship."[8] The very next year he discovered that perfect friendship in the person of Mrs. Taylor, the wife of a prosperous merchant and the mother of two young children (a third child was born soon after). Although his *Autobiography* stated flatly: "It was years after my introduction to Mrs. Taylor before my acquaintance with her became at all intimate or confidential,"[9] it is apparent from their recently published correspondence that their acquaintance became intimate and confidential almost immediately. As early as 1831 a "reconciliation" had to be effected between Mill and her husband.[1] And a love letter written by Mill to her the following summer contained every cliché of that form, including its being written in French.

For twenty years this friendship continued while Harriet remained the wife of Mr. Taylor—a loyal, affectionate, and respectful wife, Mill and Harriet insisted. Mill was in constant attendance upon her in the London house of the Taylors, he paid extended visits to her in the country in the absence of her husband, and he took long trips abroad with her, sometimes accompanied by one of the children. In spite of all this, however, and in spite of their avowed love for each other, there is every reason to accept their assurance that they were intimate in every sense but the sexual, and that Harriet was indeed the *"Seelenfreundin"* she described herself as being.[2]

In the beginning, they carried off the affair with aplomb, perhaps buoyed up by the self-righteousness of their *Seelenfreundschaft*. But in 1835, shortly before his father's illness, they were distressed to learn that even some of their

8. *Earlier Letters*, I, 28 (March 11, 1829).
9. *Autobiography*, p. 129.
1. F. A. Hayek (ed.), *John Stuart Mill and Harriet Taylor* (Chicago, 1951), p. 37.
2. Ibid., p. 56.

Radical friends were scandalized by their behavior. At the same time they were discomfited by the action of two other friends, the famous Unitarian minister William Fox and the hymn-composer Eliza Flower, who had decided that their love for each other overrode his obligations to a wife he no longer loved, and thereupon set up house together. To the implied criticism of both sides, Mill could only respond with increased guilt, frustration, and bitterness. The illness of his father, who thoroughly disapproved of this affair, brought these feelings to a focus. His own illness was small price to pay for his much abused nerves and conscience.

What the earlier fantasy of his father's death had initiated, the real death in 1836 consummated. The next five years saw the accomplishment of Mill's most imaginative, independent, and spirited work. The essays dating from this time were not only among his own finest writings, but among the finest essays of an age that excelled in the form. They were that peculiar amalgam of philosophy, history, politics, and sociology that was the distinctive quality of the English essay in the age of the great Reviews. They were the product of a lively, cultivated, interested, and engaged mind, in which all the resources of thought were brought to bear upon any subject, and in which any subject could be made to bear the burden of truth. Above all, they were free from party spirit and partisan purpose. They cut across the conventional political and philosophical lines, criticizing all doctrines with impunity and borrowing from all impartially. The result was neither destructive nor derivative, but rather an original and effective synthesis of thought.

Mill's essay on "Civilization" might serve, with only a few topical emendations, as a study of popular culture and mass society today. It was an indictment of contemporary civilization for giving to the masses the means and the will to exercise a formidable collective power, without a corresponding accession of intelligence or morality. It was also an implied indictment of Utilitarianism for assuming that progress and civilization were necessarily beneficent, and for not realizing that the rise of literacy might bring with it a decline in literature, or that the discouragement of conspicuous vice might result in the discouragement of heroic virtue. Again, there is a neat counterpoint here with the Mill of *On Liberty*. Where the later Mill looked to individuality and even eccentricity as a corrective to the mass, the earlier Mill looked to a "greater and more perfect combination among individuals," a guild of the "leading intellects of the age," to put their stamp of approval on meritorious works and thus prevent the decline of standards and the corruption of taste.[3]

The famous essays on Bentham and Coleridge are not only an indictment of Radicalism and Utilitarianism; they are an indictment of a philosophical and political temper that persists today in a variety of ideologies. Although appearing two years apart, the two essays were intended from the first as companion pieces. Bentham, "the great subversive" of his age, denying the reality and legitimacy of everything that did not conform to his peculiar scheme, was a prime exemplar of what Carlyle called "the completeness of limited men."[4] Coleridge, his antithesis, was as much a "great questioner of things established" without, however, being subversive.[5] Where Bentham was critical in the negative sense, Coleridge was critical in the inquiring sense. Where Bentham asked "Is it true?" Coleridge asked "What does it mean?"—on the presumption that the truth of a doctrine depended upon the meaning attached to it by the generations of thoughtful men who accepted it, and

3. *Essays on Politics and Culture*, p. 71.
4. Ibid., pp. 88, 129.
5. Ibid., p. 132.

that no doctrine could be presumed to be entirely untrue
that had been long accepted by intelligent men.[6] Coleridge,
Mill insisted, was the better philosopher because he had the
larger conception of human culture. He was also the better
social critic because he was the apologist of neither an
ideology nor a party: "A Tory philosopher cannot be
wholly a Tory, but must often be a better Liberal than
Liberals themselves; while he is the natural means of rescu-
ing from oblivion truths which Tories have forgotten, and
which the prevailing schools of Liberalism never knew."[7]

The politics of the Philosophic Radicals satisfied Mill as
little as their philosophy. His essay, "Reorganization of the
Reform Party," was a criticism of the Radicals for being too
sectarian both in their organization and in their program.
He took issue with them for committing themselves to
universal suffrage when a smaller measure of reform would
better promote their ends. It was necessary to redress the
grievances of the working classes, he argued, but neither
necessary nor desirable to transfer to them, in the present
state of culture, the weight of political power. What was
wanted was a "government *by means* of the middle for the
working classes.[8] What was also wanted was a "natural
Radical" party that would include the whole political spectrum from Liberal-Whigs through Ultra-Radicals.[9] Having
thus dissociated himself philosophically and politically
from the Radicals, Mill proceeded to sever his last personal
ties by selling the *London and Westminster Review*. His
next essay appeared in the *Edinburgh Review*, the *bête-
noire* of the old Radicals and of James Mill in particular.

This essay, significantly, was an eighty-page analysis of
the second volume of Tocqueville's *Democracy in*

6. Carlyle similarly rejected the question "Is it true?" in favor
of "Is it alive?" (W. H. Dunn, *James Anthony Froude* [Oxford,
1961], I, 73.)

7. *Essays on Politics and Culture*, p. 185.

8. Ibid., pp. 309–10.

9. Ibid., p. 292.

America. The proper relations of Radicals and Liberals had been a subject of contention with Tocqueville four years earlier. Now Mill was willing to concede this and much more to Tocqueville. It is instructive to compare the review of the second volume with that of the first five years earlier. In the second, Mill was far more ready to credit the dangers of democracy—although some part of the "tyranny of the majority," he suggested, might be due not so much to democracy specifically as to modern civilization, with its "sabbathless pursuit of wealth" and its "dogmatism of common sense."[1] Whatever its ultimate cause, however, he agreed with Tocqueville both in opposing "that species of democratic radicalism, which would admit at once to the highest of political franchises, untaught masses who have not yet been experimentally proved fit even for the lowest," and in favoring all measures that would educate and elevate the masses to the point where they might be gradually admitted to the franchise.[2] He also agreed with him that the best antidote to the tyranny of the majority was "a great social support for opinions and sentiments different from those of the mass"—a support to be found in the agricultural class, the leisured class, and the learned class.[3]

The essay on Tocqueville was the last of its kind for many years, the end of an epoch in Mill's life. The next two decades represented, as he put it, the "third period of my mental progress," a period of counter-reaction, when he "turned back from what there had been of excess in my reaction against Benthamism."[4] And indeed each of the works of this period may be said to represent a partial return, in one way or another, to Benthamism. His *System of*

1. Ibid., pp. 279, 282.
2. Ibid., p. 235.
3. Ibid., p. 284.
4. *Autobiography*, p. 161.

Logic reasserted the empirical and associationist episte-
mology of his father—and did so not only in the interest of
philosophy but of society as well, to counteract the intui-
tionism that was the "greatest intellectual support of false
doctrines and bad institutions."[5] His *Principles of Political
Economy* started out as a reaffirmation of Benthamite economics but then went beyond the old Radicalism to what he
came to regard as a more "fundamental" radicalism—socialism.[6] The essays later published under the title of *Utilitarianism* were first written in 1854; by modifying and modu-
lating the old philosophy, Mill also hoped to re-establish
it as the only viable philosophy. At the same time *On
Liberty* was being written—the classical testament of the
Mill of this period.

The primary characteristic of this period, as he described
it in his *Autobiography*, was not so much the influence of
Bentham as that of Harriet Taylor. In the published version
of the *Autobiography*, he spoke of his "mental progress" as
going "hand in hand with hers."[7] In the original draft,
however, the impression is not so much of their going hand
in hand as of her taking him by the hand and leading the
way. Without her, it appeared, he might never have
entered this period of his existence:

> A third and different stage of my mental progress . . .
> was essentially characterized by the predominating influ-
> ence of my wife's intellect and character. Up to this time
> I have spoken of my writings and opinions in the first
> person singular because the writings though (after we
> became intimate) mostly revised by her, and freed by her
> judgment from much that was faulty, as well as enriched
> by her suggestions, were not, like the subsequent ones,
> largely and in their most important features the direct
> product of her own mind. . . . But in the great advance

5. Ibid., p. 158.
6. Ibid., p. 161.
7. Ibid.

which I have since made in opinion I was wholly her pupil. Her bolder and more powerful mind arrived before mine at every conclusion which was derived from a more thorough comprehension of the present and insight into the future; and but for her intellect and her high moral feelings leading me on, it is doubtful if I should ever have advanced much further than the point I had now reached.[8]

Mill's public, to say nothing of private, tributes to Harriet Taylor were extravagant even by the most uxorious standards. Others, he prided himself, might discern her beauty and wit; he alone appreciated her wisdom, intelligence, poetic sensibility, and moral elevation. In spirituality, only Shelley was worthy of comparison with her, but intellectually even he was "but a child" compared to her. "Alike in the highest regions of speculation and in the smaller practical concerns of daily life, her mind was the same perfect instrument, piercing to the very heart and marrow of the matter; always seizing the essential idea or principle."[9] She was a paragon of virtues and a repository of superlatives: the most noble, the most just, the most unselfish, the most modest, the most proud, the most loving, the most considerate, the most sincere, the most sensitive, the most passionate, the most admirable person he knew or could conceive. She might have been a "consummate artist," a "great orator," or "eminent among the rulers of mankind," had she so chosen or had society been better disposed to her sex.[1] "So elevated was the general level of her faculties, that the highest poetry, philosophy, oratory, or art, seemed trivial by the side of her."[2] The last eulogy concluded with the prophecy that "if mankind continue to improve, their spiritual history for ages to come will be the

8. *The Early Draft of John Stuart Mill's Autobiography*, ed. J. Stillinger (Urbana, Ill., 1961), p. 169 *n*.

9. *Autobiography*, p. 131.

1. Ibid.

2. "Enfranchisement of Women," *Dissertations and Discussions*, II, 411–12.

progressive working out of her thoughts, and realization of her conceptions."[3]

On the face of it, no one could be so praiseworthy. And Harriet Taylor least of all, to judge by such independent evidence as we have. Her most finished literary effort, an essay on the "Enfranchisement of Women," was, even after Mill's editing, thoroughly undistinguished—as Mill himself surprisingly admitted. It had originally appeared in the *Westminster Review* (having apparently been submitted by Mill as his own work), but when he was asked to reprint it, he refused, lest, he explained, "it should be supposed to be the best we could do."[4] Later still, after her death, he reprinted it in his own volume of essays, prefacing it with the note that she herself was never satisfied with it and, highly as he estimated it, he would rather it go unacknowledged than be read "with the idea that even the faintest image can be found in it of a mind and heart which in their union of the rarest, and what are deemed the most conflicting excellencies, were unparalleled in any human being that I have known or read of." Had she lived longer, he felt assured she would have improved it immeasurably. (In fact, she took two years writing it and lived on for seven years after its publication.) Yet even this would have been unworthy of her. For nothing she could conceivably have written "would have given an adequate idea of the depth and compass of her mind."[5]

It would be agreeable to belittle Mill's infatuation as an innocent idiosyncrasy. And certainly to dwell upon Harriet Taylor's deficiencies—the vanity, arrogance, pettiness, affectation, complacency, willfulness, petulance, domestic tyranny, so plainly exhibited in her letters—would seem to suggest an obsession equal to that of Mill himself. Yet some true measure of the fantasy and the

3. Ibid., p. 412.
4. Packe, p. 347.
5. *Dissertations and Discussions*, II, 412.

reality is called for, if we are to assess Mill's own claims that she was the guiding spirit behind his major works. He saw her as presiding over the two most important areas of thought—the area of ultimate aims and ideals on the one hand, and that of the immediate and practicable on the other, while he himself occupied the humdrum middle ground of theory and logic.[6] In intellectual matters generally, he insisted, he followed where she led. Whatever was original in his work derived from her. He was but "one wheel," she the "moving engine."[7] He was her "interpreter," her "mediator," her "pupil."[8]

Again one can hardly credit such intemperate claims. Yet here the evidence bears him out—not in respect to her superiority, to be sure, but rather to her influence. His *Autobiography* spoke of the "conspicuous share" she had in the writing of *Political Economy*, the most notable chapter, on "The Probable Future of the Laboring Classes," being "entirely due to her": "She pointed out the need of such a chapter . . . ; she was the cause of my writing it; and the more general part . . . was wholly an exposition of her thoughts, often in words taken from her own lips."[9] In fact, not only this chapter but another that attracted much attention at the time, "Of Property," was written and rewritten at her dictation. The rewriting was inspired by the French Revolution of 1848, for which she conceived an instant and absolute passion. She hopefully looked for a similar revolution in Ireland; when told that such a revolution was bound to fail, she replied that a serious failure accompanied by "some loss of life" would be all to the good in inflaming the spirits of the people.[1] And

6. *Autobiography*, p. 132.
7. Hayek, pp. 165–6.
8. *Autobiography*, pp. 172, 175.
9. Ibid., p. 174.
1. Hayek, p. 125.

she even recommended the French example, and particularly the experiment in socialism, to the English.

Her sudden conversion to socialism came at an unfortunate time for Mill. His *Political Economy* had been published only a few months before, and he had there firmly denied both the feasibility and the desirability of socialism. But he had just been asked to prepare a second edition, and it was upon this that she directed her newly found fervor. Confronted with the task of adapting the old page proofs to Harriet's new convictions, Mill promptly succumbed to a "prostration of the nervous system," as his biographer put it.[2] After a brief reprieve, however, he was obliged to take up the work. The preparation of the revised edition merits close attention, for it is one of the most instructive episodes in Mill's intellectual history. It is also one of the best documented, since Mill and Harriet Taylor were separated a good deal at that time (she was traveling on the continent while her husband was mortally ill in England), and his letters to her have fortunately survived. We are thus privileged with an intimate, authentic, and altogether fascinating view of the progress of his mind on a crucial and highly influential subject.

The first edition had argued that a basic fallacy of communism and socialism (the words were used by Mill almost interchangeably) was to exaggerate the value and effect of security: "Those who have never known freedom from anxiety as to the means of subsistence, are apt to overrate what is gained for positive enjoyment by the mere absence of uncertainty."[3] When Harriet objected "strongly and totally" to this passage, Mill reminded her that it had originally been included "on your proposition and very nearly in your own words," that it seemed to him

2. Bain, p. 90.
3. *Principles of Political Economy* (Vols. II–III of *Collected Works*, Toronto, 1965), II, 978.

to be "the strongest part of the argument" against socialism, and that to alter it would be to change his entire position on the subject. At the same time he assured her that "by thinking sufficiently I should probably come to think the same [as you]—as is almost always the case, I believe always, when we think long enough."[4] "Long enough" turned out to be two or three weeks, by which time the sentence had acquired exactly the opposite meaning: "On the Communistic scheme, supposing it to be successful, there would be an end to all anxiety concerning the means of subsistence; and this would be much gained for human happiness."[5]

Similarly, the argument in the first edition that collective action should be confined to those activities which "cannot be done by individual agency," and that "where individual agency is at all suitable, it is almost always the most suitable,"[6] was altered by Mill, upon her insistence, to read: "We are as yet too ignorant either of what individual agency in its best form, or socialism in its best form, can accomplish to be qualified to decide which of the two will be the ultimate form of society."[7] (A compromise version proposed by Mill was firmly rejected by her, over his feeble protest that it had been "a favorite of mine."[8])

Or again, the first edition had portrayed a socialist community as a "well-regulated manufactory": "I believe the majority would not exert themselves for anything beyond this, and that unless they did, nobody else would, and that on this basis human life would settle itself in one invariable round."[9] When Harriet deleted this, Mill protested that without it his entire case collapsed: "All the two or three pages of argument which precede and of which this is but a

4. Hayek, pp. 134-5.
5. *Political Economy*, II, 978 *n*.
6. Ibid., II, 987 *n*.
7. Ibid., I, 208.
8. Hayek, p. 135.
9. *Political Economy*, II, 980 *n*.

summary are false and there is nothing to be said against communism at all. One would only have to turn round and advocate it—which if done would be better in a separate treatise and would be a great objection against publishing a second edition until after such a treatise."[1] Yet he did in fact delete the passage. And when finally nothing remained of the case against communism, except a caveat as to the present applicability of Fourierism, he offered to remove this too if she so desired—"even if there were no other reason than the certainty I feel that I never should long continue of an opinion different from yours on a subject which you have fully considered."[2]

The nature of her "considered" opinions may be deduced from one final example. One of her main arguments in favor of communism was that it could be achieved in the near future, since only ten years of teaching would suffice to make the present generation of schoolchildren "perfect." When Mill objected that this would require perfect people to teach them, she replied simply: "If there were a desire on the part of the cleverer people to make them perfect it would be easy." Mill could not refrain from observing that desire was not easily come by, that cleverness did not prevent a multitude of vices, and that even if the cleverest people were given absolute power to legislate and educate, perfection would still be a long way off. He then hastily closed the discussion with the promise that they would soon "have all those questions out together" and in "depth."[3]

Thus the exchange of considered opinions went, until Mill was able to assure her that he had "followed to the letter every recommendation."[4] And thus the *Political Economy* was altered from the classical text of laissez-

1. Hayek, p. 135.
2. Ibid., p. 137.
3. Ibid., p. 146.
4. Ibid., p. 144.

fairism to what has been hailed as the first serious and most influential attempt to come to terms with socialism.

The revision of the *Political Economy* came at a trying time for both of them. Mill was recovering from a variety of physical and nervous disorders. Harriet Taylor, returning to England to be with her husband before he died, was consumed by pity, self-pity, grief, and animus. Convinced that her husband's cancer was contagious, she was furious at Mill for suggesting otherwise; and another innocent attempt at consolation on his part she denounced as "the puerility of thought and feeling of any utterly headless and heartless pattern of propriety old maid."[5] Her old personal feuds were fanned by political suspicions. Everyone was lacking in seriousness and revolutionary zeal: "Tocqueville is a notable specimen of the class which includes such people as the Sterlings, Romillys, Carlyles, Austins—the gentility class—weak in moral, narrow in intellect, timid, infinitely conceited and gossiping. There are very few men in this country who can seem other than more or less respectable puppets to us."[6] And there were a host of lesser anxieties. She was obliged to move from her house in the country because "they have spoiled the appearance of it now from the outside by poor people's poor little places opposite";[7] she worried about the effects of the California gold discoveries on her husband's investments; she had to goad Mill into demanding a larger share of the profits from his book.

John Taylor died in July 1849, but it was not until March 1851 that Mill and Harriet got married. Having so long suffered from the impropriety of their relationship, they were now excessively proper, observing a longer

5. Ibid., p. 153.
6. Ibid., p. 156.
7. Ibid., p. 129.

period of mourning than was customary and absurdly
anxious about the perfect legality of their marriage ceremony. (Mill had happened to sign the register, "J. S. Mill,"
and when told that his full name was required, had squeezed
in the missing letters. A year later, haunted by the possibility that his signature had been faulty, he wrote his
wife a formal letter explaining the situation and suggesting
that they go through a church ceremony as well "so that
hereafter no shadow of a doubt on the subject can ever
arise"[8]—this at a time when they were at their most anti-
clerical.) Withdrawn from friends and family, contemptuous of ordinary social relations, both suffering poor health,
they lived a nearly solitary life in Blackheath (with Mill,
however, continuing his old job in the India Office).

It was at this time that they drew up plans for their joint
lifework. They were not beguiled by false modesty. Convinced that no one in their generation or even in the rising
generation was capable, as Mill told his wife, "of thoroughly mastering and assimilating your ideas, much less of
re-originating them," he felt it their duty to put them in
print, and "then they can wait until there are again
thinkers."[9] Since time was running short for them, he
conceived the notion of serving up their ideas in the form
of a "pemmican"—the compressed mixture of foods of the
American Indian. Thus their views on all the important
subjects (character, love, education, religion, morals, liberty, socialism, family, etc.) would be preserved in a "state
of concentrated thought—a sort of mental pemmican,
which thinkers, when there are any after us, may nourish
themselves with and then dilute for other people."[1]

Some of Mill's biographers have wondered why he published so little (two book reviews and some botanical
notes) during the period of his marriage. The answer is not

8. Ibid., p. 170.
9. Ibid., p. 185.
1. Ibid., p. 191.

ill-health, as has been supposed, but this deliberate decision to withhold publication until the whole was complete and perfect. In fact, a great deal was written: the *Autobiography, Utilitarianism, On Liberty*, two essays on religion, and one essay on women. Occasionally Mill weakened and proposed publishing part of it, but he was overruled by his wife. On November 3, 1858, Harriet Mill died. On November 30, on black-bordered writing paper, Mill offered his publisher his "little book," *On Liberty*.[2]

On Liberty was the heart of the pemmican. In his *Autobiography*, Mill explained that it was "more directly and literally our joint production than anything else which bears my name, for there was not a sentence of it that was not several times gone through by us together." But only the composition, he insisted, was joint; the basic conception of the book came from her: "The whole mode of thinking of which the book was the expression was emphatically hers." What emerged from this collaboration, he said, was "a kind of philosophical text-book of a single truth."[3]

The "single truth" of *On Liberty* was "one very simple principle": that "the sole end for which mankind are warranted, individually or collectively, in interfering with the liberty of action of any of their number, is self-protection."[4] This is a far call not only from the earlier Mill who had denied that society could be so arbitrarily limited or that human relations could be defined so simply, but also from the Mill who had only recently allowed to a socialist state such wide latitude of action. The problem of liberty, he now asserted, was uniquely the problem of democratic governments and societies. It was democracy, the reign of popular government and public opinion, that

2. Packe, p. 399.
3. *Autobiography*, pp. 176-7.
4. *On Liberty* (Everyman edn.; London, 1940), pp. 72-3.

was now the greatest threat to liberty. The "tyranny of the majority," of "prevailing opinion and feeling," was more dangerous because more encompassing than the tyranny of any magistrate, for it threatened not only liberty of action but also of thought.[5] Truth, individuality, intellectuality, genius, progress were all its victims. To be sure, Mill allowed for certain exceptions, specific occasions when society could legitimately interfere with the individual. But these were minimal; for the most part, as on matters of social welfare, the burden of the argument was overwhelmingly against the interference of government and society.

The thesis of *On Liberty* and arguments as to its validity are familiar enough. More intriguing is Mill's own attitude toward it. In his *Autobiography*, he professed the highest regard for it, describing it as the most "carefully composed" of his works and the one likely to survive the longest.[6] He even invested it with a Gibbonesque origin worthy of a classic: the idea of publishing the essay as a separate volume first came to him, he said, in Rome, while "mounting the steps of the Capitol."[7] (In fact, the idea was first broached in a letter written en route to Rome.[8]) And he made a special point of the fact that, unlike all his other books, this one appeared in edition after edition without any revision. Yet all these tributes to the book were, in effect, tributes to his wife. Having published it as a memorial to her, and having given her credit for the major part of it, he could hardly alter it without seeming to desecrate her memory. One may even suspect that the lavish tributes and credit veiled an unconscious ambivalence toward the book, for the more he paid homage to her and the more he identified her with it, the less he himself was identified with it.

5. Ibid., p. 68.
6. *Autobiography*, pp. 170, 177.
7. Ibid., p. 170.
8. Hayek, p. 216.

It is difficult otherwise to understand Mill's insistence upon the "single truth," the "simple principle," of *On Liberty*. To describe a work as "a kind of philosophic textbook of a single truth" is surely not the highest praise one can bestow upon it. This was particularly true for Mill, for whom such words could only evoke the memory of the old controversy over his father's *Essay on Government*, when Macaulay had accused the elder Mill of trying to reduce the complexities of life to a "single general rule."[9] Macaulay's critique had figured prominently in John Mill's "mental crisis" and had gone far in liberating him from his father's simplistic utilitarianism—a point Mill himself made much of in his *Autobiography*. (And the *Autobiography*, it will be recalled, was written about the same time as *On Liberty*.) By deliberately, provocatively flaunting the idea of a "single," "simple" truth, Mill was surely inviting precisely the criticism Macaulay had made, with such devastating effect, of his father.[1]

His critics were not slow in taking up his invitation. Although *On Liberty* was generally accorded the status of an instant classic, it received a good measure of criticism, on this and other grounds. Reviewers questioned the viabil-

9. T. B. Macaulay, *Works* (London, 1875), V, 268.

1. There are other intimations of ambivalence on Mill's part toward *On Liberty*. In his *Autobiography*, for example, after crediting his wife with the larger share in its composition, he went on to explain the exact nature of her influence: "She was in nothing more valuable to my mental development than by her just measure of the relative importance of different considerations." Yet the very next sentence, as if to belie what he had just said, described *On Liberty* as a "philosophic textbook of a single truth." (P. 177.) Again, praising her for her "steadying influence," he wrote: "There was a moment in my mental progress when I might easily have fallen into a tendency towards over-government." (Ibid.) Yet it was she who was responsible for his overtures toward socialism in the revised edition of the *Political Economy*. Surely to raise this point in this connection was to focus attention upon the opposite and excessive tendencies of both books—*Political Economy* veering toward "over-government," and *On Liberty* toward under-government.

ity of a purely negative conception of liberty (this criticism did not, as is commonly thought, originate with T. H. Green and his generation). They denied the possibility of distinguishing between self-regarding and other-regarding actions. They were skeptical of the proposition that truth necessarily emerged from the free clash of opinions or that the good necessarily emerged from the conflict of wills. And above all, they doubted the seriousness of the threat to liberty. *On Liberty*, it was said, might more appropriately have issued from the prison cell of a persecuted heretic than from the study of the most influential writer of the age. Macaulay found it curious that Mill should have thought individuality was being suppressed when in fact eccentricity and nonconformity seemed to be very much the fashion; surely, he protested, Mill was crying "Fire!" in Noah's flood.[2] Ten years earlier, Herbert Spencer, the most consistent individualist and laissez-fairist of the epoch, had written: "A new Areopagitica, were it possible to write one, would surely be needless in our age of the world and in this country."[3] What had been true then was still more true at this time. Mill himself was not unmoved by this argument. In that part of the *Autobiography* written after his wife's death, he felt obliged to account for the fact that *On Liberty* had appeared "at a time which, to superficial observation, did not seem to stand much in need of such a lesson," a time when new ideas were not only tolerated but encouraged. He cautioned his readers, however, that this situation might well change and that *On Liberty* was addressed to future generations possibly less tolerant than the present one.[4]

Mill's attempt to postdate the book by projecting it into the future was entirely an afterthought. Certainly there

2. G. O. Trevelyan, *The Life and Letters of Lord Macaulay* (New York, 1875), II, 386.
3. Spencer, *Social Statics* (New York, 1954), p. 133.
4. *Autobiography*, p. 177.

was nothing in the book itself to suggest that he did not think the threat to individuality a clear and present danger. Yet, curiously, at exactly the time he was writing *On Liberty*, he was involved in an episode that placed him on the side of his critics. He had been solicited by an organization calling itself the "Neophyte Writers' Society," the object of which, as Mill understood it, was to promote writing for the sake of writing rather than for any particular purpose to be served by that writing. Such an idea, Mill protested, was totally unacceptable to him:

> I set no value whatever on writing for its own sake. . . . I have, on most of the subjects interesting to mankind, opinions to which I attach importance, and which I earnestly desire to diffuse, but I am not desirous of aiding the diffusion of opinions contrary to my own. . . . There is already an abundance, not to say superabundance, of writers who are able to express in an effective manner the mischievous commonplaces which they have got to say. I would gladly give any aid in my power towards improving their opinions, but I have no fear that any opinions they have will not be sufficiently well expressed, nor in any way should I be disposed to aid in sharpening weapons when I know not in what cause they will be used.[5]

Instead of postdating *On Liberty*, one might be better advised to predate it. For it resembles not so much Mill's opinion at this time (nor, indeed, at any time), so much as the opinion of Harriet Taylor *circa* 1832, shortly after she met Mill. An unpublished manuscript signed by her had been carefully preserved over the years and was found among Mill's papers after his death. Here was the prototype in miniature of *On Liberty*:

> Whether it would be religious conformity, political conformity, moral conformity or social conformity, no matter which the species, the spirit is the same: all kinds

5. *The Letters of John Stuart Mill*, ed. Hugh S. R. Elliot (London, 1910), I, 181-2 (April 23, 1854).

agree in this one point, of hostility to individual character, and individual character if it exists at all, can rarely declare itself openly while there is, on all topics of importance a standard of conformity raised by the indolent minded many and guarded by a [?] of opinion which, though composed individually of the weakest twigs, yet makes up collectively a mass which is not to be resisted with impunity.

What is called the opinion of Society is a phantom power, yet as is often the case with phantoms, of more force over the minds of the unthinking than all the flesh and blood arguments which can be brought to bear against it. It is a combination of the many weak, against the few strong; an association of the mentally listless to punish any manifestation of mental independence.[6]

And so on, through a defense of "eccentricity" as "prima facie evidence for the existence of principle," a criticism of the concept of "toleration" as implying a basic intolerance, an assertion of the primacy of Truth in spite of the total relativism of truths, a defense of the good and the beautiful as against the social pressures toward conformity and competition, and an attack on a society that "abhors individual character" and "asks the sacrifice of body, heart and mind."[7] These words could well have come from the prison cell of a persecuted heretic—or from the drawing room of a young woman with romantic bohemian affectations.

"It is doubtful if I shall ever be fit for anything public or private again," Mill wrote just after his wife's death. "The spring of my life is broken."[8] He bought a cottage overlooking the graveyard at Avignon where she was buried, installed in it the furniture from the hotel room in which

6. Hayek, pp. 275–6.
7. Ibid., pp. 276–9.
8. Bain, p. 102.

she had died, and for the remainder of his life retired there for a few months each year. Her daughter, Helen, took over the management of his house at Blackheath and supervised his affairs.

Yet for all his pieties and memorials, for all his devotion to her memory as to a "religion,"[9] his later life gave the appearance of a renascence. Within a year, he had published *On Liberty, Dissertations and Discussions*, a pamphlet on parliamentary reform, and four essays. Some of these, to be sure, were the works of the preceding decade, but others were new and even novel. So far from being merely a "conduit" for his late wife's ideas, as he had represented himself,[1] he was in fact entering a new phase of what he liked to call his mental progress. This fourth period was inaugurated only a few months after her death with the publication of a pamphlet called *Thoughts on Parliamentary Reform*, dealing with a recently introduced bill to extend the franchise. Part of the pamphlet, he explained, had been written earlier on the occasion of a previous reform bill and had "at that time been approved and revised by her." One important feature of it, however, had not been discussed "with my almost infallible counsellor, and I have no evidence that she would have concurred in it."[2] This was the idea of plural voting: that the better educated should have more than one vote at their disposal. Mill made much more of this idea in the pamphlet than he seemed to in his *Autobiography*, the argument in its favor occupying almost a fourth of the pamphlet, and constituting, as he said, an important "question of principle" that separated him from the "democratic reformers." He agreed with the reformers that universal suffrage was an "ultimate aim," that ultimately everyone had a right to

9. *Autobiography*, p. 170.
1. Bain, p. 102.
2. *Autobiography*, p. 180.

participate in government. But he disagreed with their assumption that everyone had an equal right to participate: "It is the fact that one person is not as good as another; and it is reversing all the rules of rational conduct to attempt to raise a political fabric on a supposition which is at variance with fact."[3] A discovery that preoccupied him even more, and alienated him still further from the Radicals, was proportional representation. He acclaimed this scheme as "the greatest improvement of which the system of representative government is susceptible," because it counteracted the greatest evil of that system. By ensuring the representation of minorities, he argued, it would reduce the tyranny of the majority and strengthen "the elite of the nation."[4]

Another essay written that same year has unfortunately received almost no attention at all, even by Mill's admirers, perhaps because of its modest title. "A Few Words on Non-Intervention" is not only one of the most timely of his writings—of our time as well as of his—but also one of his most thoughtful. It is on a subject much wanting in thought: foreign policy and international morality. The immediate occasion of the article was Palmerston's opposition to the construction of the Suez Canal by the French. Mill deplored Palmerston's action, but at the same time spiritedly defended English foreign policy in general as the least aggressive, the most humane, and the most generous of any great power. He then turned to the more basic question raised by the current international situation. What should be the attitude of such an unaggressive, humane, and generous power to the wars of national liberation being waged in Europe? Italy was engaged in such a war, and Hungary, having tragically failed once, was reported to be preparing for another revolt. When is it right, he asked, for

3. *Essays on Politics and Culture*, p. 339.
4. Ibid., p. 384.

a country "to go to war for an idea"? When is it right to intervene in another country's civil war, or in a struggle "against a foreign yoke, or against a native tyranny upheld by foreign arms"?[5] The terms of the discussion—"liberation" and "intervention"—the particular issues—Suez and Hungary—and perhaps even Mill's conclusion are uncannily reminiscent of recent events and of issues that still occupy us today:

> To assist a people thus kept down is not to disturb the balance of forces on which the permanent maintenance of freedom in a country depends, but to redress that balance when it is already unfairly and violently disturbed. The doctrine of non-intervention, to be a legitimate principle of morality, must be accepted by all governments. The despots must consent to be bound by it as well as the free States. Unless they do, the profession of it by free countries comes but to this miserable issue, that the wrong side may help the wrong, but the right must not help the right. Intervention to enforce non-intervention is always rightful, always moral, if not always prudent. Though it be a mistake to *give* freedom to a people who do not value the boon, it cannot but be right to insist that if they do value it, they shall not be hindered from the pursuit of it by foreign coercion. It might not have been right for England (even apart from the question of prudence) to have taken part with Hungary in its noble struggle against Austria; although the Austrian Government in Hungary was in some sense a foreign yoke. But when, the Hungarians having shown themselves likely to prevail in this struggle, the Russian despot interposed, and joining his force to that of Austria, delivered back the Hungarians, bound hand and foot, to their exasperated oppressors, it would have been an honourable and virtuous act on the part of England to have declared that this should not be, and that if Russia gave assistance to the wrong side, England would aid the right.[6]

5. Ibid., pp. 405, 412.
6. Ibid., pp. 412-13.

The following year Mill turned to a more ambitious work. *Considerations on Representative Government*, published in 1861, was an attempt to describe the best—the practicably best—form of representative government. There was no yearning here for the "single truth" or "one very simple principle" that had characterized *On Liberty*. It was, instead, a subtle and complex inquiry into a difficult and complicated subject. Mill treated representative government, or democracy, in the manner of Tocqueville—not as a principle to be defended or attacked but as a given fact of modern civilization. He was concerned not so much with the problem of making representative government more representative, more democratic, as with the problem of making it better. And making it better generally meant, in practice, devising ways of limiting it. A representative body, Mill found, was no more suited for the legislative business of government than for the administrative. Indeed parliament was "radically unfit" for the "function of governing."[7] What it could and should do was to watch and control the government. But even here it was beset by grave dangers: the tyranny of the majority, the tendency to "collective mediocrity," and the many other "infirmities and dangers" that take up a large part of this book.[8] To mitigate these infirmities and dangers, he proposed such measures as a Commission of Legislation appointed by the Crown with exclusive responsibility for legislation; proportional representation and plural voting to give greater weight to "superior intellects and characters";[9] educational qualifications for the franchise; and the open ballot. The latter, in particular, represented a dramatic break with his earlier views, for the secret ballot had long been one of the principal demands of the Radicals. The Radicals had

7. *Representative Government* (Everyman's edn.; London, 1940), p. 239.
8. Ibid., pp. 265, 242.
9. Ibid., p. 266.

insisted upon the secret ballot on the best utilitarian grounds: every man had to be free to act upon his individual interests, since the sum of these individual interests added up to the public good. Mill, no longer convinced of the sanctity either of the individual or of his interests, conceived of the franchise as the exercise of a moral or public trust; and it was precisely to minimize personal interest and maximize public duty that he now opposed the secret ballot.

The essays on *Utilitarianism*, published at the same time (and reprinted as a volume in 1863), are in a very different tone—having originally been written in 1854 and revised in 1859–60. We do not, unfortunately, know the extent or nature of the revision, which may well explain some of the contradictions and inconsistencies of the book and the general impression that this was probably the least satisfactory of Mill's writings. "This short work has many volumes to answer for," wrote Mill's biographer who was also a prominent utilitarian.[1] And a more recent critic has wondered why Mill persisted "in maintaining general principles with which the facts admitted are clearly inconsistent."[2] Ostensibly defending Bentham's calculus of pleasure and pain as the measure of utility and the foundation of morality, Mill succeeded, in the course of the first few pages, in undermining the basis of that calculus. Pleasures, he found, were not the sole objects of desire; nor were they qualitatively identical; nor were individuals qualitatively identical—in which case, as critics were quick to point out, there could be no calculation of pleasures, nor of individuals, still less of the two combined. The rest of the book was an attempt to refine and redefine Benthamism so as to

1. Bain, p. 112.
2. A. D. Lindsay, Introduction to *Utilitarianism, On Liberty, and Representative Government* (Everyman's ed.; London, 1940), p. viii.

temper quantity with quality, the individual with society, and utility with morality. Like the *Political Economy*, and unlike *Representative Government*, Mill was notably optimistic about the prospects for reform and progress: "No one whose opinion deserves a moment's consideration can doubt that most of the great positive evils of the world are in themselves removable, and will, if human affairs continue to improve, be in the end reduced within narrow limits." These evils, which he trusted would be eliminated by the "wisdom of society combined with the good sense and providence of individuals," included poverty, the vicissitudes of fortune, and disease.[3]

If *Representative Government* may be said to mark Mill's retreat from radicalism, his last important work, the essay on "Theism," suggests a parallel retreat from rationalism. Written in 1869–70, "Theism" was published posthumously in a volume entitled *Three Essays on Religion.* Although the editor, his stepdaughter Helen Taylor, obviously intended to counteract the effect of "Theism" by the inclusion of two earlier essays—"Nature" and the "Utility of Religion," both dating from the 1850's—the real effect of the juxtaposition was to emphasize Mill's estrangement from the mood of the fifties.

The idea of writing the earlier essay on the "Utility of Religion," its title and its specific theme, had first originated with his wife. Her proposal was clear in intention if incoherent in expression:

> Would not religion, the Utility of Religion, be one of the subjects you would have most to say on—there is to account for the existence nearly universal of some religion (superstition) by the instincts of fear, hope and mystery etc., and throwing over all doctrines and theories, called religion, and devices for power, to show how religion and poetry fill the same want . . . —how all this must be

3. *Utilitarianism*, p. 14.

superseded by morality deriving its power from sympathies and benevolence and its reward from the approbation of those we respect.[4]

The essay, as Mill then wrote it, reflected most of these views. Religion, he wrote, was indefensible both on the grounds of truth and of utility, the appeal to the latter being a form of "moral bribery or subornation of the understanding."[5] There was, he concluded, nothing in Christianity that was not better supplied by the Religion of Humanity. At the same time, using her very words, he subtly altered their effect: religion, he suggested, had a more honorable origin than fear; the idea of religion as a device for power was only the "vulgarest part" of his subject; and religion, while comparable to poetry, was also distinct from it, for it addressed itself to reality in a way that poetry did not.

The later essay on "Theism" was a reconsideration of both the truth and the utility of religion. There was no proof, Mill reasoned, for the existence of a personal, omnipotent God; but there was a "degree of probability" for the existence of "an Intelligent Mind, whose power over the materials was not absolute, whose love for his creatures was not his sole actuating inducement, but who nevertheless desired their good."[6] More important, however, than the question of the existence of God was that of the utility of religious faith. And here Mill found the burden of evidence to be in favor of Christianity. Human life, small and confined as it is and was likely to be, even in the event of considerable material and moral progress, "stands greatly in need of any wider range and greater height of aspiration for itself and its destination," and it was "a part of wisdom to make the most of any, even small probabilities on this subject, which furnish imagination with any footing to

4. Hayek, pp. 195–6.
5. *Three Essays on Religion* (London, 1874), p. 71.
6. Ibid., p. 479.

support itself upon."[7] Christianity provided that probability and that support by familiarizing the imagination with the conception of a "morally perfect Being," and making that Being the "*norma* or standard" for human life. Christ, in short, was the "ideal representative and guide of humanity." And the legitimate indulgence of "supernatural hopes" was responsible for the "due ascendancy of this religion over the human mind."[8]

This last essay discomfited most of Mill's followers and has since discomfited most commentators. His biographer, James Bain, could only suppose that Mill was trying to console himself for his wife's death with the prospect of an afterlife. His great admirer, John Morley, regarded it as an "infelicitous compromise with orthodoxy," an "intellectual scandal."[9] And his great critic, James Fitzjames Stephen, ridiculed it as a "diet of anaesthetic."[1] More recently Crane Brinton dismissed it with the comment: "The wan theism of his last years is the final refuge of a mind that never had quite the courage of its own doubts."[2] In view of Mill's intellectual history, the judgment might be exactly the reverse: The theism of his last years was the candid expression of a mind that finally had the courage of its own doubts.

The last years of Mill's life were personally as well as intellectually vivifying. He renewed old friendships and even entered public life. In 1851 he had declined the offer of a seat in Commons; in 1865 he accepted it. Invited to stand as the Liberal candidate for Westminster, he accepted on condition that he would not personally campaign,

7. Ibid., p. 481.
8. Ibid., pp. 484–7.
9. John Morley, *Recollections* (New York, 1917), I, 106.
1. Packe, p. 443.
2. Brinton, *English Political Thought in the Nineteenth Century* (Cambridge, Mass., 1949), p. 103.

would not contribute to the expense of a campaign, and would not be bound either by party loyalty or by pledges from his constituency. On one of the two occasions when he did make campaign speeches, he was asked whether he had indeed written: "The lower [classes], though mostly habitual liars, are ashamed of lying."[3] He firmly replied, "I did"—whereupon the working-class audience burst into cheers. His three years in parliament were personally gratifying although politically inconsequential. Determined to be a spokesman for causes that would otherwise be unrepresented, he confined himself to such issues as women's suffrage, proportional representation, and Irish reforms. He failed to be re-elected in 1868, partly because, having refused to contribute to his own campaign, he insisted upon publicly contributing to that of the notorious atheist Bradlaugh.

When Mill died in 1873, he was the philosopher laureate of England. Students had long been nurtured on his *Logic* and *Political Economy*. *On Liberty* had been pronounced a classic at birth. And Mill himself was popularly acclaimed the spirit of the age.

But the spirit of one age is rarely the spirit of another. The individualistic liberalism so eloquently celebrated in *On Liberty* may seem less pertinent to later generations confronted with revolution, war, tyranny, and social and moral upheavals. There remains, however, the other Mill, who was less of his age, perhaps, but more of ours. This Mill was not systematic, not easily labeled. But precisely because of this, because of his complexities and subtleties, he better mirrors our own dilemmas and perplexities.

3. "Thoughts on Parliamentary Reform," *Essays on Politics and Culture*, p. 357.

LORD ACTON: THE HISTORIAN
AS MORALIST

I T IS CUSTOMARY to relate a thinker to the spirit of his age.
In the case of Lord Acton, one can hardly do otherwise.
More than most intellectuals, he was intimately involved
with the affairs of his time. By birth and breeding he was
connected with some of the most important families of Germany, Italy, France, and England. He was educated in three
countries, exposed to the most diverse traditions, acquainted
with the most eminent political leaders and thinkers of
Europe (and even some in America), privy to the gossip of
high circles and the lore of high scholarship, and passionately concerned with the most fundamental problems of the
statesman and the philosopher. His biography is pre-eminently the history of his times. But it is also the biography
of a man who was totally out of sorts with his times, who at
every critical moment transcended his own history—and
perhaps, it might be said, history itself.

Acton complained that he had no contemporaries, that
he agreed with no one. In the only sense in which he
recognized contemporaries, as intellectual compeers, there
was much truth in his lament. He could not have been
more isolated from the main currents of thought of Victorian England or of the Continent: laissez-fairism, utili-

tarianism, evangelicalism, rationalism, socialism, nationalism, imperialism. Nor were the great critics of the age
more congenial. There is a suggestion of Acton in the
"high seriousness" of Matthew Arnold—but not in the
commonsense, Protestant humanism that made of Arnold,
in the words of G. K. Chesterton, a "fanatic of moderation"; Acton's own fanaticism was of a quite different
order. Carlyle's iconoclasm might have been attractive,
were it not for the particular idols Carlyle chose to worship
in place of those he destroyed. John Stuart Mill, something
of a maverick among liberals, was not maverick enough for
Acton, not sufficiently liberated from his secular, utilitarian
heritage. Even John Henry Newman, who might, from
this distance of time, appear to be a kindred spirit, was felt
by Acton to be one of a "very grotesque company of
professing Christians."[1]

Acton's personal life reflected some of the paradoxes and
anomalies of his intellectual history. Everything about him
was slightly askew, so that even when he seemed to be most
in the center of things, his perspective was somehow awry.
Of ancient English and German stock, he was born in 1834
in Naples, his grandfather having established himself there
as the lover of the Queen of Naples and the head of a short-
lived reign of terror—a career that so distressed Acton in
later years that he refused to accept the income from the
Italian estate. His maternal ancestors, the Dalbergs, had
been the first nobles in the Holy Roman Empire but had
accepted a peerage from France during the Restoration.
Thus Acton's early years were passed at the various family
residences: Aldenham in Shropshire, Herrnsheim on the
Rhine, Naples, and Paris. To these were added, when
Acton was six, London. For Acton's father had died pre-
maturely and his mother had married Lord Leveson, later
the second Earl Granville, a prominent member of the

1. Cambridge University Library, Add. Mss. 4914. (Most of
these notes are undated.)

Whig aristocracy who was to serve as foreign minister under Russell and Gladstone.

The most important single theme, almost obsession, of Acton's life was religion. Yet the religious influences acting on him were almost as varied as the national influences. The Dalbergs were Catholics (their official genealogy traced their descent to a relative of Jesus Christ), the Actons were Catholic converts (the conversion dated back two generations), and the Leveson-Gowers were, of course, Anglican. One of the stipulations in the marriage agreement between Lady Acton and Lord Leveson was that her son be brought up in her faith. As a result, Acton had entrée to Anglican and Catholic circles equally, and was spared the religious parochialism of most English Catholics.

Even his education, while predominantly Catholic, managed to embrace the several varieties of Catholicism competing for dominance in the Church. He first attended the school in Paris directed by Monsignor Dupanloup, the celebrated Liberal Catholic; then the English Catholic school Oscott, presided over by the arch-Ultramontane and anti-Liberal, Bishop Wiseman. Encouraged by his step-father, he then sought admission to three colleges at Cambridge and was rejected by all, undoubtedly because of the strong anti-Catholic sentiment sweeping England at the time. (This was the year that Pope Pius IX restored the Catholic hierarchy in England, and Wiseman himself, to the indignation of the English, assumed the title of Archbishop of Westminster.) Many years later, Acton opened his inaugural lecture as Regius Professor of Modern History at Cambridge by remarking upon his earlier failure to be accepted there as a student. What he did not say was that had Cambridge accepted him, he would not then be delivering an inaugural lecture, or if he were, it would not be the lecture he did deliver. For Cambridge men, as Leslie Stephen, who was there at the time, testified, had the good sense to know that nothing interfered with the social intercourse of gentlemen so much as a "misplaced zeal" for religion.[2] A Cambridge-educated Acton would more probably have turned into a man of affairs on the order of his stepfather, or a man of letters on the order of Macaulay. The Acton we know would have been an unlikely product of that milieu.

Having been rejected by Cambridge, Acton went to Munich to study under Ignaz von Döllinger, the Catholic historian (and priest) who was the very antithesis of the urbane, skeptical gentleman-scholar. It was Döllinger who inspired Acton with a passion for history, who introduced him to German historical scholarship (so different from its English counterpart), and who impressed upon him the central importance of religion in the study of history. During the 1850's, under the guidance of Döllinger first as teacher and then as friend, Acton read voluminously in history, philosophy, literature, and theology, laying the basis for his reputation as the most erudite man of his generation. It was also then, from his prolonged stays on the Continent (and visits to the United States and Russia), that he began to be thought of as the man who knew everyone, as well as everything, worth knowing. At the same time he started to build up the massive library of books, monographs, and historical rarities that is presently housed in the Cambridge University Library.

In 1859, Acton simultaneously embarked on two careers: as editor of the Liberal Catholic periodical, the *Rambler,* in succession to Newman; and as a Liberal member of parliament. The second job he discharged perfunctorily. Twenty years later he would have been delighted to be active in politics and associated with Gladstone; at this time he was uninterested in politics and notably unsympathetic to Gladstone. After one undistinguished term representing an Irish borough, he failed to get renominated by

2. Stephen, *Sketches from Cambridge* (London, 1932), p. 97.

his constituency, and when he was elected for an English borough, he was unseated on a recount prompted by charges of bribery. Although Acton's fate was shared by a dozen others during this election, and the candidates were unaware of the activities of their agents, it is nevertheless ironic that Acton, having such rigorous ideas about public morality, should have been turned out of parliament on this account. It is also unfortunate that he should thus have missed being a colleague of John Stuart Mill in one of the most important parliamentary sessions of the century. Perhaps to compensate for this defeat, perhaps, as Granville intimated in a personal letter to the Queen, to strengthen the hand of the Liberal Catholics on the eve of the Vatican Council, Acton was elevated to the peerage in 1869 on the recommendation of Gladstone.

All the energy and passion lacking in Acton's parliamentary career went into his campaign to promote Liberal Catholicism by means of the *Rambler* and its successor, the *Home and Foreign Review*. His mission, as he saw it, was to instruct English Catholics in the ways of German historical scholarship. Almost every issue found occasion to point the moral: faith and knowledge, religion and science, theology and history, the church and the state, were necessarily in harmony and had nothing to fear from each other. All that was needed was for each to be true to itself and to respect the integrity of the other. By 1864 it was apparent that neither Pius IX nor the English Catholic hierarchy shared Acton's views, and he was forced to suspend publication of the *Review*. Shortly afterwards Pius issued the Syllabus of Errors that was a declaration of war against the Liberal Catholics. The last heresy denounced in the syllabus might stand as a statement of the Liberal Catholic creed: "The Roman Pontiff can and ought to reconcile himself to, and agree with, progress, liberalism, and recent civilization."[3]

The Syllabus was only an invitation to combat. The main battle was fought in 1870 at the Vatican Council over the issue of papal infallibility. During the intervening years, Acton had sharpened his instruments and prepared himself for the final encounter. Even before the meeting of the Council he laid down the challenge. The doctrine of papal infallibility, he wrote, was a perversion of history and of religion. It went counter to the spirit of the early Church; it was fostered in modern times only by the deliberate falsification of history; and its promulgation would subvert the legitimate relationship of church and pope. He could not have been more defiant of the doctrine itself or of the exalted auspices from which it emanated: "The passage from the Catholicism of the Fathers to that of the modern Popes was accomplished by willful falsehood; and the whole structure of traditions, laws, and doctrines that supports the theory of infallibility, and the practical despotism of the Popes, stands on a basis of fraud."[4]

Acton was in Rome during the Council. As a layman without diplomatic or clerical status but enjoying the closest connections in church and state, he had a unique role in the affairs of the opposition—the "Minority," as the anti-infallibilists were called. He was a coordinator of strategy and information both for the bishops within the council and for the world outside. He funneled information to ambassadors and ministers, and importuned them to protest officially against the impending decrees. And most important, he provided a record of events that was as enlightening for contemporaries as it has proved to be for historians. The "Quirinus" letters, published in the *Augsburger Allgemeine Zeitung* and almost immediately translated into

3. Gertrude Himmelfarb, *Lord Acton: A Study in Conscience and Politics* (New York, 1952), p. 61.
4. Acton, "The Pope and the Council," *North British Review*, CI (1869), 130.

English, were the joint work of Döllinger and Acton. Apart from providing a detailed and fascinating account of the day-by-day progress of the Council, they confirm one of Acton's favorite theories: that the methods of absolutism are the same everywhere. The pope and his entourage, it was revealed, did not hesitate to apply the most subtle as well as the most open pressure upon the assembly. Bishops were threatened with imprisonment and in some cases were deliberately subjected to physical discomfort. They were told that resistance to the dogma of papal infallibility was a blasphemy against the Holy Ghost. The whole stock of papal privileges—the bestowal of sees and titles, special rights, benedictions and dispensations—was tossed into the battle, and fifteen empty cardinal's hats were dangled over many more vacillating heads. Nine tenths of the prelates were silenced because they could not speak Latin readily, others by the choice of a hall in which the acoustics were notoriously bad but which provided a regal backdrop for the papal throne. The procedure and the entire order of business were decided upon by commissons appointed by the pope himself. Meetings composed of more than twenty bishops were forbidden and strict secrecy was enjoined, except in the case of Archbishop Manning and three others who enjoyed special papal dispensations to divulge information to selected confidants. And so the machinations and intrigues went on, until in July 1870 the Vatican Decrees were formally promulgated.[5] The substance of the decrees was to declare the pope infallible when he spoke *ex cathedra* on matters of faith and morals.

After much probing of conscience, most of the Minority bishops submitted to the new dogma. Those who refused

<hr/>

5. E. D. Watt, "Rome and Lord Acton: A Reinterpretation," *Review of Politics*, XXVIII (1966), disputes Acton's—and my—account of papal intrigue, but offers no scholarly evidence for such a "reinterpretation." Acton's views emerge clearly in the recently published correspondence of Acton and Döllinger: *Briefwechsel*, ed. V. Conzemius (2 vols.; Munich, 1963–5).

to submit, like Döllinger, were excommunicated. As a layman, Acton was not automatically called upon to subscribe to the decrees, and throughout 1870 and well into the following year he continued to attack them in the most outspoken fashion. He also, and no less sharply, attacked the Minority bishops who yielded to the decrees rather than face excommunication. Yet he himself did not withdraw from the church. And when the Old Catholic Church was formed by some of the excommunicated bishops, Acton did not join it.

Acton's behavior at this time and later has been much criticized, both by his own contemporaries and by historians. From private letters and notes, however, one can piece together the logic of his position and sympathize with his predicament. In one of his notes, he remarked that Döllinger had received the decree of excommunication "as a deliverance," because he "held very strongly that nobody should voluntarily sever himself from the Roman communion."[6] Elsewhere Acton took to task the French theologian Eugène Michaud, who "did not wait till his archbishop put the knife to his throat but took the initiative of that operation on himself."[7] To leave the Church voluntarily at this time, Acton reasoned, was implicitly to exonerate the behavior of Rome in all the centuries before the new dogma, since this assumed that never before had Rome been tainted by heresy.

Acton used much the same argument in 1874 when Gladstone, belatedly awakening to the evils of the decrees, accused the pope of seeking to transfer the loyalties of English Catholics to a foreign power. In a letter to *The Times*, Acton denied that the decrees had this effect. The

6. Add. Mss. 4912.
7. *Selections from the Correspondence of the First Lord Acton*, ed. J. N. Figgis and R. V. Laurence (London, 1917), p. 117.

"post-July" church, he argued, was not effectively different from the "pre-July" church, because the same conditions which had always operated as a brake on papal ambitions continued to do so. *The Times*, commenting on his letter editorially, concluded that Acton was treating the decrees as a nullity. Thereupon Archbishop Manning, himself an ardent Ultramontane, called upon Acton to clarify his position and declare his submission. Acton responded that he had no private interpretation of the decrees, did not feel obliged or qualified to engage in theological dispute, and was "content to rest in absolute reliance on God's providence in His government of the Church."[8] This did not pacify Manning, who threatened to take the matter to Rome. If Manning did carry out his threat, Rome apparently chose not to act, and the bishop of Acton's own diocese professed to be satisfied with his orthodoxy. A less influential person, it was suggested at the time, might not have fared so well.

For his part, Acton could take comfort in keeping communion with a faith to which he was passionately attached. And fortifying his argument about the essential identity of the pre-July and post-July church were two other doctrines justifying his *de facto* dissent and *de jure* compliance: the doctrine distinguishing between the mortal, fallible ecclesia and the eternally true church; and the doctrine propounded by Döllinger and Newman among others, which maintained that in the natural course of development whatever was immoral and unchristian in the church would gradually disappear. In the first draft of his letter to Manning, Acton's profession that he was content to rely on "God's providence in His government of the Church" was followed by the phrase: "and the construction she herself shall adopt in her own true time."[9] From

8. Ibid., p. 153 (Nov. 18, 1874).
9. Ibid.

his private notes, it is evident that he regarded papal infallibility as one of the fallible and transient doctrines that would eventually be given another "construction":

> It [the decree] might have been corrected if the council had continued. A declaration that it did not mean to innovate; that the decree shall not be understood or interpreted otherwise than in harmony with all tradition; that no change was intended in the constant and universal doctrine of Catholics, might still be expected. But the council closed without it. There was always room for this, und es versteht sich eigentlich von selbst.[1]

The final words—in German, as if to assure their privacy even within the privacy of his notes—leave no doubt that this was Acton's own understanding of the matter.

An additional consideration was the fact that unlike Döllinger who, as a priest, would have had to teach a doctrine that he considered false and immoral, thus risk corrupting the souls of his flock, Acton was responsible only for his own soul. And in the privacy of his soul he could take refuge in theological constructions that the church, in its wisdom, provided for just such occasions.

There was nothing equivocal, still less hypocritical (as some have suggested) about Acton's relationship to the church. On the contrary, only if one takes seriously both the gravity of his commitment and the enormity of his criticisms can one make sense of his life and work—and appreciate the tragic quality of both. For he remained in the church not in spite of his criticisms but precisely because of them: the evils of the pre-July church were the very reason for his remaining in the post-July church. And he mercilessly criticized the church while remaining in it because only thus, he believed, could he help the church redeem itself. As he privately explained to Gladstone, he wanted to "make the evils of Ultramontanism so manifest

1. Add. Mss. 5600.

that men will shrink from them, and so explain away or stultify the Vatican Council as to make it innocuous."[2]

Acton's position was logical and understandable, but it was also quixotic and not a little obsessive. Thus even those who could follow the subtlety of its logic could not, or would not, follow him to the lengths to which he carried it. The extent of his isolation was only fully borne in upon him when he found himself abandoned, as he thought, by Döllinger himself. It was Döllinger who had initiated him into the high calling of history, who had taught him that scholarship was a dedication to truth and that truth was an absolute moral commitment. And it was with Döllinger and in the common cause of historical truth that he had fought his bitter battles with the church. But not long after the last of these battles, he began to sense that Döllinger, in spite of his excommunication, was not as intransigent as he himself was. The disagreement came to a head in 1879 when Döllinger wrote a memorial tribute to Dupanloup. (It is ironic that the occasion of the quarrel should have been a commemoration of Acton's first teacher by his last.) The tribute was not a eulogy, but it was sympathetic and respectful. To Acton, it was a shameless betrayal of truth, as Dupanloup himself, in his opinion, had betrayed Liberal Catholicism. Dupanloup, like Newman, had opposed the Vatican decrees on the grounds of their "inopportuneness" and had then submitted to them—a position that Acton regarded as tantamount to Ultramontanism since it conceded the principle while deferring to expediency.

That Döllinger did not share his contempt for this "common rogue and imposter"[3] came as a great shock to Acton and precipitated an emotional and intellectual crisis from which he never entirely recovered. For five years he did

2. *Correspondence*, p. 147 (Dec. 19–20, 1874).
3. Add. Mss. 5403.

little but agonize over the affair. He worried it endlessly in letters to Döllinger and other friends, in personal encounters (he and Döllinger spent part of every summer at Tegernsee together), and in monologues that found their way into his notes. Finally, in 1884, he confessed defeat— defeat not only in respect to Döllinger but to the world at large, for everyone, he was convinced, agreed with Döllinger and no one agreed with him:

> I am absolutely alone in my essential ethical position, and therefore useless. Not because one wants support or encouragement but because anyone who asks who agrees with me, will learn that no one agrees, and that no one disputes my view with anything like the energy with which the Professor disputes it.
>
> No other person can ever be so favorably situated as the Professor. He seeks nothing, knows more, and had, assuredly, a prejudice in my favor. People whose prejudices are the other way, who know less, who are less perfectly independent will certainly not listen to me better than he.
>
> The probability of doing good by writings so isolated and repulsive, of obtaining influence for views, etc., is so small that I have no right to sacrifice to it my own tranquility and my duty of educating my children. My time can be better employed than in waging a hopeless war. And the more my life has been thrown away, the more necessary to turn now, and employ better what remains.[4]

If nothing else establishes Acton's claim to modernity, this testament would do so. For his "alienation" was as devastating as anything recorded in the more recent literature of this genre. Indeed, more devastating, for he had not the consolation of a later generation for whom alienation itself has become a rite of fraternity. Acton's alienation was far more radical and self-destructive. Not only did it sepa-

4. Ibid.

rate him from those who were personally and intellectually closest to him, but it also separated him, in a profound sense, from the enterprise of history itself. He himself thought of it as of the first order: an isolation from friends, colleagues, and the prevailing climate of opinion. But there are occasional intimations of the second: of being tragically inhibited, by the very nature of his views, from the writing of a sustained and significant work of history. Isolation would not of itself have condemned him to failure; witness the prolificacy and brilliance of some of the most persistent nay-sayers of this world. What defeated him—to anticipate the argument of this essay—was the suspicion that the truth itself was flawed, or if not flawed, too rarified to be of much service in the mundane craft of history.

The course of Acton's professional career may bear out this suspicion. Before the quarrel with Döllinger, he had given promise of becoming a major historian. By the age of forty, he had written a sizable quantity of history of a respectably scholarly nature on an impressive range of subjects—a total of almost two thousand pages of essays, lectures, book reviews, introductions, and the like. He had read and annotated countless books, documents, and manuscripts. Hundreds of boxes of notes were the raw materials for works on specific subjects: a comparison of the American and ancient democracies, a history of the Index, a compilation of German historiography, biographies of James II and of Cardinal Pole. . . . In view of his other preoccupations during these years—the *Rambler* and *Home and Foreign Review*, the Vatican Council and its aftermath—this was no mean accomplishment. But it fell far short of his own aspirations and standards.

In 1875, after his encounters with Gladstone and Manning, when he had reason to think that he could put polemics and controversies behind him, he announced his intention to start work on his magnum opus, a History of Liberty. Two years later, the first outlines of that history took shape in the form of two lectures delivered before the Bridgnorth Institution. (Bridgnorth was the town near Aldenham where Acton had made his unsuccessful bid for Parliament.) A provincial lay audience can rarely have been favored with discourse so learned and elevated. Taking as his subjects "The History of Freedom in Antiquity" and "The History of Freedom in Christianity," Acton displayed his talent for being at the same time comprehensive and detailed, factual and allusive, bold in generalization and subtle in reasoning. The following year, in a long essay on Erskine May's *Democracy in Europe*, he developed the same theme with the same confident grasp of detail and sweep of vision.

Early in 1879 Döllinger wrote the article on Dupanloup that set Acton off on his agonizing course of soul-searching. Except for one two-page book review (of Mandell Creighton's *History of the Papacy during the Period of the Reformation*—a continuation of the dialogue he had been conducting with Döllinger), he published nothing for six years. By 1882 he had begun to speak banteringly of his History of Liberty as his Madonna of the Future (a reference to Henry James's story of an artist who devotes his life to the creation of a single masterpiece which after his death is exposed as a blank canvas). But not until 1884 did the History of Liberty finally and irrevocably acquire the status of a Madonna of the Future. It was then, about the same time that he wrote the letter quoted above confessing to his isolation and defeat, that he also explained to Mary Gladstone why he could not get on with the book as she had been urging him to do:

> As to my tiresome book, please to remember that I can only say things which people do not agree with, that I have neither disciple nor sympathiser, that this is not encouragement to production and confidence, that grizzled men . . . grow appalled at the gaps in their knowledge, and that I have no other gift but that which you

pleasantly describe, of sticking eternal bits of paper into innumerable books, and putting larger papers into black boxes.[5]

This letter, taken in conjunction with the other, is unmistakable. Implicated in the "hopeless war" he had been waging was the History of Liberty. And the decision to turn away from that war, to "employ better" his remaining years, meant abandoning the History.

In 1885, Acton resumed his writing, but what he wrote were reviews and review-essays, not the History of Liberty or even any significant contribution to that History. Tributes came his way, but few were without their small ironies. In 1888 he received an honorary degree from Cambridge—fifteen years after he had received such a degree abroad, and almost forty years after he had been refused admission as a student at the university. In 1892, his good friend Gladstone, having denied his requests for diplomatic posts abroad for which he would have been eminently suited, unaccountably offered him the position of Lord-in-Waiting to the Queen, which Acton as unaccountably accepted. Three years later, Lord Rosebery, who was no friend of Acton and whose party Acton abhorred, finally gave him the honor commensurate with his calling, the chair of Regius Professor of Modern History at Cambridge. Had such a professorship come when Gladstone had it in his bestowal—in 1884, when Edward Freeman was named for the equivalent chair at Oxford—it might have rescued Acton from his abyss of despair, his sense of isolation and uselessness. (Perhaps it was his being passed over for the chair that helped precipitate the crisis at just that time.) He might even, in the congenial atmosphere of a university, have written some major work of history

5. *Letters of Lord Acton to Mary Gladstone*, ed. Herbert Paul (1st edn.; London, 1905), p. 287 (Feb. 9, 1884).

169

(although probably not, if the thesis of this paper is valid, the History of Liberty). By 1895, however, he was over sixty, an unlikely age for the writing of a first book. By this time, too, his vocation had become so nearly an avocation that the appointment as Regius Professor provoked as much surprise as his earlier appointment as Lord-in-Waiting.

Acton's inaugural lecture, "The Study of History," was apparently not much more comprehensible to the Cambridge audience of scholars and notables than his earlier Bridgnorth lectures must have been to the local gentry. Taking advantage of his cultivated audience, he indulged his taste for erudition, allusion, irony, and paradox. The *Spectator* sadly commented that he was an example of the new failing, the historian who knows too much. *The Saturday Review*, more belligerent in its philistinism, defied the most nimble mental gymnast to discover the meaning "which this inarticulate teacher has cunningly concealed"; comparing Acton unfavorably with his predecessors, it deplored the fact that the brilliant lucidity of Seeley and the imagination of Kingsley should be followed by the "Batavian splutterings of Lord Acton's awkward pen," and earnestly recommended Acton to resign the post for which he was so unsuited.[6]

One can sympathize with the reporters accustomed to the untaxing mind of a Kingsley or Seeley being suddenly confronted with a scholar addressing himself to what he regarded as the most crucial and solemn subject: the function of the historian. Certainly Acton made no concessions to the ignorance or indifference of his audience, or to the difficulty of taking in by ear what would be hard enough to follow in print. Even now, reading and rereading the lecture, one can properly understand it only by taking into account everything one knows about Acton himself. The elliptical allusions, the involutions of argument, the ap-

6. *Saturday Review*, LXXIX (1895), 822.

parent paradoxes and pervasive irony reflect not a failure of communication or a striving for profundity but rather a faithful rendition of his state of mind—an attempt to cope with the inherent difficulties and anomalies of his intellectual position.

The two series of lectures which Acton delivered to Cambridge students, published posthumously under the titles, *Lecture on the French Revolution* and *Lectures on Modern History*, were less ambitious and therefore less difficult. But even then, his colleague, Oscar Browning, who genuinely admired him and commended him for inaugurating a "great epoch in the Cambridge teaching of history,"[7] took care to parallel Acton's lectures with more elementary ones on the same subjects so that the students would be better prepared for the master. And in these lectures too the attentive reader can find the same ambiguities and difficulties.

The final irony of Acton's life was his undertaking to edit the *Cambridge Modern History*. He has been criticized for expending so much time—the last six years of his life, which was most of his tenure at Cambridge—on a project unworthy of his talents and unworthy of history itself. Yet it is a tribute to his honesty and humility that, having failed to write the "universal history" he himself took to be the mark of the serious historian, he should have been willing to take on the more menial task of editing such a universal history. Here again, in his prospectus for the *History* and in his instructions to the contributors, one finds the familiar compulsions and stresses under which his mind always labored. And again, too, one finds the ultimate personal defeat. The *History*, although including most of the best historians of England (continental historians were surprisingly few in number), lacked the unity that should have characterized a universal history, and even lacked a conspicuous distinction in its parts. Acton himself was so

7. Browning, *Memories of Later Years* (London, 1923), p. 17.

engrossed in the details of editing that he failed to write not only the chapters he had reserved for himself but even the introduction. The first volume was only partly in type when he suffered the paralytic stroke that caused his resignation. He died in June 1902, the *Cambridge Modern History*, like his own History of Liberty, a monument to his ambitions and failings.

Arnold J. Toynbee, himself a celebrant of universal history, has deplored the fact that "one of the greatest minds among modern Western historians" should have been victimized by the spirit of industrialism, sacrificed to the modern idols of the division of labor.[8] Another English historian, Max Beloff, has assigned the "decadence of English historical writing" to March 12, 1898—the date of Acton's letter to the contributors to the *History*.[9] It is not clear whether Acton can more properly be regarded, with Toynbee, as the victim of the piece, or, with Beloff, as the villain. "Lord Acton's Encyclical," as the *History* was irreverently dubbed, was in fact neither Lord Acton's nor an encyclical—which perhaps diminishes his responsibility but augments his failure. In any event, what is important for an understanding of Acton is not the *History* itself but its function as a surrogate for the history that never was written.

Toynbee suggested that the History of Liberty was not written because Acton was thwarted by the "spirit of the times": as industry required the maximum exploitation of resources, so the historian felt that he ought to exploit all the materials spawned by the archives; and as industry could only function by the division of labor, so the his-

8. Toynbee, *Study of History* (London, 1934), I, 46.
9. Beloff, "A Challenge to Historians," *Listener*, IX (1949), 816.

torian had to resort to the same device. If only Acton had lived in the age of Voltaire, Gibbon, or Turgot, Toynbee lamented, he would have produced his great history on his own. There is much truth in this, and also some injustice. In an essay on Döllinger (for which, typically, he had accumulated enough notes for a multivolume biography), Acton wrote his own epitaph: "He knew too much to write"; "he would not write with imperfect materials, and to him the materials were always imperfect."[1] Yet it is idle to bemoan the fact that Acton was not a Voltaire, Gibbon, or Turgot. A History of Liberty such as they might have produced would have been as much a defeat for Acton as not writing the history at all. For it was precisely his ambition to write a post-Rankian history: a universal history firmly grounded in primary sources, a history combining the largest vision with the most detailed and comprehensive research.

Here Acton went beyond even Ranke in his ambitions. The recent opening of the state archives, he informed the contributors to the *Cambridge Modern History*, would permit the historian to "meet the scientific demand for completeness and certainty," and "bring home to every man the last document, and the ripest conclusions of international research." Historical studies were about to enter a new and final era: "Nearly all the evidence that will appear is accessible now. . . . We approach the final stage in the conditions of historical learning."[2]

This is the vision not of a Ranke but of a Comte. To the already excessive ideals of universal history and definitive scholarship, Acton added the ideal of a positivist science, a history that was to be complete, certain, and final. And if

1. Acton, "Döllinger's Historical Work," *The History of Freedom and Other Essays* (London, 1907), pp. 434, 432.

2. Acton, *Lectures on Modern History* (London, 1950), pp. 315, 317.

this too were not enough, he incorporated into this schema, as Comte himself did, an eschatological dimension, so that the knowing and the known became one. Ultimately, he implied, the writing of history would reflect the movement of history, and historical science would encompass the meanings and morals that were implicit in history. The historian would then emerge not only as the scientist in complete possession of the facts but also as the supreme judge and moral arbiter. The end of time would be, in all senses, a day of reckoning.

The combination of universality, science (or scientism), and morality is formidable. It is also, on the surface at least, self-contradictory. As universal and monographic history are ordinarily very different, so are scientific and moralistic history. Acton was perhaps unique not so much in trying to reconcile these ideals as in seeing them as integrally related. History, he insisted, could not be genuinely scientific and objective unless it was explicitly and essentially moralistic.

It was his quarrel with the church, and more particularly with Döllinger, that impelled Acton to this view of history. Döllinger, Acton had argued, could be so tolerant of Dupanloup because, like most historians, he was a moral relativist. The besetting sin of the relativist historian was the notion that in order to immerse himself in the time and place about which he was writing, it was necessary to adopt the values of that time and place. As a result he tended to sanction whatever was done, to excuse by way of explaining, and to refrain from adverse judgment. When there was undeniable evil, he preferred to attribute it to a false ideology or defect of knowledge rather than to simple moral turpitude:

> It suited his [Döllinger's] way to distribute blame so that nobody suffered. He hated moral imputations. Folly, stupidity, ignorance, moral cowardice, the deceived conscience, did duty as long as possible. [It] suited him to

trace the gradual growth of things, so that no one was really responsible.[3]

Historians of the church, Acton reasoned, were particularly prone to this form of relativism because they were naturally loath to criticize sacred institutions and persons. But precisely in the presence of sanctity, it was necessary to maintain the highest standards. For immorality in the church was not a venial but a mortal sin and therefore all the more reprehensible. Thus where most historians tended to make allowances for the popes on the grounds that they could not be judged in the same terms as lesser men, that their power and position implied greater moral latitude, Acton reversed this formula: if any indulgence was to be meted out by the historian, it was to those lacking the moral sensibilities and responsibilities of the highest spiritual authority. By this token, the Catholic was to be judged more severely than the non-Catholic, the priest more severely than the layman, and the pope more severely than them all. The popes, Acton concluded, operating on the theory that any amount of wrong might be done for the sake of saving souls, stood accused of the most heinous crimes in history, for not only did they violate the common precepts of morality but they tainted the very source of redemption:

> Those whose motive was religious seemed to me worse than the others, because that which is in others the last resource of conversion is with them the source of guilt. The spring of repentance is broken, the conscience is not only weakened but warped. Their prayers and sacrifices appeared to me the most awful sacrilege.[4]

Catholic critics have charged that Acton had "Inquisition on the brain." And so it might seem. For he saw the Inquisition as the most important and most evil event in all of

3. Add. Mss. 4908.
4. *Correspondence,* p. 55 (Feb. 17, 1879).

history. It was then that the "principle of assassination" became "a law of the Christian Church and a condition of salvation." It was then that the papacy emerged as the "fiend skulking behind the Crucifix." Moreover it was the papacy itself that invented this unique instrument of evil:

> The Inquisition is peculiarly the weapon and peculiarly the work of the Popes. It stands out from all those things in which they co-operated, followed, or assented as the distinctive feature of papal Rome. It was set up, renewed, and perfected by a long series of acts emanating from the supreme authority in the Church. No other institution, no doctrine, no ceremony, is so distinctly the individual creation of the papacy, except the Dispensing power. It is the principal thing with which the papacy is identified, and by which it must be judged.
>
> . . . The principle of the Inquisition is murderous, and a man's opinion of the papacy is regulated and determined by his opinion about religious assassination.
>
> If he honestly looks on it as an abomination, he can only accept the Primacy with a drawback, with precaution, suspicion, and aversion for its acts.
>
> If he accepts the Primacy with confidence, admiration, unconditional obedience, he must have made terms with murder.
>
> . . . That blot [the Inquisition] is so large and foul that it precedes and eclipses the rest, and claims the first attention.[5]

With this view of the Inquisition, and with his view of moral culpability, Acton could not but extend this culpability to those historians who condoned the papacy, and by the same logic to those historians who condoned the condoning historians. It was of this final order of sin that Döllinger was found guilty. And the sin became, paradoxically, more serious the further removed it was from the original act. The historian who condoned a crime was

5. *Letters to Mary Gladstone* (1st edn.), pp. 298-300 (June 19, 1884).

perpetuating it throughout history. His guilt was greater than that of the original perpetrator of the crime not only because the effect of his sin was more enduring but also because his motive was less pressing. The sin of the historian was gratuitous, willful, total. "To commit murder," Acton noted, "is the mark of a moment, exceptional. To defend it is constant, and shows a more perverted conscience."[6]

If the historian had the largest capacity for sin, he also had the largest potentiality for good. It is not surprising that Acton, finding the church so unworthy of exercising moral authority, should have proceeded to endow the historian with that authority. Acton's historian was not only, as he said, a "hanging judge";[7] he was also a surrogate pope—indeed the only true pope.

It was Acton's penchant for morality that has made him a prime exhibit of the "Whig historian." The Whig historian, as Herbert Butterfield described him in his now classic essay, was typically Protestant, progressive, and Whig—altogether the "very model of the nineteenth-century gentleman." The working habits of the Whig historian were "to praise revolutions provided they have been successful, to emphasize certain principles of progress in the past and to produce a story which is the ratification if not the glorification of the present." Although Acton happened to be Catholic rather than Protestant, Butterfield saw nothing specifically Catholic in his ideas and much that was specifically Whig: the familiar conjunction of morality, progress, and a preference for the present over the past. To support his view that in Acton "the Whig historian

6. Add. Mss. 4939.
7. "Inaugural Lecture on the Study of History," *Essays on Freedom and Power,* ed. Gertrude Himmelfarb (Boston, 1948), p. 18.

reached his highest consciousness," Butterfield quoted Acton's statement of the proper function of history: "It deems the canonization of the historic past more perilous than ignorance or denial, because it would perpetuate the reign of sin and acknowledge the sovereignty of wrong."[8]

Had Butterfield quoted the whole of Acton's sentence, he might have discovered a species very different from the typical Whig historian. For Acton concluded his statement of the proper function of history: ". . . and conceives it the part of real greatness to know how to stand and fall alone, stemming, for a lifetime the contemporary flood."[9] And earlier in the same paragraph he described the theory of history that he took to be diametrically opposed to his own:

> A theory which justifies Providence by the event, and holds nothing so deserving as success, to which there can be no victory in a bad cause; prescription and duration legitimate; and whatever exists is right and reasonable; and as God manifests His will by that which He tolerates, we must conform to the divine decree by living to shape the future after the ratified image of the past.[1]

Surely it is this theory of providence, the theory Acton was opposing, that corresponds most closely to Butterfield's description of Whig history, even to the extent of echoing Butterfield's very words: the praise of revolutions that are successful, the use of the past to ratify the present. And surely Acton's praise for the historian who knows "how to stand and fall alone, stemming, for a lifetime, the contemporary flood," is the antithesis of Whig history. The final rebuke to the Whig may be implied in one of

8. Butterfield, *The Whig Interpretation of History* (London, 1959), pp. 3-4, v, 109-10.
9. "Inaugural Lecture," *Freedom and Power*, p. 27.
1. Ibid., p. 26.

Acton's notes: "Progress [is] the religion of those who have none."[2]

Indeed, had Acton not been put forward as the archetype of the Whig historian, one might have taken him as the arch critic of the Whig. For while Acton and the Whig were both given to moral judgments, the nature of those judgments and their relation to history were utterly dissimilar. Where the Whig derived his moral judgments from history itself, thereby ensuring the sanctification of success and the ratification of the past in terms of the present, Acton deliberately located his standard of morality outside of and above history. The source of morality, he insisted, was nothing less than the absolute, universal moral code, "that immutable law which is perfect and eternal as God Himself."[3] It was this law that he wanted to make binding on the historian: "The inflexible integrity of the moral code is, to me, the secret of the authority, the dignity, the utility of history."[4] This was the message of his inaugural lecture—that judgment was to be imposed on history, not derived from it, that morality was absolute and not relative:

The weight of opinion is against me when I exhort you never to debase the moral currency or to lower the standard of rectitude, but to try others by the final maxim that governs your own lives, and to suffer no man and no cause to escape the undying penalty which history has the power to inflict on wrong. . . . History, says Froude, does teach that right and wrong are real distinctions. Opinions alter, manners change, creeds rise and fall, but the moral law is written on the tablets of eternity.[5]

2. Add. Mss. 5648.
3. "The History of Freedom in Antiquity," *Freedom and Power*, p. 52.
4. Letter to Creighton (April 5, 1887), *Freedom and Power*, p. 365.
5. "Inaugural Lecture," *Freedom and Power*, pp. 25, 28.

Thus where morality for the Whig served as an instrument of assent—the relation between morality and history being self-confirming and self-validating—morality for Acton was supra-historical, a standing criticism of history and a perennial invitation to dissent.

Thus too, where the Whig was relativist, taking account of the circumstances and temper of the time, the exigencies of power and of the good cause, Acton was a moral absolutist. And his absolute judgments were not only the sole warrant of morality but also the sole warrant of scientific history. His notes frequently referred to murder as the "low-water mark,"[6] the ultimate, objective moral fact that carried with it an ultimate, objective moral judgment. Historians who refused to abide by this low-water mark, he insisted, were imperiling the integrity of history as much as that of morality: "I would hang them higher than Haman, for reasons of quite obvious justice; still more, still higher, for the sake of historical science."[7] To be morally lax was to "debase the currency," to "tamper with weights and measures," and finally to bring about a state of affairs in which "history ceases to be a science."[8] The ideal of the anonymous, impartial scientific history that he enjoined upon the contributors to the *Cambridge Modern History* had as its corollary the ideal of an absolute, eternal moral code:

> If men were truly sincere, and delivered judgment by no canons but those of evident morality, then Julian would be described in the same terms by Christian and pagan, Luther by Catholic and Protestant, Washington by Whig and Tory, Napoleon by patriotic Frenchman and patriotic German.[9]

6. Add. Mss. 4914.
7. Letter to Creighton (April 5, 1887), *Freedom and Power*, p. 364.
8. Ibid., pp. 26, 365.
9. Ibid., p. 19.

If anything was less Whiggish than the idea of absolute morality, it was this idea of scientific history. The true Whig historian, in this as in most respects, was G. M. Trevelyan, Macaulay's great-nephew, a student at Cambridge during Acton's tenure, and one of his successors as Regius Professor. In his memoirs Trevelyan professed the greatest admiration for and gratitude to Acton. Yet as a student, although he was in the same college as Acton and interested in modern history, he chose to do his dissertation on a medieval subject under another professor—to Acton's "regretful surprise," Trevelyan later recalled.[1] The elder Trevelyan remembered Acton as sympathetic to his idea of "literary history" and associated the disagreeable doctrine of history as a science with Bury; yet it may be that at the time he avoided working under Acton because he sensed that Acton's idea of history was in fact closer to scientific than to literary history. Again, although Trevelyan in his memoir claimed to agree with Acton "in principle" on the moral role of the historian, he qualified that principle to a considerable extent: "I am more inclined than he was to make some allowance for the standards of an age and country in judging the culpability of individuals, who for the most part do as they see others doing." To be sure, Trevelyan added, the historian should point out the defects of those standards lest he seem to be condoning them; but having pointed them out, he would think it absurd to judge the medieval persecutor as severely as he would judge a modern persecutor. "It was only the prevalence of the wicked theory that excuses the error of the mistaken men," Trevelyan concluded[2]—in a passage that Acton might well have cited as one of the *pièces justicatives* in his indictment of the modern temper.

Behind Trevelyan's conceptions of literary history and

1. Trevelyan, *An Autobiography and Other Essays* (London, 1949), p. 20.
2. Ibid., p. 79.

relativistic morality was something more basic to the Whig interpretation of history—and more antithetical still to Acton. This was the optimistic view of man that was reflected in an optimistic reading of history. In his auto-biography, Trevelyan candidly described his liking for history with "happy endings":

> I have always had a liking for those bits of history that have clear-cut happy endings,—1860 following on 1849 and completing the tale,—partly because such sections have more artistic unity than history as a whole, which is a shapeless affair; and partly no doubt because they are more cheerful to contemplate. I used to look askance at Gibbon's dreadful saying that history is 'little more than the register of the crimes, follies and misfortunes of man-kind.' . . . Nor do I even now wholly subscribe to it. But the war of 1914–18 enlarged and saddened my mind, and prepared me to write English history with a more realistic and a less partisan outlook. Yet, even after that war, the Reign of Queen Anne and the History of Eng-land up to the end of Victoria's reign, still seemed to me, when I came to write them, to be stories with happy endings.[3]

For Acton there were few happy endings in history. The Whig could so readily acquiesce in the course of history because he had a benign view of men—or at least of those men who were the bearers of history, the triumphant children of light. Acton had so often to "stand and fall alone" because the victors as much as the defeated appeared to him to be the children of darkness. Compared with him, Gibbon was an optimist. Relentlessly, obsessively, Acton kept returning to the theme: History was "an iconoclast, not a teacher of reverence"; it was the "disclosure of guilt and shame"; it was a "frightful monument of sin."[4]

3. Ibid., p. 35.
4. Review of H. C. Lea's *A History of the Inquisition of the Middle Ages, History of Freedom,* p. 568; Add. Mss. 4905.

It is curious that Butterfield should have found nothing "specifically Catholic or Christian" in Acton's idea of morality, when Acton himself accounted for his profound pessimism in terms that were alternately Catholic and Calvinist. "No priest," he noted, "accustomed to the Confessional, and a fortiori, no historian, thinks well of human nature";[5] and he marveled at the ability of the priest to bear up under the burden of his awesome knowledge. In his inaugural lecture, this view was put in its sharpest Calvinist form in the words of the Oxford theologian James Mozley:

> A Christian is bound by his very creed to suspect evil, and cannot release himself. His religion has brought evil to light in a way in which it never was before; it has shown its depth, subtlety, ubiquity; and a revelation, full of mercy on the one hand, is terrible in its exposure of the world's real state on the other. The Gospel fastens the sense of evil upon the mind; a Christian is enlightened, hardened, sharpened, as to evil; he sees it where others do not. . . . He owns the doctrine of original sin; that doctrine puts him necessarily on his guard against all appearances, sustains his apprehension under perplexity, and prepares him for recognizing anywhere what he knows to be everywhere.[6]

At best, human nature, as Acton saw it, was a poor thing; at worst, it was thoroughly bad. And what made it worse was power. It is quite proper that Acton should be generally identified by the dictum: "Power tends to corrupt and absolute power corrupts absolutely."[7] It is even proper that this dictum should be generally misquoted in the form: "All power corrupts and absolute power corrupts absolutely." For this more extreme proposition was,

5. Add. Mss. 4908.
6. *Freedom and Power*, pp. 28, 427.
7. Ibid., p. 364.

in fact, closer to his intention. If Hobbes believed, as Acton thought, that "authority is always in the right,"[8] Acton clearly believed that authority was always, or very nearly always, in the wrong—or at least that the presumption must always be that it was in the wrong:

> I cannot accept your canon that we are to judge Pope and King unlike other men, with a favorable presumption that they did no wrong. If there is any presumption it is the other way against holders of power, increasing as the power increases. Historic responsibility has to make up for the want of legal responsibility. Power tends to corrupt and absolute power corrupts absolutely. Great men are almost always bad men, even when they exercise influence and not authority: still more when you superadd the tendency or the certainty of corruption by authority.[9]
>
> By all means we should think well until forced to think ill of people. But we must be prepared for that compulsion; and the experience of history teaches that the uncounted majority of those who get a place in its pages are bad. We have to deal chiefly, in life, with people who have no place in history, and escape the temptations that are on the road to it. But most assuredly, now as heretofore, the Men of the Time are, in most cases, unprincipled, and act from motives of interest, of passion, of prejudice cherished and unchecked, of selfish hope or unworthy fear.[1]
>
> History is not a web woven with innocent hands. Among all the causes which degrade and demoralize men, power is the most constant and the most active.[2]

Acton was not quite as alone in his abhorrence of power as he sometimes made it appear. History provides a com-

8. "The History of Freedom in Christianity," *Freedom and Power*, p. 75.
9. Ibid., p. 364.
1. *Letters to Mary Gladstone* (1st edn.), p. 228 (Jan. 25, 1882).
2. Add. Mss. 5011.

pendium of epigrams to similar effect, from Tacitus ("The lust of power is the most flagrant of all the passions"), to Burckhardt ("Power is of its nature evil, whoever wields it"), and Henry Adams ("Power is poison").[3] Yet there was much justice in Acton's remark that the weight of opinion was against him when he attempted to apply the ordinary moral code to men in power. (To apply it, that is, to the public lives of those men; their private lives were not at issue.) The modern world, he believed, had learnt all too well the lesson of Machiavelli, which was that the moral code could not be applied to men in power: "The authentic interpreter of Machiavelli is the whole of later history."[4] And he proceeded to demonstrate this thesis by quotations from kings, popes, statesmen, divines, philosophers, and historians. The dossier included the most important schools and names in modern thought: Bacon, Hobbes, Locke, Pascal, Spinoza, Leibniz, Helvétius, Beccaria, Priestley, Smith, Bentham, Carlyle, Mill, Herder, Fichte, Hegel, Ranke, Sybel, Treitschke, Mommsen, Michelet, Thiers, Sainte Beuve, Renan. . . . What they had in common, and the characteristic mark of modernity, was the idea that "public life is not an affair of morality, that there is no available rule of right and wrong, that men must be judged by their age, that the code shifts with the longitude, that the wisdom which governs the event is superior to our own."[5] So overwhelming did Acton find this weight of opinion that rather than asserting himself at every point against it, he took refuge in irony—the irony of presenting

3. The Adams family had its private history of such epigrams. Shortly after the start of the American Revolution, Abigail Adams confided to her husband: "I am more and more convinced that man is a dangerous creature; and that power, whether vested in many or a few, is ever grasping, and like the grave, cries 'Give, give!'" (*Letters of Mrs. Adams, the Wife of John Adams* [4th edn.; Boston, 1848], p. 63.)

4. Introduction to L. A. Burd's edn. of *Il Principe, History of Freedom*, p. 212.

5. Ibid., p. 219.

without comment the respectable authorities who for three centuries had "borne witness to his [Machiavelli's] political veracity."[6] Indeed unless one were aware in advance of Acton's views and alert to the nuances of his style, one might think that he himself, in this essay, was endorsing the "political veracity" that came so highly recommended.

The true *Anti-Machiavel*, for Acton, was not the Whig, not even the Liberal, but the Liberal Catholic, as he understood that term. For the only security against power and against Machiavellianism was the commitment to a moral ideal so absolute as to have the force of a religious dogma. To be liberal was not enough; witness the inclusion of Mill in his roster of Machiavellians. The secular liberal was apt to think of power pragmatically, as morally neutral and justified simply by the results. It took a religious mind to see power as a kind of original sin and be wary of it as such. This is what Acton meant by Liberal Catholicism and why he attributed his alienation to his adherence to this uncommon amalgam of principles:

> I find that people disagree with me either because they hold that Liberalism is not true, or that Catholicism is not true, or that both cannot be true together. If I could discover anyone who is not included in these categories, I fancy we should get on very well together.[7]

His definition was intended to exclude most of those who went under the name of Liberal Catholic: Catholics who happened fortuitously to be Liberals, or those who believed in an attenuated form of religion. There was nothing fortuitous or attenuated about Acton's creed, which involved the most rigorous form of religious belief (the Catholicism of the Church fathers), and the most rigorous form of public morality. To be a Liberal Catholic,

6. Ibid., p. 212.
7. Add. Mss. 6871.

as he once explained to Mary Gladstone, was to subject religion to the exacting criteria of morality and to invest history and politics with the awesome values of religion:

> Have you not discovered, have I never betrayed, what a narrow doctrinaire I am, under a thin disguise of levity? . . . Politics come nearer religion with me, a party is more like a church, error more like heresy, prejudice more like sin, than I find it to be with better men.[8]

Acton had not always been so doctrinaire. There was, indeed, a time when he was close to being a Whig. But that was before the Vatican Council had impressed upon him the urgency of absolute morality. It was then, in the late fifties and sixties, that he had looked to Burke as the "law and the prophets," the exponent of a "purely Catholic view of political principles and of history"[9]—by which Acton meant a respect for facts and realities rather than speculative principles and ideals. It was then too that he had defended the South in the American Civil War on the Burkean grounds that the laws of the state could not be made conditional on absolute principles of right or reason:

> It is as impossible to sympathise on religious grounds with the categorical prohibition of slavery as, on political grounds, with the opinions of the abolitionists. In this, as in all other things, they exhibit the same abstract, ideal absolutism, which is equally hostile with the Catholic and with the English spirit. . . . The influence of these habits of abstract reasoning, to which we owe the revolution in Europe, is to make all things questions of principle and of abstract law. . . . Very different is the mode in which the Church labors to reform mankind by assimilating

8. *Letters to Mary Gladstone* (1st edn.), p. 314 (Dec. 18, 1884).
9. *Lord Acton and His Circle*, ed. Francis A. Gasquet (London, 1906), p. 60 (Feb. 4, 1859), p. 4 (Feb. 16, 1858).

realities with ideals, and accommodating herself to times and circumstances.[1]

After 1870, however, Acton so completely reversed himself that his description of the abolitionists might well be taken as a description of himself. And Burke, so far from being the "teacher of mankind,"[2] became the symbol of the modern Machiavelli. It was Burke, he complained, who initiated men into "political skepticism," subverted their faith in "political science" (i.e., a science of political ethics), encouraged them to "evade the arbitration of principle," and taught them to think of politics "experimentally," as an exercise in "what is likely to do good or harm, not what is right or wrong, innocent or sinful."[3]

At this point the issues of morality and liberty were joined. For Burke's "experimental" view of politics was associated with a Whiggish view of liberty—a liberty dependent upon history and tradition, compromise and expediency, checks and balances. This was the idea of liberty that the young Acton had found eminently praiseworthy and that the mature Acton came to distrust profoundly. True liberty, like morality, he finally decided, was a matter of absolute principle. Between the Whig and the Liberal there was all the difference in the world. Where the Whig was concerned with "legality, authority, possession, tradition, custom, opinion," the Liberal was interested only in "what ought to be, irrespective of what is." The Whig believed in the "repression of the ideal," the Liberal in its assertion. "The Whig governed by compromise; the Lib-

1. "Political Causes of the American Revolution," *Freedom and Power*, p. 246.
2. *Rambler*, IX (1858), 273.
3. Add. Mss. 4967 and 4941; *Letters to Mary Gladstone* (2nd edn.; London, 1913), p. 37 (Dec. 14, 1880), and p. 180 (Oct. 16, 1887). In public Acton was inclined to take a more lenient view of Burke. For the differences between his notes, letters, and lectures, see my article, "The American Revolution in the Political Theory of Lord Acton," *Journal of Modern History*, XXI (1949).

eral begins the reign of ideas." The Whig regarded politics as an attempt to "get advantages within the limits of ethics," the Liberal as an attempt to "realize ideals." Whiggism was not an immature version of Liberalism; it was the very opposite of Liberalism: "To a Liberal, all the stages between Burke and Nero are little more than the phases of forgotten moons."[4]

True liberty, therefore, involved a radical break with the past. The "liberties" emerging from the struggle of church and state during the Middle Ages, the "toleration" that resulted from the religious conflicts of the sixteenth and seventeenth centuries, the constitutional guarantees wrested by the English Revolutionists, were all tainted, because they were founded on force, interest, and expediency. The history of liberty proper started only with the American Revolution: "Never till then had men sought liberty knowing what they sought."[5] For the first time liberty was demanded simply and purely as a right. The threepence tax that provoked the Americans was threepence worth of pure principle. "I will freely spend nineteen shillings in the pound," Acton quoted Benjamin Franklin, "to defend my right of giving or refusing the other shilling." And Acton himself went further. The true liberal, like the American Revolutionist, he said, "stakes his life, his fortune, the existence of his family, not to resist the intolerable reality of oppression, but the remote possibility of wrong, of diminished freedom."[6] The Americans had

4. Add. Mss. 4948, 5422, 4949, 4916, 4973. Acton's distinction between Whiggism and Liberalism corresponds to Max Weber's distinction between the "ethic of responsibility" and the "ethic of ultimate ends."

5. Add. Mss. 4870. By the same token, Liberal Catholicism proper started only with the American Revolution: "Liberal Catholicism begins only when there are Liberals. Strictly then only in 1776. Liberalism was not entirely new, nor Liberal Catholicism. It had a long preamble. But a special problem arose from the time when Liberty began to be made the deciding principle of public morality." (Add. Mss. 4975.)

6. Add. Mss. 4915.

posed the ultimate problem of politics: Should a man or a nation risk everything for a purely speculative idea sanctioned by no law or religion? "The affirmative response," Acton declared, "is the Revolution, or as we say, Liberalism."[7]

This view of the American Revolution as the inauguration of a Republic of Virtue may not commend itself to historians, but the biographer of Acton will find it enormously revealing. Even more revealing is a comparison of his view of the American Revolution with that of the French Revolution. For the French Revolution, starting, as Acton believed, from the same premises as the American, terminated in a Reign of Terror rather than a Republic of Virtue. Like the Americans, the French were rebelling against the whole of the "unburied past";[8] they rejected the proposals of Necker because they did not want to purchase a few reforms at the expense of the larger principle of liberty. Yet somehow, in the very process of destroying tyranny they created a new one. And not by accident but by a fatal flaw in the Revolution itself. The attack on the Bastille prefigured the whole of the later Terror. Barnave and the other moderates were linked with Robespierre and Marat in a single chain, in which "the transitions are finely shaded and the logic is continuous."[9]

The logic of the French Revolution, of its progressive—or regressive—degeneration, Acton took to be the logic of violence. From the time that Barnave defended the "assassins" (this was Acton's term, not Barnave's) of July 14 with the ominous words, "Was this blood that they have shed so pure?" the assassins themselves were fated to atone for this original sin on the scaffold, and the revolution was doomed to degenerate into "bare cupidity and vengeance,

7. *Correspondence*, p. 278 (n.d.).
8. *Lectures on the French Revolution* (London, 1910), p. 58.
9. Ibid., p. 117.

brutal instinct and hideous passion."[1] And reinforcing this logic of violence, Acton found, was the logic of democracy: "The passion for equality made vain the hope of freedom."[2] Unlike the Americans, who wisely tempered equality by incorporating their Declaration of Rights within a mixed constitution, the French permitted nothing to stand in the way of the new democracy. Thus the monarchical claim to absolute power was superseded by a democratic claim to absolute power, a power even more dangerous than the old because it was more irresistible. In words reminiscent of Mill's *On Liberty*, Acton described the tyranny of democracy:

> It is bad to be oppressed by a minority, but it is worse to be oppressed by a majority. For there is a reserve of latent power in the masses which, if it is called into play, the minority can seldom resist. But from the absolute will of an entire people there is no appeal, no redemption, no refuge but treason.[3]

The difficulty in Acton's argument was that the logic of violence and democracy was, in his own terms, the logic of liberty itself. The rationale of the French Revolution was, to this extent, identical with that of the American Revolution. If the Americans were right "to stake the national existence, to sacrifice lives and fortunes, to cover the country with a lake of blood,"[4] the French, as he himself admitted, were all the more justified in taking the same risk. Unhappily the fatalities, for the French, turned out to be infinitely greater. But their premises had been the same, and it was these premises that Acton had enthusiastically endorsed. One might rebuke Acton as he himself, in one of his notes, rebuked Burke: "Burke was wrong to condemn

1. Ibid., pp. 91, 226.
2. *Freedom and Power*, p. 84.
3. Ibid., p. 40.
4. Review of Bryce's *The American Commonwealth, History of Freedom*, p. 586.

the Revolution because of its crimes. No great cause could resist that test."[5] And one might cite against him his own remark on another occasion: "A world has perished, a generation of men has been mown down so that the king might be Louis XVIII in place of Louis XVI, and the minister Fouché in place of Necker. According to the new doctrine of conscience it was not too dearly bought."[6]

Democracy, as much as violence, was implicit in the struggle for liberty—in the American struggle, therefore, as much as in the French. Acton admitted as much when he wrote: "The essence of the French ideal was democracy, that is, as in America, liberty founded on equality."[7] Had the French Assembly, in the early days of the Revolution, "assented, for a few political reforms, to the social degradation of democracy, they would have betrayed their constituents."[8] And Acton followed this with a defense of the French Revolution precisely in terms of the American:

> Every drop of blood shed in the American conflict was shed in a cause immeasurably inferior to theirs [that of the French], against a system more legitimate by far than that of June 23. Unless Washington was an assassin, it was their duty to oppose, if it might be, by policy, if it must be, by force, the mongrel measure of concession and obstinacy which the Court had carried against the proposals of Necker.[9]

This, to be sure, was before the fatal action of July 14. But July 14, by Acton's own account, was caused as much by the "obstinacy" of the court as by the willfulness of the revolutionaries: the same logic that compelled the revolutionaires to turn down the "mongrel" concessions of the court compelled them to implement their policies by force,

5. Add. Mss. 4967.
6. *Correspondence*, p. 279 (n.d.).
7. *French Revolution*, p. 97.
8. Ibid., p. 78.
9. Ibid.

and then to fortify force with more force. If this was the
logic of the Revolution, there was no logical stopping point
short of the Terror—for Acton no less than for the
French.

Acton was in an impossible dilemma. He could not
reasonably, logically, praise the American Revolution for
its relentless pursuit of the abstract, absolute moral idea of
liberty, and at the same time praise the American Constitution for its wise disposition of checks and balances,
countervailing forces, social traditions, and all the other
pragmatic devices for the limitation of power. The French,
it might even be argued (and Acton himself sometimes
seemed to suggest this), were truer to his idea of liberty,
for unlike the Americans, they tried to institutionalize it;
their Reign of Terror was in this sense the natural complement of the Republic of Virtue. The Americans, on the
other hand, may have averted a reign of terror only by
abandoning the idea of virtue; their constitution, then, may
be regarded as a betrayal of their revolution. (Or so it
would seem in Acton's terms. Most historians would deny
that the constitution was a betrayal of the revolution because they would deny the abstract, absolute character that
Acton attributed to the revolution.)

The dilemma, then, went to the heart of Acton's idea of
liberty. The logical conclusion of his argument would be
that it was not democracy, or violence, or any other
fortuitous circumstance that perverted the French Revolution, but rather the idea of liberty itself—liberty *as* an idea.
In his lectures and essays, Acton tried to evade this conclusion. Only in his private notes did he occasionally face up
to it:

> Government by Idea tends to take in everything, to
> make the whole of society obedient to the idea. Spaces not
> so governed are unconquered, beyond the border, uncon-
> verted, unconvinced, a future danger.[1]

1. Add. Mss. 4941.

Government that is natural, habitual, works more easily. It remains in the hands of average men, that is of men who do not live by ideas. Therefore there is less strain by making government adapt itself to custom. An ideal government, much better, perhaps, would have to be maintained by effort, and imposed by force.[2]

One has a double sense of tragedy in reading Acton: the tragedy of history, in which the most noble idea is always and necessarily perverted because it is the nature of ideas to be so perverted; and the tragedy of the historian who has not only to contemplate and report upon this perversion, but also, as judge and moralist, to participate in it, to praise the ideas whose unhappy end he knows all too well.

History, for Acton, was pre-eminently the history of ideas. Ideas alone gave "dignity and grace and intellectual value to history."[3] Modern history was marked off from earlier history by the emergence of ideas as political and social forces of a primary, determining order. And liberalism in particular was the beginning of the "reign of ideas."[4] But ideas, for Acton, were not only the essense of history; they were also the essence of revolution—which was why modern history, and especially the history of liberty, started in revolution and progressed by revolution.

History, ideas, morality, and liberty—the main components of Acton's thought, the principles to which he was most deeply committed—all came to a focus in Revolution. Again and again, in lectures, essays, private letters, and notes, he returned to this theme:

The affirmative response [of the American revolutionists] is the Revolution, or as we say, Liberalism.[5]

The principle of the higher law signifies Revolution.[6]

2. Add. Mss. 4953.
3. "Inaugural Lecture," *Freedom and Power*, p. 5.
4. Add. Mss. 4949.
5. *Correspondence*, p. 278 (n.d.).
6. *French Revolution*, p. 2.

Liberalism essentially revolutionary. Facts must yield to ideas. Peaceably and patiently if possible. Violently if not.[7]

The story of the revolted colonies impresses us first and most distinctly as the supreme manifestation of the law of resistance, as the abstract revolution in its purest and most perfect shape.[8]

The advent of the reign of general ideas which we call the Revolution. . . .[9]

. . . The equal claim of every man to be unhindered by man in the fulfillment of duty to God—a doctrine laden with storm and havoc, which is the secret essence of the Rights of Man, and indestructible soul of Revolution.[1]

Sieyès was essentially a revolutionist, because he held that political oppression can never be right, and that resistance to oppression can never be wrong.[2]

History, however, was as inimical to Acton's idea of revolution as to his idea of liberty. If liberty and morality were perverted by revolution, by the violence and excesses implicit in revolution, history was all the more surely perverted, indeed subverted, by revolution. The liberal theory of history, Acton once noted, required that "what ought to be" take precedence over "what is"; it required, that is, the installation of a "revolution in permanence."[3] The liberal historian, therefore, had to sanction this permanent revolution. But this was to ask the historian to preside over the dissolution of history—a more unthinkable situation by far than the statesman called on to preside over the dissolution of his empire.

The ambiguity in the word "history" has been deliberately retained here because it is so characteristic of Acton himself. His conception of the historian as judge and moral-

7. Add. Mss. 5654.
8. Review of Bryce, *History of Freedom,* p. 586.
9. *Freedom and Power,* p. 6.
1. Ibid., p. 12.
2. *French Revolution,* p. 161.
3. Add. Mss. 5432.

ist, as participant in the past, necessarily blurs the distinction between history as the past and history as the writing about the past, between what has been called existential history and recorded history. By effacing this distinction, Acton threatened to efface the historian himself. Committed to a permanent revolution, the historian was in effect doing what the revolutionist did: he was disburdening himself of the past. To the revolutionist this was the fulfillment of his calling. To the historian it was suicidal. In his inaugural lecture, Acton came perilously close to this denouement:

> Here we reach a point at which my argument threatens to abut on a contradiction. If the supreme conquests of society are won more often by violence than by lenient arts, if the trend and drift of things is towards convulsions and catastrophes, if the world owes religious liberty to the Dutch Revolution, constitutional government to the English, federal republicanism to the American, political equality to the French and its successors, what is to become of us, docile and attentive students of the absorbing past? The triumph of the Revolutionist annuls the historian.[4]

"The triumph of the Revolutionist annuls the historian." The words have a fateful ring. And their echo may be heard even as Acton sought to mute it by suggesting that the "unexpected" result of the Revolution might be to renovate history, if only the historian could learn to accept the Revolution as the "ripened fruit of all history."[5] The suggestion is as anticlimactic as it is unconvincing.

Summing up his earlier essays on the history of freedom in antiquity and Christianity, Acton had concluded that for almost all that time "the history of freedom was the history of the thing that was not."[6] The American Revolution, he

4. *Freedom and Power*, p. 15.
5. Ibid., p. 16.
6. Ibid., p. 83.

had then dared hope, signified the beginning of a history of freedom. But these essays were written before his confrontation with Döllinger, before the consummation of his views on morality, liberty, and history. With the final emergence of the historian as moralist and the liberal as revolutionist, Acton was more than ever alienated from a history that was the history of the thing that was not. Absolute morality meant the very nearly absolute denigration of history. The once ostensibly saving event in history, the American Revolution, retained its title to morality only by abrogating its title to historicity. More and more it assumed for Acton a mythopoeic character, the aspect of a utopian fantasy which had no historical reality of its own but which was destructive of all other reality. "All through," one of his notes read, "America meant: escape from History. They started fresh, unencumbered with political Past."[7]

For Acton too, America meant "escape from History." And this in both senses, for the denial of the legitimacy of the past implied a denial of the meaningfulness of the historical enterprise. Written history could not survive the annihilation of existential history. As the triumph of the revolution annulled liberty, so the triumph of the revolutionist annulled the historian. The History of Liberty remained "the greatest book that was never written," because the history of liberty remained "the history of the thing that was not."[8]

7. Add. Mss. 4898.

8. Acton's History of Liberty invites comparison with Croce's *History as the Story of Liberty*, an equally mythopoeic history but a written one. The difference between the two, and the reason Croce's was written while Acton's was not, was that Croce thought of history as potentially and essentially the story of liberty, while Acton thought of it as actually and essentially the story of tyranny. Croce had all the confidence of the philosophical idealist whose ideals were immanent in history; Acton had all the despair of the ethical idealist whose ideals were always being violated by history.

VI

LESLIE STEPHEN: THE VICTORIAN

AS INTELLECTUAL

Virginia Woolf's novel *To the Lighthouse* opens brightly: " 'Yes, of course, if it's fine tomorrow,' said Mrs. Ramsay. 'But you'll have to be up with the lark.' " To her six-year-old son, "these words conveyed an extraordinary joy, as if it were settled, the expedition to the lighthouse were bound to take place, and the wonder to which he had looked forward, for years and years it seemed, was, after a night's darkness and a day's sail, within touch." For some lines, the radiance of the child's world prevails; and then: " 'But,' said his father, stopping in front of the drawing-room window, 'it won't be fine.' "

Had there been an axe handy, or a poker, any weapon that would have gashed a hole in his father's breast and killed him, there and then, James would have seized it. Such were the extremes of emotion that Mr. Ramsay excited in his children's breasts by his mere presence; standing, as now, lean as a knife, narrow as the blade of one, grinning sarcastically, not only with the pleasure of disillusioning his son and casting ridicule upon his wife, who was ten thousand times better in every way than he was (James thought), but also with some secret conceit at his own accuracy of judgment. What he said was true.

It was always true. He was incapable of untruth; never tampered with a fact; never altered a disagreeable word to suit the pleasure or convenience of any mortal being, least of all his own children, who, sprung from his loins, should be aware from childhood that life is difficult; facts uncompromising; and the passage to that fabled land where our brightest hopes are extinguished, our frail barks founder in darkness, . . . one that needs, above all, courage, truth, and the power to endure.[1]

This is our first introduction to Mr. Ramsay, that egotistical, tyrannical, petty, and most disagreeable Victorian paterfamilias. It may also serve as an introduction to Virginia Woolf's father, Leslie Stephen, after whom the character of Mr. Ramsay was, surprisingly, modeled. Surprisingly, for it was of Stephen, the Victorian intellectual par excellence, that John Morley said: "His natural kindness of heart, supported by his passion for reason and fair play, made him the most considerate and faithful of men"[2]—a judgment echoed by other contemporaries. What, then, is one to make of the narrow, mean, vitriolic Mr. Ramsay, who was also the broad-minded, enlightened Mr. Stephen, author of some thirty volumes of biographical and critical works, among them the two-volume *History of English Thought in the Eighteenth Century* and the three-volume *English Utilitarians*, editor of the monumental *Dictionary of English Biography*, and contributor to it of no less than 378 distinguished articles?

A muckraker, or a parodist of the Lytton Strachey variety, might solve the problem easily enough by creating two figures, a public Dr. Jekyll and a private Mr. Hyde, of which the Mr. Hyde would be assumed to be the real person. This technique, unsatisfactory at best, would be particularly unfortunate in the case of an intellectual, for whom public and private cannot be so neatly distinguished,

1. *To the Lighthouse* (New York, 1927), p. 9.
2. Morley, *Recollections* (New York, 1917), I, 117.

for whom the public man, the thinker, is as essentially the real person as the private, domestic man. Leslie Stephen was such an intellectual, by birth, character, and vocation. He was, despite the muckraker, neither a fool, nor a fraud, nor a split personality. He was all of a piece—a Victorian man of letters.

Virginia Woolf herself never forgot that Mr. Ramsay was Mr. Stephen, an intellectual whose life and fate were, in large measure, the life and fate of his mind, and whose private terror was that peculiar to the intellectual profession, the terror of being declared counterfeit. Mr. Ramsay badgered his wife with the questions: Were his mental powers weakening? Was his last book as good as his earlier ones? And he tormented himself with the thought that his writings, voluminous though they might be, would not survive his lifetime. Leslie Stephen had similar anxieties. Himself a professional book reviewer, he could not bear, he confessed, to read reviews of his own books. Toward the end of his life, having produced a monumental body of work and about to publish still another volume, he wrote to a friend: "I always suffer from a latent conviction that I am an imposter and that somebody will find me out."[3]

Stephen had little to fear from his own contemporaries. It remained for his daughter to "find him out," and even more, perhaps, for those further removed from him in time and place. Virginia Woolf herself, however different in coloration and specific markings, was of the same species as her father. She could brilliantly expose his peculiar idiosyncrasies and deficiencies, but the general characteristics of the species escaped her because she took them to be the characteristics of the human condition. It is only from a totally different culture and society that the English intellectual, and more particularly the Victorian intellectual, emerges as a distinctive breed.

3. F. W. Maitland, *The Life and Letters of Leslie Stephen* (London, 1906), p. 413 (July 31, 1892).

To the American intellectual who has made much (perhaps too much) of his "alienation," his opposite number in England seems to enjoy an enviable ease and rapport. Where the American feels himself to be a foreigner in his own land—is often literally a foreigner, or of such recent foreign descent as to have the same effect—the Englishman is not only a pure-bred native but also, it sometimes appears, a pure-bred intellectual. It is with some awe that one contemplates the interlocking genealogies that tie together, by birth and marriage, the great names of nineteenth- and twentieth-century English culture: Macaulay, Trevelyan, Arnold, Huxley, Darwin, Wedgwood, Galton, Stephen, Wilberforce, Venn, Dicey, Thackeray, Russell, Webb, Keynes, Strachey, Toynbee . . .[4] By comparison, American culture is a series of isolated and unrelated names, the few exceptions (the Adamses, Jameses, and Lowells) being rare enough to have become the butt of jokes.

Thus where the American intellectual has a precarious hold on fame, each individual earning his title by the sweat of his brow (hence, by some Lamarckian or Darwinian process, the evolution of that peculiarly American species, the "highbrow"), the English intellectual, and pre-eminently the Victorian intellectual, seemed to come into his title and estate almost by the right of birth. At a time when few monarchs dared lay claim to the principle of legitimacy, the Victorian intellectual might do so. His legitimacy was established by family, class, education, profession, and remuneration. He could move in high society, aspire to political power, or make money, without impugning his calling. He had not the typical stigmata of intellectuals elsewhere—the academicism, bohemianism, or

4. The intricacies of their relationships have been described by Noel Annan in "The Intellectual Aristocracy," *Studies in Social History*, ed. J. H. Plumb (London, 1955). Annan's *Leslie Stephen* (London, 1952) inspired the original version of this essay. It is a model of intellectual biography—a biography that is nothing less than an intellectual history of the times.

preciosity of the Herr Professor, the feuilletoniste, or the esthete. He was no exotic, no sport. His intellectuality came as naturally to him as his language, which in turn was as natural as breathing. It was his birthright, and he was as secure in that as he was in his Englishness. If he sometimes wavered, if, like Mr. Ramsay or Mr. Stephen, he confessed his fears of being found out, being exposed as illegitimate, this could be taken, as Virginia Woolf took it, as a sign of neurosis, a private failing.

Yet it may be that this aberration of Ramsay-Stephen—indeed the whole phenomenon represented by Ramsay-Stephen—had a larger, more public significance. It may be that the very quality of legitimacy that conferred upon the Victorian the title of intellectual also, paradoxically, deprived him of the claim to it. For if to be an intellectual is as natural as breathing, it can be no more remarkable than breathing. If it has the status of an ordinary occupation, it does not enjoy the extraordinary status of a calling. If it is no special distinction which the individual must laboriously earn, if it comes to him as a right rather than a reward, if it is an incidental by-product of birth rather than the result of application and dedication, then the much-acclaimed Victorian intellectual may have been not an intellectual at all, but rather a cultured gentleman whose occupation happened to be writing.

One of the peculiarities of the English intellectual *qua* gentleman, which may account for his natural, artless manner, is the survival of the schoolboy in him. That Leslie Stephen was a product of Eton and Cambridge was one of the primary facts of his intellectual life. He had been sent to Eton when his mother, observing in him what she took to be evidence of precocious genius, consulted a physician, who diagnosed the boy's condition as the symptoms of a "disordered circulation," and prescribed a school where he could be assured of "fresh air, humdrum lessons, and a rigorous abstinence from poetry."[5] Eton, evidently, met that prescription.

It is not the mere convention of the biographer that makes it mandatory to inquire into an Englishman's school-days. Nor is it accident that the English have produced the largest literature of memoirs devoted to this subject. More than any other single factor—more than childhood, marriage, or profession—school seems to constitute the decisive, formative influence in their lives, an influence that acquires the character of a permanent emotional, social, even metaphysical condition. It is, in fact, the only relation to the metaphysical that many Englishmen experience. Thus the differences between a Leslie Stephen and a Matthew Arnold, for example, can perhaps best be understood in terms of their distinctive genera: Eton-Cambridge and Rugby-Oxford.

At Eton, as Stephen was fond of recalling, there was none of the "cant" about Christian behavior or Christian gentlemen so common at Rugby, none of the moralizing sermons to which Dr. Arnold was addicted. No one at Eton pretended that religion had anything to do with the schoolboy's life of cribbing, lying, cheating, stealing, and bullying. The old fossil droning on in the college chapel about the duties of the married state did not think the subject inappropriate because he did not assume that sermons were meant to be taken seriously. Religion, as distinct from the mere social activity of churchgoing, was a private affair.

Religion was a private affair, partly at least for the reason that science was so much a public affair. It was in the fifties, while Stephen was at Cambridge, that the Mosaic account of creation began to be seriously undermined, on the one side from geology and zoology, with their revelations about the antiquity of the universe and the evolution of species,

5. Maitland, *Life and Letters*, p. 28.

and on the other from the recently imported "Biblical Criticism" of Germany. Many of the bright young men in these middle years of Victoria's reign discovered that they could no longer subscribe to the dogmas of the Anglican Church or any other church. Those of the Rugby-Oxford temperament, like Matthew Arnold's friend, Arthur Clough, went through agonies of doubt and emerged to find their familiar world shattered. Others, generally the more sanguine products of Eton or Cambridge, experienced nothing more disturbing than the sensation of having awakened. Stephen, as he later testified, did not lose his faith; he simply awoke to the realization that he had none. A professional intellectual, he managed to live through one of the greatest intellectual revolutions of modern times, without truly experiencing it.

Under the impression that the only proper historical explanation of any event is an evolutionary one, historians have represented the English loss of faith as a gradual stripping of religion of one dogma after another until nothing remained but the memory of Christianity—the convention of a name and the habit of a ritual. If this were so, Stephen's agnosticism might be taken as a kind of diluted fourth-generation Evangelicalism: the first generation being represented by Wesleyan fundamentalism, when religion looked upon learning and culture as godless; the second by the Clapham Sect (including Macaulay's father and Stephen's grandfather), which succeeded in making piety socially and culturally respectable; and the third by men like Macaulay and James Stephen (Leslie's father), who had discarded the traditional Evangelical apparatus of conscience-probing, sin-confessing, "illuminations," and conversions. Leslie Stephen himself would have favored such an interpretation. His own spiritual journey, starting from the quiet, unostentatious piety of his home, followed by the quiet, unostentatious, lax conformism of school, ended in the quiet, reasonable, good-natured agnosticism of his maturity. The evolution of faith from belief to unbelief seemed to him to be as natural and inevitable as the process of physical growth itself.

Stephen was deceived, however, as were later historians, into confusing manners with belief. Because the generation of his elders—his own father and Macaulay, for example—had come to look upon enthusiasm with distaste, and regarded public protestations of faith, like public displays of emotion, as vulgar if not obscene, it has been assumed that their religious belief was as attenuated as the public expression of that belief. The truth is that Leslie Stephen's father, however far he had come from the primitive evangelical fervor of his ancestors, was nevertheless deeply pious, in thought as well as in behavior. Between James Stephen and Leslie Stephen there was not simply one more step in the march of enlightenment; there was a leap which no amount of good manners or good nature could obscure.

Stephen could not appreciate the enormity of the distance which separated belief from unbelief, because he could not appreciate or credit the very fact of belief. "The one thing," he wrote, "That can spoil the social intercourse of well-educated men . . . is a spirit of misplaced zeal";[6] and he was grateful that there was no Arnold at Eton and no Newman at Cambridge. He admitted that Cambridge men did not deny the existence of the soul, but he congratulated himself that they were sensible enough to know that it should be kept in its proper place. "We leave theology to theologians," he was pleased to report.[7] He himself, who did more to popularize agnosticism than any other man except Huxley, never really understood what all the fuss was about.

He never understood, as Huxley did, that a new chronology had come into being, Before-Darwin and After-Darwin, with Darwin (or more precisely, the movements

6. Stephen, *Sketches from Cambridge* (London, 1932), p. 97.
7. Ibid., p. 96.

of thought that culminated in Darwinism) marking the dividing line between belief and unbelief. Before-Darwin a bold spirit could be tempted to think of God as merely the custodian of the laws of nature; After-Darwin it took no great courage to think of the laws of nature as the custodians of the universe. Before-Darwin man could look upon himself as the creature of God fashioned in His image; After-Darwin he discovered that he had been created by laws of nature which were the laws of chance, in the image of whatever species of primate science might discover to be his next of kin. It is little wonder that Stephen and so many of his contemporaries failed to recognize the revolutionary character of their time, when the archrebel of the piece, Darwin himself, seemed to be unaware of or uninterested in the broader implications of his theory. It remained for Huxley, ten years after the appearance of *The Origin of Species*, to coin the word "agnosticism," and to discover how many of the young agnostics regarded it not as a new and upsetting revelation but rather as an old and obvious truth. Stephen was one of those to whom agnosticism was as old and obvious as common sense. It was, to quote the title of one of the essays in his *An Agnostic's Apology*, "The Religion of All Sensible Men." How could one get excited about so commonplace and sensible a thing as common sense, in a country where common sense was the common character of intellectuals and populace?

A better name for Stephen's creed than agnosticism might be Muscular Christianity—without the Christianity. Stephen once defined Muscular Christianity, in its more conventional Christian form, as the duty to "fear God and walk a thousand miles in a thousand hours."[8] He could see the point of the second part of that injunction but not of the first.

8. Ibid., p. 15.

Indeed, his quarrel with Maurice and Kingsley was that while they could rationally justify the second, their adherence to the first was sentimental and irrational. Kingsley's ideal parson, he said, was "a married man with a taste for field-sports"[9]—which was essentially Stephen's own image of the ideal philosopher.

Upon sports, Stephen, like most of his countrymen, lavished the passion and enthusiasm that they withheld from most other activities, especially religion. Sports could be indulged to excess as nothing else could. And they inspired a respect that nothing else did. Perfect in themselves, they provided a model for all else. But the model was a curious inversion of the original. For the model was sportsmanship, and sportsmanship meant that nothing—nothing but sports themselves, that is—could be indulged in passionately or to excess. Thus it was not the grudging admission but the proud boast of politicians that politics was a game, a game, however, governed by the hallowed rules of the sportsman. Gladstone was disliked by many of his colleagues because he broke the primary rule of the game: to regard it as a game. His constant appeal to principle, his tone of moral righteousness, were more offensive than the particular principles or policies he espoused. The Victorian definition of a demagogue was a politician who intruded conscience into politics.

Religion was a game in the same sense in which politics was a game, because both were skirmishes played out on the fringes of society, with society itself secure and invulnerable. Men could differ about the lesser issue of religion so long as they agreed upon the larger issues of manners and morals. It was the right of Englishmen (and the duty of liberals, Mill seemed to suggest) to indulge their idiosyncratic views about Arianism or Erastianism, the Thirty-Nine Articles and Apostolic Succession, church

9. "Charles Kingsley," *Hours in a Library* (London, 1892), III, 49.

establishments and religions of humanity, so long as they comported themselves as decent, upright, law-abiding Englishmen. The Tractarians, to be sure, took their differences, and religion itself, more seriously, and for a while it seemed that they would break through the religious consensus. But the conversion of Newman, Ward, and the others had a sobering effect on the rest, and once the converts withdrew to the parochial confines of Catholicism, they ceased to be a center of contention or a threat to the "prevailing tone . . . of quiet good sense."[1]

To Stephen, agnosticism was superior to religion because it was the more sporting and manly way of playing the game of life. For the agnostic, there were none of the easy subterfuges, the cheap consolations of religion. The agnostic had to be courageous without being foolhardy, self-sufficient but not proud. He had to know when to stand alone and when to join with others, how to exploit his good fortune and how to retreat before bad. And he had to understand that the secret of thinking was in the doing and that to be deliberate was to be decisive. The good agnostic, in short, was the good sportsman, because he knew only one rule: "The play should be played out, and as well as it could be done."[2]

It is not surprising that Stephen, interpreting agnosticism in this way, saw in it a philosophy peculiarly congenial to the English. Certainly there is no other country where both the spirit of sportsmanship and the physical activity of sports have penetrated so deeply into society as to determine the character of its intellectuals. It is almost impossible to read a memoir or biography of a Victorian writer without coming upon the inevitable walking statistics. Even Mill, that effeminate "logic-chopping machine," who had escaped the socializing institutions of the public school

1. *Sketches from Cambridge*, p. 93.
2. "A Bad Five Minutes in the Alps," *Freethinking and Plain-speaking* (London, 1908), p. 223.

and university, walked fifteen miles three days before his death at the age of sixty-seven, a modest record compared with Stephen's grandfather, who celebrated his seventieth birthday by walking twenty-five miles to breakfast, then to his office, and home again the same day. Fifty miles a day was about the average for the "Sunday Tramps" organized by Stephen. And walking was the least strenuous of the sports to which Stephen and his friends were addicted. Stephen remembered, as the most important events of his university days, the two occasions when the Trinity Hall boat, with himself as coach, went head of the river. And the most cherished memories of his later life were his mountain-climbing expeditions, on which he was joined by such other enthusiasts as Meredith, Huxley, Harrison, and Maitland. Stephen himself was the first person to scale the Schreckhorn.

Mountaineering was no idle, leisure-time amusement. It was a disciplined, exacting game with a precise set of rules and code of behavior. Mountains could only be legitimately scaled by "fair means"; the "resources of the engineer's art," the "artifices" that were even then beginning to transform mountain climbing, aroused in him a horror, he said, that could only be expressed by the epithet "unsportsmanlike."[3] Mountain climbing was, in fact, a paradigm of life itself. When Stephen put to himself the ultimate question of the meaning of life, it was to his favorite sports, rowing and mountaineering, that he looked for an answer. In "A Bad Five Minutes in the Alps," one of his most thoughtful and personal essays, he pictured himself hanging over a precipice and asking himself the value of life. As his fingers clung desperately to the edge of the rock, he contemplated the vision of eternity lying in wait for him below. He reviewed in his mind the answers of Christianity, Pantheism, and positivism's Religion of Humanity,

3. Round Mont Blanc," *Men, Books, and Mountains* (London, 1956), p. 200.

rejecting the first because it did not appreciate the goodness of man, the second because it did not appreciate his individuality, and the third because it pretended to make too much of him. It was not until he recalled the physical sensation of a race on the Thames that the answer came to him. He remembered how he had rowed on, in this race that was already lost, every muscle aching and his lungs strained almost to the breaking point, for no other reason than "some obscure sense of honor." So now, hanging over the precipice, he was overwhelmed by the instinctive thought that the "fag end of the game should be fairly played out, come what might, and whatever reasons might be given for it."[4]

If the sportsman, submitting himself to the ordeal of the Thames or the Alps, had to be satisfied with answers so vague as an "obscure sense of honor," "come what might," or "whatever reasons"—answers that were more in the nature of an admission that there were no answers—surely the philosopher, Stephen implied, could not expect better ones. From the sportsman's maxim that life was nothing but a game, it was a short step to the assertion that the game was more than life. Life was sometimes farcical; the game was always serious. In life there were extenuating circumstances and rules had exceptions; the game had to be played out strictly according to the laws. In life, responsibilities might be shirked and consequences evaded; the game took its toll inexorably. If the game, an enterprise so grave and momentous, had no meaning beyond itself, then life surely had no such meaning. Thus the philosopher yielded to the sportsman.

As the philosopher in Stephen yielded, so did the intellectual. At Cambridge he was known as a college "rough."[5]

4. *Freethinking*, p. 222.
5. Maitland, *Life and Letters*, p. 72.

In his early memoirs, he spoke of a don (identified by his friends as himself) who lectured on the Greek Testament in this manly fashion:

> "Easy all! Hard word there. Smith, what does it mean?"
> "I don't know," says Smith.
> "No more don't I," replied the aquatic, but moderately learned, tutor; "paddle on all!"[6]

He was no worse than most of his colleagues who were too busy with the administration of the college or with their private affairs to take their tutoring seriously, and whose students had to depend upon crammers to pass their examinations. He himself, like many of his contemporaries, was largely self-educated. To an American, for whom self-education implies that painful process by which an unschooled person acquires a smattering of knowledge, it may seem odd to speak of urbane, cultivated, professional intellectuals, men of good breeding, graduates of the best schools, as self-educated. Yet this was so. Stephen had to learn French and German on his own; he first read modern philosophy—mainly the English from Hobbes to Mill—while a don, between bouts of rowing and tutoring; he became acquainted with modern literature only after he was installed as a literary critic in London. Even the university man's knowledge of the ancients was more a matter of vocabulary and prosody than ideas and philosophy. Stephen told the story of his Cambridge friend and colleague, Henry Fawcett, who announced after dinner one evening: "Now I am interested in Socrates, and want to know more about him, so I am thinking of giving a lecture upon him." "But Fawcett," Stephen mildly remonstrated, "have you read his works?" "No, but I mean to."[7]

It is the faith of the self-educated man that nothing is

6. *Sketches from Cambridge*, p. 81.
7. Annan, *Leslie Stephen*, p. 43.

beyond his means, that all knowledge must submit to a firm will and good sense. This is also the creed of the amateur. The English essayist like Stephen, whose relation to ideas is that of a self-educated intellectual, may best be thought of as a professional amateur, a type familiar to Americans in certain sports.

The professional bearing of the Victorian intellectual is so conspicuous that his amateur status is apt to be over-looked. This professionalism is exhibited in the regularity and facility of his writing—the normal accreditation of a genuine, working intellectual. There cannot have been many writers like Anthony Trollope, who kept a schedule and a watch in front of him to make sure that he turned out his 250 words every quarter of an hour for a minimum of three hours. But the sense of writing as a regular occupa-tion, not beholden to inspiration or creative impulse, was and still is typical among English intellectuals. Stephen himself was no more productive than many others; he averaged three or four 8,000-word articles a week (each at one sitting, it is, incredibly, reported), apart from inci-dental writing tasks. This was the sportsmanlike way of writing: no fuss, no anguish, the game played at the ap-pointed time, so many minutes to the period, so many periods to the event.

As a writer, then, the Victorian intellectual was very much the professional; it was as a thinker that he tended to be amateur, and largely for the reason that he was so professional in his writing. No one could write profoundly on subjects worked up for the occasion at the rate of 25,000 words a week. And even if he could, the writer would not have wanted to enter too profoundly into his subjects. There was something unsporting, to his mind, in the way a German philosopher (or these days, the English complain, an American academician) worried an idea, strained for a meaning, deliberately cultivated the difficult and obscure. The Victorian essayist was sensible and urbane, preserving the amenities of discourse, the manners of a gentleman in the presence of ladies. A book or theme was explored, with no unseemly haste or heat, until the contracted number of pages were filled. Where there was a show of passion it was against those who, by affronting common sense, had ruled themselves out of the company of gentlemen. The German philosophers were most objectionable: Hegel was, Stephen confided in his diary, "in many things, a little better than an ass";[8] and he refused to believe that Coleridge could have stolen his Shakespeare criticism from Schlegel, "partly at least, for the reason which would induce me to acquit a supposed thief of having stolen a pair of breeches from a wild Highlandman."[9]

For the most part, the Germans excepted, the tone was mild and agreeable. It was as if the essayist had entered into a compact of friendship with his subject, so that Morley could be equally tender toward Rousseau and Burke, or Stephen toward almost all the great writers with whom he dealt. As a biographer, Stephen prided himself on not revealing all that an inquisitive reader might like to know, and as a critic he praised the Memorials of Charles Kingsley for its reticence. He was widely read in the literature of the eighteenth and nineteenth centuries, but he managed, as English reviewers say in praise, to carry his learning lightly. He was thoughtful yet never argumentative, sensitive but not precious, sympathetic without being committed. He had all the virtues of the gentleman—amiability, broad-mindedness and a high tolerance—which meant that he had the great vice of the essayist—literary promiscuity.

Stephen's essay on Jonathan Edwards is instructive. Here was a man who was as unlikely a candidate for his sympathy as is conceivable—a religious zealot, mystic, witch-hunter, and hair-splitting theologian. Yet Stephen never

8. Maitland, *Life and Letters*, p. 172.
9. "Coleridge," *Hours in a Library*, III, 356.

lost his temper: Edwards "is morbid, it may be, but he is not insincere"; "there is something rather touching, though at times our sympathy is not quite unequivocal. . . ."[1] Stephen was able to be good-tempered because he never really believed that a man could honestly believe in sin and hellfire as Edwards professed to. Himself a gentleman, he was generous enough to ignore these distressing lapses of taste and to assume that Edwards too was at heart a gentleman. So casually and smoothly that the reader is almost lulled into acquiescence, Stephen worked up to the remarkable judgment:

> That Edwards possessed extraordinary acuteness is as clear as it is singular that so acute a man should have suffered his intellectual activity to be restrained within such narrow fetters. Placed in a different medium, under the same circumstances, for example, as Hume or Kant, he might have developed a system of metaphysics comparable in its effect upon the history of thought to the doctrines of either of those thinkers. He was, one might fancy, formed by nature to be a German professor, and accidentally dropped into the American forests.[2]

The Victorian essayist had the temperament which Americans associate less with the literary critic than with the cultural anthropologist. A variety of beliefs, styles, and personalities came under his purview, and, in the fashion of the anthropologist, he gave them each the best of his understanding and sympathy. But he never made the mistake of believing them or accepting them at face value, much as the anthropologist takes care neither to be contemptuous of the Zulu nor deferential toward the Christian. To all his subjects he displayed the same gentle irreverence, with only the slightest hint of the superciliousness that betrays the superior man who is above the battle. Thus Stephen could say, of the greatest mind of his time: "New-

1. "Jonathan Edwards," *Hours in a Library*, I, 307, 309.
2. Ibid., I, 343.

man is good enough as a writer and ingenious enough as a sophist to be worth a little examination. I only consider him as a curiosity."[3] Or he could refer to Hobbes as "a Herbert Spencer of the seventeenth century,"[4] and describe philosophy in general as a by-product of social evolution, "the noise that the wheels make as they go round."[5]

But like the anthropologist, who often harbors behind his façade of impartiality a whole armory of beliefs and assumptions, the essayist too had his stock of prejudices which every now and then emerged in the rhetoric of the essay. In Stephen's case, they were expressed by his favorite invectives, "morbid" and "unmanly." Morbid and unmanly were anything tainted with excessive sentiment, sensibility, emotion, or exoticism. Donne's love poetry was morbid. Rousseau had a morbid tendency to introspection and a morbid appetite for happiness. Balzac's lovers were morbidly sentimental and morbidly religious. Keats, Shelley, and Coleridge were unmanly. Charlotte Brontë's Rochester and George Eliot's Tito and Daniel Deronda were all feminine. (A reviewer of Stephen's book on Eliot corrected what he took to be a typographical error in the description of a male character as womanly.)

Stephen was confident that he himself could never be charged with unmanliness. His philosophy, such as it was, was a sound, English utilitarianism. His religion was a healthy agnosticism. His esthetic principles were common sense and good nature. His highest praise of a young man was to call him "a manly and affectionate young fellow."[6] If all of this sometimes added up to Philistinism, then he admitted to being a "thorough Philistine who is dull enough to glory in his Philistinism."[7] Besides, Philistinism

---

3. Maitland, *Life and Letters*, p. 308.
4. Stephen, *Hobbes* (London, 1904), p. 73.
5. Maitland, *Life and Letters*, p. 283.
6. Ibid., p. 59.
7. "Coleridge," *Hours in a Library*, III, 357.

was a word that "a prig gives to the rest of mankind."[8] He disclaimed any comprehension of the non-literary arts; "artistic people," he once told his artistic children, "inhabit a world very unfamiliar to me."[9] And he was only so much of an intellectual as his compulsive sense of manliness permitted him to be—and manliness drove a hard bargain. The result was that Stephen, who, as Maitland put it, had a "lust for pen and ink"[1] so great that he begrudged the time spent at the dinner table, could be found uttering, and, what is more, believing, such crude philistinisms as: "To recommend contemplation in preference to action is like preferring sleeping to walking."[2] Or: "The highest poetry, like the noblest morality, is the product of a thoroughly healthy mind."[3] Writing itself, if conducted in the properly casual and sportsmanlike spirit, was not unmanly. But thinking was suspect. It was for this reason that Stephen, as he once confessed, found that he could write when he could not read—and a fortiori when he could not think.

Mr. Ramsay knew what Stephen perhaps only suspected, that as an intellectual he had failed. He did not know that this failure had been the price of his admission to the society of Victorian intellectuals. But he knew that something somewhere had gone wrong. His mind had failed him. Yet—

It was a splendid mind. For if thought is like the keyboard of a piano, divided into so many notes, or like the alphabet is ranged in twenty-six letters all in order, then his splendid mind had no sort of difficulty in running over those letters one by one, firmly and accurately, until it had

8. Maitland, *Life and Letters*, p. 170.
9. Annan, *Leslie Stephen*, p. 91.
1. Maitland, *Life and Letters*, p. 405.
2. "Wordsworth's Ethics," *Hours in a Library*, II, 293.
3. "Balzac's Novels," *Hours in a Library*, I, 234.

reached, say, the letter Q. He reached Q. Very few people in the whole of England ever reach Q. . . . But after Q? What comes next? After Q there are a number of letters the last of which is scarcely visible to mortal eyes, but glimmers in the distance. Z is only reached once by one man in a generation. Still, if he could reach R it would be something. Here at least was Q. He dug his heels in at Q. Q he was sure of. Q he could demonstrate. If Q then is Q–R— . . . R is then—what is R?

A shutter, like the leathern eyelid of a lizard, flickered over the intensity of his gaze and obscured the letter R. In that flash of darkness he heard people saying—he was a failure—that R was beyond him. He would never reach R. . . .

Feelings that would not have disgraced a leader who, now that the snow has begun to fall and the mountain top is covered in mist, knows that he must lay himself down and die before morning comes, stole upon him. . . . Yet he would not die lying down; he would find some crag of rock, and there, his eyes fixed on the storm, trying to the end to pierce the darkness, he would die standing. He would never reach R.[4]

He was doomed to failure and he would die like a man. But perhaps something, human sympathy or love, could be salvaged from this wreck of an intellectual:

Who shall blame him, if, so standing for a moment, he dwells upon fame, upon search parties, upon cairns, raised by grateful followers over his bones? Finally, who shall blame the leader of the doomed expedition, if, having adventured to the uttermost, and used his strength wholly to the last ounce and fallen asleep not much caring if he wakes or not, he now perceived by some pricking in his toes that he lives, and does not on the whole object to live, but requires sympathy, and whisky, and some one to tell the story of his suffering to at once?[5]

4. Woolf, *To the Lighthouse*, pp. 53–5.
5. Ibid., p. 57.

The failure of the intellectual was also the failure of the private man. Stephen was exposed as Mr. Ramsay. He had starved himself as an intellectual, thinking it would make him a better man. He had emaciated his sensibility, constricted his faith, stunted his imagination. When finally intellectual poverty forced him to retreat to domesticity, his spirit was poor, hard, and unyielding. But deep within him was a turbulence that erupted with painful regularity and violence. In the privacy of his home, the stoical, death-defying mountaineer confessed that he could not bear to hear the word dentist mentioned, or read newspaper accounts of the Boer War. The critic who thought it morbid and unmanly to indulge one's feelings recorded in his "Mausoleum Book" the grievances and griefs of his private life, the "hideous morbid fancies" that he had been unkind to his wives ("fancies which I know to be utterly baseless and which I am yet unable to dispense by an effort of will"), and the conviction that he was unloved and uncared for.[6] The optimistic, science-ravished utilitarian who contemplated a world free from tyranny, superstition, and exploitation, was wretched, willful, and harsh. The man who made a philosophy of common sense was prostrated by the minor crises of domestic life—a child late for dinner, an unforeseen household expenditure, a vanity offended. "I wish I were dead, I wish I were dead," his children once heard him groan in genuine misery, "I wish my whiskers would grow."[7]

There are different habitats of madness suitable for different varieties of intelligence and sensibility. There are the super-rational heights of madness on which may be found a science-ravished spirit like Comte; and there are the irrational depths in which a Dostoevski or Nietzsche may

6. Annan, *Leslie Stephen*, p. 99.
7. Ibid., p. 102.

find refuge. Victorian intellectuals dwelled, for the most part, upon the plains of madness—that deceptively peaceful countryside where philosophers paraded as journalists and writers showed off their Rugby Blues more proudly than their Oxford Firsts. Here lived those scientists and rationalists (Darwin, Huxley, Spencer) who suffered from lifelong illnesses which defied medical diagnosis and cure; novelists of domestic manners and morals (Bulwer Lytton, Thackeray, Meredith, Dickens) whose marriages were tragically unhappy; religious libertarians (Harrison, Stephen, Morley) who were zealous puritans; successful and wealthy writers (Macaulay, Dickens, Darwin) who were obsessed with the fear of bankruptcy; moral critics (Carlyle, Eliot, Mill, Ruskin) who lived in the shadow of sexual aberrations and improprieties; and in general an intellectual community suffering a larger proportion of nervous breakdowns, it would seem, than almost any other (Maine, Lecky, Kingsley, Symonds, Mill are the names that come most readily to mind, although the list can be expanded almost indefinitely). In this company of "manly and affectionate fellows," Stephen was a member in good standing.

WALTER BAGEHOT: A COMMON
MAN WITH UNCOMMON IDEAS

T HE CURRENT intellectual fashions put a premium on simplicity and activism. The subtleties, complications, and ambiguities that until recently have been the mark of serious thought are now taken to signify a failure of nerve, a compromise with evil, an evasion of judgment and "commitment." It is as if the "once-born" (to use the terms invented by Francis Newman and immortalized by William James) were reasserting themselves over the "twice-born": the once-born, simple and "healthy-minded," having faith in a beneficent God and a perfectible universe; the twice-born in awe of His mystery, impressed by the recalcitrance of men and the anomalies of social action.

In Walter Bagehot one may see a reconciliation of the two types. He was a political commentator who stopped just short of being a political philosopher, a social critic without the professional appurtenances of the sociologist but with more imagination and wisdom, an editor of the *Economist* who wrote with as much facility and perception about Shelley or Coleridge as about the rate of interest or currency reform. He once described himself as being "between sizes in politics."[1] In fact he was between sizes in everything. He was that rare species of the twice-born who could give proper due to the rights and merits of the once-born. And he did so not by a denial of his own nature but by virtue of the very subtleties, complications, and ambiguities that informed his nature. He was, as he said of St. Paul, a "divided nature."[2]

The "dark realities" of life that he often alluded to had an obvious personal reference. His mother, to whom he was deeply attached, had recurrent fits of insanity, and his half-brother was feeble-minded; both predeceased him by only a few years, so that his entire life was passed in their shadow. "Every trouble in life is a joke compared to madness," he once remarked.[3] And elsewhere he wrote: "We see but one aspect of our neighbor, as we see but one side of the moon: in either case there is also a dark half which is unknown to us. We all come down to dinner, but each has a room to himself."[4]

Yet there was nothing tragedy-ridden about Bagehot, either in his person or in his ideas. The point about the twice-born, and pre-eminently about Bagehot, is that the "dark realities" are only one-half of reality—we all have rooms to ourselves but we do also come down to dinner. Norman St. John-Stevas, his biographer and editor, distinguished between Bagehot the "mystic" and Bagehot the "man of the world," the one revealing itself in his private life, the other in his writings.[5] But this was to deny the peculiar quality of the man and the genius of his work. For

1. Mrs. Russell Barrington, *Life of Walter Bagehot* (London, 1914), p. 11.
2. "Shelley," *Literary Studies* (Everyman's edn.; London, 1911), I, 67.
3. Bagehot, *Historical Essays*, ed. Norman St. John-Stevas (Anchor edn.; New York, 1965), p. vii.
4. "Shakespeare," *Literary Studies*, I, 134.
5. *Historical Essays*, p. xv.

the characteristic of both was the ability to combine the disparate, to keep in focus at the same time both sides of the moon, to be, as he said of himself, "cheerful but not sanguine."[6] Bagehot was as much a man of the world as one could want; a man, indeed, of many worlds—banking, journalism, literature, and politics; and it was his practical experience of these worlds that gave him his remarkable intellectual power. If his writings abound in irony and paradox, it is because his sense of reality was multifaceted, shaped by the simple and the complex, the commonplace and the recondite. "Taken as a whole," he declared, "the universe is absurd"—in evidence of which he attested the disparity between "the human mind and its employments": "How can a soul be a merchant? What relation to an immortal being have the price of linseed, the fall of butter, the tare on tallow, or the brokerage on hemp? Can an undying creature debit 'petty expenses' and charge for 'carriage paid'?" To which his answer was: "The soul ties its shoes; the mind washes its hands in a basin. All is incongruous."[7]

This sense of incongruity and absurdity permeated his writings on history, politics, society, and literature. It was this that permitted him to see private vices in the guise of public virtues, to appreciate the irony of the fact that "much stupidity" might be "the most essential mental quality for a free people";[8] or to understand why it was that the statesman who carried the first Reform Act might have done so precisely because he was so bad a speaker and so slow of mind in an assembly that prized facile speech and quick wit.[9] By the same token he saw private virtues func-

6. Alistair Buchan, *The Spare Chancellor* (London, 1959), p. 107, quoting letter by Bagehot (Dec. 1, 1857).
7. "The First Edinburgh Reviewers," *Literary Studies*, I, 31.
8. "Letters on the French Coup d'Etat of 1851," *Historical Essays*, p. 403.
9. "Lord Althorp and the Reform Act of 1832," *Historical Essays*, pp. 166-7.

tioning as public vices. The intellectual lucidity and sobriety that were the great distinctions of one Liberal politician, Bagehot suggested, were also serious political defects, since the absence of passion in himself caused him to mistake the passion in others: "Such extreme calmness of mind is not favorable to a statesman; it is good to be without vices, but it is not good to be without temptations."[1]

"The world is often wiser than any philosopher," Bagehot rebuked one philosopher (John Austin) who had contempt for the "formidable community of fools" who made up the world.[2] For the same reason he rebuked the poets and writers who failed to draw upon the common experience and wisdom of the world. Shelley, for example, was too fanciful, ethereal, "unconditioned" by reality. "Before a man can imagine what will seem to be realities, he must be familiar with what are realities."[3] Shelley lacked that familiarity. "We fancy his mind placed in the light of thought, with pure subtle fancies playing to and fro. On a sudden an impulse arises; it is alone, and has nothing to contend with; . . . it bolts forward into action."[4] He was like a child who thought that anyone who was bad was very bad indeed, that anyone who did evil wished to do so, had a special impulse to do so, as the child himself felt such an impulse. And like the child, he could not conceive of the mature adult with a "struggling kind of character," who gave way to good or bad or a combination of both only after a conflict within his own double nature.[5] Shelley's poetic characters displayed the same kind of single-minded, overriding impulse that he himself exhibited in his self-styled "passion for reforming mankind":

1. "Sir George Cornewall Lewis," *Biographical Studies* (London, 1889), p. 219.
2. Ibid., p. 237.
3. "Shelley," *Literary Studies*, I, 83.
4. Ibid., I, 68–9.
5. Ibid., I, 76.

No society, however organized, would have been too strong for him to attack. He would not have paused. The impulse was upon him. He would have been ready to preach that mankind were to be 'free, equal, pure, and wise,'—in favour of 'justice, and truth, and time, and the world's natural sphere,'—in the Ottoman Empire, or to the Czar, or to George III. Such truths were independent of time and place and circumstance; some time or other, something, or somebody (his faith was a little vague), would most certainly intervene to establish them.[6]

That this was not simply an attack on Shelley's radicalism is evident from the similar charge Bagehot brought against the Tory Southey. Where Shelley's lack of common wisdom made him prone to intellectual impulsiveness, the same failing on Southey's part led to academicism and mechanical professionalism. Southey was like the German professor who could apply himself to any subject because he did not feel the need to know more of that subject than other writers had told him. "The reason why so few good books are written," Bagehot commented, "is that so few people that can write know anything." The professional thought it enough to read and write; he did not feel it his job to think or feel or know with any intimacy and depth. Bagehot's description of Southey was a damning portrait of the writer as professional: "He wrote poetry (as if anybody could) before breakfast; he read during breakfast. He wrote history until dinner; he corrected proof sheets between dinner and tea; he wrote an essay for the *Quarterly* afterwards."[7]

What Bagehot said of Southey in criticism—that he wrote poetry before breakfast—a more typical Victorian intellectual might have said in praise. Indeed Bagehot pitted himself against precisely the type of a Leslie Stephen who

6. Ibid., I, 69.
7. "Shakespeare," *Literary Studies*, I, 122.

took common sense to be a justification for philistinism. Bagehot's essay on the early *Edinburgh Review* could well have been a critique of his own generation, who shared the *Edinburgh*'s view of literature, art, and common sense.[8] It was no accident, he held, that men of this view should have created the genre of popular, ephemeral literature that was so well suited to the railway age—a magazine to be procured at a railway stall, perused en route, and disposed of at the end of the line. "People take their literature in morsels, as they take sandwiches in a journey."[9] And like the box lunch, the essays were meant to be tasty, digestible, and agreeable to all palates. It was assumed that all men—all literate men, at any rate—had the capacity to absorb the same fare, and that all ideas could be dished up in the same manner. Both the writer and the reader profited from this tidy arrangement: the writer because it permitted him to "write an article on everything," as was his boast;[1] and the reader because such an article was bound to be written, not out of condescension but out of necessity, in a form that he could most readily assimilate.

The virtues of the *Edinburgh Review*, Bagehot conceded, were considerable, particularly in the beginning. Against the Tory's "stupid adherence to the status quo," it brought to bear a cool, collected, quiet, practical, "improving" Whiggism.[2] But this cool intelligence spawned its

---

8. It is interesting, in this connection, to read Stephen's essay on Bagehot. While generally appreciative (of Bagehot's ability, for example, to enliven so dry a subject as the British Constitution), Stephen criticized his "excessive tendency to theorize" and his lapses into "cynicism"—defined as a failure to be simple, straight-forward, and "manly." (Stephen, *Studies of a Biographer* [London, 1902], III, 165, 157.) Stephen's essay on the *Edinburgh Review* is remarkably similar to Bagehot's in its judgments but significantly different in analysis.

9. *Literary Studies*, I, 2.

1. Ibid., I, 22.

2. Ibid., I, 14.

own variety of conservatism. Its "firm and placid manliness"[3] (Bagehot might have been quoting Stephen here) rejected zeal, eccentricity, and novelty, whether in the service of poetry, philosophy, religion, or politics. "This will never do"—the famous opening words of Lord Jeffrey's review of Wordsworth's "Excursion"—might have been used, were in effect used, on other occasions to condemn similarly uncongenial effusions. "So in all time," Bagehot commented, "will the lovers of polished Liberalism speak, concerning the intense and lonely prophet."[4]

"A clear, precise, discriminating intellect shrinks at once from the symbolic, the unbounded, the indefinite. The misfortune is that mysticism is true."[5] Thus Bagehot distinguished himself from both the radical rationalism of a Shelley and the liberal rationalism of a Sydney Smith. Shelley lacked not only the common sense that would have made him appreciate the complexities of human nature and social life, but also the "converting intuition" that turned men from the world without to the contemplation of a world within, "from the things which are seen to the realities which are not seen." He could so easily dismiss the idea of God because he was deficient in the "haunting, abiding, oppressive moral feeling" that was part of the reality of most men's inner lives and that made them recep-

3. Ibid., I, 19.
4. Ibid., I, 25. It is a measure of the distance we—and popular culture—have traveled that the ephemera of that age should appear to us today to be of the most exemplary solidity. Those "morsels" to be consumed casually in the course of a railway journey consisted of 20,000- to 35,000-word articles, with the magazine as a whole the equivalent of a good-sized volume. And we can hardly fail to admire the elegance of style and urbanity of manner with which those tidbits were dispensed, or the impressive number who consumed them. (The *Edinburgh Review* had a circulation of over 10,000, in a literate population of perhaps 100,000.) Yet Bagehot was right, from the perspective of his time if not entirely of ours. Jeffrey's "This will never do" was no aberration; it was the cry of the unregenerate philistine.
5. Ibid., 5, 23.

tive to the idea of God.[6] Similarly Sydney Smith was too good a liberal to be much of a divine—by which Bagehot meant a liberal in tone and temper rather than party affiliation: "Somebody has defined Liberalism as the spirit of the world. It represents its genial enjoyment, its wise sense, its steady judgment, its preference of the near to the far, of the seen to the unseen; it represents, too, its shrinking from difficult dogma, from stern statement, from imperious superstition."[7] The only kind of religion congenial to this type of liberal was a "natural religion," a "plain religion." Awe, dread, mystery were not for him. "You cannot imagine a classical Isaiah; you cannot fancy a Whig St. Dominic; there is no such thing as a Liberal Augustine."[8]

The motif running through each of Bagehot's literary essays was the two sides of the moon, the double nature of man, the dual aspect of reality. One writer was rebuked for not sharing the common experiences of man, another for not probing deeply enough into his own soul, but both came to the same thing because no one could truly know himself without knowing others or others without knowing himself. Similarly, reality and unreality were symbiotically joined, uniting the things seen with those unseen. Shakespeare was a master of reality, as that word is commonly understood; but he was also, and by the same token, a master of "Such shaping fantasies as apprehend/More than cool reason ever comprehends." It was the immaturity of Shelley that made him look on the material world as a "preposterous imposture";[9] and the wisdom of Cowper to see that "the ludicrous is in some sort the imagination of common life."[1] The tragedy of Clough was that he was unable to come to terms with the preposterous and ludi-

6. Ibid., I, 81–2.
7. Ibid., I, 27.
8. Ibid., I, 34.
9. Mr. Clough's Poems," *Literary Studies*, II, 273.
1. "Cowper," *Literary Studies*, I, 260.

crous, with the normal human condition of making the best of both worlds, with the usual compromise by which "we know that we see as in a glass darkly, but still we look on the glass."[2]

If one looks at the sheer quantity of Bagehot's writings and the variety of subjects to which he addressed himself, one might be tempted to suspect him of the same superficial fluency that he found in the *Edinburgh Review*. What redeemed him, however, was his point of view—or rather, his double point of view. This duality was not an intellectual strategy, the strategy of the disarming admission, of the lulling counterpoint of "on the one hand" and "on the other." It was a coherent, compelling vision that inevitably brought with it a complexity, subtlety, and depth that were, equally inevitably, lacking in most of the famous Reviews.

In Bagehot's political writings, the terms of this duality were common and uncommon, populace and statesman, public opinion and political wisdom. What is remarkable is not only the inseparability of the two factors, but also that he should have made so much of the first. More than any other writer engaged in discourse of this order, he persistently invoked such concepts as "popular opinion," "public opinion," "the public mind," "popular sentiment," "popular imagination," the "sense of the country" . . . And this not only in respect to the England of his own time, when it might be said that the common people were finally coming into their own as a power so that their opinions were becoming of some moment, but in respect to every period and subject he dealt with. Macaulay has been justly esteemed for his famous third chapter on the "State of England in 1685." But where Macaulay confined the people to this one chapter and rarely permitted them to

2. Ibid., II, 271.

intrude into the rest of his narrative, Bagehot gave them free range over the whole of history, bringing them into the limelight in the most unexpected times and places. This constant invocation of the populace is even more striking in view of the fact that his most memorable political writings (apart from *The English Constitution* and *Physics and Politics*) were essays on individual statesmen.

The theme of each of these essays was the relation of its hero to the public, of political wisdom to common sense. Thus Bolingbroke did not share the prejudice against the House of Hanover felt by the "unthinking people of the common sort," but he made himself the organ of that prejudice; "he became at once important in Parliament, because he was the eloquent spokesman of many inaudible persons."[3] Pitt's great gift was the ability to express "in a more than ordinary manner the true feelings and sentiments of ordinary men; not their superficial notions, nor their coarser sentiments, for with these any inferior man may deal, but their most intimate nature, that which in their highest moments is most truly themselves."[4] Burke, on the other hand, far more brilliant than Pitt, had the defect of his genius: in his mind "great ideas were a supernatural burden, a superincumbent inspiration; he saw a great truth, and he saw nothing else."[5] Adam Smith popularized political science "in the only sense in which it can be popularized without being spoiled; that is, he has put certain broad conclusions into the minds of hard-headed men, which are all which they need know, and all which they for the most part will ever care for."[6] Palmerston "was not a common man, but a common man might have been cut out of him"; and he had the good sense to know that he would succeed only so long as he kept faith with the

3. *Historical Essays*, p. 12.
4. Ibid., p. 73.
5. Ibid., p. 72.
6. Ibid., p. 106.

"common part of his mind."[7] Disraeli's misfortune was in being a political romantic: he preferred to deal with "ideal measures" and "ideal heroes," when he should have been trying to get at "the heart of a deep national conviction."[8]

If it was incumbent on the statesman to respect the wisdom of the common people, the political thinker could do no less. Yet Bagehot himself has often been charged with just this failing. His most recent biographer and editor (himself, curiously, a Conservative member of parliament) has said that Bagehot had "no sympathy with the masses of men, and his conservatism sprang in part from lack of compassion."[9] *The English Constitution* in particular has often been read in this light. The main thesis of that book—the distinction between the "dignified" and the "efficient" parts of the constitution, the one necessary for the gratification of the common people, the other for the working of the government—is assumed to be condescending and demeaning. But the condescension may be on the part of those who make this assumption, who assume that the populace is demeaned by such a description, demeaned by the mere fact of a distinction between the two aspects of the constitution. Bagehot himself, it may be claimed, was more respectful of the populace than those who found the distinction disrespectful. Indeed the common people in his account were credited with a peculiarly "intellectual," one might say, reverence for ideas. They were interested more in the theatricalities than in the mundane workings of government because they saw the theatricalities as the "embodiments of the greatest human ideas." They refused to become "absorbed in the useful" because they did not like "anything so poor." They could not be appealed to on the basis of material wants, unless those wants were thought to be the result of tyranny. They were willing, in fact, to

7. Ibid., p. 216.
8. Ibid., pp. 280-1.
9. Ibid., p. xvi.

sacrifice their material goods, their very persons, "for what is called an idea—for some attraction which seems to transcend reality, which aspires to elevate men by an interest higher, deeper, wider than that of ordinary life." It was the upper classes, by implication, who were so "poor" in mind and soul as to be contented with the useful, the material, the efficient.[1]

Bagehot minced no words. The common people were "stupid." But their stupidity was their virtue—and their wisdom as well. For not only did it spare them the futile turmoil and suicidal excesses of a more nimble-minded people such as the French; it also meant that they were never taken in by the typically French fallacy of supposing that political problems could be solved rationally, by the criteria of consistency, simplicity, or logical coherence. And English statesmen had enough in common with the people to feel the force and the good sense of their stupidity. Bagehot was not merely saying, in the fashion of later "elitist" theorists, that the good statesman was one who knew best how to exploit or manipulate the masses in the interests of good government—his, his class', or perhaps the philosopher-statesman's idea of good government. He was saying that the masses themselves had an instinct for good government which the statesman was bound to respect.

Yet the statesman had not merely to respect the people; he had also to respect himself—the uncommon as well as the common part of his mind. "An English statesman in the present day lives by following public opinion; he may profess to guide it a little; he may hope to modify it in detail; he may help to exaggerate and to develop it; but he hardly hopes for more."[2] For this very reason, however, because public opinion was so compelling and common sense so urgent, the statesman had to know when to assert

1. *The English Constitution* (World's Classics edn.; London, 1952), pp. 6–7.
2. *Historical Essays*, p. 260.

himself against the public and pit his own good sense against the common sense. This was all the more difficult for the "constitutional statesman" (democratic statesman, we would say today), so much of whose mind and time were necessarily given over to the function of persuasion, the oratorical attempt to modify and convert public opinion.

In the role of orator, Bagehot saw the essential ambivalence of the statesman. It was by means of oratory that the statesman tried to mediate not only between the public and himself but also between the two parts of his own mind. And in doing so, he exposed his great weakness. "We know that the popular instinct suspects the judgment of great orators; we know that it does not give them credit for patient equanimity; and the popular instinct is right."[3] The popular instinct, that is, correctly suspected that the orator was too subservient to popular opinion. Here again the people displayed their peculiar wisdom and virtue: their wisdom in being suspicious of the orator, and their virtue in finding cause for suspicion not so much in the attempt of the orator to impose upon them his own opinions as in his excessive solicitude for theirs.

The oratorical process, Bagehot concluded, was a necessary but profoundly disorganizing one, tempting the statesman to shift and trim in obedience to a fluctuating opinion, to advocate what he might privately dislike, to oppose at one time what he might defend at another, to defend or oppose without sufficient reflection, to lose sight of the larger design. It was particularly disorganizing to a statesman like Gladstone, whose mind was naturally "impressible, impetuous, and unfixed," "defective in the tenacity of first principle," inclined to an "elastic heroism."[4] And it was particularly dangerous at a time like Gladstone's, when

3. Ibid., p. 253.
4. Ibid., pp. 261, 254, 248.

what was wanted were deliberative, constructive, far-ranging policies, an adherence to settled principle rather than an accommodation to transient popular moods.

Bagehot's essay on Peel is a brilliant commentary on this theme. It is also a perfect specimen of his thought, a triumph of social, political, and historical analysis. No Marxist, neo-Marxist, or sociologist could hope to improve upon this account of the Lancashire businessman *qua* statesman. The son of a baronet, educated at Harrow and Christ Church, a Tory MP at the age of twenty-one, personally dissociated from the source of his fortune, Peel nevertheless showed, in the manner, language, and substance of his politics, the ineradicable "grain of the middle class," the stamp of the "transacting and trading multitude."[5] It was from this class that he derived the characteristic traits of the constitutional statesman. A "man of common opinions and uncommon abilities," having the "powers of a first-rate man and the creed of a second-rate man," he managed never to be in advance of his time but always in step with it.[6] He was a great administrator with the energy, appetite for detail, patience, tact, and adaptability of the businessman—and an absence of those "fixed opinions" that might inhibit these talents.[7] And he had the mode of oratory appropriate to his class. He could not rival the elegance, fluency, wit, or classical embellishments of an older generation of parliamentary orator, but he was a master of "middle-class eloquence," the rhetoric of exposition and arithmetic detail.[8] His oratory reflected his ideas, which were not so much his own ideas as the "quiet leavings" of other men's ideas.[9] And because his intelli-

5. Ibid., pp. 190–1.
6. Ibid., pp. 182, 185.
7. Ibid., p. 196.
8. Ibid., p. 211.
9. Ibid., p. 193.

gence was practical rather than speculative, his rhetoric was "specious," giving the impression of plausibility rather than truth.[1]

In other times—as in Gladstone's—these qualities would have been inadequate, even fatal. Peel lived at a more fortunate time, when his mind and manner were fitting to his tasks. Most of the necessary legislation involved problems of administration and regulation; and most of the necessary reforms were destructive rather than constructive, requiring the repeal of outmoded laws (Corn Laws, anti-Catholic laws, criminal statutes). In Peel, England found the precise virtues and vices that suited it:

> If we bear in mind the whole of these circumstances; if we picture in our minds a nature at once active and facile, easily acquiring its opinions from without, not easily devising them from within, a large placid adaptive intellect, devoid of irritable intense originality, prone to forget the ideas of yesterday, inclined to the ideas of today—if we imagine a man so formed cast early into absorbing, exhausting industry of detail, with work enough to fill up life, with action of itself enough to render speculation almost impossible—placed too in a position unsuited to abstract thought, of which the conventions and rules require that a man should feign other men's thoughts, should impugn his own opinions—we shall begin to imagine a conscientious man destitute of convictions on the occupations of his life—to comprehend the character of Sir Robert Peel. . . .
>
> . . . So long as constitutional statesmanship is what it is now, so long as its function consists in recording the views of a confused nation, so long as success in it is confined to minds plastic, changeful, administrative—we must hope for no better man. You have excluded the profound thinker; you must be content with what you can obtain—the business gentleman.[2]

1. Ibid., p. 201.
2. Ibid., pp. 203, 213.

Lancashire, Bagehot observed on another occasion, was sometimes called "America-and-water"; but he suspected that it was "America and very little water."[3] One hundred years later it may strike us as pure, unadulterated America. In all the discussions of "style" provoked by the American presidency in recent years, in our painful recognition of the anomalies of intellectual gratification and political effectiveness, no one has brought to the analysis of the American situation the profound common sense of Bagehot on Peel. Indeed it may be that no one has come so close to describing the American president as Bagehot did in describing Peel.

3. Ibid., p. 241.

JAMES ANTHONY FROUDE:

A FORGOTTEN WORTHY

THE HISTORIAN OF IDEAS is apt to complain of the company he keeps. Since the best minds of an age are rarely the most representative of that age, he must often deliberately cultivate the second best. Fortunately in Victorian England the gap between the two was not so large as it is today, and the second best then might compare favorably with the best now. The historian forced to associate with T. H. Huxley rather than Darwin, Arthur Clough rather than Matthew Arnold, or Froude rather than Carlyle, has little cause for grievance. Things might be much worse.

If Froude lacked the divine madness of Carlyle, he shared his hero's ebullience and passion. His twelve-volume *History of England from the Fall of Wolsey to the Defeat of the Spanish Armada* has not the originality or power of Carlyle's *French Revolution*, but it is sufficiently impressive and provocative in its own way. His *Life of Carlyle* is every bit as fascinating as Carlyle's *History of Frederick the Great* (but this may be as much a tribute to the subject as to the author). And his *Short Studies on Great Subjects*, while hardly as devastating as Carlyle's *Latter-Day Pamphlets*, engaged the enemy along a broader front. Thus, the disciple was free of the usual stigmata of the epigone. Even his personal life had a dramatic quality rivalling that of the master. The element of marital scandal, to be sure, was missing—although even here, by making public the facts about Carlyle's marriage, Froude made himself a partner to the scandal. More agonizing, however, than any tale of marital travail is the horror story of Froude's childhood.

Recent biographies of Dickens, Kipling, and Orwell have taught us to suspect that childhood horrors recounted as fact may be the horrors of fantasy. In Froude's case, although the suspicion of fantasy can never be stilled, it must be said that what independent evidence there is confirms his own account.[1] The story has all the clichés of a Victorian melodrama, a genre we have evidently not taken seriously enough. Froude's father was an archdeacon and squire with a reputation even among his friends for coldness and severity—what one associate charitably called "Stoicism." Mrs. Froude produced eight children in spite of her failing health, and died when her youngest, Anthony, was two;[2] the boy later regretted that although she was reputed to have been a great beauty, he never knew what she looked like because his father refused to have a portrait of her or even to speak of her. Anthony himself was sickly at birth and throughout his youth, despite such bracing measures as being plunged into the icy water of a spring each morning before breakfast (this at the age of three). "We were a Spartan family," he later explained,[3] remembering how he had been whipped for infantile misdemeanors and punished for his childish fears.

1. The two-volume biography by Waldo Hilary Dunn, *James Anthony Froude* (Oxford, 1961–3), intersperses Froude's "Autobiographical Fragment" with his letters and a commentary by Dunn. Most of the following account is derived from the "Autobiographical Fragment."

2. James Anthony was familiarly known as Anthony, and his brother Richard Hurrell as Hurrell.

3. Dunn, I, 17.

Something more than Spartanism, however, was at work here, particularly on the part of his oldest brother, Hurrell. It was ostensibly to cure young Anthony of cowardice that Hurrell (then seventeen or eighteen years old to Anthony's two or three) regaled him with stories of a child-eating monster dwelling in the hollow beyond the house, or held him upside down by the heels so that his head scraped the bottom of a particularly loathsome toad-filled stream, or took him out in a boat on the river and put him overboard in deep water supposedly to teach him to swim. Hurrell Froude, remembered today as the intimate of John Henry Newman and the golden boy of the Oxford Movement, was the first-born, beautiful, brilliant, the favorite of his father, and adored even by his victims. Only his mother resisted his charms. In a remarkable letter written just before her death, Mrs. Froude confessed her anxieties about her eldest son (then seventeen years old), who was "very much disposed to find his own amusement in teasing and vexing others," in what he himself called "funny torment-ing."[4] She obviously did not know the extent to which he carried this tormenting, but she had sufficient evidence in his mistreatment of herself as well as of the children, in his wild alternation of moods, and in his apparently ungovernable impulses, to fear for his sanity.

Geoffrey Faber, a historian of the Oxford Movement and a descendant of one of its most eminent members, thought that Mrs. Froude was not only excessively anxious but also responsible for the very excesses she feared. Mrs. Froude, he wrote, "was not free from the special vice of parents, the vice, namely, of trying to regulate their children's behavior by their own low standards of vitality." And it was because of her "low standards of vitality" that Hurrell Froude grew up to think of his "vigorous in-stincts" as "objects of moral suspicion," and eventually

4. Ibid., I, 21-3.

became the tortured soul portrayed in his diary.[5] (The allusion is to the homosexual and sado-masochistic tendencies revealed in his private writings.) One can sympathize with Hurrell Froude in his distress and with Geoffrey Faber in his attempt to account for that distress. Yet one must also sympathize with the mother who, by any standards of vitality, would have been dismayed by her son's behavior, and with the younger children who were the innocent victims of their brother's tormented—and tormenting—nature.

Anthony Froude must often have asked himself, while experiencing and recounting his youth, which was the more intolerable: torture suffered at the hands of strangers or that inflicted by one's closest kin. For he was amply familiar with both. As one of that despised caste known as "scholars" at Westminster, he endured the normal afflictions of hunger, flogging, and humiliation, plus such more exotic sport as being forcibly intoxicated, having his legs set on fire to make him dance, or being awakened by hot stubs of cigars pressed into his face. He was finally sent home after almost four years—not, however, because he was miserable, but rather because he was judged to be uneducable. For two more years he existed in a state of purgatory, suffering the silent contempt of his family, without companion or occupation. When his father then informed him that, for the sake of his "future," he would be sent to Oxford, he was pleased but surprised, having always assumed that his only future was an early death. Fortunately, death was one of the few things he did not fear: "When people said that it would be dreadful to appear in the presence of God, it seemed to me that we were in the presence of God already, and in our relations with so awful a being there could not be a more or a less."[6]

5. Faber, *Oxford Apostles* (New York, 1934), p. 199.
6. Dunn, I, 43.

(It was in the presence of his father that this thought came to him; earlier he had said that his feeling toward his father was "resolving itself into dread."[7])

Death was his salvation—but as it happened the death was that of Hurrell. Hurrell died before Anthony entered Oxford, so that although his memory was very much alive, Anthony was at least spared his physical presence. Oxford was pure joy and liberation. In his exuberance, Anthony even fell in love, and had already received the consent of the girl and her parents when his father, grieving over the death of Hurrell and resenting Anthony's happiness, deliberately broke up the engagement. It was at this point that Anthony finally, consciously rebelled. Until then he had acquiesced in the low opinion of him shared by schoolmates, schoolmasters, brother, and father. Now, however, he resolved that "Fate"—in the person of his father—would not master him: "Reviewing my past life, observing where I had laid myself open to the enemy, [I] determined to defy him."[8] Defiance meant proving himself, and that, in turn, meant an intensive course of work and study. In a few years he was rewarded with a fellowship at Exeter and a reputation as one of Oxford's most promising scholars.

The Oxford Movement was then at its height, and Newman and his colleagues seemed well on their way to revolutionizing—Romanizing, their opponents had it—the English Church. As a challenge to rationalism and skepticism, and in affirmation of a faith that could create and credit miracles, Newman initiated the series on the *Lives of the Saints*. He invited Froude's collaboration, perhaps as much out of respect for the memory of Hurrell as for Anthony. The episode is full of curiosities and ironies. Newman evidently did not know that Froude, having already dis-

7. Ibid., I, 40.
8. Ibid., I, 58.

covered the attractions of Evangelicalism, of Carlyle and Goethe, of the Tudor monarchs and Protestant Reformers, could hardly have been very sympathetic to his project. Yet in spite of all this, Newman was perhaps less displeased with the result than has been supposed. We do not actually know what he thought of Froude's contribution, a life of St. Neot. He would certainly have preferred not to have it known that he had advised Froude (according to Froude's account): "Rationalize where the evidence is weak, and this will gain credibility for others, where you can show that the evidence is strong."[9] And he would surely have been much more subtle in describing the relationship between myth and history; one cannot imagine Newman saying, as Froude did at the very start of his book, that the *Lives of the Saints* were "myths, edifying stories compiled from tradition, and designed not so much to relate facts, as to produce a religious impression on the mind of the hearer."[1] Yet essentially they were in agreement. The final irony of the affair (and a perfect specimen of the myths that pass as history) is the fact that the *bon mot* which has done most to discredit the *Lives* and which is generally assumed to be the final sentence of Froude's book—"This is all, and perhaps more than all, that is known of the life of the blessed St. Neot"—does not in fact appear in that book. A different version, applied to a different saint, concluded one of the lives co-authored by Newman himself: "And this is all that is known, and more than all—yet nothing to what the angels know—of the life of a servant of God."[2]

In the same year that Newman entered the Catholic Church, Froude was being carried in the opposite direction, toward a theological skepticism that saw religion as a moral and national force rather than a metaphysical doctrine. Yet even when he was the unwitting occasion for the attack on

9. Ibid., I, 77.
1. Ibid., I, 79.
2. Ibid.

Newman that led to the writing of the *Apologia* (it was in the course of a laudatory review of Froude's *History* that Charles Kingsley alluded to Newman's disrespect for truth), Froude himself had a much more complicated view of the matter—not much less complicated than Newman's own concept of truth. He explained to Kingsley that Newman was "a man of most perfect personal truthfulness," adding that since this truthfulness was of a different order from that of ordinary men, Kingsley might be excused for misunderstanding it: "No sane person could ever have divined the workings of his mind, or could have interpreted them otherwise than you, in common with so many others, did."[3] Twenty years later, in an essay on the Oxford Movement, he again tried to mediate between the claims of Newman and Kingsley, describing how the truth of the one differed from that of the other:

> Kingsley, in truth, entirely misunderstood Newman's character. Newman's whole life had been a struggle for truth. He had neglected his own interests; he had never thought of them at all. He had brought to bear a most powerful and subtle intellect to support the convictions of a conscience which was superstitiously sensitive. His single object had been to discover what were the real relations between man and his Maker, and to shape his own conduct by the conclusions at which he arrived. To represent such a person as careless of truth was neither generous nor even reasonable. . . .
>
> Kingsley, however, had passed through his own struggles. He, too, had been affected at a distance by the agitations of the Tractarian controversy. He, like many others, had read what Newman had written about ecclesiastical miracles. The foundations of his own faith had been disturbed. He was a man of science; he knew what evidence was. He believed that Newman's methods of reasoning confounded his perceptions of truth, disregarding princi-

3. *Ibid.*, II, 306.

ples which alone led to conclusions that could be trusted in other subjects, and which, therefore, he could alone trust in religion. His feelings had been, perhaps, embittered by the intrusion of religious discord into families in which he was interested, traceable all of it to the Oxford movement. He himself had determined to try every fact which was offered for his belief by the strict rules of inductive science and courts of justice; and every other method appeared to him to be treason to his intellect and to reduce truth, where truth of facts was before everything essential, to the truth of fable, or fiction, or emotional opinion.[4]

Unfortunately, Froude was not always so detached or judicious in his judgments. In a lecture on "The Science of History," he made the remark that was later quoted against him: "It often seems to me as if History was like a child's box of letters, with which we can spell any word we please. We have only to pick out such letters as we want, arrange them as we like, and say nothing about those which do not suit our purpose."[5] This was interpreted as yet another invitation to lying—a reduction of all history to the status of the *Lives of the Saints*. But he meant by it little more than a protest against the fashionable doctrine that history could be made into a science. History was not a science, Froude insisted, for it taught only one lesson, which could as well have come from the Hebrew prophets: "that the world is built somehow on moral foundations; that, in the long run, it is well with the good; in the long run, it is ill with the wicked."[6]

Like most historian-moralists, Froude projected the morality of the present into the past. For him the best of the past, "the grandest achievement in English history," was the

4. *Short Studies on Great Subjects* (London, 1899), IV, 326-8.
5. Ibid., I, 1.
6. Ibid., I, 21.

Reformation. But the Reformation was the work of two powerful sovereigns and could only have been accomplished by them; "it could never have been brought about constitutionally, according to modern methods." Indeed, had our modern constitutional methods prevailed, neither the Reformation nor the English nation would have survived: "To the last, up to the defeat of the Armada, manhood suffrage in England would at any moment have brought back the Pope."[7]

Even to speak of manhood suffrage in this context suggests that what Froude had in mind was not Tudor England but Victorian England. Yet he was not the typical, or even atypical, Victorian Conservative. Like Carlyle, he defied such labels, his contempt for democracy and liberalism being matched only by his contempt for materialism, capitalism, and the "pig philosophy" of utilitarianism. And while he favored a strong state, he opposed the imperialist movements of his time, preferring a commonwealth to an empire. He was, in fact, neither a Liberal nor a Conservative, but simply a Carlylean—a Carlyle transposed into a later generation.

Thus one can only understand Froude's *History of England*, as one can only understand Carlyle's *History of Frederick the Great*, if one appreciates the fact that they were writing "contemporary history." Yet it is not only on account of its tendentiousness, its lack of objectivity or historical distance, that Froude's work was bitterly attacked in his time and has become something of a curiosity in ours. Even more damaging to his professional reputation was a carelessness that went beyond the deliberate selection or suppression of facts. He seemed to be constitutionally incapable of transcribing a document accurately. Thus he became the principal in one of the most acrimonious academic feuds of the century—and, as it turned out, one of the most farcical ones. For his antagonist, Edward Free-

7. Dunn, I, 202.

man, proved to be quite as unscholarly as Froude. If Freeman did not so often misquote manuscripts, it was only because he refused to consult them. Froude's biographer, loyally defending his hero's scholarship and integrity, thought it eminently just that Froude should have succeeded to one of the highest academic posts, the Regius Professorship of Modern History at Oxford—in succession, as it happened, to Freeman. Perhaps a more fitting comment on this appointment may be found in the eleventh edition of the *Encyclopædia Britannica* (the sentence has been deleted from the present, more sedate edition): "Except for a few Oxford men, who considered that historical scholarship should have been held to be a necessary qualification for the office, his appointment gave general satisfaction."[8]

Even more provocative than Froude's *History* was his biography of Carlyle. Carlyle himself once wrote, in criticism of another work: "How delicate, decent, is English biography, bless its mealy mouth."[9] As if to make sure that such would not be his own fate (or perhaps as an act of atonement), he left in his *Reminiscences* an account of his ill treatment of his wife and of her acute unhappiness. Instead of publishing it, however, he entrusted the manuscript to Froude to do with as he thought best. Froude's publication of the *Reminiscences* after Carlyle's death involved him in lawsuits and public scandal; and even his four-volume biography of Carlyle, intended as tribute, was greeted with abuse. The abuse was obviously unmerited. Yet it is not enough to say, as his biographer does, that Froude wanted nothing more than to tell the whole truth.

8. *Encyclopædia Britannica* (11th edn.; New York, 1911), XI, 253.
9. Froude, *Thomas Carlyle: A History of the First Forty Years of His Life* (London, 1882), I, ix.

For in fact Froude entirely shared his critics' notions about respectability and the value of reticence. And certainly on other occasions—in discussing the domestic affairs of Henry VIII, for example—he managed to restrain his zeal for the whole truth. Clearly it was a much more complicated and ambivalent set of motives that made him pursue the subject of Carlyle's personal life at such cost to his own reputation and peace of mind, so that even during a tour of the West Indies he was kept awake night after night by the "Carlyle worry":

> Bad Carlyle fit on me. What my connection with Carlyle has cost me: my own prospects as a young man; later gave up *Fraser* [Magazine] because Carlyle wanted it for Allingham, and my work on Charles V so as to be free to write Carlyle's biography; then the ten years of worry before the book was finished, and the worry for the rest of my life. Bye and bye the world will thank me, but not in my own lifetime. I ought to shake the whole subject off me, but it is not easy to do. . . .
>
> . . . I know that my own heart and purpose was perfectly clear in that matter [the publication of the *Reminiscences*]. Why should I vex myself because I have infuriated a certain number of people? . . . I am surprised that the Carlyle business hangs heavy on me and spoils all.[1]

There was something "demonic" in the Carlyles, Froude once said;[2] and it was as if the demon had taken possession of Froude himself. Just as Carlyle fatally implicated Froude by making him responsible for the publication of the *Reminiscences*, so Froude bequeathed to his children the manuscript of *My Relations with Carlyle* with its startling disclosure of Carlyle's sexual impotence—at the same time instructing them in his will to destroy all his manuscripts, letters, and papers. His instructions, of course, were dis-

1. Dunn, II, 550-1.
2. Ibid., II, 497.

obeyed and the book was published, with the predictable results.

A demonic subject is worthy of a demonic biographer: Frederick the Great found his in Carlyle and Carlyle in Froude. The line of succession has unhappily broken off here. Although Froude's biographer, W. H. Dunn, has devoted over thirty-five years to his hero, had access to Froude's private papers, and even composed his work on Froude's own writing table, the demon has evaded him. He quotes Carlyle on the delicate, decent, mealy-mouthed biography, but is himself capable of writing: "As a decent family man, Froude naturally objected to a celibate clergy."[3] (But not, apparently, to a profligate monarchy.) And although we are assured that Froude's life is "an open book" and that "there were no skeletons in his closet"[4] (much of the writing is of this order), there is in fact at least one skeleton tucked away: a son described in Froude's letters as "made for dishonor," one "with whom no good could be done"—of whom we learn no more (in a footnote) than his name, the date and place of his death, and his occupation at that time.[5] (Froude tried to ignore the boy as much as his biographer did. Announcing the birth of a later child, he worried about the reaction of his older daughters but failed to mention this son.)

The same piety is evident in the treatment of Froude's writings, his critics getting short shrift and Froude being defended on every count. But such piety is as self-defeating for the biographer as it is denigrating for the subject. To deny the legitimacy of criticism is to make meaningless the controversies that raged about Froude, to deprive his life of its drama, and to render his demon impotent. And above

3. Ibid., I, 8.
4. Ibid., II, xiii–xiv.
5. Ibid., II, 437, 613.

all, to try to elevate Froude above Carlyle ("Froude," we are told, "emerges as an outstandingly more able and representative man than Carlyle")[6] is as sacrilegious to Froude's memory as to Carlyle's. For what then are we to make of Froude's reverence for Carlyle and of his demonic obsession with him?

One of Froude's *Short Studies* is devoted to "England's Forgotten Worthies"—the seamen who contributed to the greatness of Elizabethan England. It would be enough if Froude were restored to us not as one of the giants of Victorian England but as one of her Forgotten Worthies.

6. Ibid., I, 9.

IX

JOHN BUCHAN: THE LAST VICTORIAN

JOHN BUCHAN—novelist, biographer, historian, member of parliament, Governor-General of Canada, and, in his final years, Lord Tweedsmuir of Elsfield—died in 1940, one of the last articulate representatives of the old England. He is the paradigm (the parody, some would have it) of a species of English gentleman now very nearly extinct. The manners and morals celebrated in his books, the social prejudices unwittingly disclosed in them, and the attitudes and philosophy suggested by them have already acquired the faded tint of a period piece. Before they vanish altogether, it may be interesting to take pause, to inquire into an ethos that for some is an embarrassing memory, for others a remembrance of lost grandeur.

There is indeed matter for embarrassment in Buchan's novels. There is the clean, good life which comes with early rising, cold baths, and long immersion in fog and damp, in contrast to the red-eyed, liverish, sluggish, dissolute town dweller. There is the casual bravery, classically understated, of his heroes. ("There's nothing much wrong with me. . . . A shell dropped beside me and damaged my foot. They say they'll have to cut it off."[1]) There is the blithe provincialism and amateurishness of his spy-adventurer who complains that the natives in a Kurdish bazaar do not understand any "civilised tongue," of his member of parliament who cannot pronounce "Boche" names and confuses Poincaré with Mussolini, of the cabinet minister who will not be bothered to read the newspapers while on vacation.[2] There is the penchant for sports that requires every hero (and every respectable villain) to be a first-class shot, and looks upon politics, espionage, and war alike as an opportunity to practice good English sportsmanship. Richard Hannay, his principal hero, is much distressed at not "playing the game" when he abuses the hospitality of a particularly heinous villain; elsewhere he permits a German agent, plotting to spread anthrax germs through the British army, to escape rather than ignobly shoot him in the back; and another hero, Sandy Arbuthnot, during a tremendous cavalry attack involving Cossack, Turkish, German, and British troops, can be heard crying, "Oh, well done our side!"[3]

Even more reminiscent of the English public school boy is the curious blurring of sexual lines. All Buchan's heroes turn out to have "something girlish" about them. A husky mountain guide has hair "as flaxen as a girl's"; Peter Pienaar, the uncouth Boer adventurer, has a face "as gentle as a girl's," as does a general in the same novel; Sandy Arbuthnot has "a pair of brown eyes like a pretty girl's"; and a six and-a-half foot Negro chieftain has hands "more like a high-bred woman's than a man's."[4] Even some of his

1. *Mr. Standfast* (Penguin edn.; London, 1956), p. 312.

2. *Greenmantle* (Penguin edn.; London, 1956), p. 127; *John Macnab* (Penguin edn.; London, 1956), pp. 123, 143.

3. *Greenmantle*, p. 269.

4. *Mountain Meadow* [English title: *Sick Heart River*] (Boston, 1941), p. 155; *Greenmantle*, pp. 41, 22; *Prester John* (New York, 1938), p. 111.

historical heroes have the same ambiguous sexuality, Augustus, for example, having "features so delicately modelled as to be almost girlish."⁵ Conversely, his heroines have more than a little of the boy in them: boyish hips, boyish stride, wholesome boyish manners and interests. Even these reassuring qualities, however, cannot entirely allay the unease of the hero. When Hannay, then well in his forties, meets the bewitching Hilda von Einem he is thrown into panic at the thought of sitting beside her: "I had never been in a motor-car with a lady before, I felt like a fish on a dry sandbank."⁶ His friend, Archie Roylance, had also been "as shy as a woodcock" of those "mysterious and unintelligible" creatures. "Fresh and unstaled by disillusion," he finally falls in love with Janet, but he succumbs, the author proudly reports, not to the vulgar charms of "swelling bosoms and pouting lips and soft curves and languishing eyes"; the fresh and unstaled phrases that come to his lips are "jolly," "clean-run," "a regular sportswoman," and, as an afterthought, "amazingly good-looking."⁷ Occasionally, Buchan might be found to poke fun at this priggishness. Of Walter Scott he once said: "For women he had an old-fashioned reverence, and . . . regarded them very much as a toast to be drunk after King and Constitution." Nevertheless, he respected Scott's diffidence: "I do not suggest the severe doctrine that no man can write intimately of sex without forfeiting his title to gentility, but I do say that for Scott's type of gentleman to do so would have been impossible without a dereliction of standards."⁸

So far the Buchan ethos amuses more than it offends. It becomes displeasing when private foibles begin to impinge

5. *Augustus* (Boston, 1937), p. 4.
6. *Greenmantle*, p. 171.
7. *John Macnab*, pp. 194–5, 139, 53.
8. *Homilies and Recreations* (London, 1926), pp. 29–30.

upon public morality. The most serious item in Richard Usborne's indictment of Buchan (in *Clubland Heroes*[9]) is Buchan's preoccupation with success, his top-of-the-form ethic. A dinner party in a Buchan novel assembles a typical assortment of guests: Bonson Jane "had been a noted sportsman and was still a fine polo player; his name was a household word in Europe for his work in international finance, . . . it was rumoured that in the same week he had been offered the Secretaryship of State, the Presidency of an ancient University, and the control of a great industrial corporation." Simon Ravelstone is president of "one of the chief banking houses in the world," his son is making a big name for himself in lung surgery," and another guest is "about our foremost pundit, . . . there were few men alive who were his equals in classical scholarship."[1] So closed is the universe inhabited by these Calvinist-minded characters that they can agree to the precise rank and order of their success. Thus Sandy Arbuthnot is "one of the two or three most intelligent people in the world," Julius Victor is the "richest man in the world," Medina is the "best shot in England after His Majesty," Castor is the "greatest agent-provacateur in history," and there is one of whom it is said, with a fine conjunction of precision and vagueness, that "there aren't five men in the United States whose repute stands higher."[2]

Yet closer attention to the novels suggests that these marks of success are not the ends toward which his heroes —or villains—strive. They are the preconditions of their being heroes or villains at all, much as the characters in fairy tales are always the most beautiful, the most exalted, the most wicked of their kind. They are the starting points

9. London, 1953.
1. *Mountain Meadow*, pp. 23-7.
2. *Three Hostages* (Penguin edn.; London, 1956), pp. 25, 48; *Mountain Meadow*, p. 32.

for romance, not the termination. Indeed the theme of the more interesting of the novels is the ennui, the *taedium vitae* afflicting precisely those who have attained the highest state—precisely because they have attained that state. In *John Macnab*, three of the most eminent men in England, dispirited by a surfeit of success, deliberately engage in an adventure in illegality in order to court exposure and disgrace. And in *Mountain Meadow*, a famous American financier and an equally famous English barrister leave their comfortable establishments to suffer pain and death in the far north. All Buchan's heroes are periodically beset by fatigue and lassitude, a "death-wish" that is overcome by divesting themselves of their urban identities—success being an urban condition—and donning the shabby, anonymous clothes of the countryman. Only when the perils of nature and of the chase have roughened up the smooth patina of success, leaving the body scarred and the mind tormented, can they resume their normal lives and identities.

If Buchan's heroes are not, in fact, obsessed by success in the vulgar sense, neither are they the mindless philistines that casual memory would have us think. It is true that Sandy, revisiting Oxford in 1938, complains that the youth have become "a bit too much introverted—isn't that the filthy word?"[3] (Too *much* introverted: if Sandy is obliged to use the filthy word, he at least takes care to use the right syntax.) Yet Sandy himself is far from being an extrovert. He is given to spells of moodiness and despair, to a never-ending quest for an unattainable grail and a new identity (hence his predilection for exotic disguises).

Indeed, the introvert-intellectual is the hero of several of Buchan's works. One of these, Launcelot Make in *Mr. Standfast*, is so far gone in introversion and intellectualism as to be a pacifist. He is represented in the opening of the

3. *Mountain Meadow*, p. 7.

book as the stock intellectual, sallow of complexion and red of eye, partial to modern poetry and modern art. Yet by the end of the book, as a result of one of those typical reversals of which Buchan, like other romancers, is fond (his critics seem not to realize that the ostensible truths of the prologue have turned into the half-truths of the epilogue), Wake has emerged as the hero. He has abandoned neither his intellectualism nor his pacifism and is still incapable of the easy sentiments of patriotism and duty:

> I see more than other people see, and I feel more. That's the curse on me. You're a happy man and you get things done, because you only see one side of a case, one thing at a time. How would you like it if a thousand strings were always tugging at you, if you saw that every course meant the sacrifice of lovely and desirable things, or even the shattering of what you know to be unreplaceable? . . . For me to fight would be worse than for another man to run away.

When he dies, after a gallant exploit, Hannay delivers his eulogy: "If the best were to be taken, he would be chosen first, for he was a big man, before whom I uncovered my head."[4]

Buchan's portraits of Montrose and Cromwell are similarly tributes to the complicated man torn by conflicting ideas and emotions who barely manages to maintain a precarious balance: Montrose, starting as a Covenanter in rebellion against the king, and ending as the "noblest Cavalier" while still a Presbyterian; Cromwell, the "practical mystic," the revolutionist with a passion for law and order, the leader given to spells of withdrawal and self-doubt.[5] In history as in fiction, his heroes are by no means the simple clean-cut men of action who shoulder their way to victory. They are sensitive souls, fated to noble failures and Pyrrhic victories.

4. *Mr. Standfast*, pp. 234, 341.
5. *Montrose* (World's Classics edn.; London, 1957), pp. 16, 422.

. . .

There is no denying that Buchan is as remote as can be from the modern intellectual in his tastes and judgments. His description of the "advanced" community of Biggleswick in *Mr. Standfast* is as much a parody of such a community as it is of the writer capable of describing and judging it as he does: the pretentious, arty folk with their gimcrack houses and "demented modish" paintings, who were determined "never to admire anything that was obviously beautiful, like a sunset or a pretty woman, but to find surprising loveliness in things which I thought hideous."[6] One does not know whether to be more dismayed by this blithe confusion of the artsy-crafty with the avant-garde, or by the appalling clichés used to condemn both. One might even be tempted to assume that both the description and the judgment were intended as parodies, were it not that the judgment does essentially correspond to what Buchan himself has told us of his views. In his autobiography, he related his efforts to "get on terms with my contemporaries"—this in the 1920's—but he could only record a series of failures. Their verse (he was apparently referring to T. S. Eliot) seemed to him "unmelodious journalism, . . . a pastiche of Donne." He disliked the "hothouse world" of Proust although he granted his literary skills. He deplored the "tortuous arabesques" of the later Henry James. With the exception of *War and Peace* and a story or two by Turgenev, he found nothing of merit in the Russians and "resolved never to attempt them again." Some contemporaries, to be sure, pleased him: Sinclair Lewis and Booth Tarkington had the narrative gift of the good novelist, and some of H. G. Wells's novels "were destined to live as long as the English tradition endured." But for the rest—the "rebels and experimentalists"—he confessed a "radical defect of sympathy": "Their merits were beyond

6. *Mr. Standfast*, p. 36.

doubt, but their method and the whole world which they represented seemed to me ineffably dismal."[7]

Yet, alien as he was from the typical literature of modernity, his mind had a range and seriousness that has to be respected. It was not only Scott, Tennyson, and Macaulay whom he (and the heartier characters in his novels) fondly quoted, but also such varied writers—to select only a few of those most often cited in his pages—as Shakespeare, Hakluyt, Thomas Browne, Bunyan, Hazlitt, Walton, Thoreau, Whitman, Johnson, Chateaubriand, Calvin, and Augustine. Impatient with experiments in the arts as in politics, fearful of attempts to probe the unconscious in novels as in life, he was obviously limited in his esthetic responses. Yet it can hardly be judged philistine to prefer Homer in the Greek to T. S. Eliot in English, "low brow" to admire Tolstoi more than Dostoevski, or "anti-intellectual" to write serious works of historical scholarship that are also refreshingly literate.

What is involved is a different cultural tradition emerging in a different set of intellectual and literary manners. The English intellectual of Buchan's generation was loath to parade his intelligence; his Double First at the university had to be acquired without visible swotting or cramming. (Buchan's characters never admitted to memorizing anything; they had "fly-paper memories" to which long passages of poetry or facts adhered effortlessly.) And his writing suggested not the anguish of creation but the casualness of civilized conversation. In this relaxed manner, Buchan was able to produce fifty-seven books in the interstices of his other more absorbing occupations—the law, interrupted by a short period of service with Milner in South Africa, then business, parliament, and finally the Governor-Generalship of Canada.

Such productivity could only be attained if one wrote

---

7. *Memory Hold-the-Door* [American title: *Pilgrim's Way*] (London, 1940), pp. 211–12.

not merely *as* one spoke, but also *what* one spoke. This is the real clue to Buchan's (as to the Victorians') prodigious output. There are many today who are as rich in intellectual resources; there are few who feel so free to draw upon their capital. Buchan had confidence not only in his knowledge, but also in his opinions, attitudes, intuitions, and prejudices. What he wrote for the public was what he felt in private; he did not labor for a subtlety or profundity that did not come spontaneously, or censor his spontaneous thoughts before committing them to paper. He had none of the scruples that are so inhibiting today. He was candid about race, nation, religion, and class, because it did not occur to him that anything he was capable of feeling or thinking could be reprehensible. His creative strength was the strength of character.

It is not only productivity but also authenticity that is enhanced by this assertion of personal authority. His familiarity with the Scottish countryside does more than provide the background of many of the stories. The hunting and fishing scenes in *John Macnab*, described in great and exciting detail, are not appendages to the plot; they *are* the plot. The homely details of the domestic life of a retired Glasgow merchant, interspersed with comments about Freudianism, communism, and international politics, lend verisimilitude to the fairy-tale character of the Russian princess and the wild improbabilities of plot of *Huntingtower*. Verisimilitude, not verity—for his novels remain unashamed romances. It was his theory that fantasy and reality should be permitted to feed upon and nurture each other. This is why he did not trouble himself overmuch with plot, relying on coincidence, hunch, luck, the stock character and situation, to an extent that no popular writer today would dare to do. It is also why he did not trouble himself unduly with niceties of style, why he was unembarrassed by the cliché, the occasional longeur or discursive aside. The very laxity of plot and style served his purpose, not only to advance the tale with a minimum of effort, but also to provide the commonplace background against which the romantic adventure is best played out. In an essay on Scott, Buchan argued the case for a *punctum indifferens*, a calm center around which rages the storm of romance: "The kernel of romance is contrast, beauty and valour flowering in unlikely places, the heavenly rubbing shoulders with the earthly. The true romantic is not the Byronic hero; he is the British soldier whose idea of a *beau geste* is to dribble a football into the enemy's trenches."[8]

The modern reader probably finds it less difficult to accept Buchan's style and mode of thought than the substance of his opinions. On the subject of race especially he appears as the English gentleman of a vintage now gone sour. At least one American publisher recently considered and then had to abandon the idea of reissuing one of his most successful novels, *Prester John*, because it might offend liberal sensibilities. First published in 1910, *Prester John* is the story of a native African uprising led by a Western-educated Negro who seeks to harness the primitive religion and nationalism of the savages to set himself up as the demi-god of a native republic. If this theme is calculated to outrage the liberal, Buchan's language (the hero, a white boy, speaks of the "niggers" with their "preposterous negro lineaments"[9]) does nothing to mitigate the offense. Yet while he dwells on racial differences and assumes natural racial inferiorities and superiorities, he does so not to justify exploitation or inhumanity but rather to inculcate the duties of an enlightened humanitarianism. Laputa, the native leader, is represented as a noble figure and worthy antagonist. When he is defeated in honorable

8. *Homilies*, p. 27.
9. *Prester John*, p. 38.

battle, the classical note of the White Man's Burden is sounded:

> I knew then the meaning of the white man's duty. He has to take all risks, recking nothing of his life or his fortunes and well content to find his reward in the fulfilment of his task. That is the difference between white and black, the gift of responsibility, the power of being in a little way a king; and so long as we know this and practice it, we will rule not in Africa alone but wherever there are dark men who live only for the day and for their own bellies. Moreover, the work made me pitiful and kindly. I learned much of the untold grievances of the natives and saw something of their strange, twisted reasoning.[1]

Prester John was one of Buchan's earliest and least mature books, or possibly the fact that it was intended as a boy's book was responsible for the shrillness of its message. Elsewhere the racist overtones were more a matter of instinct and sentiment than of ideology or doctrine. Buchan was not conscious of race as a "problem" to which racism provided a solution; it was precisely because he was so unconscious of it that he could say: "A nigger band, looking like monkeys in uniform, pounded out some kind of barbarous jingle."[2] And it is precisely because we today are so acutely, unhappily conscious of it that we find this language objectionable, whether in Buchan or in a writer of such distinction and delicacy as Conrad, who had no qualms about speaking of the "repulsive mask of a nigger's soul," the "black mist," the "subtle and dismal influence" emanating from him.[3]

In spite of the usual protestations, to explain is, in large measure, to excuse. The familiar racist sentiments of

1. Ibid., p. 365.
2. *Three Hostages*, p. 97.
3. Conrad, *The Nigger of the Narcissus* (New York, 1960), pp. 43, 56.

Buchan, Kipling, even Conrad, were a reflection of a common attitude. They were descriptive not prescriptive; not an incitement to novel political action, but an attempt to express differences of culture and color in terms that had been unquestioned for generations. Today, when differences of race have attained the status of problems—and tragic problems—writers with the best of motives and finest of sensibilities must often take refuge in evasion and subterfuge. Neutral, scientific words replace the old charged ones, and then, because even the neutral ones—"Negro" in place of "nigger"—give offense, in testifying to differences that men of good will would prefer forgotten, disingenuous euphemisms are invented—"non-white" in place of "Negro." It is at this stage that one may find a virtue of sorts in Buchan: the virtue of candor, which has both an esthetic and an ethical appeal.

The same observations may be made of Buchan's alleged anti-Semitism. What some have condemned as insensitivity or condescension may also be taken as a forthright expression of opinion—or not so much opinion, because that is to dignify it as a conscious judgment, but rather impression or experience. One cannot reasonably object to references to Jewish rag dealers and pawnbrokers, Jewish Communists and financiers, when these were in fact conspicuous both as individuals and as types in an otherwise ethnically homogeneous society—unless one is prepared to impose a decree of silence on the entire subject of Jews. Nor is it reasonable to take offense at the patently fairy-tale account of an international conspiracy devised by Jewish anarchists and Jewish financiers for different and ingenious reasons, and led by a "little white-faced Jew in a bath-chair with an eye like a rattlesnake" who is avenging himself for centuries of persecution.[4] If Buchan's Jewish villains are to be kept account of, the ledger ought also to include the Jewish

4. *Thirty-Nine Steps* (Penguin edn.; London, 1956), p. 17.

heroes: the "richest man in the world," who is an entirely honorable and sympathetic figure and who is made the victim of another conspiracy precisely because his mission was to secure peace in the world; or his beautiful daughter, the fiancée of the Marquis de la Tour du Pin, one of Hannay's oldest and noblest friends.[5] And even the Jewish villain is not necessarily the nastiest of villains; in *Mr. Standfast* he is the most decent of the lot.

This is not to suggest that Buchan's novels can be acquitted of the charge of anti-Semitism. They were anti-Semitic in the same sense that they were anti-Negro. If the Jews, unlike the Negroes, were not in all ways inferior, they were most certainly different, and as one of Buchan's American heroes said of one of his Jewish heroes (vulgar Americans could be relied on to voice what polite Englishmen only thought), he simply "didn't like his race."[6] But this kind of anti-Semitism, indulged in at that time and place, was both too common and too passive to be scandalous. Men were normally anti-Semitic, unless by some quirk of temperament or ideology they happened to be philo-Semitic. So long as the world itself was normal, this was of no great consequence. It was only later, when social impediments became fatal disabilities, when anti-Semitism ceased to be the prerogative of English gentlemen and became the business of politicians and demagogues, that sensitive men were shamed into silence. It was Hitler, attaching such abnormal significance to filiation and physiognomy, who put an end to the casual, innocent anti-Semitism of the clubman. When the conspiracies of the English adventure tale became the realities of German politics, Buchan and others had the grace to realize that what was permissible under civilized conditions was not permissible with civilization *in extremis. Mountain Meadow,*

5. *Three Hostages.*
6. Ibid., p. 17.

261

his last book, composed on the eve of World War II and in the shadow of his own death, was a tract exalting "brother-hood," as that term is understood in the now orthodox liberal lexicon. It is amusing to note that among the many financiers appearing in its pages, there is not a single Jew.

Nor was it only in his later novels that Buchan displayed an admirable sense of social responsibility. Early in 1934, long before most Englishmen had even discovered the fact, Buchan publicly denounced Hitler's anti-Semitism, and, like Milner before him, espoused the cause of Zionism. It is tempting to remark upon the irony of the fact that the fictional perpetrator of Jewish-capitalist-communist conspiracies should have had his name inscribed, in solemn ceremony, in the Golden Book of the Jewish National Fund. Buchan himself would have found nothing "ironic" about this. Fiction was fiction, reality reality. Moreover his Zionism, like his fiction, was concerned not to obliterate differences but to respect them, not to deny, in more conventional liberal fashion, the Jewish identity, but to assert and promote it. His speech acknowledging the honor that had been paid him by the Jewish National Fund took as its theme the racial similarities of Scotsmen and Jews with particular reference to their high regard for learning. A participant in that ceremony, sharing the platform with Buchan, recalled his speech and also his behavior during the address following his, when Buchan leaned forward and watched, with unconcealed delight and fascination, the ample gestures and bodily movements of a Yiddish-speaking rabbi.[7]

In the clubman syndrome, acute class consciousness was second only to race consciousness. It is sometimes suggested that for Buchan this class consciousness was both aggra-

7. Private letter to me by a participant in the ceremonies.

vated and made more reprehensible by its having been acquired rather than being indigenous. The son of a modest Presbyterian minister, attending village schools, a grammar school, and finally the university at Glasgow, he was far removed from the upper-class English characters he described so lovingly. He did not even like school games, and although he did enjoy country sports—hunting, fishing, naturalizing—it was without the ritual that the rich Englishman brought to them. Only when he entered Oxford at the age of nineteen did he get a glimpse of upper-class life. And for some time it was just a glimpse. Older than most freshmen, much poorer and more puritanical, he associated at first only with the other scholarship students. It was not until his third year, when prizes and literary work had made him relatively affluent, that his circle expanded to include rowing and rugby stars as well as poets, writers, and orators. His social initiation was completed in London where he read law and then in South Africa with Milner.

What redeems Buchan from the double charge of either not knowing the clubman society he purported to describe, or if he did know it, of having gained entrée into it only by such an effort as to suggest social-climbing and snobbery, is the fact of his Scottishness. For the Scot is neither an outsider nor an interloper in the sense in which a Cockney or suburbanite might be. Like the American, he is alien enough to be assimilated and mobile enough to expect to be assimilated. His culture is not a despised subculture, but a culture in its own right. His accent and schooling are a token of national peculiarity, not of class inferiority. This is not to say that there was no climbing involved. Men accustomed to social mobility are accustomed to climbing. But it is not the same demeaning process to the foreigner that it would be to the native, does not involve the same repudiation of his past or alienation from himself.

It was his Scottishness, too, that made Buchan a Tory with a difference. For the Scottish Tory was a special breed, as he himself recognized: "A youth in Scotland who called himself a Tory was almost certain to be thinking about politics, and not merely cherishing a family loyalty."[8] He was a Tory by will and principle rather than personal or class interests. He thought the existing class structure was both inevitable and desirable. Like William Morris, he could say that he respected the working class too much to want to turn it into a middle class. And like Disraeli, he wanted to cultivate the alliance between aristocracy and working class. "Democracy and aristocracy," Buchan said, "can co-exist, for oligarchy is their common enemy."[9] The word "oligarchy" was used advisedly, for what Buchan deplored was the tendency to make of class an exclusively economic category and to use social position as an economic instrument. He had no liking for the "genuine reactionaries" of his own party who "woke to life only in the budget season."[1] Not committed to the principles of laissez-faire, he had no prejudice against socialist controls, public authorities, or welfare economics.

If class or social position was not identical with economics, neither was it fixed by birth, for history and character could alter what birth and money had established. It was the possibility, the actuality, of such alteration that attracted Buchan to the study of the English Civil War. And it was the nicety of his judgment that made him choose as his heroes Montrose rather than Charles, Cromwell rather than Lilburne: Montrose for recognizing that there were occasions when revolution was warranted, Cromwell for recognizing that there came a time in a revolution when authority had to be reasserted. Cromwell, he said, "was no Leveller or egalitarian, for the world could not do without its masters, but why reverence a brocaded puppet larded by a priest with oil, when there were men

8. *Memory Hold-the-Door*, p. 153.
9. Ibid., p. 67.
1. Ibid., p. 239.

who needed no robes or sacring to make them kingly?"[2] Authority remained, even as authorities were overthrown, and there were some more than others who were the natural repositories of authority: "It is a melancholy fact which exponents of democracy must face that, while all men may be on a level in the eyes of the State, they will continue in fact to be preposterously unequal."[3]

This declaration of inequality might have appeared in Buchan's *Cromwell;* in fact it appeared in his novel *John Macnab.* The theme of this novel is not only the natural and rightful authority exercised by some men by virtue of their breeding, experience, and character, but also the natural and rightful impulse to rebel against that authority. John Macnab's gallant wager, to kill and remove against great odds a stag and salmon from his neighbor's property, is not the paean to adventure that it may seem on the surface—sheer, gratuitous, gentlemanly adventure, *le sport* at its most absurd. It is rather a parable about authority and property and the perpetual challenge to which they are both subject. The ancient families, cherishing the tokens of their glorious antiquity and trying to remain unsullied by modern enterprise, are doomed to extinction, and justly so. The heroine describes her sister: "She's a sentimentalist and she'll marry Junius and go to America, where everybody is sentimental, and be the sweetest thing in the Western hemisphere." The old Gaelic family motto, "Sons of Dogs, come and I will give you flesh," has given way to the genteel invention of the Herald's College, "Pro Deo et Rege," and the will to fight has succumbed to the wish to survive—as a result of which Lancashire cotton spinners are succeeding to the ancient houses and heirlooms. And the Lancashire manufacturers are advised to pay heed too, for the right of property "is no right at all." Neither property nor rank nor power has a right in perpetuity. Everything is

2. *Oliver Cromwell* (London, 1934), p. 303.
3. *John Macnab,* p. 233.

held under sufferance; every privilege must be defended and legitimized anew.[4]

Misled by the romantic cast of Buchan's novels, critics have assumed that his Toryism was of the romantic variety that loves a lord, venerates the past, and despises the clerks and entrepreneurs of the middle class. In fact, his Toryism was radical rather than romantic, and he respected enterprise as he respected labor. While agreeing with Samuel Johnson that "life is barren enough surely with all her trappings; let us be therefore cautious of how we strip her,"[5] he had no fondness for trappings that interfered with the business of living, and no regrets for the regime that died in World War I: "The radicalism which is part of the Tory creed was coming uppermost, and I looked forward to a clearing out of much rubbish."[6]

If Buchan's attitude to race and class is apt to cause dismay, his attitude to nation and empire may be even more distressing. "For King and Country," the homily of generations of housemasters, is taken to be the archaic and fatuous message of his work. He himself described, in retrospect, the imperial vision of his youth: "I dreamed of a worldwide brotherhood with the background of a common race and creed, consecrated to the service of peace; Britain enriching the rest out of her culture and traditions, and the spirit of the Dominions like a strong wind freshening the stuffiness of the old lands."[7] This ideal is now commonly regarded as a utopian fantasy. But Buchan himself was no innocent, and when he confessed to his dream it was with the knowledge that his words had become irredeemable platitudes. "The 'white man's burden,'" he complained

4. Ibid., pp. 136–7.
5. *Memory*, p. 95.
6. Ibid., p. 174.
7. Ibid., p. 130.

toward the end of his life, "is now an almost meaningless phrase; then it involved a new philosophy of politics, and an ethical standard, serious and surely not ignoble."[8]

If there was rhetoric and fancy in the imperialist circles around Milner, there was also a truth and grandeur which today is too little appreciated. In his biography of Cromwell, Buchan quoted Captain John Smith: "The greatest honour that ever belonged to the greatest monarchs was the enlarging of their dominions and erecting Commonwealths"; and Harrington: "You canot plant an oak in a flower-pot; she must have earth for her roots, and heaven for her branches."[9] This is not to say that the impulse behind the imperial enterprise is always honorable, or that its consequences, whatever the impulse, are always desirable. But to impugn the motives of all imperialists is surely to have a crabbed view of both the past and the present. A respect for the integrity and independence of others is admirable, but so is a respect and faith in oneself; and while the missionary or proselytizing temperament is to be suspected and feared, it is also, on occasion, to be esteemed. If self-serving motives are attributed to the imperialists, they can also be attributed to the "Little-Englanders." Prudence and aristocratic disdain were the not particularly lofty terms in which Raymond Asquith defended Little-Englandism to Buchan:

The day of the clever cad is at hand. I always felt it would come to this if we once let ourselves in for an Empire. If only Englishmen had known their Aeschylus a little better they wouldn't have bustled about the world appropriating things. A gentleman may make a large fortune, but only a cad can look after it. It would have been so much pleasanter to live in a small community who knew Greek and played games and washed themselves.[1]

8. Ibid.
9. *Cromwell*, pp. 486, 502.
1. *Memory*, p. 62.

The dilemma of the imperial ideal was also the dilemma of the national ideal. Here too Buchan had a finer sensibility and at the same time a broader sympathy than he and his kind have generally been credited with. Thus he did not finally decide between the creeds of Cromwell and Montrose—Cromwell, as Buchan saw it, seeking to create a "spiritualized and dedicated" nation; Montrose satisfied with a homely, modest, judicious government of checks and balances.[2] He saw the glory of the first, but he realized that men might become satiated with high communal, as with high spiritual, ideals, and might prefer to devote themselves to their private concerns. He did not pretend that the first path was without its dangers, or the second without its virtues.

There was certainly a romantic streak in Buchan that invaded his politics. It was not, however, the sentimental romanticism with which the conservative is often associated—a sentimental attachment to tradition, rank, and pomp. It was rather a Gothic, almost apocalyptic vision of the dark, destructive forces contained in human beings and society. His villains are permeated by this sense of the infernal. The typical Victorian or Edwardian villain was a bounder and cad, a seducer of shopgirls, extortionist of money, sometimes a trafficker in national secrets. The Buchan villain deals in a different order of villainy. He is not a fallen gentleman but a fallen man, the personification of evil. He dabbles in black magic rather than sex, seeks not money but power, and traffics in the secrets of the soul as much as those of the nation. Compared with him, even the sadist of the contemporary thriller is frivolous, for instead of private sexual perversions, Buchan's villains are satisfied with nothing less than the subversion of society.

Long before the H-bomb, A-bomb, and even ordinary

2. *Cromwell*, p. 523.

old-fashioned aerial bombing, before the threat of fascism and in the infancy of communism, Buchan felt what later events seemed to confirm—that "civilization anywhere is a very thin crust."[3] The danger in revolution was not that it would overthrow any particular political or social institutions, but rather that it would undermine all government and society. Bolshevism itself was less menacing than the nihilism that it would release:

> A civilisation bemused by an opulent materialism has been met by a rude challenge. The free peoples have been challenged by the serfs. The gutters have exuded a poison which bids fair to infect the world. The beggar-on-horseback rides more roughshod over the helpless than the cavalier. A combination of multitudes who have lost their nerve and a junta of arrogant demagogues has shattered the comity of nations. The European tradition has been confronted with an Asiatic revolt, with its historic accompaniment of janissaries and assassins. There is in it all, too, an ugly pathological savour, as if a mature society were being assailed by diseased and vicious children.[4]

But the poison that was now infecting the world had always lain dormant in it; the diseased and vicious children are, after all, our own progeny. What terrifies Hannay in *The Three Hostages* is the fact that the villains are high in the Establishment, that they might be found next to one at a shoot in Suffolk or a dinner party in St. James'. Even when the villain in one of the spy stories was a German, Buchan took pains to absolve him from the lesser villainy of nationality (Buchan was neither a Germanophobe nor a Russophobe) and even of espionage, in order to convict him of the greater villainy of a moral depravity bordering on diabolism.

This is hardly the housemaster's credo of king and country. Again, what distinguished Buchan was his Scottishness,

3. *Huntingtower* (Penguin edn.; London, 1956), p. 130.
4. *Memory*, p. 300.

the Calvinist sense of the unquiet depths that lay beneath the human surface. He suspected that once the subconscious, lawless instincts of men were permitted to break through the barrier erected by civilization, "there will be a weakening of the power of reasoning, which after all is the thing that brings men nearest to the Almighty; and there will be a failure of nerve."[5] It was thus not the reason of state, even of a hostile state, that alarmed him, but the force of unreason itself. Shortly after World War I he foresaw the development of a new kind of propaganda, compared with which the old-fashioned Prussian militarist variety was innocuous and innocent. As Sandy Arbuthnot reminds Hannay, the new threat came from the manipulator of minds: "We are only beginning to realize the strange crannies of the human soul. The real magician, if he turned up to-day, wouldn't bother about drugs and dopes. He would dabble in far more deadly methods, the compulsion of a fiery nature over the limp things that men call their minds."[6] Buchan's villains do not simply bribe, blackmail, or torture their victims; they operate by means of hypnotism, hysteria, fanaticism, and a quasi-religious mysticism. Hannay, fortunately, is not susceptible to hypnotism, as he repeatedly comforts himself, but he is liable to his "one special funk," the mob. "I hated the thought of it—the mess, the blind struggle, the sense of unleashed passions different from those of any single blackguard. It was a dark world to me, and I don't like darkness."[7]

Hannay may be an innocent, but his creator is not. When Buchan pits the "jolly party of clean, hard, decent fellows" against the "abominable hinterland of mystery and crime,"[8] he seems to be subscribing to the decent-fellow ethic that belongs to the caricature of the phleg-

5. *Three Hostages*, p. 15.
6. Ibid., p. 61.
7. *Greenmantle*, p. 130.
8. *Three Hostages*, p. 229.

matic, obtuse Englishman. But in fact the ethic has acquired the urgency of a desperate counter-measure; it is inseparable from the evil that called it into being. As befits a good Calvinist, Buchan is hard, realistic, unsentimental, apprehensive: "It was a dogma of the elder liberalism that violence can never achieve anything, and that persecution, so far from killing a thing, must inevitably nourish it. For such optimism there is no warrant in history; time and again violence has wholly achieved its purpose, when it has been carried to its logical conclusion."[9]

What makes Buchan, and the ethos with which he is identified, so unpalatable today is not one or another cause for distaste: the idea that the good life is a matter of cold baths, rousing games, and indifferent sex; the apparent philistinism that put a high premium on success and a low premium on intelligence; an unseemly preoccupation with race and class; and a still more unseemly glorification of nation and empire. It is each of these and more: the sense of a temperament and mentality that is inimical to the prevailing "liberal imagination."[1] The liberal celebrates the like-

9. *Cromwell*, p. 355.
1. Alistair Buchan, responding to the earlier published version of this essay, took issue with my characterization of his father as antithetical to the "liberal imagination." He found it ironic that I should use this phrase, in view of the fact that his father, shortly before he died, had spoken of Lionel Trilling as "one of the best living literary critics." There is, however, nothing ironic about this. John Buchan would have admired Trilling's work precisely for the reason that I alluded to it. Trilling was not, after all, celebrating the liberal imagination in the famous work of that title. He was rather pointing to its limitations, to the fact that the political virtues of liberalism almost inevitably entailed a constriction of the emotions and imagination. The whole of this essay is, in this sense, a small footnote to Trilling's memorable work.

The Liberal Imagination, of course, was published long after Buchan's death. The book by Trilling that Buchan read and admired was *Matthew Arnold*. (See Janet Adam Smith, *John Buchan* [London, 1965], p. 469.)

nesses of men rather than their differences; individuals rather than race, class, or nation; the benevolent and malleable character of men rather than their recalcitrance. He chooses to understand rather than judge, and he is discreet where understanding fails him. He is as much repelled by intuition and prejudice as by the usages and prescriptions of tradition. He regards violence, like evil, as a negative quality, a temporary aberration, unreal both in its impulse and in its effect.

Buchan—Calvinist in religion, Tory in politics, and romantic in sensibility—is obviously the antithesis of the liberal. It is no accident that he was addicted to a genre, the romantic tale of adventure, which is itself alien to the liberal temper. For what kind of romance would it be that feared to characterize or categorize, to indulge the sense of evil, violence, and apocalypse? It is no accident, either, that the predominance of liberal values has meant the degeneration of a literary form so congenial to the Tory imagination.

VICTORIAN IDEAS
AND IDEOLOGIES

THE VICTORIAN ETHOS: BEFORE
AND AFTER VICTORIA

WHERE ONCE it was the fashion to vilify "Victorianism," today one might be tempted to deny that there
had ever been such a thing. The period, one might argue,
was too long, the tempo of change too rapid, the cast of
characters too motley to permit of generalization. How can
we lump together sixty-four years of economic, political,
social, and cultural revolution? How can we generalize
about England, Scotland, and Wales, when we cannot even
generalize about the north of England and the south? What
can we make of an age whose cultural heroines were Mrs.
Grundy and George Eliot, whose intellectual heroes were
Carlyle, Newman, Mill, and Darwin, and whose political
heroes were Gladstone and Disraeli; an age that produced
some of the most important theories of modern times, as
well as some of the most absurd practices; an age of industrial invention, scientific discovery, political emancipation,
and moral rigidity; an age of great eccentrics and of massive
conformity?

Even to take "Victorianism" in its most popular and
limited sense, as a code of moral pieties, is to invite dissent.
Some of the most eminent Victorian worthies were also the
most notorious flouters of convention: John Stuart Mill,

who courted Mrs. Taylor for almost twenty years with her husband hovering in the background; George Eliot, who lived with G. H. Lewes for more than twenty years quite as if his wife did not exist; Sarah Austin (the wife of the famous jurist), who wrote letters of such ardor and indiscretion to a visiting German prince as to invite blackmail; the historian George Grote, who celebrated the conclusion of his thirty-year-long work on ancient Greece and the fortieth anniversary of his marriage by entering into an affair with a young sculptress. And there were those who managed to offend propriety in reverse: Carlyle and Ruskin, for example, whose desire for marriage was so much more compelling than their desire for sexual relations that they lived in permanent celibacy with their wives. Nor were marital improprieties the only offense. Monckton Milnes (Lord Houghton), member of parliament, man of letters, and man about town, was as zealous in his collection of pornography as in his pursuit of high society; while Swinburne applied his genius to the composition of poetry and pornography alike.

Yet in spite of these anomalies, there was an identifiable spirit of Victorianism. The seemingly disparate social and cultural events were not without pattern. The long years of Victoria's reign reveal a line, or lines, of development. Ethics, religion, and philosophy, changing in themselves and shifting in relation to each other, merged to constitute a unique ethos. Even the violations of propriety reinforced the sense of propriety. Mill and Eliot agonized so long and strenuously over their irregular situations that they ended by representing them as the essence of true morality—indeed, by converting them into the essence of domesticity. And Swinburne not only refrained from publishing his erotica but also defended the bowdlerization of Shakespeare on the grounds that it was now possible to put the plays in the hands of children. Thus even the scandals of the age, demonstrating the Victorian's capacity to be scandalized as much as his capacity to scandalize, testified to the intensity of his moral fervor, the measure of his earnestness. Similarly, the underworld of pornography co-existed comfortably with the outer world of prudery. Indeed the one, as has recently been revealed, was the "mirror-image," the "negative analogue," of the other;[1] so that if pornography became more obtrusive, it was largely because morality had become so much the more obsessive.

Nor does it destroy this image of Victorianism to suggest that the ethic had a distinctive class character. It is true that these pieties and proprieties originated with the middle class and had their most loyal and fanatical disciples among that class. But what was more important was the dispersion of this ethic among all classes. For the first time, a substantial part of the aristocracy and of the working class (and in each case, the most influential part) shared the ideals and values of the middle class. Those quintessentially middle-class qualities—now become virtues—of prudery and prudence had transcended their class origins. Aristocratic reformers proved to be as intolerant of the frivolities of their own class as of the dissipations of the working class. Moreover, their zeal for social reform involved them, often unwittingly, in a process of self-reformation. Family prayers, intended primarily for the moral elevation of children and servants, could not fail to have an elevating, or at least sobering, effect upon parents and masters as well. Philanthropy, designed to better the conditions of the poor, had the more immediate and palpable result of improving the morals of the rich.

Nor does it detract from the significance of this ethic that some men did no more than pay lip service to it, preaching to others what they did not themselves observe, conducting family prayers rather as a public duty than out

1. Steven Marcus, *The Other Victorians* (New York, 1966), p. 283. More questionable is Marcus's claim that Victorian pornography was the positive analogue of capitalism.

of private conviction, maintaining a façade of propriety behind which vice might be indulged. As scandals, in their very nature, testify to the power of the established code, so cant and hypocrisy also testify to its power. It is a considerable achievement to convert men to the extent that they feel obliged to mask their passions or inclinations. The reformer cannot inquire into the heart and soul of his converts; he must be satisfied with their public professions and behavior. Even if the inner lives of the upper classes, or the outer lives of the lower, fell far short of the ideal, it was a great accomplishment to have converted both to the ideal as such. In this sense, the moral reformation of the Victorians was as effective as such reformations are likely to be.

In one important respect, however, the popular image of Victorianism does need amending, and that is the image of the innocent young queen, pure and unworldly, converting by her example first the cynical and debauched court and then the several estates of her realm. It is a beguiling image and in itself not unlikely—only, as it happens, untrue. For in fact the moral reformation long anteceded Victoria's reign. It anteceded her not in the sense that, as we are often told, historical events are necessarily remote and impersonal in origin, their roots being too deep and diffuse for any simple attribution of time, place, or person. There was nothing remote or impersonal about the moral reformation of England. It happened, however, to be John Wesley, rather than Queen Victoria, who was largely responsible for that reformation, and the eighteenth century, rather than the nineteenth, that inaugurated it. "Victorianism before Victoria," one historian has described the phenomenon.[2]

It was Élie Halévy, in his *England in 1815*, who focused

2. Asa Briggs, *The Age of Improvement* (London, 1959), p. 72.

attention upon the decisive role of Wesley and Wesleyanism in the history of modern England. Wesleyanism—or
"Methodism," to use the term first derisively applied to it
by its opponents and then adopted by its adherents—
started in the eighteenth century as an evangelical reform
movement within the established church. Although Wesley
never dissociated himself from the Church of England,
many of his followers did, feeding the ranks of the dissenting sects or establishing independent bodies of their own.
Thus the movement left its stamp upon the whole spectrum
of English religious institutions.[3] It had no firm theological
doctrine: Wesley tried to hold to the idea of justification
by faith while rejecting the complementary idea of pre-
destination, and his followers played upon all the possible
variations on these themes. Indeed, in its inception it was
antidoctrinal in spirit, being an attempt to revive personal
religion and scriptural faith. The doctrinal, even intellectual, weakness of Wesleyanism was precisely its strength,
for it was this that permitted it to transcend religious and
institutional barriers. Unlike most new sects, it was not
divisive but rather unifying, mediating, and accommodating.

Although Wesleyanism had no binding doctrine, it did
have firm religious and moral intentions. In one sense it was
an attempt to internalize religion and spiritualize life, to
recapture the vitality of primitive Christianity. The emphasis on personal salvation and the rejection of the concept of
an elect meant that all men, whatever their present state,

3. One of the difficulties in discussing this subject is the confusion between the original and later usage of the words
"Evangelicalism" and "Methodism." In the late eighteenth
and early nineteenth centuries, the two were generally used
interchangeably. Only later did Evangelicalism become identified with Anglicanism and Methodism with the several varieties of sects outside the Established Church. In this essay, I
have used "Evangelicalism" and "Methodism" in their common,
present-day sense, and "evangelicalism," in the lower case, as the
generic term for both.

had the duty and potentiality for reform. At the same time, the doctrine of justification by faith was interpreted in such a way as to approximate a doctrine of good works in the form of self-help and mutual help. The internalization of religion was thus accompanied by its externalization, the spiritualization of religion by its moralization and socialization. Wesley himself sometimes insisted upon the external even at the expense of the internal. "Christianity is essentially a social religion," he declared. "To turn it into a solitary religion is indeed to destroy it."[4] And he acted upon this principle when he established, among other things, a poorhouse, a soup kitchen, a dispensary for the poor, and a "contingent fund"—the latter made up of contributions by the employed for the relief of the unemployed. Before his death he had occasion to observe that some of his followers, perhaps as a result of his teachings, had accumulated what for them was considerable wealth, and he reminded them of their obligation to share their good fortune with the poor.

As the evangelical spirit infiltrated both the dissenting and the established churches, so it also infiltrated the several layers of society. Starting in the lower middle class, it soon spread to the upper. The Clapham Sect, the most influential Evangelical circle, included prominent members of parliament, bankers, lawyers, editors, writers, and philanthropists. It was no longer true, as had earlier been charged, that only the lower orders were concerned with the care of their souls. When the high and the mighty discovered that they too had souls to tend, it was the discovery of a common humanity.

The democratizing effect of evangelicalism is all the more remarkable for its having been so unintentional. Neither self-help nor mutual help was meant to imply self-government. In an age of revolution, most of Wesley's disciples were firmly committed to the established order.

4. Robert F. Wearmouth, *Methodism and the Working-Class Movements of England, 1800–50* (London, 1937), p. 160.

When a small group of Nonconformists expressed revolutionary sympathies, the Wesleyans issued a public declaration repudiating the Enlightenment as subversive of both society and faith and reaffirming their loyalty to king, country, and creed: "We are to observe that the oracles of God command us to be subject to the higher powers; and that honor to the King is there connected with the fear of God."[5] One Methodist put the matter boldly: "Wesleyanism is as much opposed to Democracy as it is to Sin."[6]

At first, Wesleyanism had been opposed to democracy not because democracy was itself sinful but rather because to be concerned with democracy, in the sense of political reform, was to be distracted from the proper concern of man: his spiritual and moral salvation. Later, however, with the outbreak of the French Revolution, it appeared that salvation depended upon a strengthening of the existing political order, particularly when the threatening example of the French Revolution was accompanied by the still more threatening advance of the Revolutionary armies. Thomas Bowdler was one of many to call for a national moral regeneration: "The only reform which can save us, if adopted in time, is a thorough reform of principles and practices."[7] Bowdler's contribution to this cause was the purgation of Shakespeare and Gibbon. But bowdlerization was not an invention of Bowdler; Wesley himself, as part of his campaign to promote literacy and encourage the dissemination of culture, had issued a series of abridged editions of famous works, in the course of which offensive passages had naturally been eliminated. Nor was bowdlerization the only or even the chief device of moral reform.

5. Élie Halévy, *England in 1815*, Vol. I of *A History of the English People in the Nineteenth Century* (London, 1949), p. 427.
6. G. M. Young, *Victorian England: Portrait of an Age* (Anchor edn.; New York, 1954), p. 103.
7. Maurice J. Quinlan, *Victorian Prelude* (New York, 1941), p. 97.

The evangelicals were just as enthusiastic in the causes of temperance, charity, Sunday and day schools, the abolition of the slave trade, Sabbatarianism, and the prohibition of such unedifying pasttimes as fortunetelling, cock fighting, bear baiting, and dueling.

The most effective and familiar case for moral reformation was made by Edmund Burke: "Manners are of more importance than law. . . . The law touches us but here and there and now and then. Manners are what vex or soothe, corrupt or purify, exalt or debase, barbarize or refine us, by a constant, steady, uniform, and insensible operation, like that of the air we breathe in."[8] But even before Burke and before the French Revolution, Hannah More was preaching about the social, even political, importance of manners and morals, and more particularly counseling the upper classes to set a good example for the lower. That the upper classes were impressed by her counsel, at least to the extent of buying her books, is suggested by the large circulation they enjoyed, in spite of their forbidding titles: *Thoughts on the Importance of the Manners of the Great to General Society* and *An Estimate of the Religion of the Fashionable World*. A similar work by William Wilberforce published in 1797, *A Practical View of the Prevailing Religious System of Professed Christians in the Higher and Middle Classes in this Country, Contrasted with Real Christianity*, went through five editions in as many months.

The urgency of moral reform did not originate in the French Revolution nor terminate with the defeat of the Revolutionary armies. The crisis of war was succeeded by domestic crises: economic depression, political dissension, riots, and suppressive measures on the part of the government. To many it appeared that not only the stability of government but the very cohesion of society was being

8. Burke, "Letters on a Regicide Peace," *Works* (London, 1910), V, 208.

impaired. Again the evangelical ethic had a soothing, amelio-rating effect. In ways subtle and crass, conscious and un-conscious, in works of great delicacy and of gross senten-tiousness, in biographies of successful businessmen and manuals for ambitious workers, the virtues of reverence, sobriety, and prudence were held up for emulation. Slowly, the moral reformation, occurring, as Burke had said it would, by "a constant, steady, uniform, and insen-sible operation," assumed the form of a social reformation.

Slowly, too, and as unwittingly, the moral and social reformation generated a social and political revolution. This was the great accomplishment of the evangelical ethic. The diffusion of what might otherwise have been a purely middle-class ethic, even more, it might be argued, than the later extension of the suffrage, initiated the democratic revolution. For it was the acceptance of a single moral code by the entire population that first breached the barriers separating the "two nations."

There were still, visibly and painfully, two nations, but there was also a visible and hopeful movement between the two. If the agricultural and industrial revolutions created the opportunities for social mobility, the ethical revolution made it easier to take advantage of these opportunities. And not only to take advantage of them but also to expand the opportunities, to institute those political and social reforms that opened up new doors and avenues of entry.

The reformers themselves, like the ethic that inspired them, cut across class and party lines, thus further contrib-uting to the general mobility. Artisans and masters (often artisans turned masters), clergymen and men of letters (again the first was often a stage toward the second), businessmen, barristers, and aristocrats, Whigs, Tories, and Radicals, Anglicans and Dissenters, found themselves asso-ciated in common causes. No one class or party had a monopoly of reform—not even of any single reform, not even of those reforms most commonly associated with a particular party or class. Behind the scenes, if not in public, there was much collusion between ostensibly opposing groups, as there was also much disaffection within ostensibly united ones. There were, to be sure, individuals— Eldon and Liverpool, for example—who were frozen into hard and fast positions. But the Lord Chancellor, however rigid he was in office, was himself a prime example of social mobility, his father having started life in a modest occupation (which may help account for the son's rigidity). And the Prime Minister, however Tory in other respects, was a thoroughgoing liberal in economic affairs and a trimmer on other subjects. On even the most controversial measures—Catholic Emancipation or the Reform Act of 1832—there was far more political and social fluidity than appeared on the surface or than is now commonly suspected.[9] (Later in the century, the same cross-class, cross-party phenomenon appeared in the form of Lib-Labism, and owed not a little to the Evangelicism of the Liberals and the Methodism of the trade unionists.)

Evangelicalism was hardly the only force contributing to this "conservative revolution"—revolution by diffusion, so to speak. But it gave an impetus and a direction to the other forces that might otherwise have been lacking. One might argue that industrialism and capitalism had sufficient incentive to bring about such a revolution—to moralize, socialize, educate, and acculturate the working classes so as to maximize their productivity and stability. But it was in fact

9. Joseph Hamburger, *James Mill and the Art of Revolution* (New Haven, 1963), is a detailed case study of the events of 1831-2 that are commonly thought to have brought England closest to the brink of revolution. What emerges from this study is an extraordinary demonstration of the way individuals, parties, and classes, ostensibly committed to different positions, in fact tacitly cooperated for the passage of the act, and the way the threat of revolution was consciously manipulated to promote a reform designed to prevent revolution.

the evangelicals who did this, who delivered the sermons, built the schools, set the example—and evangelicals who were not necessarily themselves industrialists or capitalists, and for whom the industrialist and capitalist ethic would not by itself have been sufficient inspiration. Or one might attribute the "conservative revolution" to the peculiar genius of the English parliamentary system, which permitted just such an accommodation of social forces and pressures. Macaulay, writing in 1848 while the continent was experiencing quite different varieties of revolution, explained that it was because England had "a preserving revolution in the seventeenth century that we have not had a destroying revolution in the nineteenth."[1] There is obviously a good deal of truth in this, for parliament did succeed in resolving the political problem in good Whig tradition. Yet much that happened lay outside the province of parliament, and there were clearly occasions when parliament was acted upon at least as much as it was doing the acting. Or again, with much justice, one could point to the institutional and legislative developments of the period that often, without benefit of ideology or even deliberate intention, contributed to the same effect. What evangelicalism did was to add to all these other factors the formidable weight of a religion *cum* ethics *cum* ideology.

The only other ideology that could have offered serious competition to evangelicalism was utilitarianism. But utilitarianism came on the scene as a social force in the 1820's and 1830's, long after evangelicalism had had its greatest impact. Indeed had it not been for evangelicalism, utilitarianism might never have emerged from the obscurity in which Bentham so effectively shrouded it.

1. Macaulay, *History of England, Works* (London, 1875), II, 398.

Karl Marx has left a memorable description of Bentham: "that insipid, pedantic, leather-tongued oracle of the ordinary bourgeois intelligence of the nineteenth century," the genius of "bourgeois stupidity," the philosopher of the "English shopkeeper."[2] In fact, nowhere did Bentham have less influence than in this nation of shopkeepers. The English commentator William Hazlitt was more to the point when he wrote: "His works have been translated into French—they ought to be translated into English."[3] What Hazlitt did not know was that Bentham's secretaries and editors worked in vain to translate his English into the native tongue. They failed not only because of the obscurities and involutions of Bentham's prose, but because of the un-English doctrinairism of his mind. It was not by accident that his works were often published abroad before they appeared in England and that he had a larger audience abroad than at home. Latin America, India, Spain, Russia—there he found his most enthusiastic disciples. Bentham himself was well aware of this. Early in his career he had decided that Russia was a more congenial country than England. ("I could bring more of my ideas to bear there in a month than here in my whole life."[4]) And later he actually tried to emigrate, first to Mexico and then to Venezuela.

When utilitarianism did begin to make itself felt in England, it was by abandoning the doctrine in its pure form and coming to terms with the prevailing temper and movements of reform. Its most conspicuous practical successes (legal, parliamentary, and social reforms) were achieved in conjunction with Peelites, Whigs, and Tories. And its greatest philosophical influence came when John

2. Marx, *Capital* (Modern Library edn.; New York, 1936), p. 668.

3. William Hazlitt, *The Spirit of the Age* (Dolphin edn.; New York, n.d.), p. 21.

4. M. P. Mack, *Jeremy Bentham* (New York, 1963), p. 364 (Jan. 1781). See above, p. 72.

Stuart Mill diluted it with a large dose of what was in effect evangelical ethics. Mill's *Utilitarianism* was more acceptable to the evangelical of his generation that it would have been to the utilitarian of his father's—or, indeed, to his father himself. For Mill so interpreted utilitarianism as to include "duty" in the category of "pleasure," and to make room for the pangs of conscience under the rubric of "pain." In this latter-day utilitarianism, happiness was transmuted into virtue, the greatest number was subordinated to the best-educated, and self-interest was made disinterested and altruistic. Such a philosophy may not have been quite as lofty as the more austere evangelical might have liked, but by that token it was more accessible to more men; and if it did not encourage the highest spiritual virtues, at least it discouraged the most sordid vices.

As the first dogmatic generation of utilitarians died or, with age, became less dogmatic, and as the more zealous generation of evangelicals lost their peculiar religious zeal, the two tended to merge, both as modes of thought and as social movements. Evangelicalism, after all, had had from its beginning a large admixture of utilitarianism—the pre-Benthamite variety that was so prevalent in the eighteenth century—and an even larger component of social conscience. And utilitarianism, for its part, had always had elements in common with evangelicalism: a notion of public morality as private morality writ large, a concern for the general welfare, an abiding interest in social reform. Bentham himself in his less dogmatic moments had confessed to a sympathy for evangelicalism; he once spoke of a new friend as being "what I had liked to have been, a Methodist, and what I should have been still had I not been what I am."[5] And even at his most dogmatic, when he was denouncing his own disciples (Romilly and Brougham) for deviating from the true and narrow path, he was looking

5. *Memoirs of Bentham, Works,* ed. John Bowring (London, 1838–43), X, 92 (Aug. 25, 1781).

for consolation to that staunch Evangelical, William Wilberforce.

If the diminution of utilitarianism may be traced through the careers of the two Mills, so the diminution of evangelicalism may be traced through the lives of the Macaulays. Zachary Macaulay was the archetype of the older generation and one of the leaders of the Clapham Sect. His son, the historian, was so conspicuously lacking in evangelical fervor that he, more often than Bentham, is taken to represent the spirit of the nation of shopkeepers. Yet the younger Macaulay was the most trenchant critic of utilitarianism, perhaps because he realized that a nation of shopkeepers—perhaps most of all a nation of shopkeepers —had need of a philosophy that would transcend shop-keeping. Utilitarianism, he argued, was at best a truism: people behaved as they found it useful or pleasurable to behave. At worst, it was fallacious: people also behaved, on occasion, as they thought they ought to behave; their "pleasure" was to do what was not necessarily pleasurable. Christianity had the advantage over utilitarianism in admitting the existence of the "ought" and in providing a sanction for it:

> To a man whose greatest happiness in this world is inconsistent with the greatest happiness of the greatest number is held out the prospect of an infinite happiness hereafter, from which he excludes himself by wronging his fellow-creatures here.
>
> This is practical philosophy, as practical as that on which penal legislation is founded. A man is told to do something which otherwise he would not do, and is furnished with a new motive for doing it.[6]

There was, obviously, utilitarianism of a kind, and a very pronounced kind, in this argument of Macaulay. But

6. Macaulay, "Westminster Reviewer's Defence of Mill," *Works*, V, 298.

it was an evangelized utilitarianism, and the evangelical element made all the difference. It was the spirit of Macaulay, not of Bentham, that was typical of the early Victorians—typical as much of a Thomas Arnold trying to produce "Christian gentlemen" at Rugby, as of the Christian gentlemen trying to inculcate the working classes with Useful Knowledge, Christian Knowledge, Christian Socialism, and Self-Help. The more rigorous religious thinkers— Evangelicals, Dissenters, Tractarians, Catholic converts— deplored the attenuation and hybridization of religion that they saw all around them. But even Newman, who did not conceal his preference for a religion "vastly more superstitious, more bigoted, more gloomy, more fierce," had also to admit that he himself owed a good deal to his early evangelicalism, and that Thomas Arnold was to be commended for bringing about a general "elevation of character."[7]

The curious thing is that even as religion became progressively more attenuated, as the public became more relaxed in its faith and the intellectuals more openly skeptical, the social ethic did not become correspondingly attenuated or relaxed. Indeed the ethic acquired some of the stigmata of the old religion—the gloom and fierceness that Newman yearned for. And this in spite of the fact that society no longer had practical need of such a formidable ethic. The high tide of Victorianism, the fifties and sixties, was "The Age of Equipoise," insofar as any age can war-

7. Basil Willey, *Nineteenth Century Studies* (London, 1949), p. 75; Newman, *Apologia Pro Vita Sua* (Boston, 1956), p. 273 (Appendix, "Note on Liberalism"). However much the Oxford Movement protested against a morality-centered religion, it itself owed a large debt to evangelicalism, both in feeding its ranks (many of its leaders had, like Newman, gone through an evangelical phase) and in creating a climate of seriousness that was as much a part of the High Church atmosphere as of the Low.

rant so sanguine a title.[8] In society, in politics, and in the economy there was as neat a balance as was ever to be achieved between what John Stuart Mill called the "Movement" or "Progressive" forces and the "Conservative" forces.[9] Yet it was just then, without the support of religion and without the warrant of utility, that the social ethic was most rigorous and demanding. The categorical imperative had never been so categorical nor so imperative. Macaulay's conception of "practical philosophy"—telling a man "to do something which otherwise he would not do" and furnishing him "with a new motive for doing it"—was only half realized: men were under the most imperious injunction of conscience to do that which they would not otherwise do, and the authority of that injunction was all the greater for there being no new, or old, motive to support it.

When Darwin was asked what he himself believed to be the implications of his theory for religion and morality, he said that the idea of God was "beyond the scope of man's intellect," but that man's moral obligation remained what it had always been: to "do his duty."[1] Leslie Stephen, after abandoning the effort to derive an ethic from Darwinism, finally confessed: "I now believe in nothing, but I do not the less believe in morality. . . . I mean to live and die like a gentleman if possible."[2] Frederic Harrison, the archpriest of English Positivism and agnosticism, when asked by his son what a man should do if he fell in love and could not marry, replied indignantly: "Do! Do what every gentleman does in such circumstances." And when his son per-

8. This is the title of an excellent work on the period by W. L. Burn (London, 1964).

9. Mill, "Bentham," *Essays on Politics and Culture*, ed. Gertrude Himmelfarb (New York, 1962), p. 86.

1. Darwin, *Life and Letters* (London, 1887), I, 307 (April 2, 1873).

2. F. W. Maitland, *Life and Letters of Leslie Stephen* (London, 1906), pp. 144-5.

sisted in wanting to know why love was proper only in marriage, Harrison could barely contain himself: "A loose man is a foul man. He is anti-social. He is a beast. . . . It is not a subject that decent men do discuss."[3] Harrison had only Comte to depend upon, but George Eliot, drawing upon the combined resources of Comte, Strauss, and Feuerbach, emerged with nothing more substantial than "the recognition of a binding belief or spiritual law, which is to lift us into willing obedience and save us from the slavery of unregulated passion or impulse."[4] God, she is reported to have said, was "inconceivable," immortality was "unbelievable," but duty was none the less "peremptory and absolute."[5]

Utilitarianism, Darwinism, Positivism, Rationalism, Biblical Criticism, and Atheistic Humanism—none of these succeeded either in undermining morality, as some had feared, or in providing a "new motive" for morality, as Macaulay and others had hoped. In the end what sustained the Victorian ethic was essentially what had first inspired it—an unsectarian, latitudinarian evangelicalism. After all her studies in French and German philosophy, Eliot finally turned to her native religion to account for the most important fact of life: "Evangelicalism had brought into palpable existence and operation . . . that idea of duty, that recognition of something to be lived for beyond the mere satisfaction of self, which is to the moral life what the addition of a great central ganglion is to animal life."[6]

That "central ganglion" of the moral life may well have been the nerve center of English history. It was here that irreconcilables were reconciled, passions were cooled, interests and ideologies were muted. The same "miracle of

3. Austin Harrison, *Frederic Harrison: Thoughts and Memories* (London, 1926), pp. 127-9.
4. *George Eliot's Life*, ed. J. W. Cross (Boston, n.d.), III, 179 (Oct. 20, 1873).
5. Willey, *Nineteenth Century Studies*, p. 204.
6. Ibid., p. 242.

modern England," in Halévy's famous phrase, that spared England the agonies of the first French Revolution also spared her the agonies of the succeeding French—and continental—revolutions. And it was not only by comparison with her neighbors that she survived so well for so long, but also in view of the vast changes that she herself was undergoing. The relative equanimity of the whole of the century was no less remarkable than the equipoise of the middle years. And even beyond the century, reports of the "death of liberal England" would seem to be premature, to judge by the recurrence of the reports; even now it is not certain that the corpse is entirely dead (if "liberal" be understood not as a party label but as a temper of mind). The true "miracle of modern England" is not that she has been spared revolution, but that she has assimilated so many revolutions—industrial, economic, social, political, cultural—without recourse to Revolution.

Postscript on the Halévy Thesis

THE PRESENT STATUS of the Halévy thesis is most curious. Again and again, in current historical literature, one encounters the casual but firm assumption that the thesis has been discredited or at least significantly modified. Yet in fact there has been no serious or sustained analysis of it. And the few brief critiques contradict each other more than they do the thesis itself.

Historians of Wesleyanism tend to assume one of three postures in relation to the thesis. Either they accept it for good and bad (as most liberals judge these matters)—that is, they accept the fact that a conservative and counterrevolutionary force might have had liberalizing and humanitarian effects.[1] Or they reject it for good and bad— that is, they deny that Wesleyanism had the significant influence Halévy attributed to it, apparently preferring to forego the compliment of so dubious an influence.[2] Or they accept the good and minimize the bad—accept the large measure of influence accorded to it but emphasize its "progressive" role in the radical Methodist sects, the trade-union movement, and the Labor Party (all of which Halévy himself made much of, in later portions of the *History*).

Similarly conflicting strategies are used by historians of radical disposition. Most of these follow the example of the Hammonds, who readily conceded the influence of Wesleyanism, but only for the bad. For the Hammonds, evangelicalism served the ruling classes as an instrument of suppression and reaction, and the working classes as a counsel of resignation and submission. Repressive, inhibiting, intolerant, obsessed with spiritual salvation and tormented by the fear of eternal damnation, it distracted men from their economic and social grievances and effectively destroyed any impulse to rebellion. And its attempt to impose a moral reformation was of a piece with its religious reformation. Thus the proposal to regulate the sale of liquor was seen by the Hammonds as part of a "campaign against the liberties of the poor." And Wilberforce engaged their attention not as the prime mover in the abolition of the slave trade but rather as an instigator of the

1. See for example the several books on Methodism by R. R. Wearmouth.

2. E.g., John H. S. Kent, in *Proceedings of the Wesley Historical Society* (Dec. 1964), pp. 188–9.

Combination Laws, the most important step in the "degradation" of the working class.[3] Shaftesbury, to be sure, was
exempted from much of this criticism, but their biography
of him was so excoriating of the evangelicals in general that
they had to delete from the second edition two passages
that reviewers found to be particularly unjust. Occasionally,
as in *The Town Laborer*, they relented sufficiently to admit
that Methodism might have had some unwittingly beneficial
results: "The teaching of Methodism was unfavorable to
working-class movements; its leaders were hostile and its
ideals perhaps increasingly hostile; but by the life and
energy and awakening that it brought to this oppressed
society it must, in spite of itself, have made many men better
citizens, and some even better rebels."[4]

E. P. Thompson, in *The Making of the English Working
Class*, portrays a Methodism that was even more influential
than Halévy's and more insidious than the Hammonds'.
The new religion is represented as a "component of the
psychic processes of counter-revolution," the "Chiliasm of
the defeated and the hopeless," the "opium of the masses,"
the "psychic ordeal in which the character structure of the
rebellious pre-industrial laborer or artisan was violently
recast into that of the submissive industrial worker."[5] (The
phrase "opium of the masses" is attributed matter-of-factly
and without benefit of footnote to Charles Kingsley—as if
to incorporate even this into the stream of indigenous
English radicalism.) Apart from the questionableness of
psycho-historical dicta that are at best generalizations from
extreme situations, there is the additional difficulty presented by Thompson's main proposition, which is that
England was on the brink of revolution from 1790 to 1832.
If Methodism prevailed so widely among the masses and

3. *The Town Laborer* (London, 1920), pp. 237, 231.
4. Ibid., p. 287.
5. *The Making of the English Working Class* (New York,
1964), pp. 381–2, 367–8.

penetrated so deeply into their individual and collective psyche, where did the impulse and perennial threat of revolution come from?

The dilemma can be avoided by simply denying the pervasiveness and potency of Methodism. This is the alternative strategy of the radical historian. Where Thompson subverts Halévy's intent by carrying the thesis to its extreme, reversing its values, and making virtues appear as vices, E. J. Hobsbawm takes the more straightforward course of disputing the thesis as fact. Hobsbawm's essay, "Methodism and the Threat of Revolution in Britain," was originally published in 1957 in *History Today* and has been reprinted in his recent volume *Labouring Men.*[6] Hobsbawm does not deny the conservatism of Wesleyanism, particularly in its early, Calvinistic, upper-class manifestations, but he does deny that it was powerful enough to have had the counterrevolutionary effect Halévy ascribed to it. There was no revolution, he argues, for reasons that derive from Lenin rather than Wesley: the ruling class never lost control because it knew when to compromise and concede; and the working class could not take control because it was too disorganized and divided. Wesleyanism was responsible for neither state of affairs. The ruling class did not need Evangelicalism to teach it political prudence; and among the working class, to the extent to which Methodism did prevail (which was less extensively than Halévy thought), it did so in its more radical forms. In another work, *Primitive Rebels*, Hobsbawm has distinguished between those quietest sects for whom religion was the "opium of the people" (no attribution here), and the Primitive Methodists, who were "primarily a sect of trade union cadres."[7]

There has, unfortunately, been no proper confrontation between Thompson and Hobsbawm, Thompson content-

6. (London, 1964), pp. 23-33.
7. (Manchester, 1959), pp. 134, 138.

ing himself with a passing reference to Hobsbawm's essay, and Hobsbawm taking cognizance of Thompson's view in a one-paragraph note appended to his essay in *Labouring Men*. Against Hobsbawm's statement that "Methodism advanced when Radicalism advanced," Thompson claims that, on the contrary, "religious revivalism took over just at the point where 'political' or temporal aspirations met with defeat."[8] Hobsbawm in reply has tried to mute their differences: "Mr. Thompson . . . shares my scepticism of Halévy, though for slightly different reasons." He then suggests that both phenomena occurred—sometimes Methodism and Radicalism went hand in hand, and sometimes the one was a substitute for the other. And he concludes by deferring to Thompson where their differences are irreconcilable.[9] The reader may regret that an occasion for significant historical controversy should have been passed over in favor of what one can only suppose to be a united front against a common enemy.

That the latter is the explanation for Hobsbawm's unwonted conciliatoriness and deference is further suggested by the opening sentence of his note. For even here, in a passage devoted, however inadequately, to Thompson, the initial thrust is against Halévy. Halévy, Hobsbawm observes, had himself "considerably toned down" his thesis in Volume IV of his *History*.[1] But what Halévy in fact said in Volume IV was that by 1850, the period he was then concerned with, "the religious and moral agencies we then described [in Volume I] . . . had already done their work," and he therefore proposed to turn his attention to the state of religion in 1850 to see how it compared with 1815.[2] It is difficult to see how, on the basis of this

8. *The Making of the English Working Class*, p. 389.
9. *Labouring Men*, p. 33.
1. Ibid.
2. *Victorian Years*, Vol. IV of *A History of the English People in the Nineteenth Century* (London, 1951), p. 337.

statement (and it is the only one in Volume IV to which Hobsbawm can be alluding), Halévy could be said to have "toned down" his thesis.

The question of times and dates is central to Halévy's thesis but is oddly ignored by many of his critics. Thus he is often criticized for exaggerating the religiosity of the Victorian working class. But much of the evidence of irreligion comes from the middle and later decades of the century, starting with Engels's *The Condition of the Working Class in England,* written in 1844, and going on to the findings of the census of 1851. The sentence from Engels that is invariably quoted is: "All bourgeois writers are agreed that the workers have no religion and do not go to church." But the rest of the passage, rarely if ever quoted, has even more bearing on the Halévy thesis. For Engels went on to exclude from his generalization "the Irish, a few of the older workers and those wage-earners who have one foot in the middle-class camp—overlookers, foremen and so on"; and in a subordinate clause, he casually remarked that "the clergy of all denominations have only recently lost their influence over the workers."[3] The total effect of the passage, therefore, is to confirm Halévy's thesis that an earlier generation of workers had been vitally touched by religion and that for some of them, at any rate, it had functioned not as an instrument of repression but of melioration. (To be sure, no evidence of social mobility or melioration can make Methodism palatable to those who regard the attainment of middle-class status as itself a symptom of repression and reaction.)

Halévy himself had anything but a static view of religion. Indeed the point of his thesis was that religion itself evolved into different forms and was eventually transmuted into a social ethic, so that long after the religious impulse had spent itself, its social consequences continued to be felt.

3. Trans. and ed. by W. O. Henderson and W. H. Chaloner (Oxford, 1958), p. 141.

I. K. Inglis, who has carefully analyzed the census of 1851 and documented the decline of religion in the second half of the century, does not take his findings to be at variance with Halévy; on the contrary, where he quotes Halévy, it is in agreement.[4] Others, however, making passing reference to this phenomenon, do so as if it did reflect adversely on Halévy's thesis.[5]

A more useful basis for reevaluation of the thesis would be an inquiry into all the other factors that made for stability and averted revolution in early nineteenth-century England. Charles C. Gillispie, in "The Work of Elie Halévy," maintains that Halévy "claimed too much for the moral influence of evangelical religion both by magnifying its importance as a causative factor in social history and by unduly minimizing the strength and coherence of political and economic causation." By the end of the page the criticism itself has been magnified, "a causative factor" being transformed into "a sufficient 'cause.' "[6] The second charge is almost certainly unwarranted, but the first deserves serious consideration. Although Halévy certainly did not ignore either politics or economics—the first two thirds of his book are occupied with just these two subjects—it may be, as Gillispie suggests, that he underestimated their stabilizing effects. Yet in the single page devoted to this question, Gillispie can obviously do no more than raise the possibility of criticism on this score; more than fifteen years later the validation of such criticism is still forthcoming. (The only concrete bit of evidence offered by Gillispie derives from the Hammonds, hardly an impartial authority.)

A distinguished sociologist, aware of the dissatisfaction

4. "Patterns of Worship in 1851," *Journal of Ecclesiastical History*, XI (1960); *Churches and the Working Classes in Victorian England* (London, 1963).

5. E.g., George Levine (ed.), *The Emergence of Victorian Consciousness* (New York, 1967), p. 8 *n*.

6. *Journal of Modern History*, XXII (1950), p. 243.

with the Halévy thesis, has described it as an "area of considerable scholarly controversy"[7]—on the assumption, presumably, that he had been afforded a glimpse of only the tip of the iceberg. Unfortunately there is little beneath the tip. The whole of this "area of considerable scholarly controversy" consists of a ten-page essay, several pages of a large volume, some paragraphs in a biographical article, portions of book reviews, and isolated, undocumented, but increasingly common statements to the effect that the thesis is no longer tenable.

If scholarly controversy is so conspicuously lacking, why is the dissatisfaction so pervasive? The answer may lie in the prevailing intellectual fashions. Revisionism is the temper of contemporary historical studies, and it is automatically assumed that any thesis dating back so far (the first volume of Halévy's *History* was published in 1913) must by now be obsolete. Hastening this obsolescence is the peculiarly unmodish character of this particular thesis. To assign so much importance to ideas, and especially religious ideas, seems naïve to a generation brought up on Marx, Freud, and Sartre. And to find virtue in ideas and religions that encourage gradualism, stability, and social cohesion is doubly galling to those who have a quite different order of virtues and values.

Halévy himself may have anticipated his critics when he wrote of the troubled years before World War I: "A century earlier Wesley had defeated Voltaire. Would he defeat Marx?"[8] It would have been presumptuous for Halévy, but perhaps not for us, to put the related question: Will Halévy defeat Marx as the interpreter of this crucial period in English history?

7. Seymour M. Lipset, *The First New Nation* (New York, 1963), p. 6.
8. *Imperialism and the Rise of Labour* (London, 1951), p. 361.

THE VICTORIAN *ANGST*

H OW CAN WE TAKE seriously the religious qualms of the Victorians now that the "Death of God" has been solemnized on the cover of *Time?* How can we attend to their quarrel over the Thirty-Nine Articles while we are fatally quarreling with God himself? How can we be expected to appreciate the audacity of a rationalism that strikes many of us as being no less credulous than religion itself? How can we sympathize with the attempt to create a morality without religion when we are engaged in propounding an ethic without morality? How can we share their indignation at the absurdity of the biblical miracles when we have made a principle and philosophy out of absurdity itself? How can we be patient with doubts after being exposed to the most radical and total nihilism?

Yet the curious thing is that the Victorians are still accessible and meaningful to us. The best Victorian novels, even when they turn on a moral dilemma that no longer presents itself as a dilemma, are eminently readable, dilemma and all, and with no more suspension of belief than we bring to most modern novels. And the best Victorian thinkers are similarly readable, religious qualms and all.

Indeed, it is often possible to respond more sympathetically and imaginatively to the Victorians than to the moderns. Modern forms of unbelief, like some modern novels, are so ingenious as to become *tours de force*, mechanical exercises in intellect and sensibility. In retrospect, the repudiation of the Thirty-Nine Articles may prove to have been more serious than the current celebration of polymorphous perversity. Certainly the first was more serious for the cleric or don who sacrificed his job, career, social esteem, and personal tranquillity; whereas the second, as often as not, has turned out to be the making of reputation and fortune. Cardinal Newman's novel about the travails of a Catholic convert was fittingly called *Loss and Gain.* The title had a personal as well as religious significance, implying not only the loss of one faith and gain of another, but also the loss and gain of friendships, traditions, loyalties, and sentiments. It is the conviction of a genuine loss and gain that is lacking from our own more melodramatic sagas.

A recent work brings together a miscellany of Victorians under the rubric of "Unbelievers": John Stuart Mill, A. H. Clough, Matthew Arnold, T. H. Huxley, George Eliot, Herbert Spencer, and Samuel Butler.[1] Each was different in temperament, persuasion, and ability; each had his own calculus of loss and gain. If they differed among each other, still more can they be expected to differ from us. Yet the author of this work, A. O. J. Cockshut, measuring their unbelief against what he takes to be our own standard of unbelief, finds them wanting. Only Clough, he says, was a "real doubter," doubting not only religion, but marriage, work, life itself. The others were content with smaller degrees of doubt: "Denial of Christianity was common, denial of God was fairly common, but doubt was rare." Even the celebrated Metaphysical Society, the debating forum of agnostics and clerics, had this in common: "All or almost all of its members were

1. A. O. J. Cockshut, *The Unbelievers* (New York, 1966).

untroubled by personal doubts of the truth of what they maintained." Nor did any of them question such basic tenets of the Victorian faith as Newton's laws of motion, the domestic virtues, the English parliamentary system, or the "importance of his own thoughts."[2]

This is a curious assortment of beliefs that is supposed to demonstrate the failure of Victorian unbelief. Can any unbelief withstand so rigorous a test? Our own generation of skeptics finds it easy to doubt Newton, but not Einstein; the domestic virtues, but not the political ones (colonialism being to our latter-day fundamentalists what fornication was to the Victorians); English parliamentarianism, but not participatory democracy; and surely not the importance of our own thoughts. "Nearly all the great Victorians were very emotional men," we are told, "and it is impossible for a deeply emotional man to carry skepticism beyond a certain point."[3] Are our own apocalyptic nihilists any less emotional? Or those who are playing it cool and opting out—why do they go to such lengths, take such hazardous trips, if not because they take themselves so desperately seriously?

In fact, the Victorian unbelievers carried unbelief about as far as it would humanly, sanely, go. If in the end unbelief itself became a form of belief, this is exactly what history and experience should lead us to expect. It is not really so surprising to find John Stuart Mill, the apostle of rationalism, conceding the virtue of religious piety; or George Eliot giving expression to her agnosticism in the form of Jewish characters and themes; or Matthew Arnold disbelieving in miracles and dogmatic theology but holding up the crucifixion and resurrection as symbols of moral salvation; or Spencer, the complete agnostic, making a metaphysical principle of the Unknowable itself. "To say

2. Ibid., p. 32.
3. Ibid.

that we cannot know the Absolute," wrote Spencer, "is, by implication, to affirm that there is an Absolute. In the very denial of our power to learn what the Absolute is, there lies hidden the assumption that it is; and the making of this assumption proves that the Absolute has been present to the mind, not as a nothing, but as a something."[4] This is not very far from that "negation of negation" that is the final affirmation of our own most recent and most apocalyptic nihilists.

Where the Victorians unquestionably differed from ourselves was in the form of affirmation that transcended negation, the particular belief that superseded unbelief. For the Victorian unbeliever, the transcendent belief was morality. Eliot wrote that "the idea of God, so far as it has been a high spiritual influence is the ideal of a goodness entirely human."[5] And it was this moral ideal, according to Mill, that made the best of the unbelievers "more genuinely religious, in the best sense of the word religion, than those who exclusively arrogate to themselves the title."[6]

The conventional notion has it that the Victorians were living on the moral capital of their ancestors, the diminishing capital of a religious inheritance. We can see now how inadequate this idea is. There was nothing diminished or impoverished about Victorian morality. If anything, the loss of religious zeal resulted in an intensification of moral zeal. It is as if the Victorians, by giving to mankind what they could no longer give to God, hoped to atone for the gravity of their sin and the pain of their loss. Their morality was a displacement of religion—which may explain the fanatical quality of their morality, their need to create a Religion of Humanity.

4. Ibid., p. 82.
5. *George Eliot's Life*, ed. J. W. Cross (Boston, n.d.), III, 201 (Dec. 10, 1874).
6. John Stuart Mill, *Autobiography* (New York, 1924), p. 32.

The characters in one of Ibsen's plays reflect upon their moral situation: "Where I have sinned, it is right I should expiate." "There is no judge over us. And therefore we must see to it that we judge ourselves."[7] This new atheistic morality, self-judging because it recognized no external judge, evidently completed the process that started with Protestantism. We are accustomed to the familiar distinction between Catholic and Protestant morality—the Catholic variety laxer and more tolerant because it provided the ritualistic means of atonement; Protestantism more demanding because it internalized morality together with spirituality. By the same token, atheistic (or agnostic, or rationalistic, or theistic) morality was still more demanding, carrying a burden of guilt still heavier. For here there was neither an objective ritual of atonement nor an objective measure of sin.

The displacement of religion by morality may be seen most dramatically in the crisis-of-faith novels. The subplot of most of these novels is a moral crisis paralleling the religious one. The hero, resigning from the ministry because he can no longer subscribe to the Articles or affirm the divinity of Christ, promptly finds himself engaged in some immoral or improper adventure. There is no dramatic logic connecting the two plots, the moral drama being only adventitiously related to the religious. Yet the symbolic logic is compelling. The moral crisis is in effect the human counterpart, the "objective correlative," of the religious; it is the wrath of God turned upon man, blasphemy transmuted into vice. This is why the moral issue in these novels can rarely be understood in its own terms and why the ethical doctrine is so often incoherent. The hero, who has agonizingly given up his faith because he has found God to be irrational and tyrannical, the Bible cruel and dishonest, and the Church lacking in Christian virtue, is then subjected to a secular morality, an earthly retribution, far

7. Cockshut, *Unbelievers*, pp. 152-3.

more irrational, cruel, and merciless than the most unedifying chapters in Christianity.

The desperate nature of the new morality, the internalization and subjectivization of sin, led also to the sexualization of morality. One thinks of Victorian morality as a morality of convention, in which the flouting of the proprieties was the most heinous sin. But it turns out that it was not sexual unconventionality that was condemned, but sex itself.

The passage in Zola that caused most offense to Victorians was one where no conventional moral judgment could conceivably apply: it was a scene describing the mating of a bull and cow. Dickens could more easily allude to sexual relations between an unmarried couple than between a married one because in effect there was no licit sex; it was all illicit. George Holyoake, the most belligerent atheist and radical of the century, made it one of his points in his indictment of the church that its marriage service "contains things no bride could hear without a blush *if she understood them.*"[8] (The italics were his—expressive of relief that she could not understand them, or anxiety that she might?) And in general, a major complaint against orthodox religion was the physical, corporeal, and therefore degrading character of such doctrines as baptismal regeneration, the resurrection, or the eucharistic sacrifice.

This is not of course, to say that this sexual morality (or morbidity, as we might think it) was confined to unbelievers. But it is interesting that it should have been taken up so fanatically by those who in other respects seemed so liberal, enlightened, "progressive." It is also interesting to find a similar sexual fastidiousness among an earlier generation of agnostics. William Godwin, who denounced with equal fervor religion, marriage, and property (at least until Shelley ran off with his daughter), envisaged a utopia where men would become progressively more cultivated

8. Ibid., p. 162.

and virtuous until sexuality would be eliminated entirely.[9] And James Mill, as his son observed with approval, favored a considerable increase of freedom in the relation between the sexes, in the hope that the imagination would then "no longer dwell upon the physical relation and its adjuncts, and swell this into one of the principal objects of life; a perversion of the imagination and feelings which he regarded as one of the deepest seated and most pervading evils in the human mind."[1] The son progressed beyond the father only in the ardor of his feminism; for John Stuart Mill, women were more equal than men, precisely because they were more spiritual, less physical and sensual. And when he came to defend his unconventional relationship with Harriet Taylor, it was its Platonic purity that he insisted upon.

The permutations of belief and unbelief, the mutations of faith and morality, may be strikingly illustrated in the family histories of some of the great Victorians, with brothers making for even more interesting contrasts than father and son. One is reminded of the Arnolds—the famous Matthew and the less well-known Thomas, Jr., a Catholic convert; the Wilberforces—two of William's sons being Anglican and the other two Catholic; the Froudes—Hurrell, High Church Tractarian, and Anthony, aggressive anti-Papist; and most dramatic, the Newmans—John Henry, the cardinal, and Francis, the agnostic.

It is odd that Cockshut should have neglected to include Francis Newman among his Unbelievers. A biography by William Robbins repairs this failure—and in the best possible way, by counterposing Francis to his more illustrious

---

9. Godwin, *Enquiry concerning Political Justice, and its Influence on Morals and Happiness* (3rd edn.; London, 1798), II, 516.

1. Mill, *Autobiography*, p. 75.

brother, Cardinal Newman.[2] *The Times Literary Supplement*, with the characteristic obtuseness of that journal, suggests that the contrast between the two brothers was too great to justify a joint biography and that they would each have been better served by separate books. The criticism could not be more ill-advised. The brothers cannot, in fact, be understood except in reference to each other, their minds and careers being perfectly antithetical—and complementary.

Indeed, a quadruple biography, comprising the Newmans and Froudes, might be even more revealing. John Newman was not only an intimate friend of Hurrell Froude (the extent of their intimacy was a subject of gossip in their time and speculation in ours); he also stood in much the same relation—personal and ideological—to his younger brother as Hurrell did to his.[3] John was less blatantly domineering and sadistic than Hurrell, but the psychological pattern was similar. The "Grand Master," as John designated himself in childhood games,[4] was that in all his relations with Francis. Intellectually and emotionally implacable, spurning Francis's advances and unforgiving of his religious deviations, John dominated his family even when his views were completely repugnant to it. When Francis received a Double First at Oxford (after John's failure to get a simple First), Mrs. Newman wrote John to commend him for his "labors and anxiety" on behalf of his brother: "I am more thankful on your account than on his. He is a piece of adamant. You are such a sensitive being." And John himself recorded the event as if it reflected more upon him than upon Francis: "How I have been led! how prospered! . . . I went before, failing in the Schools, to punish and humble me. Then, by gaining a fellowship here,

2. Robbins, *The Newman Brothers* (Cambridge, Mass., 1966).
3. See the essay on James Anthony Froude in this volume, pp. 238 ff.
4. Geoffrey Faber, *Oxford Apostles* (New York, 1934), p. 15.

I was enabled to take him by the hand. And now he is my 'avenger of blood'."[5]

In the case of the Froudes, it was the father who broke up his younger son's first love affair; in the case of the Newmans it was, inadvertently, the older brother. (The girl to whom Francis proposed was more attracted to John; she later became a Catholic convert and a nun.) Unlike Hurrell, John was never physically abusive toward his brother. He was only coldly and ruthlessly dismissive. He informed his Oxford congregation: "There is not a dissenter living but, inasmuch and so far as he dissents, is in a sin"; and promptly sent the sermon to his mother, who could not have escaped the implication that Francis had been consigned to perdition.[6] And in his *Apologia*, he used the example of his brother to illustrate his theory that it was necessary to "learn to hate" before one could love—to hate sin, he hastily explained; but it was his brother who personified sin: "I would have no dealings with my brother, and I put my conduct upon a syllogism. I said, 'St. Paul bids us avoid those who cause divisions; you cause divisions: therefore I must avoid you.' "[7]

The "division"-making was obviously not all on one side. If John was all too ready to damn his brother because of their differences, Francis was all too quick to create such differences. Again the analogy with the Froudes is revealing. Both younger brothers used religion as the occasion for rebellion, as the elder brothers, one suspects, used it for the assertion of authority. The analogy persists even to the oddly similar titles under which the younger brothers recorded their spiritual liberation—Anthony Froude's *Nemesis of Faith* and Francis Newman's *Phases of Faith*. Where Anthony Froude, however, was content to carry his rebel-

5. Robbins, *Newman Brothers*, p. 16.

6. Faber, *Oxford Apostles*, p. 243.

7. Newman, *Apologia Pro Vita Sua* (Riverside edn.; Boston, 1956), pp. 64–5.

lion only to the point of rejecting Anglo-Catholicism and Roman Catholicism, Francis Newman rejected all churches and all religious orthodoxies.

Indeed, Francis Newman seemed determined to reject all orthodoxies. He was not only a rationalist and agnostic; he was also a radical, democrat, anti-imperialist, feminist, humanitarian—the whole complex of attitudes that John associated with the heresy of modern liberalism. Francis was the archetypical liberal and the archetypical unbeliever. And in both capacities, he sustained his unbelief by a multiplicity of beliefs. One unbeliever described another as "an ardent Free Thinker and Radical, a teetotaller and non-smoker"—as if these qualities were naturally all of a piece.[8] In Francis Newman one finds an even more varied assortment of abnegations that seemed to add up, for him, to a single set of affirmations. He was a vegetarian of a peculiarly complicated and precise kind. He was also anti-liquor, anti-tobacco, anti-vivisection, anti-vaccination, anti-hunting, "anti-everything" as he once, in a rare moment of irony, admitted. He was also anti-sex, for the same reason that he was pro-woman. He denounced what he called the "Safe Harlot Providing Act" (the Contagious Diseases Act requiring the medical examination of prostitutes in garrison districts) as an insult to womanhood because it sanctioned sexual exploitation, and an insult to manhood because it implied that soldiers were incapable of continence: "We know that a ship-crew of young men, chiefly under the age of twenty-five, and picked for masculine vigor, may go to the Arctic regions for a year or two, and return in splendid condition without seeing a woman's face."[9]

The ultimate abnegation, beyond food, dress, pleasure, even sex, was the abnegation of self; and this was the basic moral principle, the basic affirmation of the unbeliever. We are used to associating this abnegation of self with the

8. Cockshut, *Unbelievers*, p. 162.
9. Robbins, *Newman Brothers*, p. 150.

religious zealot—the type of evangelical who, as Leslie Stephen said of his father, "once smoked a cigar and found it so delicious that he never smoked again."[1] But the unbeliever was governed by exactly the same principle. One of George Eliot's main arguments against immortality was that it was too easy and comfortable a belief. "Higher religion" she defined as that which enabled the believer to "do without the consolations that his egoism would demand";[2] and in another discussion of religion she declared it to be "preeminently desirable that we should learn not to make our personal comfort a standard of truth."[3] Francis Newman insisted that only by stripping Christianity of its "earthly husk" and restoring it to its original moral purity would men solve the real problem of the time, which was to "save cultivated Europe from Pantheism, Selfishness, and Sensuality."[4] This is why he regarded himself as a "theist" rather than "atheist": "Our highest ideal is (whether we know it or not) a God to us; and if we devote ourselves to it, we are practical Theists, whatever our creed. He who worships no ideal at all, but lives for self, is the real atheist."[5] Yet most atheists, he admitted, were no less self-denying. Holyoake's atheism, for example, could only be a "transition towards a new and better religion" since it was his "moral goodness" that gave power to his doctrine.[6]

Francis once taunted his brother with the news that "Holyoake, the Atheist Lecturer, is a great admirer of you—and of me!" To which John blandly replied that there was nothing remarkable about this: theist, atheist, and Catholic were all in search of the same thing—but it was the Catholic alone who found it. What they were in search

1. Noel Annan, *Leslie Stephen* (Cambridge, Mass., 1952), p. 14.
2. Cockshut, *Unbelievers*, p. 53.
3. *Eliot's Life*, III, 14 (May 30, 1867).
4. Basil Willey, *More Nineteenth Century Studies* (London, 1956), p. 40.
5. Robbins, *Newman Brothers*, p. 93.
6. Ibid., p. 179.

of was described by Francis in words that could as well have come from John: "to show those who know not on what to rest their faith, to what quarter they must look for solid ground," and so save them from the "desolating negations which are abroad."[7]

This, finally, is the interesting aspect of Victorian morality—and unbelief. Contemporaries often said, and historians have for the most part agreed, that unbelief was a consequence of an obsessive concern with morality, that the unbelievers were repelled by the immoralities of the church, the dishonesties of the Bible, the grossness of religious doctrine. Yet the extravagance of their moral demands, the excessive spirituality they sought in life, suggests that the reverse was more often true—that Victorian morality was a consequence of unbelief. They went to such extremes not, as is generally thought, because they feared a breakdown of morality; morality was, in fact, never so secure as then, the moral consensus never so complete. The breakdown was, rather, metaphysical, a loss of certitude about being, meaning, nature, values. Nor is it true, as contemporaries and historians have conspired to make it seem, that the metaphysical crisis was significant only because it undermined the basis of morality, or because the existence of God was assumed to be a precondition of virtue. Frederick Temple, then Bishop of Exeter, criticized the Darwinian theory of morality on the grounds that morality could not have evolved "out of anything but itself" since it was absolute and self-sufficient in exactly the same way as mathematical truth[8]—thus neatly depriving morality of a necessary basis not only in evolution but also in religion. If the bishop felt it possible to have a self-sufficient morality, a morality not grounded on religion, surely the unbe-

7. Ibid., p. 107.
8. Temple, "The Relations between Religion and Science," *Religious Controversies of the Nineteenth Century*, ed. A. O. J. Cockshut (Lincoln, Neb., 1966), p. 260.

liever could have taken the same position. It was not morality, one finally concludes, that required the security of religion; it was the unbeliever who required that security—required it not for the sake of morality but for the sake of belief itself. And lacking the security of belief, he compensated, or overcompensated, for its lack by making the most of the morality he had.

The Victorians, in fact, were suffering from the modern malady—*Angst*. It was this that was the common denominator of belief and unbelief, the common bond between a Francis Newman and a John Henry Newman. As Francis sought respite, in reason and virtue, from the "desolating negations which are abroad," so John sought sanctuary in a universal church boasting an assured apostolic succession and metaphysical, doctrinal certainty.

This quest for certainty helps explain a fact about John Newman that often perplexed his contemporaries and his commentators—the sparseness of personal mystical allusions in his writings. He once wrote that he had gone through the whole of his long, agonizing religious crisis "neither expecting nor experiencing anything supernatural," driven purely and simply by a desire for truth.[9] The confession is as extraordinary as it is credible. If he had been willing to settle for something else—for a religion that was mystically inspired or a church that was justified in terms of social expediency—he would have spared himself much labor and anguish. For he would not then have sought the complicated and subtle rationale by which metaphysical certainty could be derived from logical probability, objective knowledge from subjective belief, and theological science from historical doctrine. And he would have been spared the accusations so commonly bandied about, and not by Kingsley alone, of cunning, equivocation, hypocrisy, sophistry, shiftiness . . . But then if he had been willing to settle for something less than

9. Robbins, *Newman Brothers*, p. 76.

intellectual certitude, he would never have experienced his crisis at all, and would never have made the move that entailed so much loss as well as gain. He would not have left the church in which he had attained high honor and esteem for one that was socially demeaning, esthetically offensive, and personally humiliating. It was only because he sought to confront the "desolating negations" with the most positive affirmations that he was driven to the philosophical subtleties that were the despair of his contemporaries, and to the act of conversion that was at the same time his mortification and his salvation.

One contemporary said of John Newman: "I believe him to be at bottom far more skeptical than his brother Francis; and the extravagant credulity with which he accepts the wildest Popish legends is, as it appears to me, only another side of his bottomless unbelief."[1] The remark may be taken as a commentary not only on the Newman brothers but on all extravagances of belief and unbelief—in our time as in theirs.

1. Ibid., p. 119.

VARIETIES OF SOCIAL DARWINISM

I DEAS," a great historian has said, "have a radiation and development, an ancestry and posterity of their own, in which men play the part of godfathers and godmothers more than that of legitimate parents."[1] This dictum may well stand as the text of this essay. Without going so far as those who venture to cast doubt upon the paternity of Darwinism proper—the theory of natural selection—one would certainly be justified in questioning Darwin's paternal relationship to the variety of theories going by the name of Social Darwinism. With respect to the latter, one can charge him with no more than godfatherhood. Darwin may be likened to the old friend of the family who had amiably agreed to take part in the baptismal ceremonies and years later was dismayed to find himself responsible for an ill-assorted, erratic, and not particularly congenial set of godchildren. And yet, like the typical godfather, Darwin did have a responsibility—and not only legally and morally, but also intellectually and spiritually—for the offspring of his friends. Father and godfather, after all, have a closer intellectual affinity than many a blood relation. Surely

1. Lord Acton, *Letters to Mary Gladstone* (1st edn.; New York, 1905), p. 99 (March 15, 1880).

some of this affinity, and therefore responsibility, carries over to the godchildren.

Before sorting out the various social theories claiming descent from Darwin, one must pay one's respects to the only true and lawfully begotten theory of Darwin: the theory that was first brought to life in the *Origin of Species* and that came to maturity in the *Descent of Man*. The essential features of that theory were clearly visible at birth, and lest anyone mistake them, Darwin formally incorporated them into the patronymic. The full title of his famous book was: *On the Origin of Species by Means of Natural Selection, or the Preservation of Favoured Races in the Struggle for Life*. "Natural selection," "preservation of favoured races," "struggle for life"—only the term "survival of the fittest" was missing, although the idea was certainly implied; in a later edition of the *Origin* Darwin regretted that he had not used Spencer's "survival of the fittest" in place of his own "natural selection."

From one or another part of this multi-barreled title may be traced most of the social theories seeking legitimacy in the name of Social Darwinism—an *ex post facto* legitimacy, to be sure, the social theories having generally long ante-dated the *Origin of Species* and even Darwin himself. Yet the act of legitimization may be as important to the life and well-being of an idea as it is to a child. This process of legitimization may be demonstrated in the case of the most common variety of Social Darwinism: laissez-fairism.

The doctrine of laissez-faire—the free, unrestrained competition of individuals—was born at least three quarters of a century before the *Origin*, and indeed the *Origin* itself owed its very existence to one of the classics of laissez-fairism. It was Malthus's *Essay on Population* that, by Darwin's own admission, gave birth to the *Origin*. By a curious incestuous inversion, however, Darwin was made to legitimize both Malthus and Adam Smith. Oswald

Spengler was later to complain that the *Origin* was the "application of economics to biology" and that it reeked of the "atmosphere of the English factory."[2] Yet by the time the *Origin* and *Descent* were published, classical economic theory was being modified and social legislation was beginning to dissipate the more noxious fumes of the factory. Darwinism, therefore, did not so much reflect the current atmosphere as recall an earlier time and revive an earlier state of mind. This was the effect of one widely quoted passage from the *Descent:*

> With savages, the weak in body or mind are soon eliminated; and those that survive commonly exhibit a vigorous state of health. We civilized men, on the other hand, do our utmost to check the process of elimination; we build asylums for the imbecile, the maimed, and the sick; we institute poor-laws; and our medical men exert their utmost skill to save the life of everyone to the last moment. There is reason to believe that vaccination has preserved thousands, who from a weak constitution would formerly have succumbed to small-pox. Thus the weak members of civilized societies propagate their kind. No one who has attended to the breeding of domestic animals will doubt that this must be highly injurious to the race of man.[3]

In America the authority of Darwin was added to that of Herbert Spencer, who as social theorist and as scientist had always enjoyed higher repute in the new world than in the old. A decade before the publication of the *Origin*, Spencer had worked out the social implications of the "survival of the fittest":

> The well-being of existing humanity, and the unfolding of it into this ultimate perfection, are both secured by the same beneficent, though severe discipline, to which the

2. Spengler, *The Decline of the West* (New York, 1939), I, 373, 371.
3. Darwin, *Descent of Man* (London, 1901), pp. 205–6.

animate creation at large is subject; a discipline which is pitiless in the working out of good; a felicity-pursuing law which never swerves for the avoidance of partial and temporary suffering. The poverty of the incapable, the distresses that come upon the imprudent, the starvation of the idle, and those shoulderings aside of the weak by the strong . . . are the decrees of a large far-seeing providence.[4]

It was largely under the influence of Spencer that the American sociologist, William Graham Sumner, concluded that if we rejected the principle of the survival of the fittest, we must be prepared to accept that of the survival of the unfittest. The first was the necessary condition of liberty and civilization, the second of equality and anti-civilization; "the former carries society forward and favors all its best members, the latter carries society downward and favors all its worst members."[5] From the same premises, John D. Rockefeller was able to demonstrate that what was good for civilization was also good for business—and vice versa. The large corporation that grew by swallowing up its smaller competitors was merely exhibiting the law of the "survival of the fittest . . ., the working out of a law of nature and a law of God."[6] Even Walt Whitman, while excoriating the "depravity of the business classes," insisted that a necessary part of American democracy was its "practical, stirring, worldly, moneymaking, even materialistic character":

I perceive clearly that the extreme business energy, and this almost maniacal appetite for wealth prevalent in the United States, are parts of amelioration and progress, indispensably needed to prepare the very results I demand.

4. Spencer, *Social Statics* (New York, 1954), pp. 288–9.
5. Sumner, *Essays*, ed. A. G. Keller and M. R. Davie (New Haven, 1934), II, 56, 95.
6. Richard Hofstadter, *Social Darwinism in American Thought* (rev. edn.; Boston, 1955), p. 48.

My theory includes riches, and the getting of riches, and the amplest products, power, activity, inventions, movements, etc. Upon them, as upon sub-strata, I raise the edifice designed in these Vistas.[7]

The laissez-fairists derived their sanction from that part of Darwinism which envisaged the individual members of any given species competing against each other for the available resources—out of which competition the fittest individuals survived, perpetuated their kind, and thus contributed to the betterment and evolution of their species. But there was also going on, according to Darwin, a struggle *among* the species—an *inter*-species competition, that is, as well as an *intra*-species competition. The title of Darwin's book may be taken as exemplifying these two struggles: the first part of the title, "On the Origin of Species by Means of Natural Selection," referring to the competition within any one species; the second part, "The Preservation of Favoured Races in the Struggle for Life," to the competition among the various species. And while the first part, the intra-species competition, seemed to validate the ideology of laissez-faire, the second part, the inter-species competition, suggested a very different and, as it sometimes appeared, contrary ideology—the ideology of nationalism, imperialism, and militarism.

Darwin sometimes professed to find this second deduction from his theory as ludicrous as the first. Soon after the *Origin* was published, he poked fun at a squib in a Manchester newspaper which attributed to him the idea that " 'might is right' and therefore that Napoleon is right, and every cheating tradesman is also right."[8] Yet while he personally disapproved of Napoleon as much as he disapproved of cheating tradesmen, the proponents of the

7. Whitman, *Democratic Vistas* (New York, 1949), pp. 10, 24.
8. *Life and Letters of Charles Darwin*, ed. Francis Darwin (London, 1887), II, 262 (Jan. 4, 1860).

doctrine "might is right" could find ample justification in his theory. Darwin himself wrote, in a letter shortly before his death:

> I could show fight on natural selection having done and doing more for the progress of civilization than you seem inclined to admit. Remember what risk the nations of Europe ran, not so many centuries ago, of being over-whelmed by the Turks, and how ridiculous such an idea now is! The more civilized so-called Caucasian races have beaten the Turkish hollow in the struggle for existence. Looking to the world at no very distant date, what an endless number of the lower races will have been elimi-nated by the higher civilized races throughout the world.[9]

One can make out a strong case for Social Darwinism in this sense. Just as the hero, superman, or Führer may be assumed to have established his pre-eminence as a result of the struggle for existence within the state, so the state itself, under his leadership, will engage in a struggle with other states to establish its pre-eminence in the world. And just as the leader may be assumed to be the fittest of his species, so the triumphant nation will impose itself upon lesser, less fit, nations, and thus raise all of mankind to that higher level of civilization alluded to by Darwin. A German general drew precisely this inference from Darwin's theory:

> War is not merely a necessary element in the life of nations but an indispensable factor of culture, in which a truly civilized nation finds the highest expression of strength and vitality. . . . War gives a biologically just decision, since its decisions rest on the very nature of things. . . . It is not only a biological law, but a moral obligation, and, as such, an indispensable factor in civiliza-tion.[1]

But the doctrine was by no means confined to German generals. English scientists may be quoted to exactly the

9. Ibid., I, 316 (July 3, 1881).
1. Hofstadter, *Social Darwinism*, p. 197.

same effect. In 1900, at the height of the Boer War, the mathematican and eugenicist Karl Pearson defended the war to those of his countrymen who had doubts and qualms:

> This dependence of progress on the survival of the fitter race, terribly black as it may seem to some of you, gives the struggle for existence its redeeming features; it is the fiery crucible out of which comes the finer metal. [When wars cease] mankind will no longer progress [for] there will be nothing to check the fertility of inferior stock; the relentless law of heredity will not be controlled and guided by natural selection.[2]

And more recently, shortly before World War II, Sir Arthur Keith, the anthropologist and biographer of Darwin, confessed that although his own disposition was pacific, he feared the results of too long a period of peace. At the end of five centuries of peace, he predicted, the world would look like "an orchard that has not known the pruning hook for many an autumn and has rioted in unchecked overgrowth for endless years." He was no advocate of war, he protested, but he could not conceive of any substitute that would accomplish as much "for the real health of humanity and the building of stronger races."[3]

When German generals or English scientists, or even Darwin himself, spoke of the triumph of the "higher civilized races" in this international struggle for existence, they generally identified races with nations. But there were more precise, biological, racial implications that might be extracted from Darwin's theory. Again Darwin himself may be quoted on both sides of this issue. One may cite his

2. Bernard Semmel, *Imperialism and Social Reform* (London, 1960), p. 41.
3. Preface to Alfred Machin, *Darwin's Theory Applied to Mankind* (London, 1937), p. viii.

personal abhorrence of slavery and his ardent champion-
ship of the North in the American Civil War. "In the long
run," he wrote in 1861 to the American scientist Asa Gray,
"a million horrid deaths would be amply repaid in the cause
of humanity"—upon which gory prospect he curiously
exulted: "What wonderful times we live in!"[4] And when
the London *Times* persisted in its pro-Southern policy, he
altered the cherished habit of a lifetime and with great
sense of sacrifice canceled his subscription. Later he entered
as passionately into the cause of the Jamaican Negroes
whose revolt had been harshly suppressed by their English
governor. Yet he did not pretend to deduce his political
principles from his scientific theories, and he was well
aware that some of his closest colleagues and most loyal
disciples signed the petition in defence of the English
governor and against the Negro rebels.

In fact the theory of natural selection has played an
equivocal role in the controversy over racism. On the one
hand, by denying the separateness of species, by showing
how species evolved from each other and ultimately how
all derived from a single primordial form, the theory implicitly denied the purity of races that has been an important ingredient in most racist creeds, and affirmed the
brotherhood of man that has been the classical refutation of
racism. This brotherhood of man was, indeed, the message
which many contemporaries extracted from the *Origin*.
Asa Gray, the American friend to whom Darwin had
written so exultantly of the Northern cause, himself a
Northerner, a zealous abolitionist, and equally zealous Darwinian, confessed that when he first read the *Origin* he
could not help wincing at the thought that he was unmis-
takably related to the Hottentot and Negro. He, of course,
managed to suppress such an unworthy reaction. But
others, confronted with the same prospect, took this to be
sufficient reason for disbelieving the *Origin*.

4. *Life and Letters of Darwin*, II, 374 (June 5, 1861).

Still others, however, managed to reconcile the *Origin* and racism, and even use the *Origin* to legitimize racism. For although Darwin did derive all races, like all species, from a single ancestor, he by no means denied the present reality of distinctive races, any more than he denied the present reality of distinctive species. He did not dissolve species into an undistinguished mass of individuals; and by the same token he did not do what so many anti-racists do: that is, assume an uninterrupted racial spectrum in which each individual differs from his neighbor so slightly that only artificially, statistically, can different races be distinguished. Indeed a primary purpose of the theory of natural selection was precisely to account for the reality of species and races, to show not only how they evolved but also how they became stabilized and fixed in form, certainly in any one period and sometimes over very long periods of time.

Similarly, advocates of racial segregation and of desegregation could appeal for support to different aspects of Darwinism. The desegregationists could, and did, quote the *Origin* to the effect that crosses between varieties tend to increase the number, size, and vigor of the offspring; while segregationists cited passages demonstrating that in many circumstances such a cross would prove fatal to both varieties. When the London *Times* warned the abolitionists that the mixture of races "tends not to the elevation of the black, but to the degradation of the white man,"[5] a secretary at the American legation commented in his diary: "This is bold doctrine for an English journal and is one of the results of reflection on mixed races aided by light from Mr. Darwin's book and his theory of Natural Selection."[6]

Even if Darwinism canceled itself out, so to speak, in respect to the reality of distinct races, or the desirability of

5. *The Times*, Dec. 28, 1859.
6. Benjamin Moran, *Journal* (Chicago, 1948), I, 619.

a mixture of races, it told heavily in favor of a struggle of races and the inevitable and proper domination of the weak by the strong. Karl Pearson regarded this racial struggle as a necessary appendage to the imperialist struggle:

> History shows me one way and one way only, in which a high state of civilization has been produced, namely the struggle of race with race, and the survival of the physically and mentally fitter race. If men want to know whether the lower races of man can evolve a higher type, I fear the only course is to leave them to fight it out among themselves.[7]

Pearson's particular variety of Social Darwinism is especially intriguing because he took Darwinism to be not only a legitimization of imperialism and racism, but also of what he thought of as socialism. Against those Social Darwinists who read the lesson of the master as a vindication of laissez-fairism, Pearson read it as a refutation of laissez-fairism. Since he regarded the inter-species, the international struggle, as paramount, he argued that that struggle could only be effectively fought if the intra-species struggle, the struggle within the nation, was suppressed: "We must not have class differences and wealth differences so great within the community that we lose the sense of common interest. . . . No tribe of men work together unless the tribal interest dominates the personal and individual interest at all points where they come into conflict."[8]

Pearson's "socialism," it may be objected, had no more in common with real socialism than the National Socialism of Hitler with the socialism of the Social Democrats. But there were other socialists whose claim to the name seems more warranted, and who manifested something of the same amalgam of socialism, imperialism, and Darwinism.

7. George E. Simpson, "Darwin and Social Darwinism," *The European Past*, ed. Clough, Gay, and Warner (New York, 1964), II, 115.
8. Semmel, *Imperialism*, pp. 41-2.

And this was not because, like Pearson, they gave priority to the external, the imperial struggle and thus sought to suppress the internal, the domestic struggle, but rather because they gave priority to the attainment of domestic socialism and saw the empire as a reinforcement and extension of domestic socialism. The English Fabians were typical of this group—the Webbs, George Bernard Shaw, and others who supported first imperialism and then tariff protectionism on the grounds that both would strengthen the efficient, integrated socialist state.[9]

And then there were the Marxists, who also saw their views confirmed by Darwinism. Marx himself was so taken with the *Origin* that he proposed to dedicate *Das Kapital* to Darwin. Darwin politely declined the honor: "Though our studies have been so different, I believe that we both earnestly desire the extension of knowledge; and this, in the long run, is sure to add to the happiness of mankind."[1] To a German scientist, Darwin was more candid: "What a foolish idea seems to prevail in Germany on the connection between Socialism and Evolution through Natural Selection."[2] But Marx saw nothing foolish in the idea. Indeed he looked upon the *Origin* as a "basis in natural science for the class struggle in history,"[3] the struggle of species in nature being paralleled by the struggle of classes in history, with nature and history evolving in the same fashion. To those who protested that Marxism was a creed not of evolution but of revolution, later Marxist theorists, such as Plekhanov, pointed out that Darwinism was the exact analogue of

9. The best discussion of the socialist and "social-imperialist" variety of Social Darwinism is in Bernard Semmel's book, which gives the subject an entirely new dimension and significance.

1. Edward B. Aveling, "Charles Darwin and Karl Marx," *New Century Review*, I (1897), 243.

2. *Life and Letters of Darwin*, III, 237 (Dec. 26, 1879).

3. Marx, *Correspondence* (London, 1934), p. 125 (Jan. 16, 1861).

the Hegelian-Marxist dialectic of quantity and quality; as imperceptible increases of quantity could produce a sudden transformation of quality, so the imperceptible evolution of species produced new species, and so too the evolution of history created the moments of historical crisis or revolution.

There was another and perhaps more important sense in which Darwinism bore a real affinity to Marxism. What they both celebrated was the internal, necessary rhythm of life, the one the life of nature, the other the life of society. God was powerless to interfere with the natural laws and processes of nature, and by the same token individual men were powerless to interfere with the natural dialectic and course of history. Social Darwinism thus appeared as a vindication of social determinism, more particularly of that form of determinism known as historical materialism.

Still other socialists—anti-imperialist and anti-Marxist—claimed the authority of Darwin on still other grounds. They pointed to those passages in the *Descent* in which Darwin cited examples of altruism and cooperation on the part of individuals within the more advanced species. Altruism and cooperation, in these cases, permitted the individuals, and the species as a whole, to cope more successfully with nature, to concentrate their collective energy on the struggle with nature rather than dissipate their energy on a debilitating struggle among themselves. The struggle, these socialists reasoned, was equally debilitating whether it occurred among nations, individuals, or classes. Just as wars often resulted in the survival of the unfittest—it being precisely, as Darwin himself once wrote, the fittest young men who served in the army, were exposed to death and prevented from marrying, while the weakest remained home to propagate their kind[4]—so the social and economic struggle for existence could result in the survival of those

4. *Descent*, p. 207.

with the least desirable, the least worthy human characteristics. The lesson that these socialists learned from Darwin
was that natural selection itself favored the cooperative
rather than competitive instincts of men, and that the
evolution of society depended on the growth of cooperative
rather than competitive institutions. Thus in this view the
struggle for existence had to be pacified, domesticated, subjected to rational control, if the humanly fittest were to
survive. Evolution, that is, had to be lent a helping hand. In
John Dewey's terms, that helping hand was "intelligence."
In more conventional socialist terms, it was "planning."

Another school of thought—not socialist now, but
eugenicist—proposed to intervene even more directly and
dramatically in the evolutionary process. Francis Galton,
Darwin's cousin and the father of eugenics, said that his aim
was to "further the ends of evolution more rapidly and
with less distress than if events were left to their own
course," to "discover and expedite the changes that are
necessary to adapt circumstance to race and race to circumstance."[5] In the *Descent*, Darwin reported sympathetically
upon Galton's findings: "The very poor and reckless, who
are often degraded by vice, almost invariably marry early,
whilst the careful and frugal, who are generally otherwise
virtuous, marry late in life." Thus the former tend to
increase at a faster rate than the latter. This tendency could
cause the nation to "retrograde"—"as has too often occurred," he added, "in the history of the world."[6] Galton
and Darwin also corresponded privately on such subjects as
Galton's proposal that a registry be instituted to record
superior and inferior families, so that society would know
who should be encouraged to breed and who discouraged
or prevented from breeding. "Though I see much diffi-

5. Galton, *Inquiries into Human Faculty and its Development*
(Everyman ed.; London, n.d.), I, 218.
6. *Descent*, pp. 212, 216.

culty," Darwin wrote about this particular proposal, "the object seems a grand one; and you have pointed out the sole feasible, yet I fear utopian, plan of procedure in improving the human race."[7]

At this point the entire edifice of Social Darwinism threatens to collapse under the weight of contradiction, complication, and paradox. Laissez-fairism and socialism, racism and anti-racism, segregationism and desegregationism, militarism and pacificism, imperialism and anti-imperialism, Marxism and evolutionary socialism, social engineering and eugenics—surely they cannot all legitimately claim descent from the same ancestor. Yet, like the evolutionary tree itself, with its many branches and off-shoots, they are all related—not directly to each other but to the parent doctrine, each deriving from a different part of that doctrine, each with a lineage and legitimacy of its own. Changing the metaphor, one may say that each has a logic of its own, so that however antithetical any pair of terms may be (laissez-fairism and socialism, for example), each term within the pair has an internal consistency. There are moments, to be sure, when it is hard to keep in mind the logic and consistency. How can one reconcile the eugenicist's desire to "expedite" evolution by directing it to a predetermined end, with the essence of natural selection, which is that evolution is a self-determining, self-operating, unending process? Yet if Darwin himself was seemingly oblivious to this inconsistency, so that he was willing, in principle at least, to endorse the idea of eugenics, the eugenicists may surely be excused for invoking his name and authority.

Nor are the difficulties of Social Darwinism exhausted by an enumeration of the variously related and unrelated,

7. *More Letters of Charles Darwin,* ed. Francis Darwin (London, 1903), II, 43 (Jan. 4, 1873).

consonant and dissonant doctrines that go under that name. There is a still more basic and irreconcilable antithesis: between Social Darwinism per se, whatever the variety, and a denial of the legitimacy of the very idea of Social Darwinism. This antithesis is conveniently epitomized by two distinguished members of a single family—and, not by accident, by lectures given by these two under the same auspices exactly fifty years apart.

In 1893, T. H. Huxley, one of Darwin's most loyal disciples, delivered the Romanes Lecture at Oxford on "Evolution and Ethics," a discourse that might more properly have been entitled "Evolution *versus* Ethics." He defined evolution as that "cosmic process" by which man and nature, proceeding by struggle, selection, and survival, had arrived at their present state. Ethics, he maintained, was the very opposite of that cosmic process. Against those philosophers who tried to make of evolution the source and standard of ethical values, he argued that evolution could neither be identified with ethics nor taken as the validation of ethics.[8] Evolution, he said, was a guide not to morality but to immorality. It put a premium on those qualities that moralists could only deplore: cunning, brute force, ruthlessness, ferocity. Its laws were the laws of the jungle. It rewarded the wicked and punished the righteous, and was altogether an unedifying and even horrifying spectacle.

8. Huxley's argument was primarily directed against Herbert Spencer. In an earlier essay by Huxley on the same theme, "The Struggle for Existence in Human Society," published in 1888, Spencer was clearly identified (in both Huxley's and Spencer's private letters, although not in the essay itself) as the object of attack. By 1893, however, at the very time that Huxley was delivering his Romanes Lecture, Spencer was beginning to have second thoughts—not as to the propriety of an ethics based on evolution, but as to its practicality. In the preface to his *Principles of Ethics*, Spencer candidly admitted: "The Doctrine of Evolution has not furnished guidance to the extent I had hoped. Most of the conclusions, drawn empirically, are such as right feelings, enlightened by cultivated intelligence, have already sufficed to establish." ([London, 1893], II, v.)

Civilized man could learn from it only what to avoid and condemn.

> Social progress means a checking of the cosmic process at every step and the substitution for it of another, which may be called the ethical process; the end of which is not the survival of those who may happen to be the fittest . . . but of those who are ethically the best. . . . The ethical progress of society depends, not on imitating the cosmic process, still less in running away from it, but in combating it.[9]

Fifty years later, the syndics of Oxford University invited T. H. Huxley's grandson, the eminent scientist Julian Huxley, to deliver the Romanes Lecture on the same subject. To give point to his thesis and distinguish himself from his grandfather, Julian Huxley chose as his title "Evolutionary Ethics." In the sense, he argued, that evolution involved for the most part (although not in every instance) a movement from the less to the more complex, from the less to the more perfect, it provided an objective basis for human values and social progress, since the higher values were those that were "intrinsically or more permanently satisfying, or involve a greater degree of perfection." Thus evolution was at the same descriptive, normative, and hortatory: it told us what our values are, what they should be, and what we should do to promote them. "The facts of nature," he observed in flat contrast to his grandfather, "as demonstrated in evolution, give us assurance that knowledge, love, beauty, selfless morality, and firm purpose are ethically good."

> Evolutionary ethics must be based on a combination of a few main principles: that it is right to realize ever new possibilities in evolution . . . ; that it is right both to respect human individuality and to encourage its fullest development; that it is right to construct a mechanism for

9. T. H. Huxley, *Evolution and Ethics and Other Essays* (New York, 1898), pp. 81, 83.

further social evolution which shall satisfy these prior conditions as fully, efficiently, and as rapidly as possible.[1]

More recently, Julian Huxley carried the argument for Evolutionary Ethics to a more exalted plane by adopting, or adapting, the ideas of Teilhard de Chardin, the Jesuit priest who was a biologist, paleontologist, and ardent evolutionist. Teilhard de Chardin maintained that to study mankind—human society and human values—scientifically was to study it as part of the evolutionary process governing all phenomena. Nothing was static, everything was part of an unceasing process, and ultimately everything was part of the same process. He invented an entire vocabulary to express the various phases of this process: "cosmogenesis," the gradual and constant evolution of the cosmos; "noö-genesis," the evolution of mind and psyche; "biosphere," the context or complex of organic life; "noösphere," the context of organic life; "hominization," the process by which the original protohuman stock became (and is still becoming) more human; "ultrahominization," the process by which man will continue to develop in still unforeseen ways that will eventually bring about his own self-tran-scendence and the emergence of a new species, an ultra-man; and so on.[2]

It is this mode of thought, and some of this vocabulary, that Julian Huxley has imported into the discussion of Social Darwinism. Comparing man's present state with that of our amphibian ancestors 300 million years ago, when they were evolving from a life confined to the sea to the vastly extended opportunities of a life upon land, Huxley sees us in a similar state of transition—from the biological area of evolution into the psychosocial area, from the earth-ridden biosphere into the freedom of the noosphere. Our evolution from now on will proceed by "breakthroughs to

1. Julian Huxley, *Evolutionary Ethics* (Oxford, 1943), p. 41.
2. Pierre Teilhard de Chardin, *The Phenomenon of Man* (New York, 1959).

new dominant patterns of mental organization, of knowledge, ideas and beliefs—ideological instead of physiological or biological organization."[3] This is not to say that we are assured of a boundless evolutionary progress; for Huxley warns us of the pitfalls in our way—such fatal dangers as nuclear warfare or overpopulation. But it does suggest that all the means for overcoming these dangers are in our hands and that evolution is the first and foremost of these means.

> Evolutionary truth shows us our destiny and our duty. It shows us mind enthroned above matter, quantity subordinate to quality. It gives our anxious minds support by revealing the incredible possibilities that have already been realized in evolution's past and, by pointing to the hidden treasure of fresh possibilities that could be realized in its long future, it gives man a potent incentive for fulfilling his evolutionary role in the universe.[4]

We have come a long way, then, from the conventional alternatives of Social Darwinism—laissez-fairism and socialism, racism and anti-racism . . . But we have been confronted with a more basic alternative: whether Darwinism is, as T. H. Huxley argued, at best irrelevant to human values and social action, at worst, and more often, utterly subversive of those values and an odious example to society; or whether, as his grandson has more recently maintained, evolution remains our best, indeed our only source of private and public morality. The fact that both Huxleys share a commitment to the same values, and even agree, for the most part, on the kinds of social action best suited to preserve and enhance those values may suggest that the question is, as one says, "merely" theoretical, perhaps even "merely" semantical, and therefore not serious. The problem cannot, unfortunately, be so easily dismissed. The

3. J. Huxley, "The Evolutionary Vision," *Evolution After Darwin*, ed. Sol Tax and Charles Callender (Chicago, 1960), III, 251.
4. Ibid., p. 261.

debate over Social Darwinism is serious, however complicated and contradictory it may be. Indeed, its very complications and contradictions demonstrate, in a sense, its
seriousness. Men, intelligent men, do not generally argue
passionately about matters of little consequence. T. H.
Huxley testified to the gravity of the issue when he deliberately withheld the sanction of Darwinism from social ethics
or social policy—*any* ethics or *any* policy, even one of
which he might have approved. To withhold the sanction
of Darwinism, to deny the legitimization that had been so
eagerly sought was in effect, to try to neutralize, to keep in
check one of the most potent forces in modern society, the
authority of science.

XIII

POLITICS AND IDEOLOGY:
THE REFORM ACT OF 1867

THE REFORM ACT OF 1867 was one of the decisive events, perhaps *the* decisive event, in modern English history. It was this act that transformed England into a democracy and that made democracy not only a respectable form of government (the United States was never quite respectable), but also, in the opinion of most men, the only natural and proper form of government. And it was during the debate over this act that the case for and against democracy was most cogently argued. To be sure, the Act of 1867 had to be supplemented by others before universal suffrage was attained. But once this first step was made, no one seriously doubted that the others would follow. The Act of 1867, therefore, more than that of 1832, may deserve the title of the Great Reform Bill. For while 1832 had no necessary aftermath in 1867, 1867 did have a necessary aftermath in 1884, 1918, 1928—the later acts that genuinely universalized the suffrage, not only for Britain but for all those countries that took Britain to be the model of a parliamentary government.

It is all the more bewildering, therefore, to inquire into the actual history of this act and to find it so meandering, purposeless, fortuitous, so full of what Butterfield has called "the most useless things in the world"[1]—useless, that is, if one expects meaning or sense in history. John Morley, trying to make sense of an affair that struck him as "one of the most curious in our parliamentary history,"[2] wistfully concluded: "When we have made full allowance for blunder, caprice, chance, folly, craft, still reason and the nature of things have a share."[3] But the only element of reason or nature he could adduce was the "tide of public opinion,"[4] which, as will be seen, had little bearing upon the actual course of events culminating in the actual act of reform. A similar sense of the "reason" and "nature of things" animated the most influential historian writing of this period—G. M. Trevelyan. Determined to make this leap in the dark conform to his view of history as an "orderly and gradual" accommodation to "social facts,"[5] Trevelyan declared that "the upshot of these . . . confused Parliamentary operations of which no one of the statesmen concerned had quite foreseen the issue, was that the governing classes had recognised the needs of the new era with a wise alacrity."[6] But this interpretation, too, does

1. Herbert Butterfield, *The Whig Interpretation of History* (London, 1959), p. 15.

2. John Morley, *The Life of William Ewart Gladstone* (New York, 1903), II, 223.

3. *Ibid.,* II, 227.

4. *Ibid.*

5. G. M. Trevelyan, "The Great Days of Reform," in *The Making of English History,* ed. R. L. Schuyler and H. Ausubel (New York, 1952), p. 494.

6. G. M. Trevelyan, *British History in the Nineteenth Century* (London, 1922), p. 347. (Recently reissued as a Pelican paperback, this book still has considerable influence.) See also Frances E. Gillespie, *Labor and Politics in England, 1850–67* (Durham, N.C., 1927), p. 289: "The Act of 1867 was the culmination of a development that had been continuous since the agitation for the first reform bill. It was the inevitable result of policies forced upon all classes in the state by the facts of the social and political world."

violence to the reality, imposing order upon chaos, necessity upon contingency, and principle upon expediency.[7]

7. The chief dissenters from the "Whig interpretation of history" are: Francis H. Herrick, "The Reform Bill of 1867 and
the British Party System," *Pacific Historical Review*, III (1934),
216–33, and "The Second Reform Movement in Britain,"
Journal of The History of Ideas, IX (1948), 174–92; Joseph H.
Park, *The English Reform Bill of 1867* (New York, 1920);
G. Lowes Dickinson, *The Development of Parliament during
the Nineteenth Century* (London, 1895); and Asa Briggs, *Victorian People* (London, 1954) and *The Age of Improvement*
(London, 1959). These writers, of course, differ among themselves and from the author of the present essay.

Since this essay was written several studies have appeared
that significantly modify the traditional Whig interpretation.
The most detailed and the most subversive of the Whig interpretation is Maurice Cowling's "Disraeli, Derby and Fusion,
October 1865 to July 1866," *The Historical Journal*, VIII
(1965), which explains the behavior of the leaders of both
parties during this early period in terms of personal and fac-
tional maneuvers. Another essay contributing to this impression, although more obliquely, is James Winter's "The Cave of
Adullam and Parliamentary Reform," *English Historical Review* (Jan. 1966). Two recent books provide valuable source
material for such an anti-Whig view, although the authors
themselves, in their general theses and conclusions, do not always take this view: F. B. Smith, *The Making of the Second
Reform Bill* (Cambridge, Eng., 1966); and John Vincent, *The
Formation of the Liberal Party, 1857–68* (London, 1966). On
Smith in particular, see below, page 366, footnote 6. The most
notable departure from the Whig interpretation is a work of
much larger scope and implication, in which the Reform Act
appears only tangentially: Samuel H. Beer, *British Politics in
the Collectivist Age* (New York, 1966). Without implicating
Professor Beer in my own reading of 1867, I should like to express my gratification at finding myself in general accord with
what I regard as one of the most distinguished books of recent
years.

Counterbalancing these studies is the other tendency in recent historiography commonly associated with the "New Left"
(which has, however, large vestiges of the Old Left). This
neo-Marxist view has much in common with the Whig interpretation, both being deterministic in the same sense. The main
difference is that the Whig had the ruling classes respond to
the "social facts" and "needs of the new era" with a "wise
alacrity," while the neo-Marxist has them respond to those facts
and needs reluctantly and belatedly, as a result of workingclass
pressure and the threat of violence. The most explicit analysis

The history of the Reform Act was, in actuality, even more "curious" than Morley suggested. For it started not with blunder or caprice but with the still more nullifying fact of apathy. Throughout the 1850's and early 1860's, while the "needs of the new era" alluded to by Trevelyan were presumably becoming more urgent, the public was becoming increasingly indifferent to the need for political reform. The Reform Bills of 1859 and 1860, which would have been more in keeping with Trevelyan's notion of "orderly and gradual" change, evoked so little interest that even the reformers were disheartened. Withdrawing the second of these bills, Lord John Russell explained: "The apathy of the country is undeniable. Nor is it a transient humour; it seems rather a confirmed habit of mind."[8] Prince Albert rebuked those who were so wanting in moral principle as to take advantage of this apathy:

> Our statesmen even regard moral principle as not at all necessary on their part, because, owing to the good sense of the country, and the general loyalty and contentment and prosperity, the consequences of the want of it are not immediately felt. While this is so, the public is perilously apathetic and indifferent for and against Ministers, and the press is,—well,—as it always is.[9]

Punch diagnosed the condition as nothing more perilous than satiation and inebriation:

---

in this vein is Royden Harrison's "The Tenth April of Spencer Walpole: the Problem of Revolution in Relation to Reform, 1865–67," in *Before the Socialists* (London, 1965). Harrison maintains that in 1867 the working class "had attained precisely that level of development at which it was safe to concede its enfranchisement and dangerous to withhold it," that "a Reform Act had become essential," that "the Tory Statesmen were bowing to a process which it was beyond their power to control." (Pp. 133, 135.)

8. Spencer Walpole, *The Life of Lord John Russell* (London, 1891), II, 342.

9. Theodore Martin, *The Life of His Royal Highness the Prince Consort* (London, 1879), IV, 410.

For Reform we feels too lazy:
  Too full of beer.
Much malt liquor makes us hazy,
  Too full of beer.
We don't want no alteration
Of the present Legislation;
'Twon't affect our sittiwation,
  Too full of beer.[1]

By 1865 this habit of apathy had become so deeply confirmed that Walter Bagehot made it one of the first principles of the English constitution. He regarded it, however, as a cause for satisfaction rather than for complaint. The "most miserable creatures" in the kingdom, he wrote, "do not impute their misery to politics." Politics to them meant the Queen, and the Queen, they were sure, "is very good." Any agitator who tried to excite political passion would be more likely to be pelted than applauded. "The mass of the English people are politically contented as well as politically deferential."[2] As late as March 1866 Bagehot took this to be the state of the public temper: "There is no worse trade than agitation at this time. . . . A sense of satisfaction permeates the country because most of the country feels it has got the precise thing that suits it."[3]

Exactly three days before this passage appeared in print, Gladstone introduced in the House of Commons the bill

1. *Punch*, VI (1859), 70.
2. *Fortnightly Review*, I (1865), 327; Walter Bagehot, *The English Constitution* (World's Classics edn.; London, 1928), p. 238. Since the timing of Bagehot's remarks is significant, the citations here are to the essays as they originally appeared in the *Fortnightly Review* between June 15, 1865, and January 1, 1867. When the essays were republished as a volume later in 1867, not only were the original dates omitted but their order was changed, so that observations made before the opening of the debate on reform would seem to belong to a later stage of the controversy and vice versa. There were also significant deletions and changes in the volume.
3. *Fortnightly Review*, IV (1866), 274; *English Constitution*, p. 144.

that set in motion, as it later appeared, the train of events culminating in the Reform Act of 1867. Bagehot has often been commiserated upon the unfortunate timing that seemed to make his work obsolete even before it had been completed. Yet the fact that his work is so far from obsolete as to be one of our political classics suggests that the events, rather than his words, were somehow amiss. Bagehot, after all, wrote this passage in the full knowledge that a reform bill was imminent: the address from the throne and the speech of the prime minister had left no doubt of this. But like most political observers, he had no reason to think that this reform bill would have a different fate from that of the six other abortive measures introduced in the previous fifteen years—as indeed proved to be the case. What he did not anticipate, what no one anticipated, was that within a year of the rejection of the Liberal bill, another would be passed far more radical than anything that had ever seriously been proposed. (Serious in a practical, parliamentary sense; the Chartists' demands, like those of the Philosophical Radicals earlier, were primarily agitational.) It is this problem that Bagehot's analysis of the English people and constitution forces us to confront: How did an act so unanticipated and unsought, so uncongenial to public and parliament alike, come to pass? Did the "tide of public opinion" change so quickly and powerfully in this short period as to overcome the habitual apathy and traditional deference of the people, and if so, why?

The events most commonly cited by historians to account for such a change in public opinion are the victory of the North in the American Civil War, demonstrating the viability of democracy; the death of Palmerston, making it possible for new principles and personalities to assert themselves; and the economic depression, which inspired demands for political reform. Each of these might fruitfully yield a dissertation in itself. Here it can only be said that, as causes of the Reform Act, they are, singly or together, inadequate to the claims made for them.

The Civil War, for most members of parliament, was more often the occasion for a debater's point than a genuine change of heart toward democracy.[4] A year after Appomattox Gladstone was still complaining of public apathy, and the shifts and turns in parliament during the following year can barely be related to more immediate causes, let alone to an event so far removed in time and place. Even the staunchest reformers were not unambivalent in their reactions to the American experience or in the lessons they drew from it. While one contributor to *Essays on Reform* attributed the vitality of the American government to the strength of democracy, other contributors to the same volume were more concerned with dissociating democracy from the weaknesses and abuses of American politics—dissociating, in effect, the English reform movement from the example of America.[5] The news from America at this time dealt not with the Civil War but with its aftermath: the dissension between the president and congress, bribery at the polls, corruption and peculation among legislators, and the generally low tone of Reconstruction politics—hardly recommendations for the American system.

The death of Palmerston did revitalize politics by producing a void which competing leaders were anxious to fill, but it did not revitalize or encourage new principles.

4. The conventional thesis about the influence of the Civil War is stated in G. D. Lillibridge, *Beacon of Freedom: The Impact of American Democracy upon Great Britain, 1830–70* (Philadelphia, 1955); Henry Pelling, *America and the British Left* (New York, 1957); and a forthcoming essay by H. C. Allen, "The Impact of the Civil War and Reconstruction on Life and Liberalism in Great Britain." But what they succeed in showing is that both proponents and opponents of reform invoked America to support their prior prejudices and positions—not that they were influenced by America to change those prejudices and positions. (Another foreign influence to which Asa Briggs gives much prominence—the visit of Garibaldi to London in April 1864—is similarly inconclusive. See *The Age of Improvement*, pp. 495–6.)

5. E.g., the essays by Leslie Stephen and Bernard Cracorft, *Essays on Reform* (London, 1867).

Robert Cecil's description of the political mood under Palmerston—"The old antithesis of principle and expediency is absolutely forgotten: expediency is the only principle to which sincere allegiance is paid"[6]—applies even more aptly to the period after his death. Indeed many who witnessed the behavior of Disraeli and Gladstone in 1866–7 came to regard Palmerston as a paragon of principle. Gladstone "unmuzzled" lost none of his old habit of talking out of both sides of his mouth; while Disraeli indulged in his usual freewheeling tactics.

The third factor, the economic depression, is similarly inconclusive. As a major initiating factor in the reform movement, it is ruled out by the simple test of chronology, the Liberal reform bill having been introduced two months before the stockmarket crash and many months before the failure of the harvest. Unemployment and rising prices may have accelerated the movement in its later stages but even then the economic motif was not nearly so conspicuous as might be thought even in the public meetings, still less in the counsels of party and parliament.[7]

The fact is that the actual course of affairs culminating in the Reform Act had little to do with any of these factors. The prospects of reform varied from month to month and week to week (at one point in March 1867, from hour to hour); and these prospects had nothing to do with the triumph of Grant, the death of Palmerston, or the failure of the harvest. Indeed the first passage of arms occurred long before any of these events. It was in 1864 that Gladstone raised the flag of reform with the famous pronouncement that "every man who is not presumably incapacitated

6. Robert Cecil, "The Theories of Parliamentary Reform," *Oxford Essays* (London, 1858), p. 52.

7. See Briggs, *Age of Improvement*, p. 504, for the way economic facts may be interspersed with political events so as to give the impression that there was a causal relationship between the two, when in fact there is no evidence that the one even figured in the other. The point is further discussed below, pp. 378–83.

by some consideration of personal unfitness or of political danger is morally entitled to come within the pale of the constitution"—followed by the bland assurance that he intended, "of course," no "sudden, or violent, or excessive, or intoxicating change."[8] When his statement was interpreted as an invitation to just such a violent change, Gladstone innocently protested that his reservations about "personal unfitness" and "political danger" could as well be taken to exclude everyone. It was this spirit—reminiscent of the politician who roundly condemns both inflation and deflation and boldly commits himself to a policy of "flation"—that characterized much of the subsequent controversy and made its outcome doubtful until the very end.

Certainly there was no "sudden, or violent, or excessive, or intoxicating change" in the reform bill proposed by Gladstone in March 1866.[9] The crucial provision of the

8. Morley, *Gladstone*, II, 126.

9. Recent studies have documented the equivocations and vacillations of the Liberal Party, and of Gladstone in particular, before the introduction of this bill. It appears that the Liberals, like the Conservatives after them, toyed with the idea of a two-year parliamentary commission to inquire into—and delay action—on the issue. Only five days before their bill was introduced, the cabinet was still debating the question of a rental or rating basis for the franchise (an issue that was later made to appear so much a matter of principle), as well as the level at which the franchise would be fixed. The confusion was such that at least one official copy of the bill was actually published with the figure of £6 instead of £7. (Smith, *Second Reform Bill*, pp. 58, 66.)

In the inner circles of both parties, there was a widespread suspicion that, as one contemporary put it, Gladstone was "all for putting off Reform at first, tho' that was the question on which he was supposed to go further and to be more eager about than any of the others." Rumors circulated that he "talks Conservative and sneers at Lord Russell," that he was "prepared to take the high Conservative line," that he would have liked to replace Disraeli as Conservative leader in the House of Commons, and—only days before the bill was introduced—that he was "making advances to the Conservatives." (Unpublished Mss. quoted by Cowling, "Disraeli, Derby and Fusion," pp.

341

bill was a £7 borough franchise—the franchise to be extended to borough residents occupying premises of at least a £7 annual rental value. This was an improvement upon the existing £10 but regressive compared with earlier proposals of £6. Gladstone himself candidly explained that he chose the £7 figure because it ensured that the working class would remain a minority of the electorate, whereas under the £6 franchise it might become a majority. He also pointed out that his bill would give the working class less power than it had had before the passage of the first Reform Act. In 1830 the working class had been a majority in constituencies returning 130 members. The Act of 1832 had eliminated this workingclass electorate, and Gladstone proposed to restore it partially, to the extent of making it dominant in constituencies totaling 101 members. What Gladstone may have lacked in reforming zeal, however, he more than made up for in eloquence, acclaiming his £7 electors (144,000 workingmen by his count, 116,000 by Bright's) as "our fellow-subjects, our fellow-Christians, our own flesh and blood"[1]—which prompted the obvious query whether six-pounders were no less fellow subjects, fellow Christians, and kin of flesh and blood.

Toward the end of the debate, carried away by his own rhetoric, Gladstone warned the opposition: "You cannot fight against the future. Time is on our side."[2] The warning was gratuitous, Disraeli not being one to fight against the future or forfeit the advantage of time. Having earlier (in 1859) introduced a reform bill of his own as part of his strategy of destroying the "old Whig monopoly of Liberalism,"[3] he understood perfectly well that the present bill

---

44, 47.) These were, to be sure, only rumors; but they testify to the fact that responsible and well-informed men found them credible.

1. *3 Hansard* 182: 873 (Mar. 23, 1866).
2. Ibid., 183: 152 (Apr. 27, 1866).
3. W. F. Monypenny and G. E. Buckle, *The Life of Benjamin Disraeli* (London, 1929), I, 1576 (Oct. 24, 1858).

was designed to perpetuate that monopoly—that, as Robert Lowe said, its main object was "to render it impossible for any other Government than a Liberal one to exist in this country for the future."[4] When some Conservatives urged the adoption of the Liberal bill, plausibly reasoning that the issue would be well disposed of on such moderate terms, Disraeli firmly objected. "Such a course," he insisted, "would seat the Whigs for a lifetime."[5] Fortunately for him, the dissident Liberals—the Adullamites led by Lowe—played into his hands. By arguing against the principle of reform as well as against this particular bill, the Adullamites took upon themselves the burden of the fight and the onus of resisting the future. Disraeli happily yielded the stage to them. He did not speak at all on the first reading of the bill and took the floor only late in the eighth night of the second reading; and then he was careful to avoid the issue of reform as such, his main argument being the inadvisability of passing a franchise measure without an accompanying measure for the redistribution of seats.

Disraeli and Gladstone were, it would seem, more concerned with the future than the people whose future was being decided. *The Times* complained that even the seven-pounders seemed indifferent to the fact that they were being "presented with a very considerable slice of the British Constitution."[6] And this was not, as some historians have suggested, because the slice was not larger. Although the Reform League paid lip service to the ideal of manhood suffrage, it publicly supported the Liberal bill, with only a small faction holding out against it.[7] The Reform Union,

4. *3 Hansard* 183: 1647 (May 31, 1866).

5. Monypenny and Buckle, *Disraeli*, II, 164.

6. Quoted by Park, *English Reform Bill*, p. 94.

7. It is deceptive to say, as Harrison does: "The Government's measure not only split its own supporters, but divided the League. Beesly, out of regard for Bright, supported the Bill, others followed Ernest Jones in his bitter denunciations of it."

whose formal commitment was to household suffrage (the enfranchisement of all rate-paying householders) rather than to manhood suffrage (the enfranchisement of all adult males, rate-paying or not) was even better disposed to it. And the Radicals in parliament unanimously endorsed it. John Bright called it a "perfectly honest bill": "If it is the least the Government could offer, it may be that it is the greatest which the Government could carry through Parliament."[8]

As it happened, the Liberals were not able to carry their bill through parliament. When the Adullamites joined with the Conservatives to defeat it, Russell tendered his resignation to the Queen, explaining that he could not continue because of "the general apathy of the South of England on the subject of reform."[9] At the same time, a member of the cabinet wrote to the editor of *The Times:* "The House does not want reform, and, for aught I know to the contrary, its rabid opposition to it may faithfully represent the feeling of the country."[1]

The demonstrations that followed the defeat of the Liberal bill and the fall of the government are generally taken as evidence of a new popular militancy, a temper of mind that would be satisfied with nothing less than household suffrage. Yet the most dramatic of these demonstrations, that at Hyde Park in July, was more an assertion of the

---

(P. 82.) From this statement one might deduce that the split in the government ranks came from the fact that the bill was insufficiently radical—whereas there was not a single defection on this account; or that the League was more or less evenly "divided" between those supporting and those opposing the bill —whereas the supporters were in the overwhelming majority and represented the official position of the League.

8. G. M. Trevelyan, *The Life of John Bright* (London, 1913), p. 351 (March 25, 1866).

9. Walpole, *Russell*, II, 429 (June 19, 1866).

1. *The History of "The Times"* (London, 1935-9), II, 403.

right of assembly (the demonstrators having been forbidden access to the park) than of the right to vote.[2] The violence of this affair has been as grossly exaggerated as its significance. In fact, its true significance may be precisely this exaggeration: the other demonstrations must have been pacific indeed for contemporaries and historians alike to have been so outraged by little more than broken railings and trampled flower beds.[3] Karl Marx observed at the time that if only the railings had been used "offensively and defensively" against the police and a score of policemen had been killed, "there would have been some fun."[4] From later accounts one would hardly know that the railings had not been so used, either offensively or defensively, and that

2. The Reform League itself had had its origin, in 1864, in a similar episode involving the right of assembly. The initial move for its formation came immediately after the police had broken up a meeting protesting against the curtailment of Garibaldi's visit. And from the first the right of assembly was one of its principal demands.

3. The desperation of historians intent upon finding evidence of popular revolutionary sentiment may be seen in Harrison's attempt to make a major *cause* out of a still more minor incident: the meeting at Hyde Park on May 6, 1867. The whole of his essay is focussed on this one episode, which, as the title suggests, is held to be analogous to April 10, 1848, when the Chartist petition was presented to Parliament, and which, like that earlier date, is held to epitomize the threat of revolution. But just as one may doubt that April 10 was "one of the most famous days in the history of the nineteenth century," so one may doubt the importance of May 6. The government's "surrender of 6 May," it is said, "served as harbinger and analogue" to its "surrender on Reform." But its "surrender" on May 6 was nothing more momentous than a tactful retreat from an injudicious position; having earlier prohibited the meeting, it then tacitly permitted it—and made its change of mind known at least two days before the meeting was held. And the "surrender" on reform which supposedly followed the "surrender" of May 6 had in fact been decided upon by the government long before. Lacking even the trampled flowerbeds and broken railings of the preceding July 22, May 6, 1867, has still less claim to demonstrating the importance of "mass agitation" in the passage of the Reform Act. (Harrison, *Before the Socialists*, pp. 78, 101, 106.)

4. Karl Marx and Friedrich Engels, *Correspondence* (New York, 1935), p. 213.

there were few serious injuries, let alone fatalities.[5] Yet the distinguished literary historian J. Dover Wilson was expressing a common view when he made it seem that the affair was everything Marx had hoped it would be: "It is scarcely too much to say that the fall of the park railings did for England in July 1866 what the fall of the Bastille did for France in July 1789. The shooting of Niagara was seen to be inevitable."[6]

Trevelyan had a more moderate view of the Hyde Park episode. Having himself, many years later, witnessed the fall of the Cambridge Senate House railings from the weight of an entirely peaceable crowd, he realized that not much violence would have been required to dislodge the insecure railings at Hyde Park.[7] But he too took it for granted that from the time of this episode a radical spirit took hold of the people, who were no longer to be satisfied with such a "half-measure" or "half-hearted" measure as the Liberal bill of 1866.[8] This view is so generally held that it is today accepted almost as a truism. Yet it is as questionable in fact as in logic. What would have been, at this time, a whole measure, or even a sufficient measure of reform? If the £7 franchise was discredited as a half-measure, would a £6 franchise have been accredited as a whole or proximate measure? Where in this scale of measurement would have come some more complicated arrangement, such as the later Conservative proposal for household suffrage plus "fancy franchises"? Or would household suffrage, in the

---

5. According to Smith, one policeman later died of injuries incurred during the riots and over one hundred demonstrators were seriously hurt. (*Second Reform Bill*, p. 129.) But since the sources for this statement were the Radical press, it may well be an exaggeration. Vincent, while making light of the episode itself, nevertheless characterized it as the "Sarajevo of Reform." (*Liberal Party*, p. 192.)

6. Matthew Arnold, *Culture and Anarchy*, ed. J. Dover Wilson (Cambridge, 1957), p. xxvi.

7. Trevelyan, *Bright*, p. 361.

8. Trevelyan, *British History*, p. 344.

346

more radical form that was finally enacted, alone have qualified as a sufficient measure? Was the "shooting of Niagara"—that total capitulation to democracy that Carlyle took to be the effect of the Reform Act—indeed inevitable from the moment the Liberal bill was defeated? Yet even the Reform Act itself was in a sense a half-measure compared with the manhood suffrage demanded earlier by the Chartists and conceded later by subsequent acts of parliament.

The Hyde Park affair did result in a quickening of the public temper on the subject of reform and a greater likelihood that some measure of reform would be passed. But the particular measure remained as indeterminate as before, and no one had any idea of what it would be. Bright attested to the uncertain state of affairs when, as much as four months after the Hyde Park episode, he wrote (and Trevelyan quotes him): "I think no one can foresee what is coming. The 'shooting stars' were fore-seen—and I sat up and saw many of them—but of the session no man knoweth anything."[9] "Shooting stars" are a very different thing from the "shooting of Niagara." Like most of his contemporaries, Bright neither foresaw nor wished for the shooting of Niagara. The following March, only nine days before the introduction of the Conservative bill, he advised Disraeli that while "the oldest and wisest basis for the borough franchise is household suffrage," a £6 rental or £5 rating franchise (the rate-assessment value of premises was generally lower than the rental value), plus an unspecified lodger qualification for London, would stand a better chance of getting through parliament and would be entirely acceptable to the reformers in the country as well as to those in the House—and acceptable, he added, not as an interim measure but "for a *very long period*."[1] And even after Disraeli had come out for household suffrage

9. Trevelyan, *Bright*, p. 365 (Nov. 1866).
1. Ibid., p. 382 (March 9, 1867). Italics in the original.

(combined with fancy franchises), a delegation of reformers led by the editor of the leading trade-union weekly
officially informed Gladstone that, while household
suffrage was preferable, they would be content with any
measure of workingclass representation. There is no doubt
that in March 1867 and even later, Bright and many of the
reformers not only would have settled for but actually
would have preferred something less than household
suffrage. There is an ambiguous note in the remark of John
Stuart Mill, echoed by so many others in the course of the
debate: "I never supposed that I should see such a Reform
as this adopted in my life."[2] Bagehot was expressing a
prevalent suspicion when he wrote: "Many Radical members who had been asking for years for household suffrage
were much more surprised than pleased at the near chance
of obtaining it; they had asked for it as bargainers ask for
the highest possible price, but they never expected to get
it."[3]

What is interesting is the fact that it was not the reformers inside or outside the House who forced up the
price of reform, but rather the party leaders themselves.
Lowe described the parties as competing against each other
in a miserable auction with the constitution being "knocked
down to the lowest bidder."[4] A Conservative complained
that his colleagues were trying to "outbid the Liberal party
in the market of liberalism."[5] Grant Duff used the metaphor of a chess tournament, and Lord Shaftesbury spoke of
the parties as two tigers fighting over a carcass. Perhaps the
best image was provided by Lord Derby in December 1866
when he recommended household suffrage to Disraeli as
the best "of all possible hares to start"[6]—an image that

2. 3 *Hansard* 188: 1106 (July 5, 1867).
3. Bagehot, *English Constitution*, p. 267 (introduction to 2nd edn.).
4. 3 *Hansard* 182: 2093 (April 26, 1866).
5. Ibid., 186: 70-1 (March 18, 1867).
6. Monypenny and Buckle, *Disraeli*, II, 218 (Dec. 22, 1866).

aptly suggests the wild scramble that ensued, with not a few of the hunters to be found running with the hare and hunting with the hounds. At one point Disraeli appealed to Derby's son, Lord Stanley, to "get up an anti-lodger speech, or a speech on the subject either way," and was reassured by Stanley's reply that the only important thing was that "our Bill, or at least a Bill, is safe."[7] At the same time Gladstone, who thought household suffrage to be "beyond the wants and wishes of the time"[8] and a £5 rating franchise the most that could be safely granted, was sponsoring amendments that were to extend the franchise not only beyond the £5 point but beyond what anyone had until then conceived of as household suffrage.

Lord Stanley was right: "Our bill, or at least a bill," was passed. But even he could hardly have foreseen how rapidly and radically "our bill"—the Conservative bill of March—was transformed into "a bill"—the Reform Act. Within one week the fancy franchises and dual votes were withdrawn by Disraeli himself, and in committee the bill was so altered that, as the current witticism went, the only thing left intact was the word "whereas." The most important change was the inclusion of compound-householders— those who did not themselves pay rates but whose landlords, in effect, paid the rates for them. This one amendment had the effect of doubling the numbers who would have qualified under the original definition of the household suffrage, of enfranchising almost the entire urban working class, and of making that class a majority of the electorate not only in the boroughs but in the country at large.

•   •   •

7. Ibid., II, 269–70 (April 22, 1867).
8. Morley, *Gladstone*, II, 225. This and similar remarks should dispose of the theory that Gladstone opposed household suffrage because it was insufficiently radical.

There has been much discussion over whether the final act owed more to the Conservatives or to the Liberals. A history of the act published at the time pointed out that of the sixty-one sections of the original Conservative bill, only twenty were retained in the final act; of these, sixteen were essentially the same as the Liberal bill of 1866, the four distinctively Conservative clauses being the title, a redistribution clause disfranchising four small boroughs, a penalty for corruption, and a temporary provision regarding certain electoral registers. It was also pointed out that of Gladstone's ten objections to the original bill, nine were satisfied in line with his proposals. The author concluded by contrasting the Reform Act of 1832 with that of 1867, the first so carefully thought out that the final version was substantially the same as the original, the second completely unpremeditated—"the scheme of uninstructed sciolists, who needed, step by step, to be set right by their opponents."[9] In another work published soon afterwards, the same writer was more explicit in his conclusion and more outspoken in his indignation: "The allegation that the Reform Act of 1867 is mainly or substantially the work of the Conservative Government is one of the most impudent falsifications of history that was ever attempted."[1]

Yet this indignation seems curiously misplaced. For the author of these works, Homersham Cox, was an avowed Gladstonian and as hostile to the act itself as to the Conservatives under whose auspices it was passed. While refusing to give the Conservatives credit for the act, he clearly held them responsible—in the invidious sense—for it. And his evidence is equally ambiguous. If the final act did not conform to the original Conservative bill, it conformed still less (the sixteen similar clauses notwithstanding) to the

9. Homersham Cox, *A History of the Reform Bills of 1866 and 1867* (London, 1868), p. 282.
1. Homersham Cox, *Whig and Tory Administration during the Last Thirteen Years* (London, 1868), p. 51.

Liberal bill of 1866—which is why he thoroughly approved of the bill of 1866 and as thoroughly disapproved of the Act of 1867. And if it is true that "nobody believes that Mr. Disraeli intended it when he brought in his Reform Bill,"[2] it is equally true that nobody believed Mr. Gladstone intended it when he brought in (or had his colleagues bring in) the amendments that transformed the bill. Gladstone himself said that he had assented to the compound-householder amendment "as I would assent to cut off my leg rather than lose my life," as the "lesser of two evils."[3] The decisive point, however, is the fact that the nine changes made in accordance with Gladstone's proposals were collectively less important than the one change he sought but did not succeed in carrying: the limitation of the franchise to those meeting a minimum rental or rating requirement.

The Reform Act was indeed unpremeditated, but on both sides, the Conservative "sciolists" (opportunists, we would say today) having their counterparts among the Liberals. Gladstone worked out his party strategy during the winter recess. From Rome where he was vacationing (he remained there during these critical months when the popular reform movement was at its height), he wrote to the party whip:

> A good bill from them [the Conservatives] would save us much trouble and anxiety. A straightforward bill, such as an £8 franchise without tricks, would be easily dealt with. But their bill will be neither good nor straightforward. The mind of Disraeli, as leader of the House of Commons, and standing as he does among his compeers, will predominate in its formation. Now he has made in his lifetime three attempts at legislation—the budget of 1852, the India Bill of 1856, the Reform bill of 1859. All have been thoroughly tortuous measures. And the Ethiopian will not change his skin. His Reform bill of 1867

2. Cox, *Reform Bills*, p. 279.

3. Cox, *Whig and Tory Administration*, p. 50; *3 Hansard* 187: 717 (May 17, 1867).

will be tortuous too. But if you have to drive a man out of a wood, you must yourself go into the wood to drive him. We may have to meet a tortuous bill by a tortuous motion. This is what I am afraid of, and what I am, for one, above all things anxious to avoid.[4]

Gladstone's fears were borne out, as much by his own doing as by his opponent's. For however much he professed to dislike tortuousness, he was as masterly in the art as the "Ethiopian." Thirty years later he wrote an appropriately tortuous account of the affair. The "governing idea" of Disraeli, he then charged, "seemed to be not so much to consider what ought to be proposed and carried, as to make sure that, whatever it was, it should be proposed and carried by those now in power." At the same time, he could not conceal the fact that his own motives were no less partisan. He described the "little known" Liberal MP who had been delegated to introduce the compound-householder amendment and who did so "without an idea that it would be carried and anticipating its defeat by a majority of a hundred." And from the distance of so many years he confessed that he himself had never experienced a "stranger emotion of surprise" than when he entered the House primed for debate only to be told that Disraeli had accepted the amendment without protest—"as if," Gladstone protested, "it had been an affair of trivial importance."

> Perhaps [he reflected] we ought to have recognized that the idea of household suffrage, when the phrase had once been advertised by a government as its battle-ground, was irresistible, and that the only remaining choice was whether it should be a household suffrage cribbed, cabined, and confined by the condition of personal rate-paying, or a household suffrage fairly conforming in substance and operation to the idea that the phrase conveyed. The first was in our view totally inadmissible; the

4. Morley, *Gladstone*, II, 222-3 (Oct. 30, 1866).

second beyond the wants and wishes of the time. But the government, it must be admitted, bowled us over by the force of the phrase; and made it our next duty to bowl them over by bringing the reality of the bill into correspondence with its great profession.[5]

There was more candor in Gladstone's remarks than one generally expects of him; it is not often that he confessed to playing a game. Unfortunately, he did not entirely understand the nature of the game he was involved in since he did not properly understand the character of his opponents. The misunderstanding, as it happened, was fatal: he lost the game because he did not realize that he could not "bowl over" Disraeli as easily as Disraeli had bowled him over. The Conservatives knew their man better. As one later said: "We know he does not belong to our eleven, but we have him down as a professional bowler."[6]

Gladstone saw only one side of Disraeli: the phrasemonger. This was the Disraeli who had written, in one of his early novels: "Few ideas are correct ones, and what are correct no one can ascertain; but with words we govern men."[7] It is the Disraeli of whom his biographer remarked: "The creator of Taper and Tadpole knew well the political value of a sonorous cry."[8] Disraeli "invents phrases," Bright had contemptuously dismissed Disraeli's earlier proposal for a "lateral extension" of the franchise,[9] as Gladstone now dismissed household suffrage as a "great phrase."[1] But the inventor of phrases, the creator of Taper and

5. Ibid., II, 224-5.
6. J. L. Hammond and M. R. D. Foot, *Gladstone and Liberalism* (London, 1952), p. 102.
7. Benjamin Disraeli, *Contarini Fleming* (2nd edn.; London, 1845), p. 101.
8. Monypenny and Buckle, *Disraeli*, II, 222.
9. William Robertson, *Life and Times of the Right Hon. John Bright* (London, n.d.), p. 425.
1. Morley, *Gladstone*, II, 225.

Tadpole, was also the creator of Coningsby and Sybil. And while Disraeli himself was a consummate master of the arts of Taper and Tadpole, he despised those who knew nothing but these arts, who had none of the vision of Coningsby and Sybil. Gladstone may be excused for ignoring the evidence of the novels; most contemporaries regarded them more or less amiably as the conceits of a febrile, alien imagination. But the echoes of Coningsby and Sybil resounded throughout Disraeli's political speeches and public life, and when his great phrases became the matter of policy, Gladstone might have given thought to the possibility that there were ideas lurking behind the words.

The creed of Coningsby and Sybil consisted, basically, of nothing more exotic or esoteric than the belief that the Tories were the national party, that the aristocracy and the working class were natural allies, that the social hierarchy was independent of ephemeral political arrangements, that national character was more important than particular laws, and that both politics and society were largely governed by traditions of leadership and deference. The key words, "natural" and "national," were sounded again and again in Disraeli's speeches on the Reform Act:

> The Tory party has resumed its natural functions in the government of the country. For what is the Tory party unless it represents national feeling? If it do not represent national feeling, Toryism is nothing.[2]
> When the people are led by their natural leaders, and when, by their united influence, the national institutions fulfil their original intention, the Tory party is triumphant.[3]

This creed, so far from being a literary fantasy, was in fact a political ideology of substance and consequence—although perhaps not quite the substance and consequence

2. Monypenny and Buckle, *Disraeli*, II, 287.
3. Park, *English Reform Bill*, p. 242.

generally supposed. Its initial and most important effect was to liberate politics by divorcing it from society. Secure in his faith in a national party and a natural social order, Disraeli could contemplate with equanimity the boldest political experiment. He could take liberties with the constitution because, as he said, he put his trust not in any particular set of laws but in the national character.[4] He was not bowled over when Gladstone proposed to convert the "great phrase" of household suffrage into a "reality," because whether the franchise was fixed at seven, six, five, or no pounds was indeed, as Gladstone had charged, a matter of "trivial importance" to him. He felt free, therefore, to fix the franchise wherever expediency, opportunity, or even the sonority of a great phrase dictated. Coningsby and Sybil were the necessary complement of Taper and Tadpole; the faith of the former gave license to the latter.

It is this peculiar dependence of license upon faith that distinguishes Disraeli's opportunism from the crasser variety of a Taper or Tadpole. One disaffected Conservative, objecting to the withdrawal of one provision after another of the original bill and the adoption of one radically new amendment after another, said that the affair had taught him three things: that nothing had so little vitality as a "vital point," that nothing was so insecure as a "security," and that nothing was so elastic as the conscience of a cabinet minister.[5] But the affair may suggest not so much a lack of vitality, security, and conscience as a genuine difference over what constituted a vital point, an essential security, or a question of conscience. Similarly Cox may have been unfair when he denounced Disraeli for accepting "with alacrity" the compound-householder amendment:

4. One is reminded of Burke's famous dicta: "Nations are not primarily ruled by laws"; and "Manners are of more importance than laws." ("Thoughts on the Cause of the Present Discontents," *Works* [London, 1909], I, 306; "Letters on a Regicide Peace," *Works*, V, 208.)

5. Monypenny and Buckle, *Disraeli*, II, 279.

"Mr. Disraeli felt no difficulty in this matter. He never feels any difficulty about any matter."[6] Perhaps Disraeli had a different threshold of difficulty because he had a different priority of values, a commitment to different principles.

What has commonly been understood as Disraeli's opportunism may more accurately be rendered as latitudinarianism.[7] And latitudinarianism is as respectable a doctrine in politics as it is in theology. Not only did Disraeli take advantage of all the political latitude implicit in his social creed; he insisted upon that latitude as the only sound basis for politics. He insisted upon it, moreover, when there was no political advantage to be gained from it, when he had nothing to justify or defend. "I, for one, am no advocate of finality," he had said as early as 1848 in connection with another reform proposal.[8] The "most frequently repeated argument" of the Conservatives during the debate on the Liberal bill of 1866, according to Cox, was their objection to the "hard and fast line" of the £7 franchise.[9] The following year Disraeli said of the changes undergone by the Conservative bill: "You cannot be bound to any particular scheme, as if you were settling the duties on sugar."[1]

6. Cox, *Whig and Tory*, pp. 50–1.
7. I have chosen this term, for want of a better, in full knowledge of the fact that Disraeli himself had once used it pejoratively. In *Coningsby*, he had accused Peel of creating "a party without principles; its basis therefore was necessarily Latitudinarianism; and its inevitable consequence has been Political Infidelity." ([London, 1849], p. 98.) But the "Latitudinarianism" Disraeli was then objecting to was Peel's particular variety of liberal-Conservatism which he found indistinguishable from liberal-Whiggism. Disraeli's latitudinarianism, as I have used the word, suggests not so much a lack of principles as a lack of commitment to specific policies (a specific duty on corn or a specific suffrage qualification, for example). Moreover, it represented a distinctively non-Whig, non-Liberal attitude to society and politics.
8. *3 Hansard* 99: 951 (June 20, 1848).
9. Cox, *Whig and Tory Administration*, p. 57.
1. *3 Hansard* 188: 1605 (July 15, 1867).

In its initial impulse, then, the creed known as Tory Democracy was latitudinarian rather than democratic per se. But latitudinarianism generated and accelerated the movement toward democracy. What was possible soon became probable and what was permitted became prescriptive. One member of the cabinet noted in his diary at the time that the government was following a "laissez-aller system," yielding and adopting anything in the spirit of "in for a penny, in for a pound."[2] The expression was particularly apt, since it was literally pennies and pounds that were being frittered away. If there was no "hard and fast line" to abide by, no good reason to fix the franchise at any particular point, this itself became reason for fixing it at no point. Disraeli himself explained that, confronted with a multitude of schemes proposing to fix the franchise at "£8, £7, £6, and all sorts of pounds," he had come to the conclusion that there was no "sound resting-place" other than household suffrage.[3] As theological latitudinarianism had been impelled toward rationalism, so political latitudinarianism was now impelled toward democracy.

But there was an additional impetus toward democracy in the Tory creed. This came from the belief that the lower classes were not only naturally conservative in temperament but also naturally Conservative in politics. Thus the party had a practical interest in democracy. The Tories were democratic, one might say, because they assumed that the demos was Tory. The *Quarterly Review*, which itself opposed the Reform Act, explained why the great majority of the Conservatives favored it:

> The phantom of a Conservative democracy was a reality to many men of undoubted independence and vigour of mind. A vague idea that the poorer men are the more easily they are influenced by the rich, . . . that the ruder

2. Earl of Malmesbury, *Memoirs of an Ex-Minister* (London, 1884), II, 369.
3. *3 Hansard* 188: 1603 (July 15, 1867).

class of minds would be more sensitive to traditional emotions, . . . all these arguments . . . went to make up the
clear conviction of the mass of the Conservative party,
that in a Reform Bill more Radical than that of the Whigs
they had discovered the secret of a sure and signal triumph.[4]

A phantom, as the *Quarterly Review* realized, is as good
as reality if enough people accept it as such. It is doubtful
whether Disraeli created this phantom, as *The Times* later
suggested in its famous eulogy: "In the inarticulate mass of
the English populace, he discerned the Conservative work-
ing-man as the sculptor perceives the angel imprisoned in a
block of marble."[5] Whatever the origins and exact status
of the Conservative workingman—whether he was, as the
Conservatives liked to think, a necessary and permanent
phenomenon, or, as the Liberals hoped, a fortuitous and
transitory one—his reality by 1866 was rarely doubted. In
the debate on his own bill, Gladstone had observed that
those constituencies with the smallest workingclass populations had elected the "most advanced Liberals," while the
eight boroughs having a workingclass majority had returned five Liberals and nine Conservatives.[6] The moral
could not have escaped the Conservatives. Indeed in his
own party Disraeli was by now so far from the vanguard
that others, and not only Lord Derby, wanted to set loose
the hare of household suffrage long before Disraeli agreed
to it. His triumphal remark after the passage of the act,
that he had had to "educate" his party, is often quoted as if
he had had to convert and perhaps even to coerce the
party. What he actually said was that he had had to educate

4. *Quarterly Review*, CXXVII (1869), 541–2. This article, un-
signed in the magazine, was written by Lord Cranborne (later
Lord Salisbury), who had resigned from the Cabinet in protest
against the progressive radicalization of the bill.
5. *The Times*, April 18, 1883.
6. *3 Hansard* 182: 40 (March 12, 1866); ibid., 182: 1137 (April
12, 1866).

his party and "prepare the mind of Parliament and the country," and that this was done "not only with the concurrence of Lord Derby, but of my colleagues."[7] The process of education, in fact, must have taken place long before. By February 1867, when the question was formally put to them for the first time, not only a majority of the cabinet but a majority of the Conservatives in parliament declared themselves in favor of household suffrage.

Of all this—the nature and pervasiveness of the Tory ideology—Gladstone had only the faintest glimmerings. He persisted in thinking that the Conservatives were being led by the "mystery man," that they did not know "what course they would have to take," since that course was determined by the "secret counsels of another mind."[8] And he was convinced that there was nothing more in the secret counsels of that mysterious and tortuous mind than the desire to outwit the Liberals by pretending to outbid them—pretending, for he was convinced that the Conservatives had not the slightest intention of going through with their ostensible policy of household suffrage. He introduced his amendments confident that the Conservatives would not call his bluff. And even after they did call his bluff, after the bill was passed by the Commons, he assumed that the Conservative strategy was to have it killed in the House of Lords—this at the very time that Derby was summoning the more important Conservative peers to his sickbed to warn them that he would resign if the bill were not passed quickly and intact.[9]

Gladstone was defeated by a failure of imagination, a failure so grave that it even affected his normally acute sense of *Realpolitik*. One might have thought that his own

7. Monypenny and Buckle, *Disraeli*, II, 289.
8. Morley, *Gladstone*, II, 223, 226.
9. Malmesbury, *Memoirs*, II, 371.

position on the franchise was determined by considerations of *Realpolitik*, that he opposed household suffrage because of the admittedly Conservative bias of the lower classes. Yet it appears that this factor played so small a part in his thinking that he did not even take it seriously as an explanation of Conservative policy, indeed that he did not take it seriously enough to take the Conservative policy seriously. And he could not take the Conservatives seriously because his imagination balked at the thought that anyone, even the most tortuous "Ethiopian," could help but share his own repugnance to household suffrage. Circumscribed in his own ideas, he assumed that everyone was similarly circumscribed. His opponents might be wrong—were assuredly wrong—but they must be wrong in his terms, within the range he allowed them.

If Gladstone failed to appreciate the scope of Disraeli's mind, Disraeli knew well the limitations of Gladstone's— and the limitations which Gladstone would have imposed upon him. Explaining why the Conservatives had as much right as the Liberals to stand as the party of reform, Disraeli once said: "I was determined to vindicate the right of the party [the Conservatives] to a free hand, and not to allow them to be shut up in a cage formed by the Whigs and Radicals, confined within a magic circle which they were not to step out of at the peril of their lives."[1] It was precisely this refusal to be confined within such a circle, to play the part the Liberals had assigned to him, that made Disraeli so abhorrent to Gladstone. Gladstone's notion of a good Conservative was one who knew his place—who would propose an £8 franchise, to which Gladstone could then respond, in the proper spirit of liberality, with a £7 bill.[2] What he could not understand or tolerate was the Conservative who deliberately eschewed a fixed policy, rejected a fixed place in the political spectrum, refused even

1. Monypenny and Buckle, *Disraeli*, I, 1580.
2. See above, p. 351.

to acknowledge the need or propriety of such a fixed policy and place.

Gladstone's failure of imagination came from a crucial and characteristically Liberal failure of nerve. Lacking the Conservative's faith in the eternal verities of human nature and society, the Liberal had nothing to sustain him but the precarious arrangements of politics. And these political arrangements were all the more precarious because they were entirely and eternally at the mercy of a mass of individuals—as many individuals as there were electors. Each of these individuals was presumed to be independent of and equal to every other; each was presumed to be pursuing his private interests at the expense of everyone else's interests; and each was presumed to be exercising the maximum amount of power available to him so as to achieve the maximum satisfaction of his interests. To the Liberal, therefore, the political enterprise was eminently serious and perilous. He had to consider every reform carefully and calculate its effect, since any change in the composition of the electorate, any alteration in the political order, might jeopardize the entire structure of society. Unlike the Conservative with his cavalier "in for a penny, in for a pound" attitude, the Liberal had to take account of every penny and every pound. At one point in the debate on his own bill, Gladstone's complicated calculations and repeated invocations of the "Rule of Three Sum" moved the House to laughter, upon which Gladstone feebly retorted that he was pleased his "studies in arithmetic prove so amusing."[3] Bright once rebuked Gladstone: "You have been hunting for figures from parish offices to prove how many working men are electors . . . as if a few thousands of electors more or less were of the smallest consequence."[4] But this was precisely the point: a few thousand electors

3. *3 Hansard* 182: 53 (March 12, 1866).
4. Wilbur D. Jones, *Lord Derby and Victorian Conservatism* (Athens, Ga., 1956), p. 285.

more or less, the reduction of a pound in the franchise, the shift from a rating to rental basis were of the greatest consequence to Gladstone because they might make all the difference between a tolerable society and an intolerable one. Disraeli, on the other hand, was notably casual about numbers and figures. At critical moments he was unable to estimate how many would be enfranchised by his own proposals; and it was only after he had accepted the compound-householder amendment that the government statistician was called upon to calculate what its effect would be.[5]

It may be objected that the Conservatives were not so permissive and the Liberals not so rigid as has been made out here, that the party lines, as well as ideologies, were not so well defined, that many Liberals voted for the Reform Act and some Conservatives against it. All this is true, and given more space, many more refinements, exceptions, and qualifications might be made. But the party distinctions are basically valid, and the refinements, exceptions, and qualifications are just that and no more. Morever, the distinctions are valid concretely and specifically, not only as ideal types. They apply most strikingly, of course, to Gladstone and Disraeli, a fact of some importance in an event where so much depended on the will, temperament, and decisions of these two men. But Gladstone and Disraeli, as has been suggested, were not eccentrics, or at least not political eccentrics. They led their parties so successfully for so long because whatever their private idiosyncrasies—and they both had many—they did represent the prevailing spirit of their parties.

It is important to insist upon these ideological and temperamental distinctions because they help explain what is

5. Briggs, *Age of Improvement*, p. 511. See also Harrison, *Before the Socialists*, p. 115: "An examination of the papers of Tory Cabinet ministers reveals that Gladstone's opponents were in dire need of information and were really uncertain about the make-up of the class with which they had to deal."

surely at the heart of the matter: that the Reform Act was a Conservative measure, initiated and carried by a Conservative government. There was much truth in Gladstone's charge that the Conservatives were less interested in the particular form of the act than in taking credit for passing it. The fact remains, however, that it did take the form it did and that the Conservatives passed it in that form, whereas Gladstone and much of his party were to the end unreconciled to it in that form and agreed to its passage, as Gladstone admitted, only as one would agree to have one's leg cut off to save one's life—literally, to avoid committing political suicide.

What makes this fact even more notable is the profound resistance to it on the part of most historians. Like Gladstone, who bitterly resented Disraeli's usurpation of the role of reformer (however much he himself opposed this particular reform), so most historians have assumed that the Liberal Party was naturally, inherently, the party of progress and reform. And like Gladstone, who persisted until the end in thinking that Disraeli had no intention of permitting his great phrase to become a reality, so these historians, even after the event, have been loath to credit the Conservative accomplishment. The fantasies of the historian, however, have exceeded even those of Gladstone. For where Gladstone thought of the Liberals as the party of a £7 (or at most £5) franchise compared with the mythical £8 Conservatives, the historian feels obliged to attribute to the Liberals no less a measure than household suffrage—that is the Reform Act itself. Thus the Liberals are made out to be the rightful, legitimate parents of the act, and the Conservatives its nominal foster parents.

When Morley described the affair as "one of the most

curious in our parliamentary history,"[6] he was commenting on the anomaly of a Liberal act, as he thought it, being
passed by a Conservative government. But nothing in the
affair is quite so curious as the way this idea of what "ought
to have been" (as one historian revealingly put it)[7] has
come to prevail over what in fact was. The extreme strategy has simply been to avoid any mention of the Conservatives in connection with the act; this is more often the
device of the casual, superficial history, but may be encountered in the most respectable learned journal.[8] Occasionally, the auspices of the act having been noted, its
provisions have then been misrepresented and its effects
minimized, apparently on the assumption that a Conservative measure could not have been as radical as it was.[9] For
the most part, however, the Liberal myth has insinuated
itself in the suggestion that the act was at heart a Radical-
Liberal measure which the Conservatives abhorred but

6. See above, p. 334.

7. See quotation below, p. 365, n. 1.

8. E.g., Trygve R. Tholfsen, "The Transition to Democracy
in Victorian England," *International Review of Social History*,
VI (1961). Here the Reform Act appears as a demonstration of
the "Liberal Victorian faith"—a "belief in progress through
rational reform" and the "liberal confidence in class harmony"
—the faith that, after 1867, kept the working class loyal to the
Liberal Party and that inspired the philosophy of Lib-Labism.
Nowhere, in this account of the "Liberal" faith, is there any
mention of the fact that the act was passed by the Conservatives
rather than by the Liberals.

9. E.g., George Lichtheim: "1867 was also the year in which
the second Reform Bill gave the vote to the *upper layer* of the
British working class. It was the Tories under Disraeli's skilled
leadership who reaped most of the benefits in 1867, when the
skilled workers got the vote." (*Marxism* [New York, 1961],
pp. 98, 102; italics mine.) A more interesting compound of error,
inconsistency, and grudging admission may be found in S. G.
Checkland, *The Rise of Industrial Society in England* (London,
1964), p. 369: "Disraeli's Reform Act extended the vote to cover
the £10 householders, lodgers paying £10 rent in the towns,
and to £12 householders in the counties. Not all were satisfied
with what had been gained, but it was a notable advance over
1832. The artisan in the towns was now virtually enfranchised."

which, by Machiavellian cunning or perversity of history, they managed to appropriate:

> [Disraeli] had also to persuade his own followers to support a measure which they had all their lives been condemning, and which was, or in their view ought to have been, more dangerous to the Constitution than the one which they and the recalcitrant Whigs had thrown out in the preceding year.[1]
>
> How under these circumstances the Radicals succeeded in dictating terms to the Conservative ministers, remains one of the most complex problems of our parliamentary history.[2]
>
> Now there followed one of the most contorted and unexpected portions of even parliamentary history, ending in the enfranchisement of a great part of the British working class by the party which was controlled by its most resolute and natural enemies. . . . Disraeli, the most cunning of all Victorian politicians, leapt in first and secured it [reform] both at the time and in history books for the less probable party.[3]
>
> [Under the Conservatives, the reform issue] gave prospect at times of developing the ever ominous qualities of a class war through the operation of Tory opposition.[4]
>
> It was left, paradoxically, to his [Russell's] Conservative successor, Disraeli, as the strongest man in Derby's third cabinet, to bring in the bill which eventually became law: and in the process of becoming law it became, equally paradoxically, a much more radical measure of reform than even Disraeli wanted.[5]

It was not a matter of Disraeli's 'educating' his party, but

1. James Bryce, *Studies in Contemporary Biography* (New York, 1903), p. 14.

2. Trevelyan, *Bright*, p. 373.

3. G. D. H. Cole and R. Postgate, *The British Common People* (New York, 1939), p. 348.

4. Gillespie, *Labor and Politics*, p. 265.

5. David Thomson, *England in the Nineteenth Century* (London, 1950), p. 127.

of bamboozling it. . . . Tories were stunned. . . . Alone
of his party, Disraeli was imaginatively equipped to risk
the leap into the dark.[6]

This rewriting of history to conform to the Liberal
image has brought with it a corresponding realignment of
parties. If the Conservatives have had to be denied responsibility and credit for the Reform Act, the Liberals have had
to be absolved of responsibility and guilt for those among
themselves who preferred to turn out their own government rather than approve of even a £7 franchise. The
existence and importance of the Adullamites being undeniable, the strategy here has been to deny their status as
"real" Liberals. Thus the first, and contemporary, Liberal
historian of the Reform Act, Homersham Cox, spoke of
this "large section of members who had been elected as
Liberals"[7]—as if they had been elected under false pre-

6. Donald Southgate, *The Passing of the Whigs* (London, 1962),
pp. 318, 320. One may continue to document this attitude indefinitely—e.g., the references to a "Conservative surrender," as
if the Conservatives had reluctantly yielded to Liberal demands.
(Pelling, *America*, p. 9; Harrison, *Before the Socialists*, p. 106.)
The most recent example is Smith's *The Making of the Second
Reform Bill.* Although the body of this book provides ample
evidence to the contrary, the introduction and conclusion are
suffused with the typical Liberal assumptions. Thus "Russell,
Gladstone, and the contributors to Essays on Reform" (the
familiar amalgam of Liberals and Radicals) are credited with
the "eloquent reiteration of the incorporation theme" (the idea
that good government requires the wider participation and incorporation of the people), while Derby and Disraeli are said
to have "set out to enfranchise a small number of workingmen, sufficient to recognize their improvement and to quiet agitation, and to render their votes nugatory." (Pp. 3–4.) In fact,
the reverse was quite as true—the "incorporation" theme in
particular representing the Conservative idea of "nationality."
Similarly, the compound-householder amendment is seen as the
result of "Gladstone's intransigence" and "Disraeli's devious
stratagems" (p. 4), whereas it was quite patently the result of
Gladstone's stratagem and a complete reversal of his previous
policy. Again, Disraeli's idea that the hierarchical society would
continue whatever the suffrage is described as a "rationalization"
and "myth"; while a Liberal making the same point appears as a
"hard-headed student of politics." (Pp. 232–3.)

7. Cox, *Whig and Tory Administration*, p. 39.

tences. Later historians have been more ruthless in dissociating them from the Liberals, some identifying them as Whigs, others assimilating them to the Tories:

> Though Lowe himself was no more an aristocrat than Burke, his Adullamites were for the most part a last rally of aristocrats of the Whig decadence.[8]
> [The Liberal Party] contained a 'tail' of young men of fashion, the scions of great Whig houses who might just as well have been the scions of great Tory houses so far as their opinions were concerned.[9]
> The bulk of the wealthier commercial class and a large section of the landed class had theretofore belonged to the Liberal party. Most of them, however, were then already beginning to pass through what was called Whiggism into habits of thought that were practically Tory. They did not know how far they had gone till Lowe's speeches told them, and they welcomed his ideas as justifying their own tendencies.[1]

The idea that Lowe represented a crypto-Tory faction, an obsolete and peripheral sect of the Liberal Party that was on the verge of defection, is without logic or substance. For why should he and his faction have defected to the party that was responsible for a Reform Act far more extreme than the measure they had opposed within their own party? What these historians fail to say is that no such defection, no fusion of the Adullamites and Conservatives, took place.[2] Moreover Lowe himself remained not only a loyal but a prominent member of the Liberal Party. The very year after the passage of the Reform Act, Lowe was named Chancellor of the Exchequer in Gladstone's first ministry—a post that Gladstone himself (and Disraeli alter-

8. Trevelyan, *Bright*, p. 357.
9. Trevelyan, *British History*, p. 343.
1. Bryce, *Studies*, p. 298.
2. The many difficulties that stood in the way of fusion are described in the recent essays by Cowling and Winter.

nately) had until then occupied with such distinction.³
Later still, Gladstone persuaded the Queen to bestow a
viscountcy upon Lowe rather than the barony she had
been prepared to offer. Lowe, Gladstone explained, had
soared to such heights in 1866 that he did not deserve to be
lost in the "common ruck of official barons."⁴ These were
hardly the rewards of one whose connection with the party
was as tenuous as has generally been made out.

It was fitting that Gladstone, not ordinarily the most
forgiving of men, should have chosen the leader of the
dissidents as his own successor. For even in dissent Lowe
was, in effect, Gladstone's alter ego. So far from being
"practically Tory," his "habits of thought" were essentially, almost quintessentially, Liberal.⁵ He opposed the
Liberal bill in 1866 for the same reasons Gladstone opposed
the Conservative bill in 1867; indeed he opposed it precisely because he was convinced that the first would lead to
the second. When he warned Gladstone that the "ruinous
game of see-saw" would come to a halt only with "a
qualification so low that it will keep out nobody,"⁶ he

3. In his *British History*, Trevelyan attached great significance
to Bright's lesser cabinet position while failing to mention
Lowe's far more important one; and in his biography of Bright,
Lowe's position is referred to only in a footnote. See also
O. F. Christie, *The Transition from Aristocracy* (London,
1927), p. 160: "It had become almost impossible to say such
things [about the venality of the working class] and survive
politically. Lowe was afterwards obliged to look for a seat in
a new academic constituency." Again there is no mention of the
fact that he survived so well as to become Chancellor of the
Exchequer.

4. Philip Magnus, *Gladstone* (London, 1954), p. 178. To the
degree to which Lowe rose in Gladstone's esteem, so he declined
in Disraeli's. Shortly before his death, Disraeli was asked
whether there was anyone in London with whom he would
refuse to shake hands. "Only one," was the reply. "Robert
Lowe." (Robert Blake, *Disraeli* [New York, 1967], p. 564.)

5. Years later, Lowe wrote to Gladstone: "In almost all subjects
except the franchise I agree with you more than, I think, with
anyone else." (Winter, "The Cave of Adullam," p. 45 n.)

6. *3 Hansard* 182: 2100 (April 26, 1866).

368

knew that prospect to be as disagreeable to Gladstone as to himself.

Contemporaries did not find it as easy as later historians to impeach Lowe's Liberalism. Contributors to *Essays on Reform*, a pro-reform volume published early in 1867, had to cope with the fact that Lowe, the archetype of the Liberal-utilitarian, was their bitterest opponent. The first essayist wrote: "Never were the doctrines of Benthamism more triumphantly applied to political questions than in these [Lowe's] luminous speeches"[7]—from which he deduced that the old utilitarian Liberalism no longer provided sufficient grounds for reform and that reformers now had to base their claims upon so un-Benthamite a principle as justice. Another contributor, Leslie Stephen, reversed the argument, retaining Lowe's principles but taking exception to the use he made of them: "The ultimate test must be that upon which Mr. Lowe insisted so powerfully"—and by that test, and that test alone, reform was justified.[8]

But the issue was not merely the test of utility in the narrow sense; it was the larger presuppositions of Utilitarianism that established Lowe's claim to the title of Liberal. What he had in common with other Liberals was an image of the individual as autonomous, isolated, and self-seeking; a sense of politics as all-important, all-embracing, and therefore totally vulnerable; and an obsession with numbers that derived from this individualistic politics. When he denounced the "mere principle of numbers," the "mere worship of numbers," the "senseless homage . . . paid to mere numbers,"[9] he was really denouncing democracy as the rule of numbers, the rule of the masses. But in his fear of democracy, he exposed his own dependence

7. George C. Brodrick, "The Utilitarian Argument against Reform as Stated by Mr. Lowe," *Essays on Reform*, p. 2.
8. Leslie Stephen, "On the Choice of Representatives by Popular Constituencies," *Essays on Reform*, p. 88.
9. *3 Hansard* 183: 1639–40 (May 31, 1866).

upon the principle of numbers. Not even Gladstone, with his Rule of Three Sum, was more adept at calculations, more attentive to pennies and pounds. When Bright once intimated that there was little difference between an £8 and a £7 franchise, Lowe protested: "His £ is no joke. The honorary Member for Birmingham's £ means 100,000 men, and 100,000 men of whom he may know a great deal, but of whom we . . . know nothing at all."[1] He warned Bright that one pound was apt to lead to another, 100,000 new electors to another 100,000. Moreover, the pound itself, reduced to its weekly equivalent, amounted to no more than 3d, which was little enough to have such momentous consequences: "The £7 will eat up the £6 and the £5. The £7 franchise is 2s 9d a week, and 2s 6d a week will give £6 10s. You see: how easy it is to ascend. The difference is merely one of 3d per week, and the margin is, consequently, very small."[2]

If Lowe had not existed, one would be tempted to invent him, for he provides a perfect foil to Disraeli. And one could not improve upon Lowe's own metaphors to point up the contrast:

> It does not depend upon any Government, upon any Minister, perhaps upon any House of Commons to say where those changes will stop. One honorary Member speaks of this as a change that will last fifty years. He has put the matter as entirely out of his power as a man who, rolling a stone down the side of a mountain, fixes beforehand in his own mind the time it will take to reach the bottom.[3]
> Night and day the gate is open that leads to that bare and level plain, where every ant's nest is a mountain and every thistle a forest tree.[4]
> We are about, on this momentous occasion, to enter upon

1. Ibid., 182: 2093 (April 26, 1866).
2. Ibid., 182: 2088.
3. Ibid., 182: 2103.
4. Ibid., 183: 1650 (May 31, 1866).

a new era, when the bag which holds the winds will be untied, and we shall be surrounded by a perpetual whirl of change, alteration, innovation, and revolution.[5]

Each of these metaphors might be taken as typical of the Liberal-utilitarian mentality, the mentality which envisaged politics as a rolling stone that was uncontrollable and unpredictable, society as a bare and level plain where every ant's nest loomed large as a mountain, and civilization as a bag of winds coming undone upon the slightest pressure and exposing men to all the perils of the state of nature.

In the conventional Liberal spectrum, Bright is at the opposite pole from Lowe—the one exemplifying the dominant progressive tendency in the party, the other a retrograde, obsolete sect. Thus while Lowe's elevation to the Exchequer in 1868 has generally gone unnoticed, Bright's cabinet appointment has been taken as signifying the triumph of radicalism.[6] Yet Bright's was the lowest cabinet post (he was President of the Board of Trade); he held it for a very brief period (he was incapacitated by ill health during most of 1870 and resigned later that year); and such influence as he did exercise was, as his secretary said, "distinctly conservative," opposed to "interference or to legislation if it could possibly be avoided."[7]

5. Ibid., 188: 1540 (July 15, 1867).
6. E.g., Trevelyan, *Bright,* p. 395: "Gladstone had transformed the old Whig-Liberal party into a Liberal-Radical party on the basis of Bright's programme." Or Gillespie, *Labor and Politics,* p. 291: "The Act of 1867 gave the Radical faction the ascendancy within the Liberal party."
7. Trevelyan, *Bright,* p. 405. Other contemporaries agreed. In 1870 Bagehot wrote that "in the present cabinet, unless consistent rumor speaks false, his voice has more usually been a Conservative voice than the contrary." ("Mr. Bright's Retirement," *Bagehot's Historical Essays,* ed. Norman St. John-Stevas [New York, 1965], p. 227.) A few years later Bagehot found "few more typical Conservatives in the House of Commons than Mr. Bright." ("The Conservative Vein in Mr. Bright," *Bagehot's Historical Essays,* p. 229.) Bright's economic "conservatism"—

Both in intent and in effect, Bright's radicalism was as equivocal before the passage of the Reform Act as after. His defence of the Liberal bill of 1866 was professedly expediential. The bill, he said, was neither to his personal liking (he would have preferred household suffrage), nor "adequate to the occasion" (most reformers having expected at least a £6 franchise); but since £7 was the most they could get, and since "beggars in the House of Commons, like beggars outside of it, cannot be choosers," he had to be content with this "simple and honest measure."[8] This explanation would have been convincing had he not clung to it long after circumstances warranted it. Some weeks before the introduction of the Conservative bill, he reported to Disraeli a conversation he had had with some Conservatives in the House. He was surprised, he said, to discover "how far they were willing to go," and confessed that "at the pace they were moving, I should soon have to hold them back"; upon which Disraeli commented that these Conservatives were "fair specimens of a considerable section of the party."[9] Even after this experience, however, and after the Conservatives brought in their bill for

---

i.e., orthodox laissez-faire liberalism—has been regarded by his chief biographers, when they have attended to it at all, as an aberration, a momentary lapse from an otherwise unexceptionably liberal or radical career. The recent biography by Herman Ausubel, *John Bright: Victorian Reformer* (New York, 1966), is even more reticent on this question than Trevelyan's. John Vincent's *The Formation of the Liberal Party* is a refreshing corrective to these, for it takes seriously Bright's laissez-fairism in accounting for his attitude toward particular measures and institutions (factory acts, income tax, trade unions), and for his role in mid-Victorian politics. Vincent also provides new evidence of Bright's reservations about political reform. By concentrating on the franchise rather than the redistribution of seats, Vincent suggests, Bright was trying to neutralize the effect of reform, since redistribution would have had much more radical and democratic consequences than could be expected from a mere extension of the franchise. (P. 185.)

8. *3 Hansard* 182: 213-14, 224 (March 13, 1866).

9. *The Diaries of John Bright*, ed. R. A. J. Walling (London, 1930), p. 296.

household suffrage, Bright persisted in the claim that a £6 or £5 franchise was the most the House would accept. There may have been some justice in his argument that a £5 rating franchise was "much better than the bill of the Government as it stands"—that is, household suffrage plus fancy franchises—but not in the argument that it was "probably the best thing that could be carried."[1]

With each Conservative concession—the withdrawal of the fancy franchises, the reduction of the residence requirement from two years to one, and finally the promise to amend the bill in committee so as to provide for the compound-householders—Bright found it more difficult to hold the Conservatives back while professing to urge them forward. His rhetoric became more and more obfuscating:

> Some thought the House might alter the Bill so as to give household suffrage, but he thought the House were not in favour of any such change. He wished they were. He would support it with a great deal of pleasure; but as they were not, he should be sorry that the Bill should come out of Committee as it goes in, and without some provision for a wide extension of the suffrage in many boroughs in which it will remain limited under the Government Bill. . . . It was just possible that a proposition might be made by the Government that would render it unnecessary and undesirable to take any steps before the Bill goes into Committee. But knowing what they knew, he gave his most cordial assent to the Instruction.[2]

One would never know, from Bright's account, that the "Instruction" to which he and Gladstone gave their "most cordial assent"—indeed, instigated—was meant not to extend the suffrage but to limit it, to forestall the larger measure of household suffrage that the Conservatives were by now committed to. The Instruction was a cleverly composed document that affirmed in principle what it

1. Ibid., p. 300.
2. Cox, *Reform Bills*, p. 161.

VICTORIAN MINDS

denied in practice: insisting upon the right to vote of all rate payers, it promptly "relieved from liability to personal rating" those occupying premises below a given rateable value, "with a view to fix a line for the borough franchise."[3] Thus what sounded like an exemption from an onerous obligation was in fact an exemption from the suffrage itself, since those below the "given rateable value" (not specified in the Instruction but understood to be £5) would have neither the burden of paying rates nor, as the final clause made clear, the privilege of voting. When the "Tea-room" Liberals—a coalition of Adullamites and Radicals—forced the withdrawal of the Instruction, Bright indignantly accused them of being "more willing to express want of confidence in Mr. Gladstone than in Disraeli."[4]

Bright's tactics succeeded better with historians than with his contemporaries. One scholar has been so bemused by the rhetoric of Bright and Gladstone that he has inverted the affair, making Gladstone the author of a "radical instruction" who was "thwarted by the 'Tea–Room mutiny.'"[5] Trevelyan, who identified the Tea-Room mutineers as Radicals, nevertheless tried to preserve the illusion that Gladstone and Bright were together pursuing a Radical policy:

> Unlike the Cave [the Adullamites], the 'Tea-room' consisted of Radicals, who differed from Gladstone and Bright only as to tactics.[6]
> The Radical triumph in Committee is the more remarkable because of the painful position in which Gladstone and Bright were placed all through these critical weeks by the Whig revolt against their leadership. Bright's journal contains daily evidence that they were much more

3. Ibid., p. 160.
4. *Diaries of Bright*, p. 301.
5. Southgate, *Passing of the Whigs*, p. 319.
6. Trevelyan, *Bright*, p. 375.

374

conscious of the anxiety and discomfort of the situation than of the success that they were actually achieving.[7]

The distortions are all of a pattern: to suggest that the Liberals were the bearers of the democratic-radical faith. Thus the gap between the £10 Adullamites and the £7 Gladstonians has been magnified into a major cleavage, while that between Gladstone's (and Bright's) £5 franchise and Disraeli's household suffrage (which by then included the promise of the compound-householders) has been glossed over as a mere tactical difference. Similarly, the "painful position" of Gladstone and Bright has been ascribed to a "Whig revolt," in spite of the previous characterization of the Tea-Room group as Radicals. And the "anxiety and discomfort" attested to by Bright, caused by the desire to maintain the pretense of being radical while in fact counteracting the radicalism of others, has been made to seem less important, less real, than the "success" that Trevelyan assumed they were "actually achieving"—a "success" that they themselves at the time would gladly have foregone.

The most provocative contribution of Bright to the debate on reform is so out of keeping with this Liberal reconstruction of history that no amount of reinterpretation would have made it tolerable—which is perhaps why Trevelyan and others have chosen to ignore it completely. Before the bill went into committee, as if in premonition of what was to happen, Bright cautioned the House not to go too far; in the course of his argument, he used the term "residuum" to describe those who should be excluded from the franchise.

> At this moment, in all, or nearly all our boroughs, as many of us know, sometimes to our sorrow, there is a small class which it would be much better for themselves if they

7. *Ibid.*, p. 373.

were not enfranchised, because they have no independence whatsoever, and it would be much better for the constituency also that they should be excluded, and there is no class so much interested in having that small class excluded as the intelligent and honest working man. I call this class the residuum, which there is in almost every constituency, of almost hopeless poverty and dependence.[8]

To show that this was no passing fancy or idle bit of rhetoric, he recalled that as early as 1859 he had made the same point in calling attention to "the excessively poor—many of them intemperate, some of them naturally incapable; but all of them in a condition of dependence"; this was a class, he had said then and repeated now, "which I thought it would not be any advantage to the class itself, or to the constituency, or to the public, to admit to the franchise."[9]

Although Bright's designation of the "residuum," the class of the "excessively poor," is rarely alluded to by historians,[1] contemporaries were much provoked by it. Radicals accused Bright of betrayal, and Adullamites charged him with hypocrisy. Lowe was ready with his usual quip. Bright, he said, "had been agitating the country for household suffrage—but not meaning, as we now see by his conduct this session, to get it"; he was in the position of that Italian John (Don Giovanni) who asked the statue of the Commendatore to supper and was astonished when the statue actually arrived.[2] Bright's reply to his critics was neither so colorful nor so convincing. He opened by insisting that he had always been "unequivocally" for the proposition that "the permanent foundation for the borough franchise ought to be sought in the householders." But

8. 3 *Hansard* 186: 636–7 (March 26, 1867).
9. Ibid., p. 637.
1. Neither Trevelyan nor Ausubel mentions it.
2. 3 *Hansard* 188: 1547 (July 15, 1867).

he then went on to show how equivocal a proposition this was:

> In deference to the opinions of many persons, and because I believed that there was a class of householders in this country who were so dependent, and I am sorry to say so ignorant, that it was not likely that they would be independent electors, or would give any strength to any constituency, it would be desirable to draw a line, and I believe that the line I proposed was houses that were rented at £4 or £3 per annum. . . . I should for the present have been willing to consent to some proposition which fell short of household suffrage pure and simple. . . . I have no wish to go very far or very fast. My own impression is that, in the political changes which are inevitable in our time in all countries, and which certainly are as inevitable in this as in any other country, it is an advantage to the country that these great changes should be made rather by steps than all at once.[3]

Unlike the Liberals, the Conservatives were neither troubled nor embarrassed by the "residuum." Instead they boldly capitalized upon it. It was precisely in the interests of this class, Disraeli announced, that he sought the fullest measure of household suffrage, for "while the enfranchisement of the elite of the working classes alone would destroy his party, the enfranchisement of the residuum with the elite would renew its source of strength."[4] Later he amended this argument, making it the nation rather than the party that would benefit by the inclusion of the residuum and suffer by the creation of a "Praetorian guard."[5] It was said at the time, as it is often said now, that Disraeli was partial to the residuum because it was "most likely to be managed and *exploité* by the Conservative

3. Ibid., 188: 1550–3.
4. Park, *English Reform Bill*, p. 243, quoting *The Times*, June 12, 1867.
5. *3 Hansard* 188: 1603–4, 1609–10 (July 15, 1867).

party," whereas the elite of the working class was "almost invariably Liberals and Radicals."[6] But if this were the only consideration, the Conservatives would surely have tried to extend the suffrage to the residuum in the counties, where the opportunities for management and exploitation were even greater; yet there was no hint of such a proposal.[7] There is no doubt that party advantage played a large part in the strategy of both Conservatives and Liberals. But neither is there any doubt that ideology and temper made the Conservatives less fearful of the residuum and the Liberals more so than party interests required.

It might be said that neither party nor ideology was compelling, that both were derivative, the reflection or rationalization of economic interests. This is not the place to explore the variety of economic interests that were affected, or were thought to be affected, by the various proposals for reform. All that can be said here is that contemporaries were uncertain of the relationship between any particular economic interest and any particular political reform, and that historians have not been more successful in establishing such relationships.

The conventional view is that Conservative county landowners were willing to enfranchise the urban working class because they had nothing to lose and everything to gain by such a policy, while the Liberal merchants and manufacturers were naturally indisposed to give power to their class

6. "The Achievements and the Moral of 1867," *North British Review*, XLVII (1867), 211-12.

7. There is another, and to a certain extent contradictory, thesis that finds significance in the fact that the Conservatives sponsored the Act of 1867 enfranchising the urban working class and the Liberals the Act of 1884 enfranchising the agricultural laborers—each giving away, so to speak, what belonged to the other. But this does not take account of the tendency of the agricultural laborers to vote *with* their Conservative landlords rather than *against* them. The facility of constructing such plausible but contradictory theses casts suspicion upon them all.

enemies. In a general and rather vague sense, this theory is plausible and, probably, true. Unfortunately the kind of study that would determine the degree of its validity—a Namierite inquiry into the lives of members of parliament—has never been undertaken, perhaps because the generalization has been too readily accepted.[8] What evidence there is suggests that the generalization is in any case too imprecise to account for what most needs explaining: the particular divergencies and convergencies of policy. Did Lowe, Gladstone, and Bright represent distinctive economic or social classes, and if so, how explain their differences and at the same time their similarities? How did Lowe, the son of a rector and the epitome of the classless intellectual, whose only apparent interest was his ideology and whose only commitment was to an aristocracy of intellect, come to represent a group described as the "last rally of aristocrats of the Whig decadence"?[9] And if this Whig aristocracy was beginning to merge with the Tory aristocracy, as is generally assumed, why did the Adullamites differ so radically from the Tories on the issue of reform? What made Whig landowners more hostile to reform than Tory landowners? Conversely, what made Conservative manufacturers more receptive to reform than Liberal manufacturers? One historian, demonstrating that Disraeli's strongest support came from Conservatives from urban constituencies—merchants, shipowners, and manufacturers—explained: "The pressure of constituency affected the character of the representatives selected. Conservatives were bound to become more 'democratic' when they sat for large towns."[1] But in that event, why were not

8. The appendices and index to Southgate's book come closest to a Namierite analysis. But the information is too fragmentary and unrelated to questions of public policy to be of much assistance in the present inquiry. Vincent's work is more pertinent and goes far in breaking down the conventional view of the class differentiations of the parties.

9. See above, p. 367.

1. Briggs, *Victorian People*, p. 302.

the preeminently urban, mercantile, and manufacturing Liberals affected in the same way?

It might be thought that the economic interests of at least one party in this controversy—the urban working class—could be easily identified and assessed. A common notion of these interests was expressed by *The Times:*

> Almost universally without the first elements of political knowledge, it is readily concluded that they [the workers] will use the franchise for the objects which animal life or their social condition will enable them to appreciate. They are hard-worked and ill-fed, so their cry at the hustings will be for eight hours instead of nine, and sixpence more a day. They are envious, and they will want to have divided among them the land and the incomes of their more fortunate neighbors. They want employment so they will ask for infinite paper money, to keep up enterprise.[2]

Yet even here the matter is more complicated than might be thought. The solecism of the first sentence, so unlike *The Times*, is provokingly ambiguous: Who was it who so dismally lacked the "first elements of political knowledge" —the workers who would make such extravagent demands, or those who assumed that the workers would do so? In fact, *The Times* itself did not think the workers would do so. So far from subscribing to these fears of excesses, *The Times* made it clear that it had remarked upon them only to show how unduly alarmist they were.

Thirty years earlier a prominent Chartist had pronounced universal suffrage to be a "knife-and-fork," "bread-and-cheese" matter: the right of every worker to "a good coat on his back, a good hat on his head, a good roof for the shelter of his household, a good dinner upon his table, no more work than will keep him in health while at it, and as much wages as will keep him in the enjoyment of plenty, and all the blessings of life that reasonable men

2. *The Times*, May 23, 1867.

could desire."[3] By 1866 such utopian illusions were rare. Most workingclass leaders aspired not to universal or even manhood suffrage but to household suffrage or less; and they anticipated nothing more in the way of material bliss than the alleviation of particular grievances. The thesis that the Reform Act was inspired by socialist demands has been most forcibly stated by A. V. Dicey, and his authority is still invoked to this effect. But Dicey, typically, arrived at this thesis by amalgamating the Acts of 1867 and 1884 as part of a single "reform movement": "The Reform Acts, 1867–1884, were carried in deference to the wishes and by the support of the working classes, who desired, though in a vague and indefinite manner, laws which might promote the attainment of the ideals of socialism or collectivism."[4] And historians after him, equally typically, have quoted him as if his generalization could be applied to 1867 alone.[5] Yet it is little enough true even of 1884–still less of 1867.

There were, to be sure, in the winter and spring of 1866–7, the inevitable appeals to economic justice, equality, an end to unemployment, and an alleviation of hardship. But only in a sense so "vague and indefinite" as to be almost meaningless can such talk be related to "socialism or collectivism." Moreover, much of it was directed against landlordism, the land monopoly, and the laws of primogeniture–which were hardly grievances of the urban workers to whom these declamations were addressed and whose franchise was being sought. In fact, rhetoric of this kind was consciously avoided and even denounced by many workingclass leaders. For every speech invoking the

3. Donald Read, "Chartism in Manchester," *Chartist Studies*, ed. Asa Briggs (London, 1962), p. 34.
4. A. V. Dicey, *Lectures on the Relation between Law and Public Opinion in England during the Nineteenth Century* (2nd edn.; London, 1962), p. 254.
5. Gillespie, *Labor and Politics*, p. 282: "The evidence goes far to justify Dicey's judgment that the reform of 1867 was sought by labor to secure legislation in favor of collectivism, its object being social rather than political."

franchise as a means of protecting the economic interests of the workers, one can produce another speech arguing that the workers had proved themselves worthy of the franchise by their indifference to economic affairs and their hostility to economic innovations.[6]

The situation, then, was infinitely complicated. And it was made all the more complicated by the fact that although there was seldom a clear economic mandate or compelling interest for this or that policy, there was what might be called an "ideology" of interests. However confused or conflicting their own interests, motives, or policies might be, most Liberals shared the utilitarian philosophy of self-interest, according to which all men were seeking a maximum realization of their interests by means of a maximum utilization of their power. It is this ideology of interests, more than any particular set of interests, that united the various factions of Liberals and distinguished them from the Conservatives. While Gladstone, Lowe, and Bright were trying to calculate the precise effect of this or that reform, on the assumption that each measure of reform would bring into play a measurable interest and power, the Conservatives, having no such utilitarian conceptions, had no need of such calculations.[7] Tory landlords were as vulnerable as Whig landlords—or even Liberal manufacturers—to attacks upon land, property, primogeniture, the currency, and the like. But they worried less about them because they did not believe the masses to be covetous of

6. E.g., Edmond Beales, the president of the Reform League: "The working classes themselves are deeply interested in the preservation of law and order, of the rights of capital and property; of the honour and power and wealth of our country. They are as members of co-operatives, building and other societies daily becoming themselves capitalists and land-owners; there are among them men of large intellectual capacity and earnest unaffected Christian principle." (Harrison, *Before the Socialists*, p. 114.)

7. In describing Gladstone as a "utilitarian," I am, needless to say, referring only to his social and political views—not, for example, to his opinions of religion or the Church.

property, privilege, or power. Indeed, the Conservatives assumed that the masses identified themselves, both in interest and in power, with their betters, that economic advantage or political strength counted less in their order of values than established traditions and authorities. *The Times*, toward the end of the editorial quoted above, explained why the workers could be trusted with the vote:

> The plain truth of the matter is that all the private relations of the working man will be engrafted into our political system. He will vote with his master, his employer, his preacher, his society, and possibly sometimes commit the unpardonable crime of voting as his landlord asks him to vote. . . . Our social system, therefore, . . . is our real sheet anchor, and that on which we may fearlessly ride.[8]

"When the leap in the dark is made," one Liberal wrote at the time, "when the franchise is given to cottagers who pay a weekly rent of eighteen pence, when we have, not merely household suffrage, but hovel suffrage also, nobody knows who are to be the future governors of England."[9] The Conservative had no such doubts. His leap in the dark was made in the confidence that he would land securely on his feet. Whatever the suffrage—£10, £6, household, or hovel—whatever the interests or forces called into play, he was confident that the "future governors of England" would be not very different from the past governors of England.

The Liberal put a premium upon interest because he put a premium upon intelligence: he assumed that the elector should be intelligent enough to know his interests and to

8. *The Times*, May 23, 1867.
9. Cox, *Reform Bills*, p. 278. The phrase "leap in the dark" was first used by Macaulay in connection with the first Reform Act. (*Works* [London, 1875], VIII, 41.)

act upon them. The Conservative had no such regard either for interests or for intelligence. John Stuart Mill, called upon to explain his reference to the Conservatives as the "stupidest party," said that he did not mean that Conservatives are "generally stupid," but that "stupid persons are generally Conservative."[1] There was some truth in Mill's remark, although not necessarily in the invidious sense he intended it. The Conservative ideology was better expressed in Bagehot's statement that "the most essential mental quality for a free people, whose liberty is to be progressive, permanent and on a large scale," was "much stupidity"[2]—a quality he elsewhere defined as "the dull traditional habit of mankind that guides most men's actions."[3]

The case of Bagehot is particularly revealing, his personal ambivalence toward Liberalism and Conservatism being paralleled by an ambivalence toward intelligence and stupidity. While the main text of the *English Constitution* may be taken as the classical Conservative argument in favor of "stupidity," the introduction to the second edition expressed the classical Liberal abhorrence of stupidity. Between the text of that work and the later introduction, there had intervened the Reform Act, and it was in explaining his opposition to that act that Bagehot came close to vitiating the principles he had earlier expounded. He showed himself distrustful and fearful of the newly enfranchised masses, quite as if there were no "dull traditional habit" to guide them. The Englishman's capacity for deference he now attributed exclusively to the lower middle class. And the stupidity he had earlier taken to be the saving grace of a free people now appeared as cause for the gravest anxiety:

1. *3 Hansard*, 183: 1592 (May 31, 1866).
2. Bagehot, "Letters on the French Coup d'Etat of 1851," *Works*, ed. Mrs. Russell Barrington (London, 1915), I, 100.
3. Bagehot, *English Constitution*, p. 8.

It must be remembered that a political combination of the lower classes, as such and for their own objects, is an evil of the first magnitude; that a permanent combination of them would make them (now that so many of them have the suffrage) supreme in the country; and that their supremacy, in the state they now are, means the supremacy of ignorance over instruction and of numbers over knowledge.[4]

Although Bagehot rejected the Reform Act and Mill accepted it, the ideology in both cases was identical: it was the Liberal ideology of intelligence. There were obvious philosophical tensions in an ideology that held both interests and intelligence to be supreme; yet this dual loyalty was at the heart of utilitarianism. For the utilitarian, intelligence, or reason, was a necessary instrument and adjunct of interest. Mill described his father as having "an almost unbounded confidence" in two things: representative government and free discussion—the first to secure the interests of the people, the second to permit "reason" and "educated intelligence" to determine their true interests.[5]

4. Ibid., p. 272. There is one passage in the body of the *English Constitution* that seems to express a similar anxiety. A community "in which the bulk of the people are ignorant" is described as being in a state of "unstable equilibrium"; and if the ignorant masses are permitted to rule, "you may bid farewell to deference forever." (Pp. 239-40.) In book form, this statement appears in the final paragraph of the chapter on cabinet government. But in the original version in the *Fortnightly Review*, the chapter continues for another two pages and concludes on a more familiar and optimistic note: "In another and a better age, a lower class, more intelligent than ours, will doubtless leave to a higher class, more improved than ours, the principal show in political affairs; but our lower class already do so without being intelligent. They are overcome by the pomp of society, the force of tradition, and the apparent grandness of our dignified institutions; and so yield to our real rulers an obedience and respect which there is nothing in the outside of these real rulers to attract, which is the more marvelous the more we consider it, and which is the source of a hundred peculiarities, and a hundred blessings. (*Fortnightly Review*, I [1865], 331.)

5. J. S. Mill, *Autobiography* (New York, 1924), p. 74.

The son went even further, regarding representative government as itself an instrument of education. Other Liberals might disagree with the Mills on the best mode of representation, as they disagreed among themselves on the best mode of reform. But they were united in the conviction that reason, education, and intelligence were the basis of a sound polity.

In 1859, on the occasion of an earlier reform bill, John Stuart Mill had argued that while it was just for every competent adult to have a voice in public affairs, it was not just that everyone have an *equal* voice, that to vote was to exercise power over others as well as oneself, and that there was no equal claim to such power because people were not equally worthy of exercising it. Least worthy were those least educated, least accustomed to the use of reason and intelligence—which is to say, the lower classes: "No lover of improvement can desire that the *predominant* power should be turned over to persons in the mental and moral condition of the English working classes."[6] Six years later, accepting the nomination for Westminster, he declared that he favored giving the vote to "all grown persons, both men and women, who can read, write, and perform a sum in the rule of three, and who have not, within some small number of years, received parish relief." But he was not "for giving the suffrage in such a measure that any class, even though it be the most numerous, could swamp all other classes taken together." The best reform, he suggested, would be one

6. J. S. Mill, "Thoughts on Parliamentary Reform," *Essays on Politics and Culture*, ed. Gertrude Himmelfarb (New York, 1962), pp. 344–5. Several years earlier he had added these sentences to his *Principles of Political Economy:* "As soon as any idea of equality enters the mind of an ordinary English working man, his head is turned by it. When he ceases to be servile, he becomes insolent." In 1865 Mill altered "ordinary" to "uneducated"; with this emendation the sentences were retained in the final edition of 1871. (*Collected Works of John Stuart Mill,* II, *Principles of Political Economy,* ed. J. M. Robson [Toronto, 1965], 109.)

that would allow the working class "a clear half of the national representation."[7]

Mill did not permit himself such candor during the debates of 1866–7, perhaps because he did not want to give comfort to the enemies of reform, perhaps because he felt that a mode of discourse appropriate to the independent intellectual was not appropriate to a member of parliament, or perhaps simply because he had learned discretion from the recent electoral campaign when a sentence from his 1859 essay—"the lower [classes], though mostly habitual liars, are ashamed of lying"[8]—had been widely quoted against him. He supported the Liberal bill of 1866, although it would have given the working class less than one half of the national representation. And as late as March 1, 1867, at a time when the Conservatives had already decided on household suffrage, he withdrew from the Reform League, both on account of its incitement to violence and because of its excessive demands. He rebuked it for not realizing that "any Reform Bill capable of being passed at present and for some time to come must be more or less of a compromise," that "ultimate success can only in this country be obtained by a succession of steps," and that the middle class could hardly be expected to approve the "passage all at once from the present distribution of political power to one exactly the reverse, the effects of which they feel quite unable to foresee."[9] When he did ultimately give his approval to the Reform Act, it was not without grave compunctions about the evils of numbers and ignorance.

His most determined effort to mitigate these evils took

7. *The Letters of John Stuart Mill,* ed. Hugh S. R. Elliott (London, 1910), II, 23 (April 19, 1865).

8. Mill, "Recent Writers on Reform," *Essays on Politics and Culture,* p. 357.

9. *Letters of Mill,* II, 77–8.

the form of an amendment providing for proportional representation to "diminish and counteract the tyranny of majorities."[1] When he had first come across the plan of proportional representation some years earlier, he had seized upon it as a means of giving greater representation to the "available intellectual strength of the country" and of bringing into the House of Commons the "*élite* of the nation."[2] It solved, he said, the "difficulty of popular representation" and "raised up the cloud of gloom and uncertainty which hung over the futurity of representative government and therefore of civilization."[3]

> It is an uphill race, and a race against time, for if the American form of democracy overtakes us first, the majority will no more relax their despotism than a single despot would. But our only chance is to come forward as Liberals, carrying out the democratic idea, not as Conservatives, resisting it.[4]

It was the Conservatives, as it happened, who in 1867 were "carrying out the democratic idea," while the one most bent upon "resisting" it was the Liberal Lowe. And it was Lowe who proved to be Mill's strongest ally on the issue of proportional representation:

> All our other arrows have been shot; not one remains in the quiver; so that if this does not hit, there will be nothing left but one simple uniform franchise to be entrusted to, and left in, the hands of the lowest class of society.[5]
> It appears, indeed, our only hope. Nothing remains behind. This is the last offer that can be made before you

1. *3 Hansard* 188: 1103 (July 5, 1867).
2. Mill, "Recent Writers on Reform," *Essays on Politics and Culture*, p. 384.
3. *Letters of Mill*, I, 215 (March 3, 1859).
4. Michael St. John Packe, *The Life of John Stuart Mill* (London, 1954), p. 418 (Feb. 5, 1860).
5. *3 Hansard* 188: 1037 (July 4, 1867).

put it out of your power to do anything to remedy the violence of the changes you are making.[6]

Proportional representation was not, however, quite the last arrow in the quiver. When all other attempts to create an intellectual elite failed, when plural votes for university graduates were swept away together with all the other fancy franchises (Mill's disciple, Henry Fawcett, was the last to defend this particular fancy franchise), and when proportional representation was rejected, there was one remaining recourse. If the educated minority could not be given more power, the newly empowered majority would have to be given more education. Again Mill found an ally in Lowe. And again Lowe made out the most dramatic case for "the most universal measure of education that can be devised":

> I believe it will be absolutely necessary that you should prevail on our future masters to learn their letters. . . . I was opposed to centralization, I am ready to accept centralization; I was opposed to an education rate, I am ready now to accept it; I objected to inspection, I am now willing to create crowds of inspectors. This question is no longer a religious question, it has become a political one. It is indeed the question of questions; it has become paramount to every other question that has been brought before us.[7]

Lowe's remarks were echoed by other Liberals, no less devoted than he to the principles of laissez faire. In his election address in 1867, Bagehot declared that the state would have to intervene far more than had yet been contemplated in order to provide the necessary education on the necessary scale: "After the first Reform Act, the cry was 'Register! Register! Register!' The cry should now be, 'Educate! Educate! Educate!'"[8]

6. Ibid., 188: 1041.
7. Ibid., 188: 1549 (July 15, 1867).
8. Bagehot, *Works*, X, 394.

The Conservatives did not take up this cry. They were not opposed to popular education, or even to state-supported popular education, as became evident in the following decade. But they had no sense of the urgency of such education, partly because they did not think of the new electorate as their "future masters," partly because they did not assign the same importance to the principle of intelligence. It is significant that the only notable remark of a Conservative on the subject of education at this time was Disraeli's boast that he had "educated his party"—these were the only masters he knew.

In one sense the "stupidest party" was vindicated. Although the Conservatives lost the elections of 1868, they won those of 1874 and afterwards more than held their own—and this at a time when industrialization, democracy, trade-unionism, social reforms, and the like might have been expected to throw the balance in favor of the Liberals.[9] The masses, it appeared, were less inclined to "a perpetual whirl of change, alteration, innovation and revolution,"[1] less given to calculations of interests and numbers, more respectful of institutions and persons, more imbued with the dull traditional habits of mind, than most Liberals had suspected. That so much of English government and society should have remained intact while so much else changed was a proper cause for gratification among Conservatives. Indeed, that the Conservative Party should have remained intact while the Liberal Party disintegrated was a tribute to Disraeli's ideology and politics.

Yet, however little the politics of democracy seemed to differ from the politics of aristocracy, there was a significant difference. The Liberals may have been mistaken

9. Smith documents the increasing Conservative strength in the large towns after 1867. (*Second Reform Bill*, pp. 237 ff.)
1. See above, p. 371.

about the nature of the difference, but not about the fact. In the final debate on reform, Lowe defined the "new era" in terms of the new role assumed by the parties:

> We have inaugurated a new era in English politics this session, and depend upon it, the new fashion will henceforth be the rule and not the exception. This session we have not had what we before possessed—a party of attack and a party of resistance. We have instead two parties of competition who, like Cleon and the Sausage-seller of Aristophanes, are both bidding for the support of Demos.[2]

Bagehot carried this analysis one step further, by showing the effect of party competition upon the Demos for whose favor they were competing:

> In plain English, what I fear is that both our political parties will bid for the support of the working-man; that both of them will promise to do as he likes if he will only tell them what it is; that, as he now holds the casting-vote in our affairs, both parties will beg and pray him to give that vote to them. I can conceive of nothing more corrupting or worse for a set of poor ignorant people than that two combinations of well-taught and rich men should constantly offer to defer to their decision, and compete for the office of executing it. *Vox populi* will be *vox diaboli* if it is worked in that manner.[3]

Bagehot and Lowe were right in defining the logic of the new situation; they only erred in assuming that the reality would necessarily correspond to the logic. The new electorate, as it happened, did not take advantage either of the possibilities of change and violence in the new era, or of the new role available to it. The masses did not become, as Bagehot had feared, the rulers (the decision makers) and the parties merely the executives. In the new game of politics as in the old, the parties still carry the ball and decide upon the moves, while the electors are still more or

2. *3 Hansard* 187: 797 (May 20, 1867).
3. Bagehot, *English Constitution*, p. 271.

less interested spectators. The essential innovation of the new era and the new role assigned to the electors has been to make the spectators double as umpires. Even here, the spectators have not fully availed themselves of their powers, being content, for the most part, to sit back and enjoy the spectacle, intervening as umpires only when called upon, and abiding by the established rules of the game. It is, curiously, the players themselves, the competing teams, who invite, almost compel, the intervention of the spectators by playing to the grandstand, thus creating the conditions and occasions for intervention.

If the people still display some reticence, if they have not yet acquired a taste for power nor become willful and erratic in its exercise, the provocation and potentiality of power remain. And it is this provocation and potentiality, rather than the actual exercise or abuse of power, that distinguish the new politics. Almost a hundred years since the passage of the Reform Act, we are still in the uncertain and ominous position described by Bagehot when he said that the Tories "may have got hold of a real force, but have not the slightest notion how to ascertain the law of that force's expansion."[4]

4. Bagehot, "Lord Salisbury on Moderation," *Works*, IX, 174.

INDEX

i

Gertrude Himmelfarb was born in New York City and studied at Brooklyn College and the University of Chicago. She is now professor emeritus of history at the Graduate School of the City University of New York. She has written extensively on Victorian England. Her other books are *On Looking into the Abyss, Poverty and Compassion, The New History and the Old, Marriage and Morals Among the Victorians, The Idea of Poverty, On Liberty and Liberalism, Darwin and the Darwinian Revolution,* and *Lord Acton.*

ELEPHANT PAPERBACKS

American History and American Studies
Stephen Vincent Benét, *John Brown's Body*, EL10
Henry W. Berger, ed., *A William Appleman Williams Reader*,
    EL126
Andrew Bergman, *We're in the Money*, EL124
Paul Boyer, ed., *Reagan as President*, EL117
Robert V. Bruce, *1877: Year of Violence*, EL102
George Dangerfield, *The Era of Good Feelings*, EL110
Clarence Darrow, *Verdicts Out of Court*, EL2
Floyd Dell, *Intellectual Vagabondage*, EL13
Elisha P. Douglass, *Rebels and Democrats*, EL108
Theodore Draper, *The Roots of American Communism*, EL105
Joseph Epstein, *Ambition*, EL7
Lloyd C. Gardner, *Spheres of Influence*, EL131
Paul W. Glad, *McKinley, Bryan, and the People*, EL119
Daniel Horowitz, *The Morality of Spending*, EL122
Kenneth T. Jackson, *The Ku Klux Klan in the City, 1915–1930*,
    EL123
Edward Chase Kirkland, *Dream and Thought in the Business
    Community, 1860–1900*, EL114
Herbert S Klein, *Slavery in the Americas*, EL103
Aileen S. Kraditor, *Means and Ends in American Abolitionism*,
    EL111
Leonard W. Levy, *Jefferson and Civil Liberties: The Darker Side*,
    EL107
Seymour J. Mandelbaum, *Boss Tweed's New York*, EL112
Thomas J. McCormick, *China Market*, EL115
Walter Millis, *The Martial Spirit*, EL104
Nicolaus Mills, ed., *Culture in an Age of Money*, EL302
Nicolaus Mills, *Like a Holy Crusade*, EL129
Roderick Nash, *The Nervous Generation*, EL113
William L. O'Neill, ed., *Echoes of Revolt: The Masses,
    1911–1917*, EL5
Glenn Porter and Harold C. Livesay, *Merchants and
    Manufacturers*, EL106
Edward Reynolds, *Stand the Storm*, EL128
Geoffrey S. Smith, *To Save a Nation*, EL125
Bernard Sternsher, ed., *Hitting Home: The Great Depression in
    Town and Country*, EL109
Athan Theoharis, *From the Secret Files of J. Edgar Hoover*, EL127
Nicholas von Hoffman, *We Are the People Our Parents Warned
    Us Against*, EL301
Norman Ware, *The Industrial Worker, 1840–1860*, EL116
Tom Wicker, *JFK and LBJ: The Influence of Personality upon
    Politics*, EL120
Robert H. Wiebe, *Businessmen and Reform*, EL101
T. Harry Williams, *McClellan, Sherman and Grant*, EL121
Miles Wolff, *Lunch at the 5 & 10*, EL118
Randall B. Woods and Howard Jones, *Dawning of the Cold
    War*, EL130

European and World History
Mark Frankland, *The Patriots' Revolution*, EL201
Lloyd C. Gardner, *Spheres of Influence*, EL131
Gertrude Himmelfarb, *Victorian Minds*, EL205
Thomas A. Idinopulos, *Jerusalem*, EL204
Ronnie S. Landau, *The Nazi Holocaust*, EL203
Clive Ponting, *1940: Myth and Reality*, EL202

ELEPHANT PAPERBACKS

Literature and Letters
Stephen Vincent Benét, *John Brown's Body*, EL10
Isaiah Berlin, *The Hedgehog and the Fox*, EL21
Anthony Burgess, *Shakespeare*, EL27
Philip Callow, *Son and Lover: The Young D. H. Lawrence*, EL14
James Gould Cozzens, *Castaway*, EL6
James Gould Cozzens, *Men and Brethren*, EL3
Clarence Darrow, *Verdicts Out of Court*, EL2
Floyd Dell, *Intellectual Vagabondage*, EL13
Theodore Dreiser, *Best Short Stories*, EL1
Joseph Epstein, *Ambition*, EL7
André Gide, *Madeleine*, EL8
John Gross, *The Rise and Fall of the Man of Letters*, EL18
Irving Howe, *William Faulkner*, EL15
Aldous Huxley, *After Many a Summer Dies the Swan*, EL20
Aldous Huxley, *Ape and Essence*, EL19
Aldous Huxley, *Collected Short Stories*, EL17
Sinclair Lewis, *Selected Short Stories*, EL9
William L. O'Neill, ed., *Echoes of Revolt: The Masses,
    1911–1917*, EL5
Ramón J. Sender, *Seven Red Sundays*, EL11
Wilfrid Sheed, *Office Politics*, EL4
Tess Slesinger, *On Being Told That Her Second Husband Has
    Taken His First Lover, and Other Stories*, EL12
B. Traven, *The Bridge in the Jungle*, EL28
B. Traven, *The Carreta*, EL25
B. Traven, *The Cotton-Pickers*, EL32
B. Traven, *General from the Jungle*, EL33
B. Traven, *Government*, EL23
B. Traven, *March to the Montería*, EL26
B. Traven, *The Night Visitor and Other Stories*, EL24
B. Traven, *The Rebellion of the Hanged*, EL29
Anthony Trollope, *Trollope the Traveller*, EL31
Rex Warner, *The Aerodrome*, EL22
Thomas Wolfe, *The Hills Beyond*, EL16

Theatre and Drama
Robert Brustein, *Reimagining American Theatre*, EL410
Robert Brustein, *The Theatre of Revolt*, EL407
Irina and Igor Levin, *Working on the Play and the Role*, EL411
Plays for Performance:
    Aristophanes, *Lysistrata*, EL405
    Pierre Augustin de Beaumarchais, *The Marriage of Figaro*,
        EL418
    Anton Chekhov, *The Seagull*, EL407
    Fyodor Dostoevsky, *Crime and Punishment*, EL416
    Euripides, *The Bacchae*, EL419
    Georges Feydeau, *Paradise Hotel*, EL403
    Henrik Ibsen, *Ghosts*, EL401
    Henrik Ibsen, *Hedda Gabler*, EL413
    Henrik Ibsen, *The Master Builder*, EL417
    Henrik Ibsen, *When We Dead Awaken*, EL408
    Heinrich von Kleist, *The Prince of Homburg*, EL402
    Christopher Marlowe, *Doctor Faustus*, EL404
    The Mysteries: Creation, EL412
    The Mysteries: The Passion, EL414
    Sophocles, *Electra*, EL415
    August Strindberg, *The Father*, EL406